Ranga Chand's World of Mutual Funds

Ranga Chand's World of Mutual Funds

AN INVESTOR'S GUIDE

1998 Edition

Published in 1997 by Stoddart Publishing Co. Limited
34 Lesmill Road, Toronto, Canada M3B 2T6

Distributed in Canada by General Distribution Services Limited
34 Lesmill Road, Toronto, Canada M3B 2T6
Tel. (416) 445-3333 Fax (416) 445-5967
Email Customer.Service@ccmailgw.genpub.com

Distributed in the U.S. by General Distribution Services Inc.
85 River Rock Drive, Suite 202, Buffalo, New York 14207
Toll-free tel. 1-800-805-1083 Toll-free fax 1-800-481-6207
Email gdsinc@genpub.com

01 00 99 98 97   1 2 3 4 5

Cataloguing in Publication Data

Chand, Ranga
Ranga Chand's world of mutual funds: an investor's guide

1998 ed.
ISBN 0-7737-5908-5

1. Mutual funds. I. Title II. Title: World of
mutual funds.

HG4530.C482 1997   332.63'27   97-931971-4

The **Heavy Hitters** is a registered trademark of
Chand Carmichael & Company Limited

Cover design: Pekoe Jones
Author photograph: Peter Paterson
Computer graphics: Mary Bowness

Printed and bound in Canada

To Sylvia, Jason, and Hamish

CONTENTS

● ●

APPENDICES

About the Author

ACKNOWLEDGEMENTS

●●●●●●●●●●●●●●●●●●●●●●●●●●●●●●●●●●●●●

I WOULD LIKE to express my thanks to Jack Stoddart, Nelson Doucet, Donald G. Bastian, and Angel Guerra of Stoddart Publishing for their continuing support and belief that the public needs an *independent*, *comprehensive*, and *objective* investment guide to mutual funds. As always, I am especially grateful to Kevin Linder, my editor at Stoddart, for his extremely helpful editorial advice and significant contribution to the content of this book.

I am particularly indebted to my wife and business partner, Sylvia D. Carmichael, who, through her research and editing, contributed enormously to this book, and to our son, Jason, for his ongoing computer assistance.

The main source of data on which the analysis for this book is based was supplied by Globe HySales, a division of Globe Information Services. I am very grateful to Kevin Grennan for helping me meet my various publishing deadlines.

A special thank you to all the readers who took the time and trouble to get in touch with me with their comments and questions. As always, your feedback is very much appreciated.

I am especially grateful to Hamish for ensuring that I continue to get my daily walk.

INTRODUCTION

● ●

TODAY, THERE ARE approximately $55 billion dollars invested in Under-achievers — mutual funds that hold the dubious distinction of consistently delivering below-average returns. And some of those dollars could be yours! Before you invest another dime, there are a few crucial points you need to know. The first is that the difference in returns between investing in the average Heavy Hitter — a mutual fund that consistently delivers above-average returns over several time periods — and the average Underachiever is *substantial.* To get some idea of what we are talking about, take a look at the performance of Canadian equity mutual funds over the past five years. During this period, the average Heavy Hitter fund in this category posted an annual return of 18.1%, compared with only 11.9% for the average Underachiever. In dollar terms, for an initial investment of $10,000, the average Heavy Hitter Canadian equity fund would have returned a total of $22,975 over the five-year period. For the same investment, the average Underachiever would have returned only $17,545. *A difference of $5,430 or 30.9%!* And remember, we are talking *averages* here. Obviously, if we compared only the top-performing Heavy Hitters with the chronic Underachievers, the difference would be even larger. And these differences are not exclusive to Canadian equity mutual funds; they occur in *all* fund categories.

Before you make the mistake of thinking that your chances of investing in an Underachiever — assuming you're not already — are remote, think again! Our research clearly shows that this is not the case. Of the more than 600 mutual funds on the market with a five-year performance history, approximately *one-third* are Underachievers.

Clearly, as investors we all need factual, comprehensive, and unbiased information. The *World of Mutual Funds* fills all those needs, allowing you to independently check out the relative performance of any fund. If you are relying on a fund company for objective advice, you simply won't get it. Like all businesses, mutual fund companies will naturally promote and sell only their own products — whether they are good, bad, or mediocre. The onus of uncovering this information is, and always has been, on the investor.

The *World of Mutual Funds*, by being fully comprehensive, explicitly identifies not only 194 Heavy Hitters but also 176 Underachievers. The unique quantitative research methodology developed to evaluate the funds takes into account both compound and annual rates of return, the degree of risk, and how a fund's performance compares with the appropriate benchmark. In this way, investors know which funds to zero in on and, just as important, which funds to avoid. The methodology also allows investors who already own units in *any* fund to quickly and easily compare its performance with that of similar funds. This is obviously crucial information you need to have before you make any investment decisions.

Many articles that appear in the print media often promote one company over another. Should we as investors rely on these articles, or should we simply view them as infomercials? In the Mutual Fund Company Scorecard (Appendix 3), investors will, perhaps for the first time, be able to quickly see how many Heavy Hitters, Underachievers, and Rookie Camp members (promising newcomers) each mutual fund company holds. This will allow you to judge for yourself the overall performance record of 155 mutual fund companies. Moreover, you can use this appendix for a quick independent check before you buy any recommended fund.

This book is divided into five parts. Part One, Investing in Mutual Funds, briefly introduces you to mutual fund investing and covers the different types of funds and common management styles.

Part Two, The Selection Process, lays out the methodology used to evaluate the funds and describes the rating system by which the Heavy Hitters are ranked. Here you will also find a listing of all the Heavy Hitters and the Underachievers, plus the Heavy Hitter fund companies, those with the most Heavy Hitters and *no* Underachievers.

Parts Three and Four, How Canadian Mutual Funds Rate and How International Mutual Funds Rate, analyse and rank funds in 16 categories, using data as of May 31, 1997. Here you will find easy-to-read information on each Heavy Hitter, covering factors such as how often a fund has beaten its appropriate benchmark, who manages it, and what investment style is followed. You will also learn its best and worst returns over the past five calendar years, whether its volatility and management expense ratio are above or below the average for its category, and if any restrictions apply. In each chapter the Rankings/ Returns table lists all funds alphabetically. This will allow you to easily compare the rankings and returns of your funds over three different time periods. Each chapter also contains a Heavy Hitters vs Underachievers table giving the difference in returns between the two.

Part Five, The Essentials of Mutual Fund Investing, provides information on such topics as costs, the prospectus, and investment strategies. Chapter 33 walks you through the process of building a Heavy Hitter fund portfolio, from identifying your financial objectives and determining your asset allocation to selecting the Heavy Hitters. Finally, Chapter 35 focuses on indexing.

Appendix 1 contains some interesting and revealing fast fund facts, and Appendix 2 contains a useful glossary of investment terms. As noted above, Appendix 3, the Mutual Fund Company Scorecard, alphabetically lists 155 mutual fund companies, provides a complete list of their funds, both domestic and international, and identifies how many Heavy Hitters, Underachievers, and Rookie Camp members each company holds. Funds with less than a five-year history are shown in italics. This allows investors who are considering one of these newer funds to quickly review a fund company's performance record with its more established funds before making a buying decision. Individuals who prefer to invest with only one or two companies will find that this appendix gives them a good overview of which companies might be suitable.

Don't be afraid to mark up this book (assuming, of course, that you have bought it). Use a marker to highlight funds you are interested in and scribble notes to yourself. Use this book as a reference guide and above all make sure you consult it *before* you feel the urge to act impulsively on a hot tip or succumb to aggressive marketing. I firmly believe that every investor should have access to factual, comprehensive, and unbiased information. I hope you will find the information in this book both useful and illuminating. I certainly have.

PART ONE

• •

INVESTING IN MUTUAL FUNDS

1

What Are Mutual Funds?

A MUTUAL FUND is a cooperative means for many people with common financial goals to pool their savings. This pool of money is managed by professional money managers who invest the pool, depending on the objectives of the fund, in anything from Government of Canada treasury bills to shares in major Canadian corporations or foreign companies worldwide. These fund objectives generally cover income, growth, or safety of principal, or some combination of the three.

Individuals can purchase mutual fund units from financial institutions, insurance companies, brokers, financial planners, and the mutual fund's own sales force. Funds that do not charge a sales commission to buy, sell, or exchange fund units are called no-load funds. Unit sales of no-load funds are largely dominated by financial institutions. Load funds, on the other hand, charge investors a sales commission either at the time of purchase or on redemption and are generally offered by mutual fund companies that have limited or no distribution network of their own. These companies must rely on independent salespeople such as brokers and financial planners to sell their funds. The load or sales commission compensates the salesperson for his or her advice and time.

When a mutual fund earns money, it distributes the earnings to its unitholders. Earnings come from interest paid by bonds, money-market instruments such as treasury bills, and dividends on stocks, and from capital gains from selling securities at a higher price than the fund originally paid. All earnings are paid out to unitholders in proportion to the number of units held. In this way, unitholders with small amounts of invested money get the same return per dollar as those who invest hundreds of thousands. Unitholders can also make a capital gain or loss when selling back their units to the fund, depending on whether the unit price has increased or decreased since the units were purchased.

Investing in a mutual fund, however, is not the same as investing in a five-year GIC. The unit price of most funds will fluctuate, some quite dramatically, and there is no guaranteed rate of return.

Because mutual funds are "securities," not "deposits," they are not insured by the Canada Deposit Insurance Corporation (CDIC). However, unitholders' invested funds are held in trust by a custodian, either a Canadian chartered bank or trust company, and are protected under banking and trust laws. Securities regulations also require that companies that sell mutual fund units keep clients' funds separate from their own assets. Moreover, fund managers are prohibited from using fund assets in any way other than to make investments for the unitholders' benefit.

In addition, investors are protected by the Canadian Investor Protection Fund (CIPF) against a firm's insolvency, provided that their account is held with a mutual fund distributor or securities dealer who is a member of either the Investment Dealers Association of Canada (IDA) or one of Canada's four stock exchanges. This fund currently compensates each client up to $500,000. Clients of companies that are not members of the above self-regulatory organizations (SROs) are protected by various funds held by security commissions across Canada. However, the maximum compensation allowed is generally much lower. In Ontario, for example, the National Contingency Trust Fund can reimburse investors up to a maximum of $5,000. Both the CIPF and the National Contingency Trust Fund are designed to reimburse individuals in instances in which their mutual fund company collapses or their money is stolen in transit, but not against market losses.

2

● ●

Why Invest in Mutual Funds?

TIME, MONEY, AND the necessary expertise are required in varying amounts in order to build a successful investment portfolio. However, if you're fortunate enough to have large amounts of investment money at your disposal, it doesn't really matter about the other two requirements. You can hire your own money manager. For people who can't, mutual funds level the playing field. Investing in mutual funds allows individuals with limited money, time, and investment know-how to own shares in a variety of domestic and foreign securities, all managed by a professional money manager.

For most investors, the key factors for choosing mutual funds are diversification, professional management, liquidity, and ease of investment and record keeping.

Diversification

With only a limited amount of money available for investment, building a well-diversified portfolio is extremely difficult. At best, you may hold two or three stocks and possibly a bond. If one investment fails to perform as expected, the results can be decidedly unpleasant and could seriously derail any investment plan. By investing the same amount of money in mutual funds, you can obtain instant diversification through funds that own bonds or shares in many different companies and countries. This diversification greatly reduces risk — if one company or country's economy does badly, the others may do well — and increases the potential for growth of any investment portfolio. As an individual investor you would require tens of thousands of dollars to accomplish similar diversification.

Professional Management

Mutual funds are managed by either one person or a team. These professionals bring years of experience to the task of managing and making money. After extensive analysis of all available data, they choose which securities meet their fund's objectives and when to buy and sell. This type of financial management was, until mutual funds came on the scene, available only to large institutional investors and wealthy individuals.

Liquidity

This refers to how easily and quickly an asset, such as mutual fund units, can be converted to cash. Since mutual funds must redeem all or any of your units on demand, they are extremely liquid. The only exceptions are a few real-estate funds, where unitholders would have to wait until the properties held were appraised. To cash in your units, all you have to do is follow the procedure given in the fund prospectus, generally a written notification. After receiving your request, the fund company will send you a cheque for the price your shares were worth on the day the company received the redemption notice. This could be greater or less than the price originally paid, depending on the market.

Ease of Investment

Buying a mutual fund is not complicated. For those with sufficient investment knowledge, a mutual fund can be bought by mail. Those who would prefer advice in selecting an appropriate fund can take their pick from a variety of sources such as financial institutions, insurance companies, brokers, financial planners, and registered mutual fund specialists with individual fund companies. Most mutual fund companies also offer toll-free telephone assistance to prospective investors.

Record Keeping

Most people don't have enough time to keep track of their investments. With mutual funds all your record keeping is done for you. All funds provide unitholders with quarterly statements detailing all transactions, income earned and capital-gains distributions, and the total value of all funds held. Moreover, when you buy or sell units, you will receive written confirmation detailing the number of units involved, the price paid, and the date of the transaction. Unitholders also receive yearly statements detailing the tax status of all earnings from the fund, including dividends and capital-gains information. Each year the fund company issues a T3 (Relève 16 in Quebec) slip for tax purposes, listing the type and amount of income you must report on your income-tax return.

3

· ·

The Different Types of Mutual Funds

MUTUAL FUNDS INVEST in almost anything you can buy or sell on your own, such as treasury bills, bonds, stocks, real estate, and precious metals. Some funds invest only in Canada, while others search the world looking for the best investment opportunities. With over 1,400 mutual funds on the market, it's easy to get confused. However, while no two mutual funds are exactly alike, they fall into several broad-based categories.

Canadian Mutual Funds

Money-Market Funds. These funds invest principally in short-term (less than one year) debt securities such as federal and provincial treasury bills, Guaranteed Investment Certificates (GICs), and bankers' acceptances (promissory notes issued by Canadian companies and bank-guaranteed). In other words, the money you invest in these funds is used for short-term loans to various Canadian companies and government bodies. The aim of a money-market fund is to provide investors with as high a rate of interest income as possible, typically two or three percentage points higher than savings accounts, with the lowest possible risk. Funds that invest in federal treasury bills are the safest, followed by provincial treasury bills, and debentures issued by major corporations.

Some money-market securities mature in 24 hours, others in several months, or up to one year. These shorter maturity terms allow a fund manager to reinvest at higher rates if current interest rates are rising. If interest rates are falling, however, yields will decline as maturing securities are reinvested at a lower rate.

These funds are suitable for people who may need their cash in the near future or are waiting to take advantage of a market correction. Unlike for other mutual funds, the unit price of Canadian money-market funds does not fluctuate, and is intended to remain fixed at $10. These funds are a good low-risk, short-term parking place, but over the long term provide the lowest real rate of return.

Because the performance of these funds tends to cluster in a fairly narrow band, it makes little sense to pay a sales commission. Clearly, the consistent performers that have the lowest management expense ratio and do not charge a sales fee will have the edge.

Bond Funds. These funds invest in short-term (1–3 years), medium-term (3–10 years), and long-term (over 10 years) bonds and debentures of federal, provincial, and municipal governments and large corporations. The aim of a bond fund is to provide investors with maximum interest income and, to a lesser extent, capital gains from buying and selling bonds. The income payments to unitholders reflect the interest rates of the bonds held in the fund.

The performance of these funds is influenced by interest-rate movements. When interest rates go down, the unit price of bond funds will go up. This is because if interest rates are lower now than they were a year ago, last year's bonds are more attractive and consequently will command a higher price than originally paid. Conversely, when interest rates go up, the unit price will fall. Short-term funds have the least risk, followed by medium- and then long-term funds.

Mortgage Funds. As with bond funds, the aim of mortgage funds is to provide regular income. These funds generally concentrate on residential first mortgages, the most secure type, although some funds include commercial and industrial mortgages. Because fund managers rarely trade the mortgages they hold, capital-gains potential is low. Mortgage funds tend to be less volatile than most bond funds because of the shorter maturity dates of the investments held.

Dividend Funds. These funds invest in dividend-paying preferred shares of Canadian corporations and in common shares that are expected to yield a high level of dividend income. As with equity funds, there is also the potential for long-term capital growth through higher share prices of the funds' holdings. Dividend funds that carry a P1 or P2 rating issued by the Canadian Bond Rating Service and Dominion Bond Rating Service have the highest degree of safety. Because dividend income is taxed at a much lower rate than other types of investment income, these funds are best held outside of a registered plan. This type of fund would be suitable for investors seeking additional income with the potential for growth. Dividend funds are sensitive to stock-market fluctuations.

Equity Funds. Equity funds invest primarily in stocks and are commonly referred to as "growth funds." These funds invest in a wide range of Canadian companies through common and preferred shares, and the main objective of equity funds is to provide investors with long-term growth. Conservative equity funds typically invest in large well-established corporations with long histories of profitability. Aggressive growth funds, on the other hand, invest in the common shares of small emerging companies, often referred to as "small cap," that are expected to grow rapidly. The primary objective of aggressive growth funds is to provide investors with maximum capital gains.

Because of the volatility of the stock market and depending on the assets held, returns on equity funds may vary widely from year to year. They are, therefore, not suitable for individuals with a short investment time frame or limited investment dollars. Canadian equity funds are more volatile than income and money-market funds but less volatile than investing in individual stocks.

Special Equity Funds. These funds focus exclusively on specific industries and sectors of the economy and invest in companies in specialized areas such as real estate, resources, and precious metals. Due to the specialized nature of these funds, returns tend to be extremely volatile. If a specific industry is doing well, investors can make large capital gains. However, they can also make equally large losses. The experienced investor will have at most only a small percentage of his or her portfolio in these funds.

Precious Metals Funds typically invest in gold, silver, platinum, palladium, and rhodium, and shares of mining exploration and production companies. Due to the volatile and often speculative nature of the underlying securities, investors should consider placing no more than 5% of their assets in this type of fund. Investors who stick to this limit will be in a better position to ride out any sharp decline in returns such as occurred at the height of the Bre-X debacle, when fund returns dropped by as much as 30.9%.

Resources Funds invest in securities of Canadian companies involved in metals and minerals, oil and gas, forestry products, and water resources. Resources funds may also invest in precious metals. Because of the cyclical nature of these industries, returns will be volatile.

Real-Estate Funds invest in commercial and industrial real estate. Returns are generated by the income from these investments (rental and leasing) and potential capital gains from selling the properties held for profit. Due to the slump in real estate in the late 1980s, many of these funds have been liquidated or converted into closed-end funds called real-estate investment trusts (REITs). Units in some real-estate funds are also not as easily redeemed as units in other types of mutual funds. Investors must wait until a real-estate fund has its properties appraised and the unit price established. This could be either monthly or quarterly. Once the appraisals are completed, investors are then able to redeem their units.

Balanced Funds. This type of fund seeks to provide a competitive total return through a balance of bonds, stocks, and money-market holdings. The mix of assets held will change according to market conditions to maximize growth without excessive risk exposure. A typical balanced fund would include government and corporate bonds for income, and Canadian stocks for capital gains. These funds are suitable for people with limited investment dollars or who prefer a more diversified portfolio of stocks and bonds in one fund.

Balanced funds are less volatile than equity funds but more volatile than money-market and income funds. They are affected by interest-rate movements and stock-market performance.

International Mutual Funds

There are a number of reasons for investing internationally, but the most compelling is that Canada represents less than 3% of the world's stock and bond market. It makes little sense, therefore, to ignore the tremendous investment opportunities in the global marketplace. Investing internationally also allows investors to hedge against a decline in the Canadian dollar.

U.S. Money-Market Funds. These funds invest in short-term securities, similar to their Canadian counterparts, but denominated in U.S. dollars, providing investors with a hedge against any drop in value of the Canadian dollar. In this way, if the Canadian dollar declines against the U.S. dollar, this will boost returns, even though interest rates may be lower in the United States. If the Canadian dollar strengthens, however, returns will suffer. This type of fund is also suitable for people who need regular access to U.S. dollars.

International Money-Market Funds. For investors who wish to venture further afield, there are a few funds that invest in interest-bearing securities denominated in a variety of currencies such as the British pound, the French franc, and the Deutschmark. This diversification reduces the risk inherent in investing in only one country and currency.

International Bond Funds. International bond funds typically include medium- and long-term bonds and debentures and are designed to provide investors with regular interest-income payments and also the potential for capital growth and currency gains.

The performance of these funds is geared not only to interest-rate fluctuations, like their Canadian counterparts, but also to currency developments. On the foreign exchange front, when the Canadian dollar weakens against the other currencies in an international bond fund's portfolio, the value of the foreign bonds rises in terms of the Canadian dollar. As a result the fund will realize a currency gain that will boost its total rate of return. When the dollar strengthens, the opposite happens. The value of foreign bond prices in Canadian dollars falls, and the fund will experience a currency loss. If interest rates were also rising in the country of investment, this would further decrease returns.

This type of fund is suitable for investors looking for steady income with the possibility of capital gains and as a hedge against a decline in the Canadian dollar.

International Equity Funds. These funds invest in shares of companies around the world. There are also many funds that invest in a particular country or region such as the United States, the Pacific Rim, or Latin America. The primary objective of these funds, like their Canadian counterparts, is to provide investors with long-term capital appreciation. The value of these funds will be affected not only by political uncertainties and market conditions, however, but also by exchange-rate fluctuations — just like international bond funds. When the Canadian dollar falls in value against the currency of the country your fund holds assets in, you gain. When the Canadian dollar goes up in value, this will eat into your returns. Management expenses are also higher for international funds, due to the added cost of having overseas advisers and operating in foreign markets.

International Balanced Funds. These funds provide a competitive total return through balanced diversification in international bonds, stocks, and currencies. A typical asset mix of 60% bonds and 40% stocks would change according to market conditions to maximize potential growth without excessive risk exposure. International balanced funds are suitable for investors who do not want to commit to a single international fund and would prefer a more diversified portfolio in one fund. Generally speaking, these funds are less volatile than international equity funds but more volatile than international money-market and income funds. International balanced funds are affected by interest-rate changes, stock-market performance, currency fluctuations, and the economic conditions of the countries of investment.

Segregated Funds

A segregated fund is a mutual fund offered by a life insurance company. The assets of the fund are segregated (hence the name) from the other assets of the company. Unlike mutual funds that are not protected by insurance, a segregated fund may guarantee that at maturity, or on your death, you, or your estate, will receive not less than 75%, and sometimes 100%, of the total amount originally invested. Segregated funds, like other mutual funds, invest in all asset classes, domestically and internationally. Sales commissions for segregated funds can be high and are usually non-negotiable. Also, bear in mind that life insurance funds offered through subsidiaries, rather than the life insurance company itself, may not be segregated and will not be guaranteed.

4

Management Styles

ALTHOUGH THE MOST important determinant of the performance of equity-based mutual funds is the performance of the stock market as a whole, a particular manager's investment style is not something that should be ignored. Investors are well advised to look at a manager's investment philosophy as well as a fund's past performance figures before making a buying decision. Fund managers usually adhere to one of the following approaches.

Growth

These managers look for companies with a good track record of rapid growth in sales and earnings and the potential for more of the same. Typically a growth stock will have a higher-than-average price-to-earnings ratio and trade at a price well above book value. The belief is that the future growth of the company will, in a relatively short time frame, justify its current high price and provide even higher prices in the future. Growth investments will often be in the small-to-medium-capitalization companies.

Value

Managers who follow a value approach search for assets that are under-valued or where the manager feels the market may not be appreciating the full potential for that company or industry. Typically these stocks sell at low price-to-earnings ratios or book value, or may have hidden assets such as real-estate or trademark rights. The strategy is to buy the assets cheap and sell them when their market value rises.

Sector

These managers focus on specific industries such as high technology or chemicals that, based on their analysis, will experience the greatest growth. The investment portfolio will then be built around individual companies within these selected industries. Some sector investors attempt to forecast which areas of a market will do well in the short term. Their strategy is to get in at the bottom before other investors catch on.

Many managers use a blend investment style, employing a combination of value, growth, and sector strategies.

Top-Down

Managers who use a top-down approach first analyse the economy and market outlooks and then select markets and industries that they feel will outperform. These managers are more concerned with the big picture than with individual companies.

Bottom-Up

Fund managers who follow a bottom-up management style start by selecting promising individual companies, with little or no emphasis on the larger picture. Only stocks or bonds that meet these managers' investment criteria are purchased. If they can't find what they want, they will hold cash until they do.

Some fund managers combine top-down and bottom-up styles by determining not only the countries and industries in which to invest but also the individual companies.

Interest-Rate Anticipation

When actively employed this technique covers forecasting and analysing the direction of the change in interest rates, the degree of the change across maturities, and the timing of the change. Any anticipated drop in interest rates would dictate an increase in the duration of the bond portfolio, and the opposite action would be called for when rates are expected to rise. The greater the shift of the duration prior to the change in rates, provided the manager's forecast and timing are correct, the greater the incremental returns.

Spread Trading

This approach involves switching bond issues to take advantage of higher yields or to decrease risk without adversely affecting the yield. Spread traders analyse and closely monitor credit risk, historical yield relationships, and the yield curve. Unlike interest-rate anticipators, spread traders are very active market participants.

Although many managers remain true to their investment philosophy, others use a combination of two or more styles. None of these investment styles is better or worse, only different. Read the prospectus and annual report or call the fund company if you have any questions on a particular manager's style.

Part Two

· ·

THE SELECTION PROCESS: IDENTIFYING THE HEAVY HITTERS AND UNDERACHIEVERS

5

•••••••••••••••••••••••••••••••••

What Is a Heavy Hitter?

WITH MORE THAN 1,400 mutual funds to choose from, it is no wonder that most individual investors find the process not only confusing but also extremely time consuming. Many investors, when deciding which fund to purchase, often base their judgment solely on its short-term performance. Some base their decision on the basis of five-year returns while others simply give up and go with the hot fund of the month. Either way, the decision arrived at is at best unsatisfactory and at worst dangerous. In this chapter we discuss the methodology developed to identify the Heavy Hitter funds. This methodology is based solely on facts. It takes into account both compound and annual rates of return, the degree of risk, and how a fund's performance compares with the appropriate market index.

Compound vs Arithmetic Returns

Before getting into the methodology, we need to address the important issue of why we use the compound rate of return instead of the simple average annual return to judge the performance of funds. Many investors are understandably confused about which is the appropriate measure to use. Articles constantly appear in the press warning them that compound returns are misleading because they tend to hide, or smooth out, fluctuations in a fund's performance over time. Logic would seem to dictate, then, that by looking at annual returns you get a better handle on a fund's performance. If that's the case, why not use the simple average to measure a fund's annual returns over a period of time? While this may sound like a trivial question, it is actually a very important one. Let's look at what these two different measures tell us:

- The compound average return indicates the rate at which wealth grows over time.
- The arithmetic average indicates the annual average return from investing.

As investors we want, and need, to know the rate at which our money grows over time. The method used to calculate this compound average return is the geometric mean. The arithmetic, or simple, average, on the other hand, while it will give you a rough indication of wealth creation, is actually the measure that is misleading. To illustrate this point, let's assume you start with an initial investment of $2,000. At the end of the first year your investment rises by 25% to $2,500, but in the second year it suffers a loss of 20% and drops back to $2,000. The annual average arithmetic change is +2.5%. According to this measure, your investment has averaged gains of 2.5% a year, which is, of course, absurd. Your true return is obviously zero. And if you use the geometric mean formula, that's precisely the answer you will get.

Typically, you will also find that over longer time frames the average return is higher than the compound return. A study in the United States, by Ibbotson & Associates, found that over a period of 63 years, from 1925 to 1988, the compound return for U.S. common stocks was 10% a year, whereas the arithmetic mean showed a return of 12.1%. Similarly, for small-company stocks the compound return was 12.3%, whereas the arithmetic mean or average return was 17.8%. A difference of over five percentage points! Clearly, as a gauge of wealth creation the arithmetic mean is misleading and is not the measure to use. This does not mean, however, that one should ignore annual numbers. On the contrary, they contain valuable insights about a fund's performance. More about this later.

Screening the Heavy Hitters — The First Step

With over 1,400 funds to analyse, determining the Heavy Hitters is no small task. The first basic selection criterion is that *a fund must have at least a five-year performance history*. A fund with a five-year track record gives you relevant information about how it has performed during the ups and downs of the economic cycle, the volatility of the fund's returns, and whether the risks of investing in it are worth the reward. Newer funds don't have enough history for you to make an informed decision about their overall performance. However, we do flag those promising new funds with at least a three-year track record that are potential near-future members of the Heavy Hitters club. These funds are included in our "Rookie Camp" category — that is, they appear to have what it takes but have not yet proven themselves over a five-year period.

To qualify as a Heavy Hitter, *a fund must consistently post, within its category, an above-average return over each and every one of the past one-, three-, and five-year periods.* Rankings based on only one time frame can be misleading. When you look at funds with at least a five-year history and rank them, for example, only by their five-year compound rate of return, the results can be deceptive. A fund may have done extremely well in any one of those five years but bombed out or performed poorly in the other four. That one year's stellar performance could, however, easily boost the five-year compound return and give an erroneous impression of the fund's performance. The Heavy Hitter methodology by contrast greatly reduces this possibility by looking at three separate time frames. Therefore, even if a fund delivered an above-average return over a three- and five-year period, and only marginally failed to meet the mark in the latest one-year period, it still would not qualify as a Heavy Hitter. The selection criterion is stringent and eliminates close to 90% of the funds currently available.

The Second Step

As stated earlier, because compound returns tend to hide or smooth over the peaks and valleys of a fund's performance, it is also important to look at annual performance data. This is like focusing on the small print. You get to see easily what was indiscernible before. In our methodology, once a fund passes the one-, three-, and five-year screening process, it becomes a Heavy Hitter. Then each Heavy Hitter is put under a magnifying glass and rated according to its benchmark, volatility, and quartile performance on a calendar year basis over the past five years.

Benchmark Performance. Comparing a fund's returns with an appropriate benchmark gives additional valuable information on a fund's performance. The most commonly used benchmarks are market indexes such as the TSE 300, the S&P 500, and the Morgan Stanley World Index. By comparing, for example, the Canadian equity Heavy Hitter funds with the TSE 300 Index one can see how often a particular fund has beaten the index over the past five years. This gives investors a good gauge with which to judge the performance of a fund during periods when the TSE was declining, as well as when it was increasing. The most appropriate benchmark, or a combination, is used for each category, such as the ScotiaMcLeod Universe Bond Index for bond funds and the S&P 500 Total Return Index for U.S. equity funds. Benchmarks are not precise, but nevertheless give investors valuable information. We award two points for each year that a fund beats its benchmark. Funds that beat their designated benchmarks in each of the five years from 1992 to 1996 receive the maximum of 10 points.

Volatility. As investors we are all interested in the question of risk. How volatile are the returns of our fund? How does its degree of volatility compare with that of other funds in the same category? Is the risk worth the reward? One widely accepted measure of risk is standard deviation. Standard deviation measures the volatility of a fund's actual monthly returns relative to the average, or mean, monthly return for the fund over the period. Standard deviation allows one to compare funds with similar objectives over a particular time frame. It can also be used as an indication of how much more risk a fund in one category has versus a fund in another.

To arrive at a volatility rating, we compare a fund's standard deviation with all other funds' standard deviations and classify it into one of ten deciles. A low volatility rating of 1 would indicate a fund with a more stable monthly rate of return. The higher the volatility rating, the wider the swings in return. Because the Heavy Hitters are by definition all above-average performers, those with lower volatility ratings are awarded higher points. Given the choice, most investors would prefer to receive superior returns with lower risk. Therefore, funds with a volatility rating of 1, the lowest, receive a maximum of 10 points. On the other hand, funds with a volatility rating of 10, the highest, receive only one point.

Quartile Performance. The third criterion used in rating the Heavy Hitters is how often a fund has achieved either first-quartile (top 25%) or second-quartile (top 50%) returns performance in its category. We award two points for each year of first-quartile performance and one point for each year of second-quartile performance. A Heavy Hitter fund that delivers a first-quartile performance every year over the past five years receives the maximum of 10 points. No points are awarded for third- or fourth-quartile performances.

The Heavy Hitter Scoreboard

All Heavy Hitter funds are ranked according to total points scored, up to a maximum of 30, and are awarded one to three stars as shown below.

★★★	24–30 points
★★1/2	21–23 points
★★	18–20 points
★1/2	15–17 points
★	14 points or fewer

To see an example of this process, let's take a look at the Saxon Stock Fund ★★★, a Canadian equity fund, to see how it achieved its three-star rating. This fund has a volatility rating of 3, which gives it a score of 8 points. It beat the benchmark, the TSE 300 Total Return Index, four out of the five years from 1992 to 1996 and received 8 out of 10 points for this category. For quartile performance the Saxon Stock Fund achieved quartile 1 in four of the five years, scoring 8 points. Total points scored: 24.

To help investors narrow down their choices, we have also included in each chapter detailed information on all the Heavy Hitter funds. This includes important factors such as each fund's investment style, the manager and how long he or she has been with the fund, asset size, portfolio composition, best and worst year returns, and how much the fund charges in management expenses for every $100 in assets.

It is also important for investors to bear in mind that every Heavy Hitter, regardless of its rating, is an above-average fund.

Monitoring the Heavy Hitters

Heavy Hitters, like all funds, need to be monitored on a regular basis. Some funds will slip out of the Heavy Hitter category temporarily because of a lapse in performance, which is normal. As investors we must accept that *every* fund will from time to time have periods of underperformance. A few may drop out completely, because of a systemic problem resulting in a continuous decline in performance. It is important to check the Rankings/Returns table in the appropriate chapter to see how your particular fund is measuring up against its peers.

Because our methodology allows no exceptions, any fund that slips, however marginally, in its one-year performance won't make the Heavy Hitter list, and this includes former Heavy Hitters. A good example would be the Templeton Growth Fund. A Heavy Hitter in the 1996 edition of the *World of Mutual Funds*, the fund didn't quite make it last year due to a below-average one-year return. Its three- and five-year returns were well above average. However, as noted in the 1997 edition, "this fund clearly has an excellent track record and its lapse in performance does not mean that you should rush out and sell your units." This year, the Templeton Growth Fund returns to the Heavy Hitter ranks with above-average returns in all three time periods. As stated earlier, these *temporary* lapses in performance are normal. They are not an indication to redeem units. No fund will deliver above-average returns every single month. And many funds will (and do) underperform for extended periods of time before bouncing back.

However, if any fund were to deliver below-average returns month in and month out, over (say) a 12-to-18-month period, and your numerous calls to your sales representative had not reassured you, then it would obviously be time to seriously consider moving on or, at the very least, looking at other funds for your next investment.

Under the Heavy Hitter screening process, either a fund meets the criteria or it doesn't. This rigidity is one of the major strengths of the methodology. Investors should know if a fund's performance has slipped, even if it's only temporary. This is what monitoring is all about. After all, you don't want to wake up one morning to find that the bottom has fallen out of your investment portfolio. That's why it is crucial to track your fund's performance on a regular basis.

6

● ●

The Heavy Hitters at a Glance

USING OUR RESEARCH methodology, we have identified a total of 194 funds that are Heavy Hitters. Eighty-nine are load funds and 105 are no-load funds. These Heavy Hitters manage a total of $84 billion in assets and include 145 Canadian and 49 international funds. Of the 145 Canadian Heavy Hitters, 92 are no-load funds and 53 are load funds. In contrast, 36 of the 49 international Heavy Hitters are load funds and only 13 are no-load funds.

Among the Canadian Heavy Hitters, TD's Green Line Canadian Money Market is the largest, with $5.3 billion in assets, and AMI's Private Capital Equity Fund is the smallest, with $1.5 million in assets. Among the international Heavy Hitters, the Templeton Growth Fund is the largest, with $7.6 billion in assets, and the Mutual Amerifund is the smallest, with $6.6 million in assets.

There are 57 funds on the market with assets of more than $1 billion. Twenty-one of the billion-dollar funds are Heavy Hitters — 10 Canadian and 11 international. Six of the 10 Canadian billion-dollar Heavy Hitters are no-load funds. In contrast, only one of the 11 international billion-dollar Heavy Hitters is a no-load fund.

Readers should consult the relevant chapter for information on a Heavy Hitter's performance, volatility, investment style, and management expenses. For information on how many Heavy Hitters a particular fund company has, consult Appendix 3.

THE BILLION-DOLLAR HEAVY HITTERS

CANADIAN MUTUAL FUNDS

	Assets ($bns)
Green Line Canadian Money Market (N)	5.3
Trimark Select Balanced Fund	3.8
First Canadian Mortgage Fund (N)	2.0
CIBC Premium T-Bill Fund (N)	1.9
CIBC Mortgage Fund (N)	1.7
AIC Advantage Fund	1.5
Investors Government Bond Fund	1.5
PH&N Balanced Pension Trust (N)	1.4
PH&N Bond Fund (N)	1.3
Spectrum United Canadian Equity	1.0

INTERNATIONAL MUTUAL FUNDS

Templeton Growth Fund Ltd.	7.6
Trimark Select Growth Fund	5.1
Templeton International Stock Fund	3.4
Trimark Fund	2.7
MD Growth Fund (N)	2.7
Fidelity Far East Fund	1.9
Investors North American Growth	1.6
Fidelity International Portfolio	1.6
Templeton Emerging Markets Fund	1.3
Investors Pacific International	1.2
Fidelity Growth America Fund	1.1

(N) denotes a no-load fund

CANADIAN HEAVY HITTERS

CANADIAN EQUITY FUNDS

Load Funds (13):
- AIC Advantage Fund ★★1/2
- Empire Equity Growth Fund 3 ★★1/2
- Equitable Life Seg. Common Stock ★★1/2
- Bissett Canadian Equity Fund ★★1/2
- Guardian Growth Equity Fund A ★★
- Clean Environment Equity Fund ★★
- Standard Life Ideal Equity Fund ★★

CANADIAN HEAVY HITTERS *continued*

- Pursuit Canadian Equity Fund ★★
- Cundill Security Fund ★1/2
- Spectrum United Canadian Equity ★1/2
- National Life Equities Fund ★1/2
- Empire Premier Equity Fund 1 ★1/2
- Maritime Life Growth - A & C ★

No-Load Funds (17):
- Saxon Stock Fund ★★★
- ABC Fundamental Value Fund ★★1/2
- Phillips Hager & North Vintage ★★1/2
- GBC Canadian Growth Fund ★★1/2
- Tradex Equity Fund Ltd. ★★1/2
- McLean Budden Pooled Cdn. Equity ★★1/2
- Industrial Alliance Stocks Fund ★★
- Phillips Hager & North Cdn. Equity Plus ★★
- Phillips Hager & North Cdn. Equity ★★
- Trust Pret & Revenu Canadian Fund ★★
- InvesNat Canadian Equity Fund ★1/2
- McLean Budden Equity Growth Fund ★1/2
- AMI Private Capital Equity ★
- Ethical Growth Fund ★
- Ferique Equity Fund ★
- Green Line Canadian Equity Fund ★
- Green Line Canadian Index Fund ★

CANADIAN SMALL-TO-MID-CAP EQUITY FUNDS

Load Funds (2):
- Bissett Small Cap Fund ★★1/2
- Guardian Enterprise Fund A ★1/2

No-Load Funds (2):
- Mawer New Canada Fund ★★
- Sceptre Equity Growth Fund ★★

CANADIAN HEAVY HITTERS *continued*

CANADIAN DIVIDEND FUNDS

Load Funds (4):
- Maxxum Dividend Fund ★★★
- AGF Dividend Fund ★★1/2
- Industrial Dividend Growth Fund Ltd. ★★
- Dynamic Dividend Growth Fund ★1/2

No-Load Funds (3):
- Phillips Hager & North Div. Income ★★1/2
- Scotia Excelsior Dividend Fund ★1/2
- Royal Trust Growth and Income Fund ★1/2

CANADIAN BALANCED FUNDS

Load Funds (11):
- Bissett Retirement Fund ★★★
- Maxxum Canadian Balanced Fund ★★1/2
- Trimark Select Balanced Fund ★★1/2
- Industrial Pension Fund ★★
- Caldwell Securities Associate Fund ★★
- Cassels Blaikie Canadian Fund ★★
- Global Strategy Income Plus Fund ★1/2
- NN Asset Allocation Fund ★1/2
- Clean Environment Balanced Fund ★1/2
- Templeton Balanced Fund ★
- National Life Balanced Fund ★

No-Load Funds (16):
- ABC Fully Managed Fund ★★★
- Saxon Balanced Fund ★★★
- Beutel Goodman Private Balanced ★★1/2
- McLean Budden Pooled Balanced Fund ★★1/2
- McLean Budden Registered Balanced ★★1/2
- Phillips Hager & North Bal. Pens. Tr. ★★1/2
- Sceptre Balanced Growth Fund ★★
- McLean Budden Balanced Fund ★★
- Phillips Hager & North Balanced ★★
- Leith Wheeler Balanced Fund ★★

CANADIAN HEAVY HITTERS *continued*

- Scotia Excelsior Total Return Fund ★1/2
- Industrial Alliance Diversified ★1/2
- Ferique Balanced Fund ★1/2
- Mawer Cdn. Balanced RSP Fund ★1/2
- AMI Private Capital Optimix ★
- Ontario Teachers Group Balanced ★

CANADIAN BOND FUNDS

Load Funds (11):
- AGF Canadian Bond Fund ★★1/2
- Bissett Bond Fund ★★
- Spectrum United Long-Term Bond Fund ★★
- Industrial Bond Fund ★1/2
- Equitable Life Segregated Accum. Inc. ★1/2
- Maxxum Income Fund ★1/2
- Hyperion High Yield Bond Fund ★1/2
- NN Bond Fund ★1/2
- National Life Fixed Income Fund ★
- Talvest Bond Fund ★
- Investors Government Bond Fund ★

No-Load Funds (25):
- Batirente - Section Obligations ★★★
- Fonds Optimum Obligations ★★1/2
- Phillips Hager & North Bond Fund ★★1/2
- Altamira Bond Fund ★★
- Altamira Income Fund ★★
- MD Bond Fund ★★
- Beutel Goodman Income Fund ★★
- McLean Budden Pooled Fixed Income ★★
- Ferique Bond Fund ★1/2
- GBC Canadian Bond Fund ★1/2
- AMI Private Capital Income ★1/2
- Co-operators Fixed Income Fund ★1/2
- Ethical Income Fund ★1/2
- Green Line Canadian Bond Fund ★1/2
- National Trust Canadian Bond Fund ★1/2

CANADIAN HEAVY HITTERS *continued*

- First Canadian Bond Fund ★
- Green Line Canadian Gov't Bond Fund ★
- McLean Budden Fixed Income Fund ★
- Atlas Canadian Bond Fund ★
- Mawer Canadian Bond Fund ★
- Royal Trust Bond Fund ★
- RoyFund Bond Fund ★
- Sceptre Bond Fund ★
- BNP (Canada) Bond Fund ★
- HRL Bond Fund ★

CANADIAN MORTGAGE FUNDS

Load Funds (1):
- Investors Income Portfolio Fund ★★

No-Load Funds (4):
- Ontario Teachers Group Mortgage Inc. ★★1/2
- CIBC Mortgage Fund ★1/2
- First Canadian Mortgage Fund ★1/2
- GWL Mortgage Fund (G) NL ★

CANADIAN MONEY-MARKET FUNDS

Load Funds (9):
- Bissett Money Market Fund ★★1/2
- Talvest Money Fund ★★
- Elliott & Page Money Fund ★★
- C.I. Money Market Fund ★★
- Industrial Cash Management ★★
- BPI T-Bill Fund ★1/2
- Trans-Canada Money Market (Sagit) ★1/2
- Trimark Interest Fund ★1/2
- Manulife Vistafund 1 Short Term Sec. ★1/2

No-Load Funds (24):
- Ontario Teachers Group Fixed Value ★★★
- Fonds de Professionnels Short Term ★★★
- Ferique Short Term Income Fund ★★★

CANADIAN HEAVY HITTERS *continued*

- Pursuit Money Market Fund ★★1/2
- Beutel Goodman Money Market Fund ★★1/2
- Capstone Cash Management Fund ★★1/2
- AMI Private Capital Money Market ★★
- CDA Money Market (Canagex) ★★
- Maxxum Money Market Fund ★★
- NN Money Market Fund ★★
- Phillips Hager & North Cdn. Money Mkt. ★★
- Green Line Cdn. Money Market ★★
- HRL Instant $$ Fund ★★
- MD Money Fund ★★
- Sceptre Money Market Fund ★1/2
- InvesNat Treasury Bill Plus Fund ★1/2
- Lotus (MKW) Income Fund ★1/2
- CIBC Premium T-Bill Fund ★1/2
- General Trust of Canada Money Mkt. ★1/2
- Fonds Ficadre Money Market ★
- Mawer Canadian Money Market Fund ★
- McLean Budden Money Market Fund ★
- Green Line Canadian T-Bill Fund ★
- Hongkong Bank Money Market Fund ★

SPECIAL EQUITY FUNDS

Load Funds (2):
- 20/20 Canadian Resources Fund
- Universal Canadian Resource Fund

No-Load Funds (1):
- Royal Energy Fund

INTERNATIONAL HEAVY HITTERS

INTERNATIONAL EQUITY FUNDS

Load Funds (13):
- Templeton Growth Fund Ltd. ★★1/2
- Templeton International Stock Fund ★★1/2
- Trimark Fund ★★1/2
- Trimark Select Growth Fund ★★

INTERNATIONAL HEAVY HITTERS *continued*

- Empire International Fund ★★
- Canada Life U.S. & Int. Equity S-34 ★★
- Investors Growth Portfolio Fund ★1/2
- Investors North American Growth ★1/2
- Investors Special Fund ★1/2
- Dynamic International Fund ★1/2
- Fidelity International Portfolio ★1/2
- Special Opportunities Fund ★1/2
- National Life Global Equities Fund ★1/2

No-Load Funds (3):
- MD Growth Fund ★★1/2
- Cornerstone Global Fund ★1/2
- Mawer World Investment Fund ★1/2

EMERGING-MARKET FUNDS
Load Funds (1):
- Templeton Emerging Markets Fund ★★

EUROPEAN FUNDS
Load Funds (2):
- Dynamic Europe Fund ★
- Vision Europe Fund ★

ASIAN FUNDS
Load Funds (5):
- Fidelity Far East Fund ★★
- Investors Pacific International ★★
- C.I. Pacific Fund ★1/2
- C.I. Pacific Sector Shares ★1/2
- Hyperion Asian Fund ★1/2

U.S. EQUITY FUNDS
Load Funds (9):
- Chou Associates Fund ★★
- Fidelity Growth America Fund ★★
- AIC Value Fund ★1/2

INTERNATIONAL HEAVY HITTERS *continued*

- Investors U.S. Growth Fund ★1/2
- AGF American Growth Fund ★
- Hyperion Value Line U.S. Equity ★
- Dynamic Americas Fund ★
- Mutual Amerifund ★
- BPI American Equity Value Fund ★

No-Load Funds (9):
- Phillips Hager & North U.S. Equity ★★1/2
- RoyFund U.S. Equity Fund ★★
- Green Line U.S. Index Fund ($US) ★
- McLean Budden Pooled American Equity ★
- Ethical North American Equity Fund ★
- Royal Trust American Stock Fund ★
- Cornerstone U.S. Fund ★
- McLean Budden American Growth Fund ★
- Atlas American Large Cap Growth Fund ★

INTERNATIONAL BALANCED FUNDS

Load Funds (2):
- Investors Growth Plus Portfolio ★1/2
- AGF American Tactical Asset Alloc. ★1/2

INTERNATIONAL BOND FUNDS

Load Funds (3):
- Guardian International Income A ★★1/2
- Dynamic Global Bond Fund ★★
- Admax World Income Fund ★1/2

INTERNATIONAL MONEY-MARKET FUNDS

Load Funds (1):
- AGF U.S. Dollar Money Market ($US)

No-Load Funds (1):
- Phillips Hager & North $US Money Mkt.

( ) number of funds

7

● ●

Heavy Hitter Fund Companies

THERE ARE A number of fund companies that stand out from the crowd
due to a preponderance of Heavy Hitters. To make our list on the
domestic side, a company must have no Underachievers (see Chapter
8) and a minimum of three Heavy Hitters. On the international side,
since there are considerably fewer funds to draw from, the minimum
number of Heavy Hitters is reduced to two (again no Underachievers).
Based on these criteria, out of a total of 155 fund companies, only 10
have made the grade for domestic funds and six for international. On
the Canadian side, eight of the 10 Heavy Hitter companies are no-
load. In contrast, on the international side only two of the six
companies are no-load. Only one company — Phillips Hager &
North — has Heavy Hitter funds in both categories.

HEAVY HITTER FUND COMPANIES

CANADIAN MUTUAL FUNDS

- Phillips Hager & North* (8)
- McLean Budden* (8)
- Bissett & Associates (5)
- Maxxum Group of Funds (4)
- Sceptre Investment Counsel* (4)
- Mawer Investment Management* (4)
- AMI Private Capital* (4)

HEAVY HITTER FUND COMPANIES *continued*
- Ordre des Ingenieurs du Quebec* (4)
- Beutel Goodman Managed Funds* (3)
- Ontario Teachers Group (3)

INTERNATIONAL MUTUAL FUNDS
- Dynamic Mutual Funds (4)
- Fidelity Investments (3)
- Templeton (3)
- Trimark (2)
- Phillips Hager & North* (2)
- Laurentian Bank Investment Services Inc.* (2)

( ) number of Heavy Hitters
* denotes a no-load fund company

Canadian Mutual Funds

Phillips Hager & North Ltd. This no-load fund company has made the Heavy Hitter Fund Companies list for the third year in a row. Of a total of eight domestic funds with a five-year performance history, all eight of Phillips Hager & North's funds are Heavy Hitters. Included in this group are three Canadian equity, two balanced, one dividend, one bond, and one money-market fund. With assets of $5.7 billion, the company has a total of 13 funds. Phillips Hager & North has a minimum initial investment requirement of $25,000 for non-RRSP accounts and $5,000 for RRSP accounts. The company charges management fees that average only 0.93% of assets, which is below the group average of 1.93% for all Canadian funds. Expenses range from a low of 0.48% for PH&N's money-market fund to a high of 1.76% for its Vintage Equity Fund.

McLean Budden Limited. For the second year in a row this no-load company has made the Heavy Hitter Fund Companies list. Of a total of eight domestic funds with a five-year performance history, all eight are Heavy Hitters. Included in this group are three balanced, two equity, two bond, and one money-market fund. Four of the eight are pooled funds which have a minimum initial investment requirement of $500,000. The remaining four funds have a minimum initial investment requirement of $5,000. With assets of $1.1 billion, the company has a total of 13 funds and charges management fees that average 1.16% of assets for its Canadian funds, which is below the group average. Management expenses range from a low of 0.75% for its money-market fund to a high of 1.75% of its balanced and equity growth funds.

Bissett & Associates Investment Management Ltd. This Calgary-based fund company joins the ranks of the Heavy Hitters this year. Of a total of five domestic funds with a five-year performance history, all five are Heavy Hitters. Included in this group are an equity, a small-cap, a balanced, a bond, and a money-market fund. With assets of $276 million, the company has a total of eight funds. The company charges below-average management fees that average 1.07% for its Canadian funds. Expenses range from a low of 0.44% for its retirement fund to a high of 1.90% for its small-cap fund. The funds have a minimum initial investment requirement of $10,000 and are available for sale only in Alberta, British Columbia, and Ontario. No sales commissions apply when the funds are purchased directly from the company.

Maxxum Group of Funds. This company is one of only three to make the Heavy Hitter Fund Companies list for the third year in a row. Of a total of seven domestic funds with a five-year performance history, four are Heavy Hitters. Included in this group are a balanced, a dividend, a bond, and a money-market fund. With assets of $725 million, the company has a total of nine funds, which are sold on a front- or back-end load basis. The company charges below-average management expenses that average 1.88% of assets for its Canadian funds. Expenses range from a low of 0.85% for its money-market fund to a high of 2.25% for its natural resource and precious metals funds.

Sceptre Investment Counsel. This no-load company makes the Heavy Hitter Fund Companies list for the second year in a row. Of a total of four domestic funds with a five-year performance history, all four are Heavy Hitters. Included in this group are a balanced, a bond, a small-cap, and a money-market fund. With assets of $760 million, the company has a total of six funds. The company charges below-average management expenses that average 1.24% of assets for its Canadian funds. Expenses range from a low of 0.75% for its money-market fund to a high of 1.51% for its equity fund. The funds have a minimum initial investment requirement of $5,000.

Mawer Investment Management. This Calgary-based investment firm joins the ranks of the Heavy Hitters this year. Of a total of six domestic funds with a five-year performance history, four are Heavy Hitters. Included in this group are a balanced, a small-cap, a bond, and a money-market fund. With assets of $300 million, this no-load company has a total of 10 funds. The company charges below-average management expenses that average 0.97% of assets for its Canadian funds. Expenses range from a low of 0.57% for its money-market fund to a high of 1.34% for its small-cap fund. The funds have a minimum initial investment requirement of $25,000.

AMI Private Capital. This company joins the ranks of the Heavy Hitters this year. Of a total of four domestic funds with a five-year performance history, all four are Heavy Hitters. Included in this group are an equity, a balanced, a bond, and a money-market fund. With assets of $9 million, this no-load company has a total of four funds. The company charges below-average management expenses that average 1.38% of assets for its Canadian funds. Expenses range from a low of 0.75% for its money-market fund to a high of 1.75% for its other funds. The funds have a minimum initial investment requirement of $50,000.

Ordre des Ingenieurs du Quebec. This Quebec-based professional engineers' association makes the Heavy Hitter Fund Companies list for the third year in a row. Of a total of four domestic funds with a five-year performance history, all four are Heavy Hitters. Included in this group are a balanced, a bond, an equity, and a money-market fund. The balanced and money-market funds are managed by the Montreal firm T.A.L. Investment Counsel Ltd., the bond fund is managed by the investment firm Canagex Inc., and the equity fund by Phillips Hager & North and Montrusco Associates. With assets of $497 million, the association has a total of seven funds, which are sold on a no-load basis. For its Canadian funds, management fees average only 0.58% of assets and range from a low of 0.44% for its money-market fund to a high of 0.87% for its equity fund. The funds can be purchased only by the association's members.

Beutel Goodman Managed Funds. This company makes the Heavy Hitter Fund Companies list for the second year in a row. Of a total of five domestic funds with a five-year performance history, three are Heavy Hitters. Included in this group are a balanced, a bond, and a money-market fund. With assets of $430 million, the company has a total of nine funds, which are sold on a no-load basis. For its Canadian funds, management fees average 1.42% of assets, which is below the group average, and range from a low of 0.63% for its income and money-market funds to a high of 2.56% for its small-cap fund. The minimum initial investment requirement for these funds is $2,500.

Ontario Teachers Group Inc. This teachers' association joins the ranks of the Heavy Hitters this year. Of a total of five domestic funds with a five-year performance history, three are Heavy Hitters. Included in this group are a balanced, a mortgage, and a money-market fund, all managed by the investment firm AMI Private Capital. With assets of $260 million, the company has a total of six funds, which are sold on a no-load basis. For its Canadian funds, management fees average 0.85% of assets, which is below the group average, and range from a low of 0.50% for its money-market fund to a high of 1.00% for its balanced, equity, and small-cap funds. The funds are available for sale only to members of the Ontario Teachers Association.

International Mutual Funds

Dynamic Mutual Funds. This company makes the Heavy Hitter Fund Companies list on the international side for the second year in a row. Of a total of five international funds with a five-year performance history, four are Heavy Hitters. Included in this group are an international equity, a European, an international bond, and a U.S. equity fund. With assets of $6.1 billion, the company has a total of 23 funds, which are sold on a front- or back-end load basis. For its international funds, management fees average 2.54% of assets, which is above the group average of 2.26%, and range from a low of 1.75% for its international bond fund to a high of 3.57% for its Asian equity fund.

Templeton Management Limited. This company makes the Heavy Hitter Fund Companies list for the third year in a row. Of a total of five international funds with a five-year performance history, three are Heavy Hitters. Included in this group are two international equity funds and one emerging-markets fund. With assets of $13.2 billion, the company has a total of 14 funds, which are sold on a commission basis. The company charges above-average management expenses that average 2.41% of assets for its international funds and range from a low of 2.0% for its

Templeton Growth Fund to a high of 3.30% for its emerging-markets fund.

Fidelity Investments Canada Ltd. This company makes the Heavy Hitter Fund Companies list for the second year in a row. Of a total of three international funds with a five-year performance history, all three are Heavy Hitters. Included in this group are an international equity, an Asian, and a U.S. equity fund. With assets of $9.7 billion, the company has a total of 20 funds, which are sold on a commission basis. The company charges above-average management expenses that average 2.62% of assets for its international funds and range from a low of 1.25% for its international money-market fund to a high of 3.50% for its Latin America Growth Fund.

Trimark Investment Management Inc. This fund company scores again for the third time in a row. Of a total of two international funds with a five-year performance history, the Trimark Fund and the Trimark Select Growth Fund, both are Heavy Hitters. With assets of $25 billion, the company has a total of 14 funds, which are sold on a commission basis. The company charges above-average management expenses that average 2.31% of assets for its international funds and range from a low of 1.52% for its Trimark Fund to a high of 2.74% for its Indo-Pacific Fund.

Phillips Hager & North Ltd. PH&N has two international funds with a five-year performance history, an international money-market and a U.S. equity fund, and both are Heavy Hitters for the second year in a row. For its international funds, management expenses average only 1.0% of assets and range from a low of 0.52% for its international money-market fund to a high of 1.49% for its International Equity Fund. As noted above, the company has a minimum initial investment requirement of $25,000 for non-RRSP accounts and $5,000 for RRSP accounts.

Laurentian Bank Investment Services Inc. (now Cornerstone Management Inc.). This fund company joins the ranks of the Heavy Hitters this year. Of a total of two international funds with a five-year performance history, the Cornerstone Global Fund and the Cornerstone U.S. Fund, both are Heavy Hitters. With assets of $293 million, this no-load company has a total of six funds. For its international funds, management expenses average 2.79% of assets, which is above the group average of 2.26%.

8
• •

What Is an Underachiever?

MANY PEOPLE HOLD units in mutual funds that consistently provide poor returns. Obviously, those investors do so unknowingly. Before you make the mistake of thinking that this must be a rare occurrence, or only something that happens to a few misguided souls, you should contemplate a few hard facts. There are currently 176 mutual funds that are members of the Underachievers club. These funds hold assets totalling $55 billion and charge combined management fees of about $1.1 billion!

Identifying those funds that underperform relative to their peers is not an arbitrary process. As in the case of the Heavy Hitters, our first basic selection criterion is that a fund must have at least a five-year performance history before it can be classified as an Underachiever. In order to join the ranks of the Underachievers, *a fund must consistently post, within its category, below-average returns over each and every one of the past one-, three-, and five-year periods.*

The difference in returns between holding units in a Heavy Hitter and an Underachiever can be substantial. For example, for an initial investment of $10,000, the average Heavy Hitter Canadian equity fund would have returned a total of $22,975 over the past five years. For the same investment, the average Underachiever would have returned $17,545 — for a difference of $5,430 or 30.9%.

Similarly, for an initial investment of $10,000, the average Heavy Hitter international equity fund would have returned a total of $21,185 over the past five years. The average Underachiever in contrast would have returned $15,386 — for a difference of $5,799 or 37.7%. Clearly, then, for an investor it's important not only to know which funds have performed well but also to be able to identify which funds, compared to their peers, have performed poorly.

If you own units in an Underachiever, don't panic! They're not all hopeless cases. Some funds will be marginal Underachievers, posting returns that are only slightly below the average. Others, however, are chronic cases, where you may want to consider cutting your losses and moving on.

The Underachiever Companies

To make the list below, a company must have a minimum of four Underachievers and no Heavy Hitters among those of its funds with a five-year performance history. Only one fund company has the dubious distinction of meeting these criteria.

THE UNDERACHIEVER COMPANIES

- Laurentian Fund Management (10)
  (now Strategic Value Funds Management)

( ) number of Underachievers

Strategic Value Funds Management Inc. (formerly Laurentian Fund Management Inc.). Out of a total of 11 funds with a five-year history, Strategic Value has 10 Underachievers, which cut across all asset classes. The company has a total of 19 funds, manages $1.9 billion in assets, and charges management expenses that average 2.57% of assets, well above the group average of 2.06% for all 1,431 mutual funds.

There are also a number of fund companies that stand out due to a preponderance of Underachievers. The following companies each have a minimum of nine Underachievers.

- Royal Bank
- Sagit Management Ltd.
- Manulife Financial

While the Royal Bank also has six Heavy Hitters, the other two companies each have only one Heavy Hitter amongst their funds with a five-year performance history.

On a final note, consult the Rankings/Returns table in the appropriate chapter in Parts Three and Four, where all Underachievers are highlighted, and check how your particular fund has performed over the last one-, three-, and five-year periods compared to the average for its category. This information, combined with some questioning telephone calls to your salesperson, should put you in a position to make a more knowledgeable decision regarding your investment.

9

....

The Underachievers at a Glance

USING OUR RESEARCH methodology, we have identified a total of 176 funds that are Underachievers. One hundred and nine are load funds and 67 are no-load funds. These Underachievers manage a total of $55 billion in assets and include 136 Canadian and 40 international funds. Of the 136 Canadian Underachievers, 84 are load funds and 52 are no-load funds. Of the 40 international Underachievers, 25 are load funds and 15 are no-load funds. For information on how many Underachievers a particular fund company has, readers should consult Appendix 3.

Eleven of the 57 funds on the market with assets of $1 billion are Underachievers and all are Canadian mutual funds.

THE BILLION-DOLLAR UNDERACHIEVERS
CANADIAN MUTUAL FUNDS

	Assets ($bns)
• Royal Balanced Fund (N)	5.4
• Investors Dividend Fund	3.4
• Trimark RSP Equity Fund	3.4
• Investors Retirement Growth Portfolio	2.3
• Investors Retirement Plus Portfolio	1.8
• CIBC Money Market Fund (N)	1.7
• London Life Diversified	1.7

THE BILLION-DOLLAR UNDERACHIEVERS *continued*

	Assets ($bns)
• Investors Income Plus Portfolio	1.3
• Industrial Growth Fund	1.2
• Industrial Horizon Fund	1.2
• Canada Trust Everest Money Market (N)	1.0

(N) denotes a no-load fund

Eight of these mega-Underachievers are load funds. Investors Group, Canada's largest fund company, has four billion-dollar funds that are Underachievers. Mackenzie Financial Corporation has two and the Royal Bank, CIBC, Canada Trust, Trimark, and London Life each have one billion-dollar Underachiever fund.

CANADIAN UNDERACHIEVERS

CANADIAN EQUITY FUNDS

Load Funds (26):
- Admax Canadian Performance Fund
- Admax Canadian Select Growth Fund
- AGF Canadian Equity Fund
- AGF Canadian Growth Fund
- All-Canadian Capital Fund
- BPI Canadian Equity Value Fund
- C.I. Canadian Sector Shares
- Canadian Protected Fund
- Fidelity Capital Builder Fund
- Global Strategy Canada Growth Fund
- Industrial Growth Fund
- Industrial Horizon Fund
- Investors Retirement Growth Portfolio
- Jones Heward Fund Ltd.
- Laurentian Canadian Equity Fund Ltd.
- London Life Canadian Equity
- Manulife Vistafund 1 Cap. Gains Growth
- Manulife Vistafund 1 Equity Fund
- Manulife Vistafund 2 Cap. Gains Growth

CANADIAN UNDERACHIEVERS *continued*

- Manulife Vistafund 2 Equity Fund
- Metlife MVP Equity Fund
- Middlefield Growth Fund
- Talvest Canadian Equity Value Fund
- Trans-Canada Value Fund (Sagit)
- Trimark RSP Equity Fund
- University Avenue Canadian Fund

No-Load Funds (10):
- All-Canadian Compound
- Altamira Capital Growth Fund
- CDA Common Stock Fund
- CIBC Canadian Equity Fund
- Co-operators Canadian Equity Fund
- GWL Canadian Equity Fund (G) NL
- GWL Equity Index Fund (G) NL
- ICM Equity Fund
- Royal Trust Canadian Stock Fund
- Scotia Excelsior Cdn. Blue Chip

CANADIAN SMALL-TO-MID-CAP EQUITY FUNDS

Load Funds (4):
- Cambridge Growth Fund (Sagit)
- Cambridge Special Equity (Sagit)
- Industrial Equity Fund Ltd.
- Laurentian Special Equity Fund

No-Load Funds (2):
- Altamira Special Growth Fund
- Canada Trust Everest Special Equity

CANADIAN DIVIDEND FUNDS

Load Funds (7):
- AGF High Income Fund
- Dynamic Dividend Fund
- Guardian Monthly Dividend Fund A
- Investors Dividend Fund

CANADIAN UNDERACHIEVERS *continued*

- Laurentian Dividend Fund Ltd.
- Spectrum United Dividend Fund
- Trans-Canada Dividend Fund (Sagit)

No-Load Funds (1):
- CIBC Dividend Fund

CANADIAN BALANCED FUNDS

Load Funds (13):
- BPI Canadian Balanced Fund
- Cambridge Balanced Fund (Sagit)
- Guardian Canadian Balanced Fund A
- Industrial Mortgage Securities
- Investors Income Plus Portfolio
- Investors Retirement Plus Portfolio
- Jones Heward Canadian Balanced Fund
- London Life Diversified
- Manulife Vistafund 1 Diversified
- Manulife Vistafund 2 Diversified
- Metlife MVP Balanced Fund
- Talvest Canadian Asset Allocation
- Transamerica Balanced Inv. Growth

No-Load Funds (12):
- Altamira Balanced Fund
- Altamira Growth & Income Fund
- First Canadian Asset Allocation
- Fonds de Professionnels Balanced
- GWL Diversified Fund (G) NL
- GWL Equity/Bond Fund (G) NL
- HRL Balanced Fund
- Royal Balanced Fund
- Royal Trust Advantage Balanced Fund
- Royal Trust Advantage Growth Fund
- Royal Trust Advantage Income Fund
- Scotia Excelsior Balanced Fund

CANADIAN UNDERACHIEVERS *continued*

CANADIAN BOND FUNDS

Load Funds (15):
- BPI Canadian Bond Fund
- Concorde Revenu
- Elliott & Page Bond Fund
- Empire Bond Fund
- Laurentian Government Bond Fund
- Laurentian Income Fund
- Manulife Vistafund 2 Bond Fund
- Maritime Life Bond - A & C
- Metlife MVP Bond Fund
- Mutual Bond Fund
- Pursuit Canadian Bond Fund
- Spectrum United Short-Term Bond
- Talvest Income Fund
- Templeton Canadian Bond Fund
- Trans-Canada Bond Fund (Sagit)

No-Load Funds (5):
- Fonds de Professionnels Bond
- Green Line Short Term Income Fund
- InvesNat Short Term Government Bond
- Scotia Excelsior Defensive Income
- Westbury Canadian Bond Fund

CANADIAN MORTGAGE FUNDS

Load Funds (1):
- Concorde Hypotheques

No-Load Funds (5):
- Fonds Desjardins Hypotheques
- General Trust of Canada Mortgage
- Green Line Mortgage Fund
- Industrial Alliance Mortgage Fund
- Royal Trust Mortgage Fund

CANADIAN UNDERACHIEVERS *continued*

CANADIAN MONEY-MARKET FUNDS

Load Funds (13):
- AGF Money Market Account
- C.I. Short-Term Sector Shares
- Fidelity Cdn. Short Term Asset Fund
- Imperial Growth Money Market Fund
- Industrial Alliance Ecoflex Fund M
- Industrial Short-Term Fund
- Manulife Vistafund 2 Short Term Sec.
- Maritime Life Money Market - A & C
- Metlife MVP Money Market Fund
- NAL-Canadian Money Market Fund
- National Life Money Market Fund
- NN T-Bill Fund
- Spectrum United Canadian T-Bill

No-Load Funds (17):
- Atlas Canadian Money Market Fund
- Atlas Canadian T-Bill Fund
- BNP (Canada) Canadian Money Market
- Canada Trust Everest Money Market
- CIBC Canadian T-Bill Fund
- CIBC Money Market Fund
- Cornerstone Gov't Money
- Empire Money Market Fund
- Fonds Desjardins Monetaire
- GWL Money Market Fund (G) NL
- Industrial Alliance Money Mkt. Fund
- Investors Money Market Fund
- Laurentian Money Market Fund
- Royal Trust Canadian Money Market
- RoyFund Canadian Money Market Fund
- Scotia Excelsior Money Market Fund
- Scotia Excelsior T-Bill Fund

CANADIAN UNDERACHIEVERS *continued*

SPECIAL EQUITY FUNDS

Load Funds (5):
- All-Canadian Resources Corporation
- Allstar Adrian Day Gold Plus Fund
- Goldfund Ltd. (CSA Mgmt.)
- Goldtrust (CSA Mgmt.)
- Working Ventures Canadian Fund Inc.

INTERNATIONAL UNDERACHIEVERS

INTERNATIONAL EQUITY FUNDS

Load Funds (6):
- Cambridge Global Fund (Sagit)
- Laurentian Commonwealth Fund Ltd.
- Laurentian International Fund Ltd.
- Spectrum United Global Equity Fund
- Spectrum United Global Growth Fund
- Universal World Equity Fund

No-Load Funds (8):
- Altamira Global Diversified Fund
- Canada Trust Everest Int'l Equity
- Capstone Int'l Investment Trust
- Fonds Desjardins International
- GBC International Growth Fund
- General Trust of Canada International
- Mackenzie Sentinel Global Fund
- McLean Budden Pooled Offshore Equity

EMERGING-MARKET FUNDS

Load Funds (1):
- C.I. Emerging Markets Fund

EUROPEAN FUNDS

Load Funds (1):
- Hyperion European Fund

INTERNATIONAL UNDERACHIEVERS *continued*

ASIAN FUNDS

Load Funds (3):
- Admax Korea Fund
- Cambridge Pacific Fund (Sagit)
- Investors Japanese Growth Fund

No-Load Funds (1):
- Royal Japanese Stock Fund

U.S. EQUITY FUNDS

Load Funds (8):
- AGF Special U.S. Class
- Bissett American Equity Fund
- Cambridge American Growth (Sagit)
- Century DJ Fund
- First American (Guardian Timing)
- Industrial American Fund
- Laurentian American Equity Fund Ltd.
- University Avenue Growth Fund

No-Load Funds (5):
- CIBC U.S. Equity Fund
- General Trust of Canada U.S. Equity
- Scotia Excelsior American Growth
- Trust Pret & Revenu American Fund
- Zweig Strategic Growth

INTERNATIONAL BALANCED FUNDS

Load Funds (4):
- Caldwell Securities International
- Laurentian Global Balanced Fund
- Protected American Fund
- Talvest Global Asset Allocation

INTERNATIONAL BOND FUNDS

Load Funds (2):
- Global Strategy Diversified Bond

INTERNATIONAL UNDERACHIEVERS *continued*

- Global Strategy World Bond Fund

No-Load Funds (1):
- Scotia CanAm Income Fund

( ) number of funds

10

· ·

Rookie Camp Members at a Glance

To **HELP INVESTORS** make better-informed buying decisions for funds with less than a five-year track record, this chapter lists those funds that, based on our analysis, have shown above-average performance. To qualify as a Rookie Camp member, a fund must have at least a three-year track record and post, within its category, an above-average return over each of the past one-, two-, and three-year periods.

Using our research methodology, we have identified 78 funds that are members of the Rookie Camp group. Forty-six are load funds and 32 are no-load funds. This group of up-and-comers manages $16 billion in assets and includes 42 Canadian and 36 international funds. Three fund companies — the Mackenzie Financial Corporation, the Toronto-Dominion Bank, and the Primerica Life Insurance Company of Canada — each have five Rookie Camp members. Of the 35 funds that were identified as Rookie Camp members in last year's edition of *World of Mutual Funds*, 15 now have a five-year track record. Of this group, nine have gone on to become Heavy Hitters.

CANADIAN ROOKIE CAMP MEMBERS

CANADIAN EQUITY FUNDS

Load Funds (5):
- Cote 100 Amerique

52

CANADIAN ROOKIE CAMP MEMBERS *continued*

- Cote 100 REER
- Standard Life Equity Mutual Fund
- Optima Strategy Canadian Equity
- Ivy Canadian Fund

No-Load Funds (7):
- Batirente - Section Actions
- First Canadian Growth Fund
- Fonds Optimum Actions
- Green Line Value Fund
- Leith Wheeler Canadian Equity Fund
- MD Select Fund
- Mutual Premier Blue Chip Fund

CANADIAN SMALL-TO-MID-CAP EQUITY FUNDS

Load Funds (5):
- Colonia Special Growth Fund
- Cote 100 EXP
- Hyperion Small-Cap Canadian Equity
- Metlife MVP Growth Fund
- Millennium Next Generation Fund

CANADIAN DIVIDEND FUNDS

Load Funds (1):
- Bissett Dividend Income Fund

No-Load Funds (1):
- RoyFund Dividend Fund

CANADIAN BALANCED FUNDS

Load Funds (8):
- Common Sense Asset Builder 1
- Common Sense Asset Builder 2
- Common Sense Asset Builder 3
- Common Sense Asset Builder 4
- Common Sense Asset Builder 5
- Investors Asset Allocation Fund

CANADIAN ROOKIE CAMP MEMBERS *continued*

- Ivy Growth & Income Fund
- Standard Life Balanced Mutual Fund

No-Load Funds (1):
- MD Balanced Fund

CANADIAN BOND FUNDS

Load Funds (3):
- C.I. Canadian Bond Fund
- Optima Strategy Cdn. Fixed Income
- Standard Life Bond Mutual Fund

No-Load Funds (3):
- Beutel Goodman Private Bond
- Lotus Bond Fund
- Mawer Canadian Income Fund

CANADIAN MORTGAGE FUNDS

Load Funds (1):
- Ivy Mortgage Fund

No-Load Funds (3):
- Hongkong Bank Mortgage Fund
- National Trust Mortgage Fund
- Scotia Excelsior Mortgage Fund

SPECIAL EQUITY FUNDS

Load Funds (1):
- Admax Global Health Sciences Fund

No-Load Funds (3):
- First Canadian Resource Fund
- Green Line Resource Fund
- Green Line Science & Tech. Fund

INTERNATIONAL ROOKIE CAMP MEMBERS

INTERNATIONAL EQUITY FUNDS

Load Funds (4):
- Clean Environment Int'l Equity Fund
- Ivy Foreign Equity Fund
- Optima Strategy Int'l Equity
- Trimark - The Americas Fund

No-Load Funds (5):
- Fonds de Professionnels Int'l Equity
- Greystone Managed Global Fund
- ICM International Equity Fund
- OHA Foreign Equity Fund
- PH&N North American Equity Fund

EMERGING-MARKET FUNDS

Load Funds (4):
- 20/20 Latin America Fund
- Global Strategy Diversified Latin
- Global Strategy Latin America Fund
- Spectrum United Emerging Markets

EUROPEAN FUNDS

No-Load Funds (1):
- Atlas European Value Fund

ASIAN FUNDS

Load Funds (3):
- AGF China Focus Fund
- Dynamic Far East Fund
- NN Can-Asian Fund

No-Load Funds (2):
- Green Line Asian Growth Fund
- Sceptre Asian Growth Fund

INTERNATIONAL ROOKIE CAMP MEMBERS *continued*

U.S. EQUITY FUNDS

Load Funds (4):
- Metlife MVP U.S. Equity Fund
- NAL-U.S. Equity Fund
- NN Can-Am Fund
- Optima Strategy U.S. Equity

No-Load Funds (5):
- Canada Trust Everest AmeriGrowth
- Co-operators U.S. Equity Fund
- Mawer U.S. Equity Fund
- MD U.S. Equity Fund
- Scotia CanAm Growth Fund

INTERNATIONAL BALANCED FUNDS

Load Funds (4):
- AGF European Asset Allocation
- Dynamic Global Partners Fund
- Fidelity Asset Manager Fund
- Universal World Balanced RRSP

INTERNATIONAL BOND FUNDS

Load Funds (3):
- C.I. Global Bond RSP Fund
- C.I. World Bond Fund
- Fidelity Emerging Markets Bond Fund

No-Load Funds (1):
- Green Line Global RSP Bond Fund

( ) number of funds

11

• •

Reality Check:
The Performance Record of the
Ten Largest Fund Companies

THE TEN LARGEST fund companies manage about $161 billion in assets, which represents close to 56% of the $290 billion currently invested in mutual funds. Is this due to excellence in performance, aggressive marketing, convenience, or simply investor loyalty? Our research results show that all companies in this group have at least one Underachiever in their line-up of funds. Trimark and Templeton have the lowest number of Underachievers, one each, whereas the Investors Group, the Royal Bank, and Mackenzie Financial Corporation each have at least eight Underachievers. Canada Trust stands out among the top ten as the only fund company with no Heavy Hitters amongst its funds with a five-year performance history.

Eight of the ten companies have at least one fund that qualifies as a Rookie Camp member, with Mackenzie and TD Securities topping the list with five each.

THE PERFORMANCE RECORD OF THE TEN LARGEST
MUTUAL FUND COMPANIES IN CANADA

(RANKED BY ASSET SIZE)

		No. of Heavy Hitters	No. of Under- achievers	No. of Rookie Camp Members	Total No. of Funds	Assets ($bns)
1	Investors Group	8	6	1	47	28.7
2	Trimark Investment Management Inc.	4	1	1	14	25.0
3	Royal Mutual Funds Inc.	6	10	1	36	22.3
4	Mackenzie Financial Corporation	5	8	5	56	18.9
5	Templeton Management Limited	4	1	0	14	13.2
6	TD Securities Inc.	7	2	5	33	12.6
7	AGF Management Limited	6	5	3	39	11.4
8	CIBC Securities Inc.	2	5	0	28	10.5
9	Fidelity Investments Canada Limited	3	2	2	20	9.8
10	CT Investment Management Group	0	3	1	18	8.9

Source: The Investment Funds Institute of Canada

The bottom line for investors: Don't confuse a good marketing strategy with good performance. Judge each fund on an individual basis and, above all, don't assume *anything*.

PART THREE

● ●

HOW CANADIAN MUTUAL FUNDS RATE

12

· ·

Canadian Equity Funds

EQUITY FUNDS INVEST in the stocks of Canadian corporations, with the primary objective of providing capital gains for investors through increases in stock prices. There are currently 208 equity funds on the market. Together these funds manage a total of close to $68 billion in assets.

Over the five calendar years from 1992 to 1996, the best year for Canadian equity funds was 1993, when returns averaged 31.3%. In contrast, the worst year was 1994, when returns averaged -2.2%. The average annual compound rate of return over the five-year period was 13%.

Canadian equity funds have an average volatility rating of 3.6, which is below the average of 4.1 for all equity funds. The average fee for management expenses is $2.12 for every $100 in assets, which is up marginally from last year's average of $2.11.

The Heavy Hitters

There are 30 Canadian equity funds that have qualified for membership in the Heavy Hitters club this year. Each of these funds has consistently delivered *above*-average returns over the past one-, three-, and five-year periods. Collectively these Heavy Hitters manage a total of $7.1 billion in assets. The AIC Advantage Fund is the largest, with more than $1.5 billion in assets, and the AMI Private Capital Fund is the smallest, with about $1.5 million in assets. Thirteen of the 30 Canadian equity Heavy Hitters are no-load funds.

● ●

Table 1

THE HEAVY HITTERS

CANADIAN EQUITY FUNDS

		Bench- mark*	Vola- tility	Performance Quartile 1	Quartile 2	Overall Rating
1	Saxon Stock Fund (R) (N)	4	3	4	0	★★★
2	ABC Fundamental Value Fund (R) (N)	4	3	3	1	★★1/2
3	Phillips Hager & North Vintage (C) (N)	4	4	4	0	★★1/2
4	AIC Advantage Fund (C)	4	5	4	1	★★1/2
5	GBC Canadian Growth Fund (R) (N)	4	4	3	1	★★1/2
6	Tradex Equity Fund Ltd. (C) (N)	4	4	3	1	★★1/2
7	Empire Equity Growth Fund 3 (R)	4	4	3	1	★★1/2
8	Equitable Life Seg. Common Stock	4	4	3	1	★★1/2
9	Bissett Canadian Equity Fund (R)	4	3	2	2	★★1/2
10	McLean Budden Pooled Cdn. Equity (R) (N)	3	4	2	2	★★1/2
11	Industrial Alliance Stocks Fund (C) (N)	3	3	2	2	★★
12	Guardian Growth Equity Fund A	3	3	3	0	★★
13	Clean Environment Equity Fund (R)	3	4	3	0	★★
14	Standard Life Ideal Equity Fund	3	3	2	1	★★
15	PH&N Canadian Equity Plus Fund (R) (N)	3	4	1	3	★★
16	Phillips Hager & North Cdn. Equity (R) (N)	3	4	2	1	★★
17	Trust Pret & Revenu Canadian Fund (N)	3	3	1	2	★★
18	Pursuit Canadian Equity Fund	3	4	1	3	★★
19	Cundill Security Fund	2	2	2	0	★1/2
20	Spectrum United Canadian Equity	2	3	1	3	★1/2
21	National Equities Fund	2	3	1	3	★1/2
22	Empire Premier Equity Fund 1	2	4	2	1	★1/2
23	InvesNat Canadian Equity Fund (R)	2	4	1	2	★1/2
24	McLean Budden Equity Growth (N)	2	4	1	2	★1/2
25	AMI Private Capital Equity (N)	1	3	1	2	★
26	Ethical Growth Fund (R) (N)	1	3	1	2	★
27	Ferique Equity Fund (R) (N)	2	4	1	1	★
28	Green Line Canadian Equity Fund (N)	2	4	1	1	★
29	Maritime Life Growth - A & C	2	4	0	3	★

Table 1

THE HEAVY HITTERS *continued*

CANADIAN EQUITY FUNDS

		Bench-mark*	Vola-tility	Performance Quartile 1	Performance Quartile 2	Overall Rating
30	Green Line Canadian Index Fund (N)	0	4	0	4	★

*TSE 300 Total Return Index; (R) — Restricted; (C) — Closed to new members; (N) — No-load fund; Benchmark — number of times that a fund beat the benchmark from 1992 to 1996; Volatility — measures swings in fund returns on a scale of 1 to 10 (1 = low, 10 = high); Performance — number of times that a fund was in the first (top 25%) or second quartile (top 50%) from 1992 to 1996.

The benchmark used to compare Canadian equity fund returns is the TSE 300 Total Return Index. Over the past five calendar years, the TSE 300 posted its highest return of 32.6% in 1993 and its lowest return of -1.4% in 1992. Returns were also negative in 1994, when the index dipped by 0.2%.

Saxon Stock Fund ★★★

This fund, the number-one Heavy Hitter Canadian equity fund and the only one to receive three stars, was launched in 1985 and has been managed by Richard Howson since March 1989. With $21 million in assets, it follows a bottom-up/value investment strategy. Investments in industrial products, metals and minerals, consumer products, and financial services account for about 87% of the fund's assets.

Its best year was 1993, when it posted a return of 43.8%, and its worst year was 1994, when its return was -4.4%. The fund's average annual compound return over the past five years was 21.1%. A no-load fund, it charges management expenses of $1.75 for every $100 in assets, which is lower than the group average of $2.12. The fund has a minimum initial investment requirement of $5,000 and is available for sale only in Alberta, British Columbia, and Ontario.

ABC Fundamental Value Fund ★★1/2

Launched in 1989, this fund has been managed by Irwin Michael since its inception. The fund has $223 million in assets and follows a bottom-up/value investment strategy. Investments in consumer products, oil and gas, metals and minerals, and financial services account for over 60% of the fund's assets.

In 1993, its best year, the fund posted a return of 121.7%, and in 1994, its worst year, it returned 3.0%. Over the past five years, it yielded an average annual compound return of 30.1%. This no-load fund charges below-average management expenses of $2 for every $100 in assets and has a minimum initial investment requirement of $150,000.

Phillips Hager & North Vintage Fund ★★1/2

This fund was launched in 1986 and has been managed by Ian Mottershead since its inception. With $128 million in assets, it follows a growth investment strategy. Sixty-two percent of the fund's assets are made up of investments in financial services, industrial products, oil and gas, and merchandising.

The fund posted its highest return, 39.2%, in 1996, and its lowest, 1.4%, in 1994. Over the past five years, its average annual compound return was 20.7%. This is a no-load fund which charges management expenses of $1.76 for every $100 in assets, lower than the group average of $2.12. The fund is closed to new investors.

AIC Advantage Fund ★★1/2

This fund was launched in 1985 and is managed by the team of Michael Lee-Chin, Jonathan Wellum, and Neil Murdoch. With $1.5 billion in assets, it follows a bottom-up/value/growth investment strategy. Investments in financial services, mutual fund companies, and tele-communications account for 70% of the fund's assets.

Its best year was 1996, when it posted a return of 66.5%, and its worst year was 1994, when its return was -12.6%. The fund's average annual compound return over the past five years was 33.0%. A load fund, it charges management expenses of $2.45 for every $100 in assets, which is higher than the group average of $2.12. The fund has been closed to new investors since September 1996.

GBC Canadian Growth Fund ★★1/2

Started in 1988, this fund has been managed by Ian Souter, Scott Taylor, Jeff Tory, Ian Aitken, and Mike Shannon since its inception. The fund has $174 million in assets and follows a bottom-up/growth investment strategy. Investments in oil and gas, technology, industrial products, and metals and minerals account for over 55% of the fund's assets.

In 1996, its best year, the fund posted a return of 35.3%, and in 1994, its worst year, it returned -5.8%. Over the past five years, it yielded an average annual compound return of 19.8%. This no-load fund charges below-average management expenses of $1.85 for every $100 in assets and has a minimum initial investment requirement of $100,000.

Tradex Equity Fund ★★1/2

This fund was launched in 1960 and has been managed by Phillips Hager & North since July 1992. With $92 million in assets, it follows a growth/bottom-up/top-down investment strategy. Over 60% of the fund's assets are made up of investments in financial services, U.S. equities, industrial products, and oil and gas.

The fund posted its highest return, 36.0%, in 1996, and its lowest, 1.7%, in 1994. Over the past five years, its average annual compound return was 18.7%. This is a no-load fund which charges management expenses of $1.35 for every $100 in assets, lower than the group average of $2.12. This fund, which is restricted to federal and provincial government employees, was closed to new investors in March 1997.

Empire Equity Growth Fund 3 ★★1/2

This fund was launched in 1971 and has been managed by Catharina van Berkel since 1993. With $16 million in assets, it follows a bottom-up/value investment strategy. Investments in financial services, industrial products, oil and gas, and precious metals account for over 50% of the fund's assets.

Its best year was 1993, when it posted a return of 34.0%, and its worst year was 1994, when its return was -5.1%. The fund's average annual compound return over the past five years was 17.1%. A load fund, it charges well-below-average management expenses of $1.28 for every $100 in assets. The fund is closed to new investors.

Equitable Life Segregated Common Stock Fund ★★1/2

Started in 1966, this segregated fund has been managed by Robert Hannill of the investment firm Guardian Capital Group Ltd. since May

65

1997. The fund has $22 million in assets and follows a bottom-up/growth investment strategy. Investments in financial services, industrial products, and oil and gas account for over 50% of the fund's assets.

In 1996, its best year, the fund posted a return of 32.7%, and in 1994, its worst year, it returned 4.9%. Over the past five years, it yielded an average annual compound return of 17.2%. This load fund, sold on a front-end basis, charges well-below-average management expenses of $1.04 for every $100 in assets and is available to existing contract holders only.

Bissett Canadian Equity Fund ★★1/2

This fund was launched in 1983 and has been managed by Michael Quinn and Fred Pynn since April 1986. With $86 million in assets, it follows a growth/bottom-up investment strategy. Over 50% of the fund's assets are made up of investments in industrial products, financial services, and oil and gas.

The fund posted its highest return, 36.0%, in 1996, and its lowest, -2.3%, in 1994. Over the past five years, its average annual compound return was 20.1%. A no-load fund if bought directly from the company, it charges management expenses of $1.33 for every $100 in assets, lower than the group average of $2.12. The fund has a minimum initial investment requirement of $10,000 and is available for sale only in the provinces of Alberta, British Columbia, and Ontario.

McLean Budden Pooled Canadian Equity Fund ★★1/2

This fund was launched in 1980 and is managed by the McLean Budden Canadian equities team of Mary Hallward, Lewis Jackson, Bruce Murray, and Bob Nadon. With $238 million in assets, it follows a growth/bottom-up investment strategy. Investments in industrial products, financial services, and consumer products account for about 53% of the fund's assets.

Its best year was 1996, when it posted a return of 41.9%, and its worst year was 1994, when its return was -3.1%. The fund's average annual compound return over the past five years was 18.7%. A no-load fund, it charges well-below-average management expenses of $1.00 for every $100 in assets. The fund has a minimum initial investment requirement of $500,000.

Industrial Alliance Stocks Fund ★★

Started in 1969, this segregated fund has been managed by Luc Fournier since 1991. The fund has $41 million in assets and follows a top-down/value/sector investment strategy. Investments in metals and minerals, oil and gas, industrial products, and financial services account for 51% of the fund's assets.

In 1993, its best year, the fund posted a return of 34.0%, and in 1994, its worst year, it returned 2.2%. Over the past five years, it yielded an average annual compound return of 17.0%. This no-load fund charges below-average management expenses of $1.58 for every $100 in assets.

Guardian Growth Equity Fund A ★★

This fund was launched in 1988 and has been managed by John Priestman since February 1989. With $65 million in assets, it follows a bottom-up/growth investment strategy. About 56% of the fund's assets are made up of investments in oil and gas, industrial products, financial services, and metals and minerals.

The fund posted its highest return, 39.9%, in 1996, and its lowest, -4.5%, in 1994. Over the past five years, its average annual compound return was 19.1%. A load fund, sold on a front-end basis, it charges management expenses of $2.24 for every $100 in assets, higher than the group average of $2.12.

Clean Environment Equity Fund ★★

This fund was launched in 1992 and has been managed by Ian Ihnatowycz since its inception. With $80 million in assets, it follows a bottom-up/value investment strategy. Investments in environment and transportation, consumer products, industrial products, and metals and minerals account for over 60% of the fund's assets.

Its best year was 1993, when it posted a return of 40.3%, and its worst year was 1994, when its return was -13.7%. The fund's average annual compound return over the past five years was 18.7%. A load fund, it charges management expenses of $3.00 for every $100 in assets, which is considerably higher than the group average of $2.12.

Standard Life Ideal Equity Fund ★★

This segregated fund was started in 1986 and is managed by Standard Life's Canadian equity team. The fund has $114 million in assets and follows a bottom-up/blend investment strategy. Investments in foreign bonds, financial services, industrial products, and oil and gas account for about 45% of the fund's assets.

In 1996, its best year, the fund posted a return of 27.0%, and in 1992, its worst year, it returned 0.5%. Over the past five years, it yielded an average annual compound return of 15.2%. This load fund charges below-average management expenses of $2.00 for every $100 in assets.

Phillips Hager & North Canadian Equity Plus Fund ★★

This fund, PH&N's second Canadian equity fund to make the Heavy Hitter list this year, was launched in 1971 and has been managed by the firm's Canadian equity research team since its inception. With $171 million in assets, it follows a growth investment style. About 55% of the fund's assets are made up of investments in financial services, industrial products, merchandising, and oil and gas.

The fund posted its highest return, 28.6%, in 1996, and its lowest, 2.1%, in 1992. Over the past five years, its average annual compound return was 16.5%. This is a no-load fund which charges management expenses of $1.18 for every $100 in assets, well below the group average of $2.12. The fund has a minimum initial investment requirement of $25,000 for non-RRSP accounts and $5,000 for RRSP accounts.

Phillips Hager & North Canadian Equity Fund ★★

This fund, PH&N's third Canadian equity Heavy Hitter, was launched in 1971 and is managed by the firm's Canadian equity research team. With $581 million in assets, it follows a growth investment strategy. Investments in financial services, industrial products, and oil and gas account for 53% of the fund's assets.

Its best year was 1996, when it posted a return of 30.0%, and its worst year was 1992, when its return was -0.2%. The fund's average annual compound return over the past five years was 16.5%. A no-load fund, it charges well-below-average management expenses of $1.09 for every $100 in assets. The fund has a minimum initial investment requirement of $25,000 for non-RRSP accounts and $5,000 for RRSP accounts.

Trust Pret & Revenu Canadian Fund ★★

This fund was started in 1956 and has been managed by Ubald Cloutier since May 1995. The fund has $61 million in assets and follows a bottom-up/growth investment strategy. Investments in oil and gas, financial services, industrial products, and metals and minerals account for 55% of the fund's assets.

In 1996, its best year, the fund posted a return of 28.5%, and in 1994, its worst year, it returned -2.6%. Over the past five years, it yielded an average annual compound return of 15.5%. This no-load fund charges below-average management expenses of $1.93 for every $100 in assets.

Pursuit Canadian Equity Fund ★★

This fund was launched in 1983 and is managed by Ian Dalrymple of the investment firm Nigel Stephens Counsel Inc. With $9 million in assets, it follows a bottom-up/blend investment strategy. Sixty percent of the fund's assets are made up of investments in computer software, financial services, oil and gas, and telecommunications.

The fund posted its highest return, 31.7%, in 1993, and its lowest, -4.8%, in 1994. Over the past five years, its average annual compound return was 17.4%. This is a load fund, sold on a front-end basis, which charges management expenses of $1.50 for every $100 in assets, lower than the group average of $2.12. This fund has a minimum initial investment requirement of $10,000.

Cundill Security Fund ★1/2

This fund was launched in 1979 and has been managed by Tim McElvaine since July 1992. With $31 million in assets, it follows a bottom-up/value investment strategy. Investments in Canadian equities account for about 56% of the fund's assets.

Its best year was 1993, when it posted a return of 39.9%, and its worst year was 1992, when its return was -12.2%. The fund's average annual compound return over the past five years was 19.2%. A load fund, sold only on a front-end basis, it charges management expenses of $2.06 for every $100 in assets, which is slightly lower than the group average of $2.12.

Spectrum United Canadian Equity Fund ★1/2

This fund was started in 1971 and has been managed by Kiki Delaney of the investment firm Delaney Capital Inc. since October 1992. The fund has $1.1 billion in assets and follows a bottom-up/blend investment strategy. Investments in oil and gas, industrial products, and financial services account for about 47% of the fund's assets.

In 1993, its best year, the fund posted a return of 42.9%, and in 1994, its worst year, it returned -0.7%. Over the past five years, it yielded an average annual compound return of 17.2%. This load fund charges above-average management expenses of $2.35 for every $100 in assets.

National Equities Fund ★1/2

This segregated fund was launched in 1961 and has been managed by Thomas Dea since August 1996. With $116 million in assets, it follows a top-down/value investment strategy. About 55% of the fund's assets are made up of investments in regulated industries, oil and gas, and financial services.

The fund posted its highest return, 30.9%, in 1993, and its lowest, -1.1%, in 1992. Over the past five years, its average annual compound return was 16.0%. A load fund, sold on a deferred basis, it charges management expenses of $2.00 for every $100 in assets, lower than the group average of $2.12.

Empire Premier Equity Fund 1 ★1/2

This segregated fund was launched in 1964 and has been managed by Catharina van Berkel since 1993. With $227 million in assets, it follows a bottom-up/value investment strategy. Investments in financial services, industrial products, oil and gas, and precious metals account for over 50% of the fund's assets.

Its best year was 1996, when it posted a return of 30.9%, and its worst year was 1994, when its return was -3.3%. The fund's average annual compound return over the past five years was 15.7%. A load fund, sold on a front-end basis, it charges below-average management expenses of $1.54 for every $100 in assets.

InvesNat Canadian Equity Fund ★1/2

This National Bank fund was started in 1988 and has been managed by Sylvain Belanger since May 1997. The fund has $202 million in assets and follows a bottom-up/blend investment strategy. Investments in oil and gas, metals and minerals, forest products, and industrial products account for 40% of the fund's assets.

In 1996, its best year, the fund posted a return of 25.7%, and in 1994, its worst year, it returned -1.0%. Over the past five years, it yielded an average annual compound return of 14.9%. This no-load fund charges management expenses of $2.12, the group average, for every $100 in assets.

McLean Budden Equity Growth Fund ★1/2

This fund was launched in 1989 and is managed by McLean Budden's Canadian equities team. With $16 million in assets, it follows a bottom-up/growth investment strategy. Sixty-two percent of the fund's assets are made up of investments in industrial products, financial services, and oil and gas.

The fund posted its highest return, 37.9%, in 1996, and its lowest, -3.9%, in 1994. Over the past five years, its average annual compound return was 16.2%. This is a no-load fund which charges management expenses of $1.75 for every $100 in assets, lower than the group average of $2.12. This fund has a minimum initial investment requirement of $5,000.

AMI Private Capital Equity Fund ★

This fund was launched in 1987 and is managed by the investment firm AMI Partners Inc. With $1.5 million in assets, it follows a top-down/blend investment strategy. Investments in equities account for about 98% of the fund's assets.

Its best year was 1996, when it posted a return of 31.9%, and its worst year was 1992, when its return was -2.2%. Returns were also negative in 1994. The fund's average annual compound return over the past five years was 16.0%. A no-load fund, it charges below-average management expenses of $1.75 for every $100 in assets. The fund has a minimum initial investment requirement of $50,000.

Ethical Growth Fund ★

This fund was started in 1986 and is managed by Larry Lumm and Alastair Dunn of the investment firm Connor, Clark & Lumm Investment Management Inc. The fund has $507 million in assets and follows a growth investment strategy. Investments in industrial products, oil and gas, and financial services account for about 45% of the fund's assets.

In 1996, its best year, the fund posted a return of 28.2%, and in 1992, its worst year, it returned -4.3%. Returns were also negative in 1994. Over the past five years, it yielded an average annual compound return of 15.3%. This no-load fund charges slightly above-average management expenses of $2.14 for every $100 in assets. The fund is not available for sale in Quebec.

Ferique Equity Fund ★

This fund, sponsored by the Ordre des Ingenieurs du Quebec, a professional engineers' association, was launched in 1975 and is co-managed by Phillips Hager & North and Montrusco Associates. With $115 million in assets, it follows a top-down/blend investment strategy. About 55% of the fund's assets are made up of investments in oil and gas, financial services, industrial products, and metals and minerals.

The fund posted its highest return, 24.9%, in 1996, and its lowest, -0.8%, in 1992. Over the past five years, its average annual compound return was 14.8%. This is a no-load fund which charges management expenses of $0.59 for every $100 in assets, considerably lower than the group average of $2.12. The fund is available for purchase only by the association's members.

Green Line Canadian Equity Fund ★

This Toronto-Dominion Bank fund was launched in 1988 and is managed by its Canadian equity team. With $656 million in assets, it follows a bottom-up/blend investment strategy. Investments in Canadian equities account for 81% of the fund's assets.

Its best year was 1993, when it posted a return of 40.0%, and its worst year was 1994, when its return was -4.6%. Returns were also negative in 1992. The fund's average annual compound return over the past five years was 15.3%. A no-load fund, it charges management expenses of $2.11 for every $100 in assets, which is marginally lower than the group average of $2.12.

Maritime Life Growth Fund A & C ★

This segregated fund was started in 1968 and is managed by a number of investment firms, including Knight, Bain, Seath & Holbrook Capital Management Inc. and Bolton Tremblay. The fund has $228 million in assets and follows a bottom-up/blend investment strategy. Investments in financial services, oil and gas, and industrial products account for 50% of the fund's assets.

In 1993, its best year, the fund posted a return of 31.6%, and in 1994, its worst year, it returned -7.0%. Over the past five years, it yielded an average annual compound return of 14.8%. This no-load fund charges above-average management expenses of $2.30 for every $100 in assets and has a minimum initial investment requirement of $5,000 for non-RRSP accounts and $1,000 for RRSP accounts.

Green Line Canadian Index Fund ★

This fund, the Toronto-Dominion Bank's second Canadian equity Heavy Hitter, was launched in 1985 and is managed by their Canadian equity team. With $335 million in assets, the fund tracks the TSE 300 Total Return Index, which consists of stocks of major Canadian companies.

The fund posted its highest return, 31.0%, in 1993, and its lowest, -2.9%, in 1992. Returns were also negative in 1994. Over the past five years, its average annual compound return was 14.9%. This is a no-load fund which charges management expenses of $1.10 for every $100 in assets, well below the group average of $2.12.

The Rookie Camp

Twelve of the promising newer Canadian equity funds, each with at least a three-year track record, are in the Rookie Camp this year. Each of these funds, listed below, posted *above*-average returns over the past one-, two-, and three-year periods.

Batirente – Section Actions Fund, sponsored by the St-Laurent Financial Corporation, follows a top-down/value investment strategy and is managed by Carmand Normand. A no-load fund, it has $3 million in assets and charges below-average management expenses of $1.61 for every $100 in assets.

Cote 100 Amerique Fund, sponsored by Cote 100 Inc. of St. Bruno, Quebec, was launched in 1992 and is managed by Guy LeBlanc. With $20 million in assets, the fund follows a growth investment strategy. It is a no-load fund and charges below-average management expenses of $1.38 for every $100 in assets.

Cote 100 REER Fund is also sponsored by Cote 100 Inc. A no-load fund, it has $28 million in assets and charges below-average management expenses of $1.41 for every $100 in assets.

First Canadian Growth Fund, sponsored by the Bank of Montreal, was launched in 1993 and follows a bottom-up/value investment strategy. The fund has been managed by Michael Stanley since its inception. A no-load fund, it has $701 million in assets and charges above-average management expenses of $2.21 for every $100 in assets.

Fonds Optimum Actions, sponsored by Placements Optimum du St-Laurent Inc. of Montreal, was launched in 1994. With $1 million in assets, the fund follows a top-down/blend investment strategy. It is a no-load fund and charges below-average management expenses of $1.62 for every $100 in assets. The fund is available for sale only in Quebec.

Green Line Value Fund, sponsored by the Toronto-Dominion Bank, has $365 million in assets and follows a blend investment strategy. A no-load fund, it charges slightly above-average management expenses of $2.13 for every $100 in assets.

Ivy Canadian Fund, sponsored by the Mackenzie Financial Corporation, was launched in 1992 and follows a bottom-up/blend investment strategy. The fund is managed by Jerry Javasky. A load fund, it has $3.7 billion in assets and charges above-average management expenses of $2.37 for every $100 in assets.

Leith Wheeler Canadian Equity Fund, sponsored by Leith Wheeler Investment Counsel Ltd. of Vancouver, was launched in 1994. With $6 million in assets, the fund follows a bottom-up/value investment strategy. It is a no-load fund and charges below-average management expenses of $1.40 for every $100 in assets. The fund is available for sale only in Alberta and British Columbia.

MD Select Fund, sponsored by MD Management Ltd., is managed by Guardian Capital Inc. A no-load fund, it has $236 million in assets and charges well-below-average management expenses of $1.31 for every $100 in assets. The fund is available for sale only to members of the Canadian Medical Association and their families.

Mutual Premier Blue Chip Fund, a segregated fund sponsored by Mutual Life of Canada, was launched in 1992. A no-load fund, it has $561 million in assets and charges above-average management expenses of $2.29 for every $100 in assets.

Optima Strategy Canadian Equity Fund, sponsored by Loring Ward Investment Counsel Ltd. of Winnipeg, follows a bottom-up/value investment strategy. A load fund, it has $295 million in assets and charges well-below-average management expenses of $0.41 for every $100 in assets.

Standard Life Equity Mutual Fund, sponsored by Standard Life Mutual Funds Ltd., was launched in 1992. The fund has $15 million in assets and follows a bottom-up/blend investment strategy. A load fund, sold only on a deferred basis, it charges below-average management expenses of $2.00 for every $100 in assets.

The Underachievers

There are 36 Canadian equity funds that have failed to measure up to their peers. These Underachievers have consistently delivered *below-average* returns over the past one-, three-, and five-year periods. Collectively these Underachievers manage $16.1 billion in assets. The Trimark RSP Equity Fund is the largest, with $3.4 billion in assets, and the Canadian Protected Fund is the smallest, with $1.7 million. Ten of the 36 Underachievers are no-load funds.

Table 2

THE UNDERACHIEVERS

CANADIAN EQUITY FUNDS

- Admax Canadian Performance Fund
- Admax Canadian Select Growth Fund
- AGF Canadian Equity Fund
- AGF Canadian Growth Fund
- All-Canadian Capital Fund
- All-Canadian Compound
- Altamira Capital Growth Fund*
- BPI Canadian Equity Value Fund
- C.I. Canadian Sector Shares
- Canadian Protected Fund
- CDA Common Stock*
- CIBC Canadian Equity Fund*
- Co-operators Canadian Equity Fund*
- Fidelity Capital Builder Fund
- Global Strategy Canada Growth Fund
- GWL Canadian Equity Fund (G) NL*
- GWL Equity Index Fund (G) NL*
- ICM Equity Fund*
- Industrial Growth Fund
- Industrial Horizon Fund
- Investors Retirement Growth Portfolio
- Jones Heward Fund Ltd.
- Laurentian Canadian Equity Fund Ltd.
- London Life Canadian Equity
- Manulife Vistafund 1 Cap. Gains Growth
- Manulife Vistafund 1 Equity Fund
- Manulife Vistafund 2 Cap. Gains Growth
- Manulife Vistafund 2 Equity Fund
- Metlife MVP Equity Fund
- Middlefield Growth Fund*
- Royal Trust Canadian Stock Fund*
- Scotia Excelsior Cdn. Blue Chip*
- Talvest Canadian Equity Value Fund

Table 2

THE UNDERACHIEVERS *continued*

CANADIAN EQUITY FUNDS

- Trans-Canada Value Fund
- Trimark RSP Equity Fund
- University Avenue Canadian Fund

* denotes a no-load fund

Heavy Hitters vs Underachievers

Table 3 shows the difference in returns, over three time periods, between the Heavy Hitters and Underachievers in this category. As can be seen, the Heavy Hitters posted returns that were, on average, significantly higher than the Underachievers'. In dollar terms, for an initial investment of $10,000, the average Heavy Hitter Canadian equity fund would have returned a total of $22,975 over the past five years. For the same investment, the average Underachiever would have returned $17,545 — for a difference of $5,430 or 30.9%.

With respect to costs, the average Heavy Hitter charged management expenses of $1.74 for every $100 in assets, compared with $2.14 for the average Underachiever.

Table 3

HEAVY HITTERS vs UNDERACHIEVERS

CANADIAN EQUITY FUNDS

(Returns %)

	1-Year	3-Year*	5-Year*
• Heavy Hitters	28.5	18.1	18.1
• Underachievers	11.8	10.0	11.9

* annualized

CANADIAN EQUITY FUNDS
RANKINGS/RETURNS

Rank			Name of Fund	Returns (%)			Assets
(118)	(145)	(176)		(20.9)	(14.2)	(14.7)	
5-Yr	3-Yr	1-Yr		1-Yr	3-Yr	5-Yr	($mns)
2	60	33	ABC Fundamental Value Fund (HH)	27.6	15.3	30.1	222.6
103	117	160	Admax Canadian Performance Fund (UA)	7.1	11.4	11.5	38.0
117	138	154	Admax Canadian Select Growth Fund (UA)	9.9	7.8	7.0	7.3
108	128	170	AGF Canadian Equity Fund (UA)	2.1	9.1	10.9	723.5
98	108	115	AGF Canadian Growth Fund (UA)	19.8	12.0	11.9	321.9
10	112	143	AGF Growth Equity Fund	13.8	11.7	19.4	847.3
1	1	1	AIC Advantage Fund (HH)	64.4	37.9	33.0	1549.4
-	-	2	AIC Diversified Canada Fund	53.9	-	-	608.5
114	142	175	All-Canadian Capital Fund (UA)	-2.7	5.2	10.0	13.8
115	143	174	All-Canadian Compound (UA)	-2.5	4.9	9.8	12.2
-	141	140	All-Canadian Consumer Fund	14.3	5.7	-	0.9
112	97	60	Allstar AIG Canadian Equity Fund	24.3	12.8	10.1	4.5
6	68	113	Altafund Investment Corp.	20.0	14.8	20.6	320.7
104	132	159	Altamira Capital Growth Fund (UA)	7.4	8.6	11.5	137.1
18	110	158	Altamira Equity Fund	7.8	11.8	17.7	2547.3
-	88	11	Altamira North American Recovery	33.9	13.4	-	98.6
32	20	17	AMI Private Capital Equity (HH)	32.0	17.7	16.0	1.5
-	122	167	APEX Equity Growth Fund	4.6	9.7	-	64.7
61	33	8	Associate Investors Ltd.	34.4	16.9	13.9	10.1
77	21	25	Atlas Canadian Large Cap Growth	29.1	17.7	13.3	161.6
-	-	129	Atlas Canadian Large Cap Value Fund	17.0	-	-	25.6
-	-	150	Azura Growth RSP Pooled	11.9	-	-	26.9
-	71	28	Batirente - Section Actions (RC)	28.5	14.7	-	2.7
81	89	82	Beutel Goodman Canadian Equity	22.1	13.4	13.0	46.0
8	5	9	Bissett Canadian Equity Fund (HH)	34.1	20.8	20.1	85.8
62	48	43	BNP (Canada) Equity Fund	25.8	16.0	13.8	6.8
69	104	145	BPI Canadian Equity Value Fund (UA)	13.6	12.3	13.5	391.5
-	-	152	BPI Canadian Opportunities RSP Fund	10.5	-	-	128.3
-	125	156	C.I. Canadian Growth Fund	8.7	9.5	-	1153.6
63	130	157	C.I. Canadian Sector Shares (UA)	7.9	8.9	13.8	55.8
80	72	116	CAMAF (Cdn. Anaest.)	19.4	14.7	13.1	39.0
76	70	67	Canada Life Canadian Equity S-9	23.1	14.8	13.4	628.4
57	105	64	Canada Trust Everest Stock Fund	23.7	12.3	14.1	840.2
118	144	173	Canadian Protected Fund (UA)	-0.2	3.6	6.4	1.7

CANADIAN EQUITY FUNDS
RANKINGS/RETURNS cont'd

Rank			Name of Fund	Returns (%)			Assets
(118)	(145)	(176)		(20.9)	(14.2)	(14.7)	
5-Yr	3-Yr	1-Yr		1-Yr	3-Yr	5-Yr	($mns)
86	61	78	CCPE Growth Fund R	22.3	15.3	12.8	41.4
106	136	161	CDA Common Stock (UA)	7.0	8.3	11.1	51.1
94	51	37	Chou RRSP Fund	27.4	15.8	12.1	1.3
111	118	100	CIBC Canadian Equity Fund (UA)	20.8	11.3	10.5	712.8
14	27	49	Clean Environment Equity Fund (HH)	25.4	17.4	18.7	79.4
65	99	109	Co-operators Canadian Equity Fund (UA)	20.3	12.6	13.7	13.8
-	100	35	Colonia Equity Fund	27.5	12.6	-	24.1
52	58	128	Concorde Croissance	17.4	15.4	14.3	34.9
60	50	135	Cornerstone Cdn. Growth	15.7	15.9	13.9	83.7
-	17	61	Cote 100 Amerique (RC)	24.3	18.3	-	20.2
-	13	19	Cote 100 REER (RC)	30.7	18.8	-	28.3
11	38	41	Cundill Security Fund (HH)	27.2	16.7	19.2	30.9
3	111	138	Dynamic Canadian Growth Fund	14.9	11.7	25.4	885.3
45	123	92	Dynamic Fund of Canada	21.1	9.7	14.7	247.7
27	40	131	Elliott & Page Equity Fund	16.8	16.6	16.6	962.6
54	56	27	Empire Elite Equity Fund 5	28.7	15.5	14.2	527.8
24	25	13	Empire Equity Growth Fund 3 (HH)	32.8	17.4	17.1	16.1
35	37	18	Empire Premier Equity Fund 1 (HH)	31.6	16.7	15.7	226.5
-	79	102	Equitable Life Canadian Stock Fund	20.7	14.3	-	68.8
21	14	44	Equitable Life Seg. Common Stock (HH)	25.8	18.6	17.2	22.3
38	15	51	Ethical Growth Fund (HH)	25.3	18.3	15.3	507.3
43	49	90	Ferique Equity Fund (HH)	21.4	15.9	14.8	114.9
-	-	163	Ferique Growth Fund	6.7	-	-	11.0
105	127	148	Fidelity Capital Builder Fund (UA)	12.3	9.2	11.2	657.5
55	73	75	First Canadian Equity Index	22.5	14.6	14.1	338.4
-	36	31	First Cdn. Growth Fund (RC)	27.8	16.7	-	701.2
85	67	76	Fonds de Professionnels Cdn. Equity	22.4	14.9	12.9	92.7
79	76	72	Fonds Desjardins Actions	22.6	14.5	13.1	121.9
-	116	153	Fonds Desjardins Croissance	10.2	11.4	-	39.7
91	57	29	Fonds Desjardins Environnement	28.4	15.4	12.7	45.7
71	54	117	Fonds Ficadre Actions	19.2	15.6	13.5	12.3
-	62	22	Fonds Optimum Actions (RC)	30.0	15.2	-	1.1
9	22	66	GBC Canadian Growth Fund (HH)	23.3	17.7	19.8	174.2
73	35	24	General Trust of Canada Cdn. Equity	29.5	16.7	13.4	40.5

CANADIAN EQUITY FUNDS
RANKINGS/RETURNS *cont'd*

Rank			Name of Fund	Returns (%)			Assets
(118)	(145)	(176)		(20.9)	(14.2)	(14.7)	
5-Yr	3-Yr	1-Yr		1-Yr	3-Yr	5-Yr	($mns)
90	96	121	Global Strategy Canada Growth Fund (UA)	18.7	12.8	12.7	632.6
95	69	48	Green Line Blue Chip Equity Fund	25.5	14.8	12.1	318.2
39	74	30	Green Line Canadian Equity Fund (HH)	27.9	14.6	15.3	656.0
41	65	73	Green Line Canadian Index Fund (HH)	22.6	15.0	14.9	334.9
-	8	7	Green Line Value Fund (RC)	35.7	20.0	-	364.8
-	75	62	Growsafe Canadian Equity Fund	24.1	14.5	-	53.6
-	-	50	GS Canadian Equity Fund	25.4	-	-	210.0
-	-	169	GT Global Canada Growth Class	2.2	-	-	501.7
12	43	12	Guardian Growth Equity Fund A (HH)	32.8	16.3	19.1	64.8
-	-	15	Guardian Growth Equity Fund B	32.2	-	-	147.0
-	-	118	GWL Canadian Equity Fund (G) DSC	19.0	-	-	104.7
64	107	120	GWL Canadian Equity Fund (G) (UA)	18.7	12.0	13.7	242.3
-	-	77	GWL Equity Fund (M) DSC	22.3	-	-	29.2
-	-	83	GWL Equity Fund (M) NL	22.0	-	-	28.4
-	-	46	GWL Equity Fund (S) DSC	25.5	-	-	20.9
-	-	53	GWL Equity Fund (S) NL	25.2	-	-	32.0
-	-	96	GWL Equity Index Fund (G) DSC	21.0	-	-	19.2
72	90	101	GWL Equity Index Fund (G) (UA)	20.7	13.3	13.4	66.8
-	-	139	GWL Larger Co. Fund (M) DSC	14.5	-	-	7.4
-	-	141	GWL Larger Co. Fund (M) NL	14.2	-	-	8.9
-	-	81	GWL N. A. Equity Fund (B) DSC	22.1	-	-	9.8
-	-	86	GWL N. A. Equity Fund (B) NL	21.8	-	-	13.8
23	113	47	Hongkong Bank Equity Fund	25.5	11.6	17.2	145.6
99	114	10	HRL Canadian Fund	34.1	11.6	11.8	2.4
46	95	142	ICM Equity Fund (UA)	14.2	12.9	14.7	231.7
82	98	88	Imperial Growth Canadian Equity	21.5	12.7	12.9	76.6
-	66	104	Industrial Alliance Ecoflex Fund A	20.6	14.9	-	132.5
25	55	91	Industrial Alliance Stocks Fund (HH)	21.4	15.5	17.0	41.3
19	77	149	Industrial Future Fund	12.1	14.4	17.7	654.5
75	124	147	Industrial Growth Fund (UA)	12.3	9.5	13.4	1252.1
74	115	133	Industrial Horizon Fund (UA)	16.5	11.4	13.4	1159.5
42	32	26	InvesNat Canadian Equity Fund (HH)	28.9	16.9	14.9	202.3
34	82	71	Investors Canadian Equity Fund	22.7	13.8	15.9	3663.7
66	84	110	Investors Retirement Growth Portfolio (UA)	20.2	13.6	13.7	2281.5

CANADIAN EQUITY FUNDS
RANKINGS/RETURNS *cont'd*

Rank			Name of Fund	Returns (%)			Assets
(118)	(145)	(176)		(20.9)	(14.2)	(14.7)	
5-Yr	3-Yr	1-Yr		1-Yr	3-Yr	5-Yr	($mns)
53	78	80	Investors Retirement Mutual Fund	22.1	14.4	14.2	2979.5
47	39	32	Investors Summa Fund	27.7	16.7	14.6	196.5
-	24	63	Ivy Canadian Fund (RC)	23.7	17.4	-	3752.0
67	131	144	Jones Heward Fund Ltd. (UA)	13.8	8.9	13.5	76.0
-	-	136	LaSalle Equity Fund	15.3	-	-	1.3
101	109	103	Laurentian Canadian Equity Fund Ltd. (UA)	20.7	11.8	11.6	243.9
-	26	3	Leith Wheeler Canadian Equity Fund (RC)	39.6	17.4	-	5.5
59	106	132	London Life Canadian Equity (UA)	16.5	12.2	13.9	967.3
-	-	70	Lutheran Life Canadian Equity Fund	22.8	-	-	7.5
26	137	155	Mackenzie Sentinel Canada Equity	8.9	8.1	17.0	13.0
-	29	119	Manulife Cabot Blue Chip Fund	18.9	17.2	-	13.4
-	11	108	Manulife Cabot Canadian Equity Fund	20.4	18.9	-	36.9
102	135	168	Manulife Vistafund 1 Cap. Gains Gr. (UA)	2.4	8.3	11.5	77.8
113	126	165	Manulife Vistafund 1 Equity Fund (UA)	6.3	9.4	10.1	53.1
109	139	171	Manulife Vistafund 2 Cap. Gains Gr. (UA)	1.6	7.5	10.7	384.0
116	133	166	Manulife Vistafund 2 Equity Fund (UA)	5.5	8.5	9.3	323.3
-	-	105	Maritime Life Cdn. Equity - A & C	20.5	-	-	111.3
44	64	42	Maritime Life Growth - A & C (HH)	26.0	15.0	14.8	227.7
88	101	74	Mawer Canadian Equity Fund	22.5	12.6	12.8	18.7
16	63	162	Maxxum Canadian Equity Growth Fund	6.9	15.1	18.2	168.8
31	18	14	McLean Budden Equity Growth Fund (HH)	32.6	18.2	16.2	15.6
13	6	6	McLean Budden Pooled Cdn. Equity (HH)	36.1	20.7	18.7	238.5
48	121	94	MD Equity Fund	21.1	10.3	14.6	1671.2
-	45	23	MD Select Fund (RC)	29.6	16.1	-	235.6
-	-	137	Merrill Lynch Canadian Equity Fund	14.9	-	-	100.9
110	120	124	Metlife MVP Equity Fund (UA)	18.4	10.9	10.5	45.5
89	140	146	Middlefield Growth Fund (UA)	12.8	7.0	12.7	24.9
-	-	98	Millennia III Canadian Equity 1	20.9	-	-	99.8
-	-	99	Millennia III Canadian Equity 2	20.8	-	-	10.5
50	28	87	Mutual Equifund	21.7	17.3	14.3	117.9
-	46	68	Mutual Premier Blue Chip Fund (RC)	22.9	16.1	-	561.2
51	34	130	NAL-Canadian Equity Fund	16.8	16.8	14.3	106.5
-	-	36	NAL-Equity Growth Fund	27.4	-	-	85.0
33	41	40	National Equities Fund (HH)	27.3	16.6	16.0	116.2

CANADIAN EQUITY FUNDS
RANKINGS/RETURNS *cont'd*

Rank			Name of Fund	Returns (%)			Assets
(118)	(145)	(176)		(20.9)	(14.2)	(14.7)	
5-Yr	3-Yr	1-Yr		1-Yr	3-Yr	5-Yr	($mns)
96	92	38	National Trust Canadian Equity Fund	27.4	13.2	11.9	185.9
-	4	164	Navigator Value Inv. Retirement	6.5	21.6	-	52.1
83	47	58	NN Canadian 35 Index	24.7	16.0	12.9	48.7
100	102	79	NN Canadian Growth	22.2	12.4	11.7	33.7
-	-	151	O'Donnell Growth Fund	11.2	-	-	178.7
-	103	127	OHA Canadian Equity Fund	17.8	12.3	-	20.7
56	52	45	Ontario Teachers Group Diversified	25.8	15.6	14.1	44.1
-	2	4	Optima Strategy Canadian Equity (RC)	38.9	22.8	-	295.4
28	31	55	PH&N Canadian Equity Plus Fund (HH)	24.8	17.0	16.5	171.3
29	30	54	Phillips Hager & North Cdn. Equity (HH)	24.9	17.0	16.5	581.5
5	3	21	Phillips Hager & North Vintage (HH)	30.1	22.3	20.7	127.5
20	12	16	Pursuit Canadian Equity Fund (HH)	32.0	18.8	17.4	9.3
58	53	52	Royal Life Equity Fund	25.2	15.6	14.1	115.9
78	81	112	Royal Trust Canadian Stock Fund (UA)	20.1	13.9	13.1	950.4
37	91	125	RoyFund Canadian Equity Fund	18.2	13.3	15.4	2008.1
4	16	84	Saxon Stock Fund (HH)	21.9	18.3	21.1	21.1
107	119	114	Scotia Excelsior Cdn. Blue Chip (UA)	19.9	11.2	10.9	368.7
17	10	123	Scotia Excelsior Cdn. Growth Fund	18.4	19.0	17.8	841.0
-	-	5	Scudder Canadian Equity Fund	38.1	-	-	38.5
22	59	56	Spectrum United Canadian Equity (HH)	24.8	15.4	17.2	1043.6
68	23	20	Spectrum United Canadian Investment	30.3	17.6	13.5	89.4
92	94	69	Spectrum United Canadian Stock Fund	22.8	13.1	12.5	155.7
-	42	57	Standard Life Equity Mutual Fund (RC)	24.7	16.4	-	14.8
40	19	95	Standard Life Ideal Equity Fund (HH)	21.1	17.8	15.2	114.1
-	-	93	STAR Cdn. Maximum Equity Growth	21.1	-	-	
-	-	122	STAR Reg. Maximum Equity Growth	18.5	-	-	
-	-	89	Stone & Co. Flagship Stock Fund	21.5	-	-	48.5
97	87	126	Talvest Canadian Equity Value Fund (UA)	17.8	13.6	11.9	135.9
-	129	172	Talvest New Economy	0.2	8.9	-	139.1
7	7	106	Teachers' RSP - Equity Section	20.5	20.0	20.4	12.7
70	83	59	Templeton Canadian Stock Fund	24.4	13.7	13.5	175.5
15	9	34	Tradex Equity Fund Ltd. (HH)	27.6	19.8	18.7	92.2
93	134	134	Trans-Canada Value Fund (UA)	16.3	8.4	12.4	4.2
30	80	85	Trimark Canadian Fund	21.8	14.0	16.4	2417.2

CANADIAN EQUITY FUNDS
RANKINGS/RETURNS *cont'd*

Rank			Name of Fund	Returns (%)			Assets
(118)	(145)	(176)		(20.9)	(14.2)	(14.7)	
5-Yr	3-Yr	1-Yr		1-Yr	3-Yr	5-Yr	($mns)
49	93	111	Trimark RSP Equity Fund (UA)	20.1	13.2	14.4	3411.8
-	86	107	Trimark Select Canadian Growth Fund	20.4	13.6	-	4830.9
36	44	97	Trust Pret & Revenu Canadian Fund (HH)	21.0	16.2	15.5	60.6
-	-	39	Universal Canadian Growth Fund Ltd.	27.3	-	-	886.9
84	145	176	University Avenue Canadian Fund (UA)	-11.1	3.3	12.9	16.3
87	85	65	Westbury Canadian Equity Fund	23.5	13.6	12.8	65.4

( ) under Rank indicates total number of funds; ( ) under Returns (%) indicates average annual return;

(HH) — Heavy Hitter; (UA) — Underachiever; (RC) — Rookie Camp member.

CANADIAN EQUITY FUNDS/SUMMARY

Name of Fund	MER	Load	RRSP	Vola-tility	Company Number (App. 3)
ABC Fundamental Value Fund (R)	2.00	N	R	4	1
Admax Canadian Performance Fund	2.61	Y	R	4	69
Admax Canadian Select Growth Fund	2.63	Y	R	3	69
AGF Canada Class (R)	2.50	Y	F		3
AGF Canadian Equity Fund	2.99	Y	R	4	3
AGF Canadian Growth Fund	2.43	Y	R	3	3
AGF Growth Equity Fund	2.82	Y	R	4	3
AIC Advantage Fund (C)	2.45	Y	R	5	4
AIC Advantage Fund II	2.71	Y	R		4
AIC Diversified Canada Fund	2.55	Y	R		4
All-Canadian Capital Fund	2.00	Y	R	3	138
All-Canadian Compound (C)	N/A	N	R	3	138
All-Canadian Consumer Fund	1.96	Y	R	3	138
Allstar AIG Canadian Equity Fund	3.00	Y	R	4	5
Altafund Investment Corp.	2.30	N	R	5	6
Altamira Capital Growth Fund	2.00	N	R	4	6
Altamira Equity Fund	2.28	N	R	4	6
Altamira North American Recovery	2.30	N	R	4	6
AMI Private Capital Equity	1.75	N	R	3	7
APEX Canadian Stock Fund (R)	2.55	Y	R		126
APEX Equity Growth Fund (R)	2.95	N	R	4	126
Associate Investors Ltd.	2.09	N	R	3	75
Atlas Canadian Large Cap Growth	2.47	N	R	3	9
Atlas Canadian Large Cap Value Fund	2.66	N	R		9
Azura Growth RSP Pooled (R)	2.23	Y	R		127
Batirente - Section Actions (R)	1.61	N	R		131
Beutel Goodman Canadian Equity	2.20	N	R	4	12
Bissett Canadian Equity Fund (R)	1.33	Y	R	3	13
BNP (Canada) Equity Fund	2.47	N	R	4	14
BPI Canadian Equity Value Fund	2.68	Y	R	4	15
BPI Canadian Opportunities RSP (C)	2.50	Y	R		15
C.I. Canadian Growth Fund	2.39	Y	R	4	28
C.I. Canadian Sector Shares	2.44	Y	F	3	28
CAMAF (Cdn. Anaest.)	1.43	N	R	4	20
Canada Life Canadian Equity S-9	2.25	Y	R	3	18

CANADIAN EQUITY FUNDS/SUMMARY *cont'd*

Name of Fund	MER	Load	RRSP	Vola-tility	Company Number (App. 3)
Canada Trust Everest Stock Fund	1.86	N	R	3	19
Canadian Protected Fund (R)	2.40	Y	R	2	62
CCPE Growth Fund R (R)	1.35	N	R	3	21
CDA Canadian Equity (R)	1.55	N	R		22
CDA Common Stock (R)	0.96	N	R	4	22
Chou RRSP Fund	2.27	Y	R	3	27
CIBC Canadian Equity Fund	2.05	N	R	4	29
CIBC Canadian Index Fund	1.00	N	R		29
Clarington Canadian Equity Fund	2.75	Y	R		30
Clean Environment Equity Fund (R)	3.00	Y	R	4	31
Co-operators Canadian Equity Fund (R)	2.07	N	R	4	33
Colonia Equity Fund	2.43	Y	R	4	32
Concorde Croissance (R)	2.18	Y	R	3	59
Cornerstone Cdn. Growth	2.50	N	R	4	73
Cote 100 Amerique (R)	1.38	Y	F	4	34
Cote 100 REER (R)	1.41	Y	R	4	34
Cundill Security Fund	2.06	Y	R	2	111
Dynamic Canadian Growth Fund	2.49	Y	R	4	40
Dynamic Fund of Canada	2.47	Y	R	4	40
Dynamic Quebec Fund	2.00	Y	R		40
Elliott & Page Equity Fund	1.95	Y	R	4	41
Empire Elite Equity Fund 5	2.57	Y	R	4	42
Empire Equity Growth Fund 3 (R)	1.28	Y	R	4	42
Empire Premier Equity Fund 1	1.54	Y	R	4	42
Equitable Life Canadian Stock Fund	2.25	Y	R	4	43
Equitable Life Seg. Common Stock	1.04	Y	R	4	43
Ethical Growth Fund (R)	2.14	N	R	3	44
Ferique Equity Fund (R)	0.59	N	R	4	109
Ferique Growth Fund (R)	0.87	N	R		109
Fidelity Capital Builder Fund	2.53	Y	R	4	46
Fidelity True North Fund	2.48	Y	R		46
First Canadian Equity Index	1.48	N	R	4	11
First Cdn. Growth Fund	2.21	N	R	4	11
Fonds de Professionnels Cdn. Equity (R)	0.75	N	R	4	50
Fonds Desjardins Actions (R)	1.94	N	R	4	37

CANADIAN EQUITY FUNDS/SUMMARY *cont'd*

Name of Fund	MER	Load	RRSP	Vola-tility	Company Number (App. 3)
Fonds Desjardins Croissance (R)	2.03	N	R		37
Fonds Desjardins Environnement (R)	2.12	N	R	4	37
Fonds Ficadre Actions	2.12	Y	R	3	128
Fonds Optimum Actions (R)	1.62	N	R		107
GBC Canadian Growth Fund (R)	1.85	N	R	4	52
General Trust of Canada Cdn. Eq. (R)	2.10	N	R	4	98
Global Strategy Canada Growth Fund	2.69	Y	R	3	54
Global Strategy Cdn. Opportunities	2.75	Y	R		54
Green Line Blue Chip Equity Fund	2.27	N	R	3	139
Green Line Canadian Equity Fund	2.11	N	R	4	139
Green Line Canadian Index Fund	1.10	N	R	4	139
Green Line Value Fund	2.13	N	R	4	139
Growsafe Canadian Equity Fund	2.30	Y	R	3	141
GS Canadian Equity Fund	2.80	Y	R		70
GT Global Canada Growth Class	2.57	Y	R		60
Guardian Growth Equity Fund A	2.24	Y	R	3	61
Guardian Growth Equity Fund B	2.92	Y	R		61
GWL Aggressive Portfolio (G) DSC	2.70	Y	R		57
GWL Aggressive Portfolio (G) NL	2.94	N	R		57
GWL Canadian Equity Fund (G) DSC	2.40	Y	R		57
GWL Canadian Equity Fund (G) NL	2.64	N	R	4	57
GWL Equity Fund (M) DSC	2.58	Y	R		57
GWL Equity Fund (M) NL	2.82	N	R		57
GWL Equity Fund (S) DSC	2.52	Y	R		57
GWL Equity Fund (S) NL	2.76	N	R		57
GWL Equity Index Fund (G) DSC	2.40	Y	R		57
GWL Equity Index Fund (G) NL	2.65	N	R	4	57
GWL Larger Co. Fund (M) DSC	2.58	Y	R		57
GWL Larger Co. Fund (M) NL	2.82	N	R		57
GWL N. A. Equity Fund (B) DSC	2.52	Y	R		57
GWL N. A. Equity Fund (B) NL	2.76	N	R		57
Hongkong Bank Equity Fund	1.96	N	R	3	63
HRL Canadian Fund	1.75	N	R	3	64
Hyperion Cdn. Equity Growth	2.62	Y	R		136

CANADIAN EQUITY FUNDS/SUMMARY *cont'd*

Name of Fund	MER	Load	RRSP	Vola-tility	Company Number (App. 3)
ICM Equity Fund	0.12	N	R		68
IG Beutel Goodman Cdn. Equity Fund	3.17	Y	R		70
IG Sceptre Canadian Equity Fund	2.83	Y	R		70
Imperial Growth Canadian Equity (C)	1.96	Y	R	3	65
Industrial Alliance Ecoflex Fund A	2.39	Y	R	3	66
Industrial Alliance Stock Fund - 2	2.94	N	R		66
Industrial Alliance Stocks Fund (C)	1.58	N	R	3	66
Industrial Future Fund	2.38	Y	R	3	80
Industrial Growth Fund	2.38	Y	R	4	80
Industrial Horizon Fund	2.38	Y	R	4	80
Infinity Canadian Fund	2.95	Y	R		67
Infinity Wealth Management Fund	2.95	Y	F		67
InvesNat Canadian Equity Fund (R)	2.12	N	R	4	98
Investors Canadian Equity Fund	2.46	Y	R	3	70
Investors Retirement Growth Portfolio	0.18	Y	R	3	70
Investors Retirement Mutual Fund	2.40	Y	R	3	70
Investors Summa Fund	2.43	Y	R	3	70
Ivy Canadian Fund	2.37	Y	R	2	80
Jones Heward Fund Ltd.	2.50	Y	R	4	72
LaSalle Equity Fund (R)	1.00	Y	R		151
Laurentian Canadian Equity Fund Ltd.	2.65	Y	R	3	135
Leith Wheeler Canadian Equity Fund (R)	1.40	N	R		74
London Life Canadian Equity	2.00	Y	R	4	76
Lutheran Life Canadian Equity Fund (R)	2.60	N	R		78
Mackenzie Sentinel Canada Equity (C)	1.98	N	R	4	80
Manulife Cabot Blue Chip Fund	2.50	N	R		84
Manulife Cabot Canadian Equity Fund	2.50	N	R		84
Manulife Vistafund 1 Cap. Gains Gr.	1.63	Y	R	4	83
Manulife Vistafund 1 Equity Fund	1.63	Y	R	4	83
Manulife Vistafund 2 Cap. Gains Gr.	2.38	Y	R	4	83
Manulife Vistafund 2 Equity Fund	2.38	Y	R	4	83
Maritime Life Aggr. Equity - B	2.30	Y	R		85
Maritime Life Aggr. Equity - A & C	2.30	Y	R		85
Maritime Life Cdn. Equity - A & C	2.30	Y	R		85

CANADIAN EQUITY FUNDS/SUMMARY *cont'd*

Name of Fund	MER	Load	RRSP	Vola-tility	Company Number (App. 3)
Maritime Life Cdn. Equity - B	2.30	Y	R		85
Maritime Life Growth - A & C	2.30	Y	R		85
Maritime Life Growth - B	2.30	Y	R		85
Mawer Canadian Equity Fund (R)	1.07	N	R	4	86
Maxxum Cdn. Equity Growth Fund	2.15	Y	R	4	87
McLean Budden Equity Growth Fund	1.75	N	R	4	89
McLean Budden Pooled Cdn. Equity (R)	1.00	N	R	4	89
MD Equity Fund (R)	1.28	N	R	4	90
MD Select Fund (R)	1.31	N	R	3	90
Merrill Lynch Canadian Equity Fund	2.88	Y	R		70
Metlife MVP Equity Fund	2.23	Y	R	4	92
Middlefield Growth Fund	2.78	Y	R	4	93
Millennia III Canadian Equity 1	2.72	Y	R		65
Millennia III Canadian Equity 2	2.90	N	R		65
Monarch Canadian Fund	2.41	Y	R		28
Monarch Canadian Sector Shares	2.46	Y	F		28
Mutual Equifund	1.79	Y	R	4	97
Mutual Premier Blue Chip Fund	2.29	N	R	4	97
NAL-Canadian Equity Fund	1.75	Y	R	4	83
NAL-Equity Growth Fund	2.00	Y	R		83
National Equities Fund	2.00	Y	R	3	99
National Trust Cdn. Equity Fund (R)	1.60	N	R	4	100
National Trust Cdn. Index Fund (R)	0.80	N	R		100
Navigator Value Inv. Retirement (R)	2.88	Y	R	5	101
NN Canadian 35 Index	2.00	Y	R	4	102
NN Canadian Growth	2.25	Y	R	4	102
North-West Life Ecoflex A	2.39	Y	R		103
O'Donnell Growth Fund	2.75	Y	R		104
OHA Canadian Equity Fund	0.90	N	R	4	105
Ontario Teachers Group Diversified (R)	1.00	N	R	4	106
Optima Strategy Canadian Equity (R)	0.41	Y	R	3	77
Pacific Total Return Fund (R)	2.90	Y	R		110
PH&N Canadian Equity Plus Fund (R)	1.18	N	R	4	112
Phillips Hager & North Cdn. Equity (R)	1.09	N	R	4	112

CANADIAN EQUITY FUNDS/SUMMARY *cont'd*

Name of Fund	MER	Load	RRSP	Vola-tility	Company Number (App. 3)
Phillips Hager & North Vintage (C)	1.76	N	R	4	112
Pursuit Canadian Equity Fund	1.50	Y	R	4	117
Royal Life Equity Fund	2.37	Y	R	3	120
Royal Trust Canadian Stock Fund	1.95	N	R	3	119
RoyFund Canadian Equity Fund	2.10	N	R	3	119
Saxon Stock Fund (R)	1.75	N	R	3	122
Scotia Excelsior Cdn. Blue Chip	2.03	N	R	3	124
Scotia Excelsior Cdn. Growth Fund	2.09	N	R	4	124
Scudder Canadian Equity Fund (R)	1.25	N	R		125
Spectrum United Canadian Equity	2.35	Y	R	3	129
Spectrum United Canadian Investment	2.33	Y	R	3	129
Spectrum United Canadian Stock Fund	2.33	Y	R	3	129
Standard Life Equity Mutual Fund (R)	2.00	Y	R	3	133
Standard Life Ideal Equity Fund	2.00	Y	R	3	132
STAR Cdn. Maximum Equity Growth	N/A	Y	R		80
STAR Cdn. Maximum Long-Term Growth	N/A	Y	R		80
STAR Reg. Maximum Equity Growth	N/A	Y	R		80
Stone & Co. Flagship Stock Fund	2.85	Y	R		134
Strategic Value Canadian Equity	2.75	Y	R		135
Talvest Canadian Equity Value Fund	2.40	Y	R	4	136
Talvest New Economy	2.50	Y	R	4	136
Teachers' RSP - Equity Section (C)	1.00	N	R	4	95
Templeton Canadian Stock Fund	2.44	Y	R	3	137
The Goodwood Fund (R)	1.00	Y	R		116
The McElvaine Investment Trust (R)	0.40	N	R		111
Tradex Equity Fund Ltd. (C)	1.35	N	R	4	140
Trans-Canada Value Fund	2.89	Y	R	5	121
Trimark Canadian Fund	1.52	Y	R	3	143
Trimark RSP Equity Fund	2.00	Y	R	4	143
Trimark Select Canadian Growth Fund	2.25	Y	R	3	143
Trust Pret & Revenu Canadian Fund	1.93	N	R	3	145
Universal Canadian Growth Fund Ltd.	2.41	Y	R		80
University Avenue Canadian Fund	2.60	Y	R	4	146
Valorem Canadian Equity-Value (R)	2.00	Y	R		152

CANADIAN EQUITY FUNDS/SUMMARY *cont'd*

Name of Fund	MER	Load	RRSP	Vola-tility	Company Number (App. 3)
Value Contrarian Canadian Equity (R)	2.00	Y	R		147
Westbury Canadian Equity Fund (R)	2.42	N	R	4	148
Average	2.12			3.6	

(R) — Restricted; (C) — Closed to new investors; MER — Management Expense Ratio; Load — fee charged; RRSP: R = 100% eligible, F = eligible as foreign content only, N = not eligible; Volatility — measures swings in performance on a scale of 1 to 10 (1 = low, 10 = high). Blank space indicates that fund is less than three years old. Fund company addresses may be found by number in Appendix 3.

13

○ ○

Canadian Small-to-Mid-Cap Equity Funds

THIS GROUP OF funds invests in the stocks of small- and medium-sized Canadian companies with a market capitalization — the number of shares multiplied by the price per share — of less than $500 million.

Because small companies start from a much smaller base, they can often grow at a much faster rate than larger companies. For example, it is much easier for a company with revenues of $20 million to double its sales than it is for a company with revenues of $20 billion. However, the short-term records of many small companies make this type of fund more speculative than other equity funds.

There are currently 60 Canadian small-to-mid-cap funds on the market. These funds manage $10.4 billion in assets. Over the five calendar years from 1992 to 1996, the best year for Canadian small-to-mid-cap equity funds was 1993, when returns averaged 55.7%. In contrast, the worst year was 1994, when returns averaged -10.0%. The average annual compound rate of return over the five-year period was 19%.

Canadian small-to-mid-cap equity funds have an average volatility rating of 4.6, which is above the average of 4.1 for all equity funds. The average fee for management expenses is $2.36 for every $100 in assets, which is up from last year's average of $2.32.

The Heavy Hitters

There are four Canadian small-to-mid-cap funds that have qualified for membership in the Heavy Hitters club this year. Each of these funds has consistently delivered *above*-average returns over the past one-, three-, and five-year periods. Collectively these Heavy Hitters manage a total of $530 million in assets. The Sceptre Equity Growth Fund is the largest, with $374 million in assets, and the Mawer New Canada Fund is the smallest, with $39 million in assets. Two of the four Heavy Hitters are no-load funds.

● ●

Table 1

THE HEAVY HITTERS

CANADIAN SMALL-TO-MID-CAP EQUITY FUNDS

		Bench-mark*	Vola-tility	Performance Quartile 1	Quartile 2	Overall Rating
1	Bissett Small Cap Fund (R)	4	4	2	3	★★1/2
2	Mawer New Canada Fund (R) (N)	4	4	2	1	★★
3	Sceptre Equity Growth Fund (N)	3	4	2	1	★★
4	Guardian Enterprise Fund A	2	4	2	1	★1/2

* Nesbitt Burns Canadian Small-Cap Index; (R) — Restricted; (C) — Closed to new members; (N) — No-load fund; Benchmark — number of times that a fund beat the benchmark from 1992 to 1996; Volatility — measures swings in fund returns on a scale of 1 to 10 (1 = low, 10 = high); Performance — number of times that a fund was in the first (top 25%) or second quartile (top 50%) from 1992 to 1996.

The benchmark used to compare Canadian small-to-mid-cap equity fund returns is the Nesbitt Burns Small-Cap Index. Over the past five calendar years, the index posted its highest return of 48.3% in 1993 and its lowest return of -8.6% in 1994.

Bissett Small Cap Fund ★★1/2

This fund, the number-one Heavy Hitter small-cap fund and identified as a Rookie Camp member in last year's edition of *World of Mutual Funds*, was launched in 1992 and has been managed by David Bissett since its inception and Jean Vollendorf since December 1996. With $58 million in assets, it follows a bottom-up/growth investment strategy. Investments in industrial products, oil and gas, consumer products, and financial services account for close to 60% of the fund's assets.

Its best year was 1993, when it posted a return of 112.5%, and its worst year was 1994, when its return was -8.6%. The fund's average annual compound return over the past five years was 32.0%. A no-load fund if bought directly from the company, it charges management expenses of $1.90 for every $100 in assets, which is lower than the group average of $2.36. This fund has a minimum initial investment requirement of $10,000 and is available for sale only in the provinces of Alberta, British Columbia, and Ontario.

Mawer New Canada Fund ★★

This fund was started in 1988 and has been managed by William MacLachlan since November 1996. The fund has $23 million in assets and follows a bottom-up/growth investment strategy. Investments in industrial products, oil and gas, precious metals, and financial services account for over 60% of the fund's assets.

In 1993, its best year, the fund posted a return of 63.7%, and in 1994, its worst year, it returned -2.8%. Over the past five years, it yielded an average annual compound return of 22.5%. This no-load fund charges well-below-average management expenses of $1.34 for every $100 in assets and has a minimum initial investment requirement of $25,000 for both RRSP and non-RRSP accounts.

Sceptre Equity Growth Fund ★★

This fund was launched in 1987 and has been managed by Allan Jacobs since May 1993. With $374 million in assets, it follows a bottom-up/value/sector investment strategy. About 60% of the fund's assets are made up of investments in industrial products, oil and gas, merchandising, and financial services.

The fund posted its highest return, 41.0%, in 1993, and its lowest, -2.1%, in 1992. Over the past five years, its average annual compound return was 25.5%. A no-load fund if purchased directly from the sponsor, it charges management expenses of $1.51 for every $100 in assets, lower than the group average of $2.36. The fund has a minimum initial investment requirement of $5,000 for both RRSP and non-RRSP accounts.

Guardian Enterprise Fund A ★1/2

This fund was launched in 1972 and has been managed by Gary Chapman since December 1994. With $59 million in assets, it follows a bottom-up/growth investment strategy. Investments in industrial products, consumer products, and oil and gas account for 55% of the fund's assets.

Its best year was 1996, when it posted a return of 44.6%, and its worst year was 1994, when its return was -9.9%. The fund's average annual compound return over the past five years was 20.5%. A load fund, sold only on a front-end basis, it charges below-average management expenses of $2.03 for every $100 in assets.

The Rookie Camp

Five of the promising newer Canadian small-to-mid-cap equity funds, each with at least a three-year track record, are in the Rookie Camp this year. Each of these funds, listed below, posted *above*-average returns over the past one-, two-, and three-year periods.

Colonia Special Growth Fund, a segregated fund sponsored by the Colonia Life Insurance Company, was launched in 1993 and follows a bottom-up/growth investment strategy. The fund is managed by Ultravest Investment Counsellors Inc. A load fund, sold only on a deferred basis, it has $28 million in assets and charges above-average management expenses of $2.43 for every $100 in assets.

Cote 100 EXP Fund, sponsored by Cote 100 Inc. of St. Bruno, Quebec, was launched in 1994 and is managed by Guy LeBlanc. With $28 million in assets, the fund follows a growth investment strategy. It is a no-load fund and charges above-average management expenses of $2.60 for every $100 in assets. The fund has a minimum initial investment requirement of $5,000.

Hyperion Small-Cap Canadian Equity Fund, sponsored by Talvest Fund Management Inc., has been managed by Sebastian Van Berkom since its inception in January 1994. The fund has $77 million in assets and follows a bottom-up/growth investment strategy. A load fund, it charges above-average management expenses of $2.50 for every $100 in assets.

Metlife MVP Growth Fund, a segregated fund sponsored by the Metropolitan Life Insurance Co., was launched in 1993 and follows a bottom-up/blend investment strategy. The fund is managed by AMI

Partners Inc. A load fund, sold only on a deferred basis, it has $78 million in assets and charges below-average management expenses of $2.23 for every $100 in assets.

Millennium Next Generation Fund, sponsored by Morrison Williams Investment Management Ltd., was launched in 1993 and is managed by Leslie Williams and Barry Morrison. With $21 million in assets, the fund follows a top-down/blend investment strategy. It is a load fund, sold only on a front-end basis, and charges above-average management expenses of $2.50 for every $100 in assets. The fund is available for sale only in the province of Ontario.

The Underachievers

There are six Canadian small-to-mid-cap funds that have failed to measure up to their peers. These Underachievers have consistently delivered *below*-average returns over the past one-, three-, and five-year periods. Collectively these Underachievers manage $1.1 billion in assets. Canada Trust's Everest Special Equity Fund is the largest, with $364 million in assets, and the Cambridge Special Equity Fund is the smallest, with $8.8 million. Two of the six Underachievers are no-load funds.

Table 2

THE UNDERACHIEVERS

CANADIAN SMALL-TO-MID-CAP EQUITY FUNDS

- Altamira Special Growth Fund*
- Cambridge Growth Fund
- Cambridge Special Equity
- Canada Trust Everest Special Equity*
- Industrial Equity Fund Ltd.
- Laurentian Special Equity Fund

---

* denotes a no-load fund

Heavy Hitters vs Underachievers

Table 3 shows the difference in returns, over three time periods, between the Heavy Hitters and Underachievers in this category. As can be seen, the Heavy Hitters posted returns that, on average, far out-stripped the Underachievers'. In dollar terms, for an initial investment of $10,000, the average Heavy Hitter Canadian small-to-mid-cap fund would have returned a total of $30,640 over the past five years. For the same investment, the average Underachiever would have returned $16,474 — for a difference of $14,165 or 86.0%.

With respect to costs, the average Heavy Hitter charged management expenses of $1.70 for every $100 in assets, compared with $2.47 for the average Underachiever.

Table 3

HEAVY HITTERS vs UNDERACHIEVERS

CANADIAN SMALL-TO-MID-CAP EQUITY FUNDS

(Returns %)

	1-Year	3-Year*	5-Year*
• Heavy Hitters	22.9	21.7	25.1
• Underachievers	-10.2	1.4	10.5

* annualized

CANADIAN SMALL-TO-MID-CAP EQUITY FUNDS RANKINGS/RETURNS

Rank			Name of Fund	Returns (%)			Assets
(19)	(37)	(55)		(11.8)	(13.9)	(18.7)	
5-Yr	3-Yr	1-Yr		1-Yr	3-Yr	5-Yr	($mns)
-	-	48	20/20 RSP Aggr. Smaller Companies	-7.4	-	-	377.0
-	8	52	20/20 RSP Aggressive Equity	-12.8	22.0	-	333.7
13	28	39	Altamira Special Growth Fund (UA)	8.9	8.8	13.7	321.2
-	-	44	Atlas Canadian Emerging Growth Fund	6.7	-	-	118.8
-	-	19	Atlas Canadian Emerging Value Fund	18.5	-	-	29.8
-	-	4	Beutel Goodman Small Cap Fund	29.9	-	-	12.0
3	9	3	Bissett Small Cap Fund (HH)	32.6	20.4	32.0	57.8
7	10	49	BPI Canadian Small Companies Fund	-8.3	18.5	21.5	724.8
19	37	54	Cambridge Growth Fund (Sagit) (UA)	-36.3	-8.4	2.3	32.4
18	36	55	Cambridge Special Equity (Sagit) (UA)	-52.4	-6.3	5.9	8.8
16	33	38	Canada Trust Everest Special Equity (UA)	9.2	6.7	12.0	364.4
-	26	26	CDA Aggressive Equity	16.5	10.2	-	8.2
14	31	31	CIBC Capital Appreciation Fund	13.6	7.9	12.9	376.2
-	2	8	Colonia Special Growth Fund (RC)	26.6	28.0	-	28.0
-	6	5	Cote 100 EXP (RC)	28.5	24.0	-	28.3
-	-	33	Cote 100 REA - Action	12.5	-	-	8.8
-	-	30	Ethical Special Equity Fund	14.9	-	-	65.7
-	-	14	Fidelity Canadian Growth Company	20.3	-	-	851.2
-	22	18	First Cdn. Special Growth Fund	19.5	12.7	-	230.0
-	30	12	Fonds d'Investissement REA	21.1	7.9	-	44.5
12	25	17	General Trust of Canada Growth Fund	19.7	10.2	15.1	15.5
-	-	1	Global Strategy Cdn. Small Cap	38.9	-	-	217.1
8	7	11	Guardian Enterprise Fund A (HH)	21.6	23.6	20.5	58.6
-	-	13	Guardian Enterprise Fund B	21.0	-	-	137.5
-	-	25	GWL Growth Equity Fund (A) DSC	16.7	-	-	19.6
-	-	27	GWL Growth Equity Fund (A) NL	16.3	-	-	30.1
-	-	22	GWL Smaller Company Fund (M) DSC	17.0	-	-	12.0
-	-	24	GWL Smaller Company Fund (M) NL	16.7	-	-	14.3
-	-	21	Hongkong Bank Small Cap Growth Fund	17.3	-	-	52.2
-	14	7	Hyperion Small-Cap Canadian Equity (RC)	27.3	16.0	-	77.4
11	35	46	Industrial Equity Fund Ltd. (UA)	0.6	0.1	16.1	209.0
-	-	10	Ivy Enterprise Fund	22.2	-	-	186.7
15	32	41	Laurentian Special Equity Fund (UA)	8.5	7.4	12.8	153.2
-	21	34	Lotus (MKW) Canadian Equity Fund	12.5	13.1	-	7.8

CANADIAN SMALL-TO-MID-CAP EQUITY FUNDS
RANKINGS/RETURNS *cont'd*

Rank			Name of Fund	Returns (%)			Assets
(19)	(37)	(55)		(11.8)	(13.9)	(18.7)	
5-Yr	3-Yr	1-Yr		1-Yr	3-Yr	5-Yr	($mns)
-	18	15	Manulife Cabot Canadian Growth Fund	20.2	13.6	-	16.0
-	23	28	Manulife Cabot Emerging Growth Fund	16.1	12.7	-	7.1
1	1	43	Marathon Equity Fund	7.1	28.4	37.5	290.2
5	15	32	Mawer New Canada Fund (HH)	13.4	15.1	22.5	39.4
-	16	16	Metlife MVP Growth Fund (RC)	19.9	15.0	-	78.4
-	4	35	Millennium Next Generation Fund (RC)	12.1	26.0	-	21.0
2	5	51	Multiple Opportunities Fund	-12.7	24.4	35.9	14.7
-	12	23	Mutual Premier Growth Fund	17.0	17.9	-	930.9
-	27	40	National Trust Special Equity Fund	8.6	9.0	-	42.4
-	-	45	O'Donnell Canadian Emerging Growth	5.4	-	-	649.9
17	24	20	Ontario Teachers Group Growth	17.6	11.5	11.6	20.9
-	20	53	Pacific Special Equity Fund	-18.4	13.3	-	15.2
9	13	2	Quebec Growth Fund	37.6	16.8	18.6	13.7
-	17	50	Resolute Growth Fund	-11.8	14.0	-	4.8
-	29	42	Royal Canadian Growth Fund	8.4	8.4	-	696.7
-	34	47	Royal Canadian Small Cap	0.1	6.4	-	272.5
-	-	37	Royal Life Canadian Growth Fund	9.8	-	-	44.1
10	19	6	Saxon Small Cap (Howson Tattersall)	28.3	13.5	18.2	10.8
4	3	9	Sceptre Equity Growth Fund (HH)	24.3	27.7	25.5	374.0
6	11	36	Spectrum United Canadian Growth	11.2	18.2	21.8	1065.5
-	-	29	Standard Life Growth Equity Fund	15.0	-	-	7.8

( ) under Rank indicates total number of funds; ( ) under Returns (%) indicates average annual return; (HH) — Heavy Hitter; (UA) — Underachiever; (RC) — Rookie Camp member.

CANADIAN SMALL-TO-MID-CAP EQUITY FUNDS/SUMMARY

Name of Fund	MER	Load	RRSP	Vola-tility	Company Number (App. 3)
20/20 RSP Aggr. Smaller Companies	2.64	Y	R		3
20/20 RSP Aggressive Equity (C)	2.45	Y	R	7	3
Altamira Special Growth Fund	1.80	N	R	4	6
Atlas Canadian Emerging Gr. Fund (C)	2.50	N	R		9
Atlas Canadian Emerging Value Fund	2.61	N	R		9
Atlas Cdn. Small-Cap Growth Fund	2.89	N	R		9
Beutel Goodman Small Cap Fund	2.56	N	R		12
Bissett Small Cap Fund	1.90	Y	R	4	13
BPI Canadian Small Companies Fund (C)	2.84	Y	R	5	15
Cambridge Growth Fund	2.89	Y	R	5	121
Cambridge Special Equity	2.88	Y	R	9	121
Canada Trust Everest Special Equity	2.18	N	R	4	19
CDA Aggressive Equity (R)	1.00	N	R		22
CDA Special Equity (R)	1.45	N	R		22
CIBC Capital Appreciation Fund	2.40	N	R	3	29
Clarington Canadian Small-Cap Fund	2.75	Y	R		30
Colonia Special Growth Fund	2.43	Y	R	5	32
Cote 100 EXP (R)	2.60	Y	R		34
Cote 100 REA - Action (R)	2.60	Y	N		34
Ethical Special Equity Fund (R)	2.61	N	R		44
Fidelity Canadian Growth Company	2.65	Y	R		46
First Cdn. Special Growth Fund	2.17	N	R	4	11
Fonds d'Investissement REA (R)	2.36	Y	R	3	53
General Trust of Canada Growth (R)	2.13	N	R	4	98
Global Strategy Cdn. Small Cap (C)	2.75	Y	R		54
Guardian Enterprise Fund A	2.03	Y	R	4	61
Guardian Enterprise Fund B	2.75	Y	R		61
GWL Growth Equity Fund (A) DSC	2.94	Y	R		57
GWL Growth Equity Fund (A) NL	3.18	N	R		57
GWL Smaller Company Fund (M) DSC	2.58	Y	R		57
GWL Smaller Company Fund (M) NL	2.82	N	R		57
Hongkong Bank Small Cap Growth	2.31	N	R		63
Hyperion Small-Cap Canadian Equity	2.50	Y	R		136
IG Beutel Goodman Cdn. Small-Cap	2.86	Y	R		70

CANADIAN SMALL-TO-MID-CAP EQUITY FUNDS/SUMMARY *cont'd*

Name of Fund	MER	Load	RRSP	Vola-tility	Company Number (App. 3)
Industrial Equity Fund Ltd.	2.41	Y	R	5	80
Investors Canadian Small-Cap Fund	2.79	Y	R		70
Ivy Enterprise Fund	2.43	Y	R		80
Laurentian Special Equity Fund	2.65	Y	R	4	135
Lotus (MKW) Canadian Equity Fund (R)	2.10	N	R	5	79
Manulife Cabot Canadian Growth	2.50	N	R		84
Manulife Cabot Emerging Growth	2.50	N	R		84
Marathon Equity Fund (C)	2.00	N	R	6	48
Mawer New Canada Fund (R)	1.34	N	R	4	86
Metlife MVP Growth Fund	2.23	Y	R	4	92
Millennium Next Generation Fund (R)	2.50	Y	R	4	96
Multiple Opportunities Fund (R)	2.74	N	R	8	94
Mutual Premier Growth Fund	2.28	N	R	4	97
National Trust Special Equity Fund (R)	2.50	N	R	4	100
O'Donnell Canadian Emerging Growth	2.75	Y	R		104
Ontario Teachers Group Growth (R)	1.00	N	R	4	106
Pacific Special Equity Fund	2.90	Y	R	6	110
Quebec Growth Fund (R)	1.90	Y	R	4	95
Resolute Growth Fund (R)	2.00	Y	R	6	36
Royal Canadian Growth Fund	2.30	N	R	4	119
Royal Canadian Small Cap	2.27	N	R	4	119
Royal Life Canadian Growth Fund	2.00	Y	R		120
Saxon Small Cap (R)	1.75	N	R	3	122
Sceptre Equity Growth Fund	1.51	N	R	4	123
Spectrum United Canadian Growth (C)	2.35	Y	R	4	129
Standard Life Growth Equity Fund	2.00	Y	R		133
Average	2.36			4.6	

(R) — Restricted; (C) — Closed to new investors; MER — Management Expense Ratio; Load — fee charged; RRSP: R = 100% eligible, F = eligible as foreign content only, N = not eligible; Volatility — measures swings in performance on a scale of 1 to 10 (1 = low, 10 = high). Blank space indicates that fund is less than three years old. Fund company addresses may be found by number in Appendix 3.

14

● ●

Canadian Balanced Funds

AS THEIR NAME implies, these funds invest in a well-diversified portfolio of short- and long-term bonds and Canadian stocks. Balanced income funds place their emphasis on bonds for higher income potential; balanced growth funds place greater emphasis on stocks for higher capital-growth potential. By investing in a combination of stocks and bonds, balanced funds are considerably less volatile than funds that invest solely in the stock market.

There are currently 182 Canadian balanced funds on the market. These funds manage a total of $50.6 billion in assets. Over the five calendar years from 1992 to 1996, the best year for Canadian balanced funds was 1993, when returns averaged 22.4%. In contrast, the worst year was 1994, when returns averaged -2.8%. The average annual compound rate of return over the five-year period was 11.0%. The average fee for management expenses is $2.08 for every $100 in assets, which is up from last year's average of $1.94.

The Heavy Hitters

There are 27 Canadian balanced funds that have qualified for membership in the Heavy Hitters club this year. Each of these funds has consistently delivered *above*-average returns over the past one-, three-, and five-year periods. Collectively these Heavy Hitters manage a total of $8.7 billion in assets. The Trimark Select Balanced Fund is the largest, with more than $3.8 billion in assets, and the AMI Private Capital Optimix Fund is the smallest, with $4.2 million in assets. Sixteen of the 27 Heavy Hitters are no-load funds.

• •

Table 1

THE HEAVY HITTERS

CANADIAN BALANCED FUNDS

		Bench-mark*	Vola-tility	Performance Quartile 1	Quartile 2	Overall Rating
1	Bissett Retirement Fund (R)	4	2	2	3	★★★
2	ABC Fully Managed Fund (R) (N)	4	3	4	0	★★★
3	Saxon Balanced Fund (R) (N)	4	3	4	0	★★★
4	Maxxum Canadian Balanced Fund	4	3	3	1	★★1/2
5	Beutel Goodman Private Balanced (R) (N)	3	2	3	1	★★1/2
6	McLean Budden Pooled Balanced Fund (R) (N)	3	3	3	2	★★1/2
7	McLean Budden Registered Balanced (R) (N)	3	3	3	2	★★1/2
8	Trimark Select Balanced Fund	3	3	2	3	★★1/2
9	Phillips Hager & North Bal. Pens. Tr. (R) (N)	2	2	4	0	★★1/2
10	Industrial Pension Fund	3	3	3	0	★★
11	Sceptre Balanced Growth Fund (N)	3	3	3	0	★★
12	Caldwell Securities Associate Fund	3	4	3	0	★★
13	Cassels Blaikie Canadian Fund	2	2	2	2	★★
14	McLean Budden Balanced Fund (N)	3	3	2	1	★★
15	Phillips Hager & North Balanced (R) (N)	2	2	1	4	★★
16	Leith Wheeler Balanced Fund (R) (N)	2	2	1	3	★★
17	Global Strategy Income Plus Fund	2	2	2	0	★1/2
18	Scotia Excelsior Total Return Fund (N)	2	3	2	1	★1/2
19	NN Asset Allocation Fund	1	3	2	2	★1/2
20	Clean Environment Balanced Fund (R)	2	3	2	0	★1/2
21	Industrial Alliance Diversified (C) (N)	2	3	1	2	★1/2
22	Ferique Balanced Fund (R) (N)	1	3	1	3	★1/2
23	Mawer Cdn. Balanced RSP Fund (R) (N)	1	2	0	4	★1/2
24	AMI Private Capital Optimix (N)	1	3	1	2	★
25	Templeton Balanced Fund	1	3	1	1	★
26	Ontario Teachers Group Balanced (R) (N)	1	3	0	3	★
27	National Balanced Fund	0	3	1	2	★

* TSE 300 Total Return Index/ScotiaMcLeod Universe Bond Index (equally weighted); (R) — Restricted; (C) — Closed to new members; (N) — No-load fund; Benchmark — number of times that a fund beat the benchmark from 1992 to 1996; Volatility — measures swings in fund returns on a scale of 1 to 10 (1 = low, 10 = high); Performance — number of times that a fund was in the first (top 25%) or second quartile (top 50%) from 1992 to 1996.

The benchmark used to compare Canadian balanced fund returns is the TSE 300 Total Return Index/ScotiaMcLeod Universe Bond Index (equally weighted). Over the past five calendar years, the index posted its highest return of 25.4% in 1993 and its lowest return of -2.3% in 1994.

Bissett Retirement Fund ★★★

This fund, a Rookie Camp member in last year's *World of Mutual Funds*, was launched in 1991 and has been managed by Michael Quinn since its inception. With $23 million in assets, 40% of the portfolio is invested in equities, 15% in U.S. equities, and 36% in bonds.

Its best year was 1996, when it posted a return of 22.2%, and its worst year was 1994, when its return was -1.8%. The fund's average annual compound return over the past five years was 15.0%. A no-load fund when purchased directly from the sponsor, it charges management expenses of $0.44 for every $100 in assets, which is well below the group average of $2.08.

ABC Fully Managed Fund ★★★

This fund was started in 1988 and has been managed by Irwin Michael since its inception. The fund has $74 million in assets, with 68% of the portfolio invested in equities and 30% in fixed-income securities.

In 1993, its best year, the fund posted a return of 64.4%, and in 1992, its worst year, it returned -1.5%. Over the past five years, it yielded an average annual compound return of 22.5%. This no-load fund charges below-average management expenses of $2.00 for every $100 in assets and has a minimum initial investment requirement of $150,000.

Saxon Balanced Fund ★★★

Launched in 1985, this fund has been managed by Richard Howson since March 1989. With $9 million in assets, 61% of the fund's portfolio is invested in equities, 23% in fixed-income securities, and 16% in cash. The fund posted its highest return, 34.4%, in 1993, and its lowest, -3.2%, in 1994. Over the past five years, its average annual compound return was 17.6%. This is a no-load fund which charges management expenses of $1.75 for every $100 in assets, lower than the group average of $2.08. The fund has a minimum initial investment requirement of $5,000 and is available for sale only in Alberta, British Columbia, and Ontario.

Maxxum Canadian Balanced Fund ★★1/2

This fund was launched in 1988 and is managed by the team of Martin Anstee, Gerald Boychuk, and Douglas Crawford. With $115 million in assets, 56% of the portfolio is invested in equities, 34% in fixed-income securities, and 10% in cash.

Its best year was 1993, when it posted a return of 29.8%, and its worst year was 1994, when its return was -8.4%. The fund's average annual compound return over the past five years was 13.3%. A load fund, it charges management expenses of $2.15 for every $100 in assets, which is above the group average of $2.08.

Beutel Goodman Private Balanced Fund ★★1/2

This fund, which was started in 1989, has been managed by Stephen Clements since its inception. The fund has $45 million in assets, with 33% of the portfolio invested in U.S. equities, 21% in Canadian equities, and 38% in fixed-income securities.

In 1996, its best year, the fund posted a return of 19.3%, and in 1994, its worst year, it returned -0.1%. Over the past five years, it yielded an average annual compound return of 14.9%. This no-load fund charges well-below-average management expenses of $1.10 for every $100 in assets, has a minimum initial investment requirement of $250,000, and is not RRSP eligible.

McLean Budden Pooled Balanced Fund ★★1/2

Launched in 1993, this fund is managed by McLean Budden's asset mix team of Craig Barnard, Mary Hallward, Lewis Jackson, Doug Mahaffy, and Bob Nadon. With $199 million in assets, 35% of the fund's portfolio is invested in Canadian equities, 17% in foreign equities, and 44% in fixed-income securities.

The fund posted its highest return, 22.4%, in 1996, and its lowest, -2.7%, in 1994. Over the past five years, its average annual compound return was 14.3%. This no-load fund charges management expenses of $1.00 for every $100 in assets, considerably lower than the group average of $2.08. The fund has a minimum initial investment requirement of $500,000.

McLean Budden Registered Balanced Fund ★★1/2

This fund, the second McLean Budden pooled balanced fund to make the Heavy Hitter list this year, is also managed by the firm's asset mix team. With $47 million in assets, 31% of the portfolio is invested in equities, 36% in government bonds, and 15% in foreign bonds.

Its best year was 1993, when it posted a return of 21.7%, and its worst year was 1994, when its return was -2.7%. The fund's average annual compound return over the past five years was 14.7%. A no-load fund, it charges well-below-average management expenses of $1.00 for every $100 in assets. The fund has a minimum initial investment requirement of $500,000.

Trimark Select Balanced Fund ★★1/2

This fund was started in 1989 and is managed by the Trimark investment team headed by Robert Krembil. Other members of the team include Rick Serafini, Patrick Farmer, Phillip Taller, Vito Maida, and Wally Kusters. The fund has $3.8 billion in assets, with 40% of the portfolio invested in Canadian equities, 19% in foreign equities, and 27% in fixed-income securities.

In 1993, its best year, the fund posted a return of 27.4%, and in 1994, its worst year, it returned 1.5%. Over the past five years, it yielded an average annual compound return of 14.1%. This load fund charges above-average management expenses of $2.23 for every $100 in assets.

Phillips Hager & North Balanced Pension Trust Fund ★★1/2

Launched in 1988, this fund is managed by the Phillips Hager & North investment team. With $1.4 billion in assets, 41% of the fund's portfolio is invested in PH&N's bond fund and another 38% in the PH&N Pooled Pension Fund.

The fund posted its highest return, 19.8%, in 1996, and its lowest, 0.4%, in 1994. Over the past five years, its average annual compound return was 13.7%. This is a no-load fund which charges management expenses of $0.50 for every $100 in assets, considerably lower than the group average of $2.08. The fund is available for defined contribution pension plans only.

Industrial Pension Fund ★★

This fund, sponsored by the Mackenzie Financial Corporation, was launched in 1971 and is managed by William Proctor. With $106 million in assets, 74% of the portfolio is invested in equities, 13% in fixed-income securities, and 13% in cash.

Its best year was 1993, when it posted a return of 50.5%, and its worst year was 1992, when its return was -2.7%. The fund's average annual compound return over the past five years was 17.5%. A load fund, it charges management expenses of $2.44 for every $100 in assets, which is above the group average of $2.08.

Sceptre Balanced Growth Fund ★★

This fund was started in 1986 and has been managed by Lyle Stein since March 1993. The fund has $154 million in assets, with 38% of the portfolio invested in Canadian equities, 13% in foreign equities, and 33% in fixed-income securities.

In 1996, its best year, the fund posted a return of 26.0%, and in 1994, its worst year, it returned -4.2%. Over the past five years, it yielded an average annual compound return of 14.9%. This no-load fund charges below-average management expenses of $1.43 for every $100 in assets and has a minimum initial investment requirement of $5,000.

Caldwell Securities Associate Fund ★★

Launched in 1990, this fund has been managed by Thomas Caldwell and Dennis Freeman since its inception. With $89 million in assets, 70% of the fund's portfolio is invested in equities and 30% in cash.

The fund posted its highest return, 27.0%, in 1993, and its lowest, -3.4%, in 1992. Over the past five years, its average annual compound return was 15.1%. This is a load fund, sold only on a deferred basis, which charges management expenses of $2.98 for every $100 in assets, higher than the group average of $2.08.

Cassels Blaikie Canadian Fund ★★

This fund was launched in 1984 and is managed by Carol McGillivray. With $16 million in assets, 60% of the portfolio is invested in equities and 37% in fixed-income securities.

Its best year was 1996, when it posted a return of 19.9%, and its worst year was 1994, when its return was -1.0%. The fund's average annual compound return over the past five years was 12.7%. A load fund, sold only on a front-end basis, it charges management expenses of $1.04 for every $100 in assets, which is well below the group average of $2.08.

McLean Budden Balanced Fund ★★

This fund was started in 1989 and has been managed by McLean Budden's asset mix team since its inception. The fund has $15 million in assets, with 52% of the portfolio invested in equities and 42% in fixed-income securities.

In 1996, its best year, the fund posted a return of 21.6%, and in 1994, its worst year, it returned -4.2%. Over the past five years, it yielded an average annual compound return of 12.9%. This no-load fund charges below-average management expenses of $1.75 for every $100 in assets and has a minimum initial investment requirement of $5,000.

Phillips Hager & North Balanced Fund ★★

Launched in 1991, this fund has been managed by the Phillips Hager & North investment team since its inception. With $350 million in assets, 31% of the fund's portfolio is invested in Canadian bonds, 23% in other mutual funds, and 6% in corporate bonds.

The fund posted its highest return, 20.2%, in 1993, and its lowest, -0.4%, in 1994. Over the past five years, its average annual compound return was 13.3%. This is a no-load fund which charges management expenses of $0.91 for every $100 in assets, considerably lower than the group average of $2.08. The fund has a minimum initial investment requirement of $25,000 for non-RRSP accounts and $5,000 for RRSP accounts.

Leith Wheeler Balanced Fund ★★

This fund was launched in 1987 and is managed by the firm's investment committee. With $46 million in assets, 50% of the portfolio is invested in equities and 40% in fixed-income securities.

Its best year was 1993, when it posted a return of 23.5%, and its worst year was 1994, when its return was -1.7%. The fund's average annual compound return over the past five years was 12.9%. A no-load fund, it charges management expenses of $1.16 for every $100 in assets, which is well below the group average of $2.08. The fund has a minimum initial investment requirement of $50,000 and is available for sale only in Alberta and British Columbia.

Global Strategy Income Plus Fund ★1/2

This fund, identified as a Rookie Camp member in last year's *World of Mutual Funds*, was started in 1992 and has been managed by Tony Massie since April 1992. The fund has $725 million in assets, with 72% of the portfolio invested in equities and 21% in fixed-income securities. In 1993, its best year, the fund posted a return of 28.7%, and in 1994, its worst year, it returned -2.9%. Over the past five years, it yielded an average annual compound return of 14.9%. This load fund charges above-average management expenses of $2.63 for every $100 in assets.

Scotia Excelsior Total Return Fund ★1/2

Launched in 1989, this fund, the only bank fund to make the Heavy Hitter list in this category, is managed by the Montrusco Associates investment team. With $577 million in assets, 60% of the fund's portfolio is invested in equities, 20% in fixed-income securities, and 20% in cash.

The fund posted its highest return, 31.1%, in 1993, and its lowest, -4.8%, in 1994. Over the past five years, its average annual compound return was 14.5%. This is a no-load fund which charges management expenses of $2.27 for every $100 in assets, higher than the group average of $2.08.

NN Asset Allocation Fund ★1/2

This segregated fund was launched in 1987 and has been managed by Ted Gibson since November 1992. With $108 million in assets, 43% of the portfolio is invested in equities, 39% in fixed-income securities, and 18% in cash.

Its best year was 1993, when it posted a return of 20.8%, and its worst year was 1994, when its return was -3.4%. The fund's average annual compound return over the past five years was 12.4%. A load fund, sold only on a deferred basis, it charges management expenses of $3.00 for every $100 in assets, which is well above the group average of $2.08.

Clean Environment Balanced Fund ★1/2

This fund was started in 1992 and has been managed by Ian Ihnatowycz since its inception. The fund has $29 million in assets, with 45% of the portfolio invested in equities, 11% in fixed-income securities, and 44% in cash.

In 1993, its best year, the fund posted a return of 38.4%, and in 1994, its worst year, it returned -8.0%. Over the past five years, it yielded an average annual compound return of 16.6%. This load fund charges well-above-average management expenses of $3.00 for every $100 in assets.

Industrial Alliance Diversified Fund ★1/2

Launched in 1987, this segregated fund is managed by Luc Fournier and Benoit Desrochers. With $251 million in assets, 56% of the fund's portfolio is invested in equities and 33% in fixed-income securities.

The fund posted its highest return, 23.9%, in 1993, and its lowest, -0.7%, in 1994. Over the past five years, its average annual compound return was 12.7%. This is a no-load fund which charges management expenses of $1.58 for every $100 in assets, lower than the group average of $2.08.

Ferique Balanced Fund ★1/2

This fund, sponsored by the Ordre des Ingenieurs du Quebec, a professional engineers' association, was launched in 1981 and is managed by the Montreal-based firm T.A.L. Investment Counsel Ltd. With $255 million in assets, 66% of the portfolio is invested in equities and 32% in fixed-income securities.

Its best year was 1993, when it posted a return of 19.9%, and its worst year was 1994, when its return was -0.3%. The fund's average annual compound return over the past five years was 13.0%. A no-load fund, it charges management expenses of $0.44 for every $100 in assets, which is considerably below the group average of $2.08. The fund is available for purchase only by the association's members.

Mawer Canadian Balanced RSP Fund ★1/2

This fund was started in 1988 and has been managed by Don Ferris since its inception. The fund has $65 million in assets, with 58% of the portfolio invested in equities and 35% in fixed-income securities.

In 1993, its best year, the fund posted a return of 19.8%, and in 1994, its worst year, it returned -2.3%. Over the past five years, it yielded an average annual compound return of 12.2%. This no-load fund charges well-below-average management expenses of $0.89 for every $100 in assets and has a minimum initial investment requirement of $25,000.

AMI Private Capital Optimix Fund ★

Launched in 1987, this fund is managed by the firm's investment team. With $4 million in assets, 60% of the fund's portfolio is invested in equities and 36% in fixed-income securities.

The fund posted its highest return, 20.7%, in 1993, and its lowest, -3.5%, in 1994. Over the past five years, its average annual compound return was 12.6%. This is a no-load fund which charges management expenses of $1.75 for every $100 in assets, lower than the group average of $2.08. The fund has a minimum initial investment requirement of $50,000.

Templeton Balanced Fund ★

This fund was launched in 1990 and is managed by George Morgan and Neil Devlin. With $40 million in assets, 66% of the portfolio is invested in equities and 32% in fixed-income securities.

Its best year was 1993, when it posted a return of 31.0%, and its worst year was 1994, when its return was -3.0%. The fund's average annual compound return over the past five years was 12.6%. A load fund, sold only on a front-end basis, it charges management expenses of $2.34 for every $100 in assets, which is above the group average of $2.08

Ontario Teachers Group Balanced Fund ★

This fund was started in 1985 and has been managed by the Toronto investment firm AMI Partners Inc. since December 1985. The fund has $52 million in assets, with 54% of the portfolio invested in equities, 35% in fixed-income securities, and 11% in cash.

In 1993, its best year, the fund posted a return of 18.1%, and in 1994, its worst year, it returned -2.9%. Over the past five years, it yielded an average annual compound return of 12.9%. This no-load fund charges well-below-average management expenses of $1.11 for every $100 in assets and is available only to members of the Ontario Teachers Group.

National Balanced Fund ★

Launched in 1992, this segregated fund is managed by Thomas Dea and Nang Cheung. With $104 million in assets, 52% of the fund's portfolio is invested in equities and 33% in fixed-income securities.

The fund posted its highest return, 23.2%, in 1993, and its lowest, -3.7%, in 1994. Over the past five years, its average annual compound return was 12.2%. This is a load fund, sold only on a deferred basis, which charges management expenses of $2.00 for every $100 in assets, slightly lower than the group average of $2.08.

The Rookie Camp

Nine of the promising newer Canadian balanced funds, each with at least a three-year track record, are in the Rookie Camp this year. Each of these funds, listed below, posted *above*-average returns over the past one-, two-, and three-year periods.

Common Sense Asset Builder Funds 1, 2, 3, 4, and 5 are segregated funds sponsored by Primerica Life Insurance Company. The funds were launched in 1994 and are managed by Jerry Javasky of the Mackenzie Financial Corporation. The asset mixes of these funds vary, with fixed-income securities dominating the Common Sense Asset Builder 1 Fund and investments in equities dominating the Common Sense Asset Builder 5 Fund. Load funds, sold only on a deferred basis, they have combined assets of $120 million and charge above-average management expenses of $2.10 for every $100 in assets.

Investors Asset Allocation Fund, sponsored by the Investors Group, was launched in 1994 and has been managed by Eric Innes since its inception. A load fund, with $1.5 billion in assets, it charges above-average management expenses of $2.73 for every $100 in assets.

Ivy Growth & Income Fund, sponsored by the Mackenzie Financial Corporation, was launched in 1992 and has been managed by Jerry Javasky since May 1997. A load fund, with $1.1 billion in assets, the fund charges slightly above-average management expenses of $2.13 for every $100 in assets.

MD Balanced Fund, sponsored by MD Management Ltd., was launched in 1992 and is managed by the investment firm Connor, Clark & Lumm Investment Management Inc. A no-load fund, it has $657 million in assets and charges well-below-average management expenses of $1.30 for every $100 in assets. The fund is available for sale only to members of the Canadian Medical Association and their families.

Standard Life Balanced Fund, sponsored by Standard Life Mutual Funds Ltd., was launched in 1992 and is managed by the firm's investment team. With $15.5 million in assets, the fund follows a blend/bottom-up investment strategy. A load fund, sold only on a deferred basis, it charges below-average management expenses of $2.00 for every $100 in assets.

The Underachievers

There are 25 Canadian balanced funds that have failed to measure up to their peers. These Underachievers have consistently delivered *below*-average returns over the past one-, three-, and five-year periods. Collectively these Underachievers manage $15.1 billion in assets. The Royal Balanced Fund is the largest, with $5.4 billion in assets, and the Cambridge Balanced Fund is the smallest, with $19.8 million. Twelve of the 25 Underachievers are no-load funds.

Table 2

THE UNDERACHIEVERS

CANADIAN BALANCED FUNDS

- Altamira Balanced Fund*
- Altamira Growth & Income Fund*
- BPI Canadian Balanced Fund
- Cambridge Balanced Fund
- First Cdn. Asset Allocation*

Table 2

THE UNDERACHIEVERS *continued*
CANADIAN BALANCED FUNDS

- Fonds de Professionnels Balanced*
- Guardian Canadian Balanced Fund A
- GWL Diversified Fund (G) NL*
- GWL Equity/Bond Fund (G) NL*
- HRL Balanced Fund*
- Industrial Mortgage Securities
- Investors Income Plus Portfolio
- Investors Retirement Plus Portfolio
- Jones Heward Canadian Balanced Fund
- London Life Diversified
- Manulife Vistafund 1 Diversified
- Manulife Vistafund 2 Diversified
- Metlife MVP Balanced Fund
- Royal Balanced Fund*
- Royal Trust Advantage Balanced Fund*
- Royal Trust Advantage Growth Fund*
- Royal Trust Advantage Income Fund*
- Scotia Excelsior Balanced Fund*
- Talvest Canadian Asset Allocation
- Transamerica Balanced Inv. Growth

* denotes a no-load fund

Heavy Hitters vs Underachievers

Table 3 shows the significant difference in returns, over three time periods, between the Heavy Hitters and Underachievers in this category. In dollar terms, for an initial investment of $10,000, the average Heavy Hitter Canadian balanced fund would have returned a total of $19,509 over the past five years. For the same investment, the average Underachiever would have returned $16,032 — for a difference of $3,477 or 21.7%.

With respect to costs, the average Heavy Hitter charged management expenses of $1.66 for every $100 in assets, compared with $1.89 for the average Underachiever.

Table 3

HEAVY HITTERS vs UNDERACHIEVERS

CANADIAN BALANCED FUNDS

(Returns %)

	1-Year	3-Year*	5-Year*
• Heavy Hitters	21.1	14.7	14.3
• Underachievers	10.7	9.5	9.9

* annualized

CANADIAN BALANCED FUNDS
RANKINGS/RETURNS

Rank			Name of Fund	Returns (%)			Assets
(99)	(119)	(156)		(16.6)	(12.5)	(12.1)	
5-Yr	3-Yr	1-Yr		1-Yr	3-Yr	5-Yr	($mns)
1	9	17	ABC Fully Managed Fund (HH)	22.2	16.2	22.5	73.0
-	-	59	Acadia Balanced Fund	18.2	-	-	16.3
-	115	144	Admax Asset Allocation Fund	8.8	7.7	-	8.1
62	82	62	AGF Canadian Tactical Asset Alloc.	18.1	12.0	11.3	803.8
18	32	151	AGF Growth & Income Fund	3.8	13.9	14.1	626.2
63	114	146	Altamira Balanced Fund (UA)	7.5	7.9	11.3	89.7
93	118	155	Altamira Growth & Income Fund (UA)	-1.5	4.9	9.3	240.1
35	25	24	AMI Private Capital Optimix (HH)	21.1	14.2	12.6	4.2
-	113	149	APEX Balanced Allocation Fund	6.5	8.0	-	117.9
50	23	27	Atlas Canadian Balanced Fund	21.1	14.6	11.7	87.5
-	-	125	Azura Balanced RSP Pooled	13.3	-	-	35.0
-	-	140	Azura Conservative Pooled	10.8	-	-	6.9
59	45	73	Batirente - Section Diversifiee	17.4	13.4	11.4	53.8
46	76	74	Beutel Goodman Balanced Fund	17.4	12.1	11.8	154.7
10	15	11	Beutel Goodman Private Balanced (HH)	24.1	15.6	14.9	44.9
8	8	20	Bissett Retirement Fund (HH)	21.6	16.5	15.0	23.2
94	116	150	BPI Canadian Balanced Fund (UA)	4.5	7.3	9.0	72.7
-	105	143	C.I. Canadian Balanced	9.3	9.9	-	465.1
-	-	82	C.I. Canadian Income Fund	16.8	-	-	111.4
7	20	19	Caldwell Securities Associate Fund (HH)	21.8	14.9	15.1	88.6
99	119	156	Cambridge Balanced Fund (Sagit) (UA)	-17.8	-3.2	4.9	19.8
51	52	66	Canada Life Managed Fund S-35	17.7	13.1	11.7	1055.4
58	79	77	Canada Trust Everest Balanced Fund	17.0	12.0	11.4	1458.5
41	80	100	Capstone Investment Trust	15.6	12.0	12.2	7.2
32	16	10	Cassels Blaikie Canadian Fund (HH)	24.3	15.3	12.7	15.9
53	41	57	CCPE Diversified Growth Fund R	18.4	13.6	11.6	35.7
52	47	67	CDA Balanced (KBSH)	17.7	13.3	11.6	49.2
83	81	68	CIBC Balanced Fund	17.7	12.0	10.3	921.4
4	44	8	Clean Environment Balanced Fund (HH)	25.6	13.5	16.6	28.7
21	18	96	Co-operators Balanced Fund	16.0	15.2	13.6	34.3
-	-	41	Colonia Strategic Balanced Fund	19.4	-	-	17.4
-	17	12	Common Sense Asset Builder 1 (RC)	23.6	15.2	-	29.9
-	7	6	Common Sense Asset Builder 2 (RC)	28.1	16.5	-	35.1
-	2	5	Common Sense Asset Builder 3 (RC)	30.1	17.0	-	30.4

CANADIAN BALANCED FUNDS
RANKINGS/RETURNS *cont'd*

Rank			Name of Fund	Returns (%)			Assets
(99)	(119)	(156)		(16.6)	(12.5)	(12.1)	
5-Yr	3-Yr	1-Yr		1-Yr	3-Yr	5-Yr	($mns)
-	4	4	Common Sense Asset Builder 4 (RC)	30.2	16.8	-	16.7
-	3	3	Common Sense Asset Builder 5 (RC)	30.3	17.0	-	6.7
-	-	132	Concorde Balanced Fund	12.4	-	-	34.6
69	59	123	Cornerstone Balanced Fund	13.4	12.8	11.0	67.4
5	101	108	Dynamic Partners Fund	14.5	10.2	16.1	1981.2
12	98	135	Dynamic Team Fund	12.0	10.6	14.8	260.6
14	63	115	Elliott & Page Balanced Fund	13.8	12.7	14.5	285.0
-	77	36	Empire Asset Allocation Fund	20.0	12.1	-	125.9
60	56	37	Empire Balanced Fund	19.9	13.0	11.4	218.9
-	-	101	Equitable Life Asset Allocation	15.3	-	-	44.7
56	35	75	Ethical Balanced Fund	17.3	13.7	11.5	338.1
28	14	50	Ferique Balanced Fund (HH)	18.8	15.8	13.0	254.7
-	-	15	Fidelity Canadian Asset Allocation	22.6	-	-	618.9
87	71	91	First Cdn. Asset Allocation (UA)	16.3	12.3	9.9	345.2
92	91	134	Fonds de Professionnels Balanced (UA)	12.0	11.0	9.4	437.5
-	-	137	Fonds de Professionnels Growth & Income	11.5	-	-	54.5
-	-	131	Fonds Desjardins Divers. Audacieux	12.6	-	-	197.7
-	-	142	Fonds Desjardins Divers. Modere	10.1	-	-	343.2
-	-	148	Fonds Desjardins Divers. Secure	6.6	-	-	244.7
57	70	79	Fonds Desjardins Equilibre	17.0	12.4	11.4	495.2
84	55	129	Fonds Ficadre Equilibre	12.9	13.0	10.2	42.8
68	67	104	Fonds Optimum Equilibre	14.9	12.5	11.1	23.4
74	72	72	General Trust of Canada Balanced	17.5	12.3	10.8	76.0
9	13	9	Global Strategy Income Plus Fund (HH)	24.5	15.8	14.9	724.7
66	22	47	Green Line Balanced Growth	19.1	14.7	11.1	320.6
82	50	40	Green Line Balanced Income Fund	19.8	13.1	10.4	167.6
-	110	122	Greystone Managed Wealth Fund	13.5	8.9	-	2.5
-	106	118	Growsafe Canadian Balanced Fund	13.7	9.5	-	65.8
-	-	14	GS Canadian Balanced Fund	22.6	-	-	291.0
-	-	2	GT Global Canada Income Class	31.2	-	-	512.6
86	103	133	Guardian Canadian Balanced Fund A (UA)	12.3	10.0	9.9	83.6
-	-	136	Guardian Canadian Balanced Fund B	11.7	-	-	258.7
-	-	86	GWL Balanced Fund (B) DSC	16.6	-	-	13.7
-	-	90	GWL Balanced Fund (B) NL	16.3	-	-	15.6

CANADIAN BALANCED FUNDS
RANKINGS/RETURNS *cont'd*

Rank			Name of Fund	Returns (%)			Assets
(99)	(119)	(156)		(16.6)	(12.5)	(12.1)	
5-Yr	3-Yr	1-Yr		1-Yr	3-Yr	5-Yr	($mns)
-	-	43	GWL Balanced Fund (M) DSC	19.3	-	-	10.3
-	-	48	GWL Balanced Fund (M) NL	19.0	-	-	12.0
-	-	70	GWL Balanced Fund (S) DSC	17.5	-	-	16.6
-	-	76	GWL Balanced Fund (S) NL	17.2	-	-	28.7
-	-	106	GWL Diversified Fund (G) DSC	14.8	-	-	76.1
85	99	109	GWL Diversified Fund (G) NL (UA)	14.5	10.6	10.0	336.3
-	-	93	GWL Equity/Bond Fund (G) DSC	16.2	-	-	75.9
61	86	98	GWL Equity/Bond Fund (G) NL (UA)	15.9	11.5	11.3	254.8
-	-	153	GWL Growth & Income Fund (A) DSC	2.0	-	-	13.0
-	-	154	GWL Growth & Income Fund (A) NL	1.7	-	-	16.3
-	-	33	GWL Growth & Income Fund (M) DSC	20.2	-	-	11.9
-	-	38	GWL Growth & Income Fund (M) NL	19.9	-	-	19.7
26	75	69	Hongkong Bank Balanced Fund	17.5	12.2	13.2	259.9
96	108	113	HRL Balanced Fund (UA)	14.1	9.4	8.8	36.0
22	53	130	ICM Balanced Fund	12.8	13.1	13.3	159.6
72	66	56	Imperial Growth Diversified Fund	18.4	12.5	10.8	12.2
33	58	80	Industrial Alliance Diversified (HH)	16.9	12.9	12.7	250.7
-	73	94	Industrial Alliance Ecoflex Fund D	16.1	12.3	-	451.0
37	69	26	Industrial Balanced Fund	21.1	12.4	12.3	393.6
77	78	83	Industrial Income Fund	16.7	12.0	10.6	2796.1
91	109	138	Industrial Mortgage Securities (UA)	11.4	9.2	9.4	695.6
3	10	7	Industrial Pension Fund (HH)	28.0	15.9	17.5	106.4
78	60	53	InvesNat Retirement Balanced Fund	18.6	12.8	10.6	526.2
-	33	35	Investors Asset Allocation Fund (RC)	20.1	13.8	-	1503.5
98	102	111	Investors Income Plus Portfolio (UA)	14.3	10.1	8.6	1301.7
27	88	61	Investors Mutual of Canada	18.1	11.3	13.1	935.1
79	100	116	Investors Retirement Plus Portfolio (UA)	13.8	10.4	10.5	1796.9
-	1	22	Ivy Growth & Income Fund (RC)	21.3	17.1	-	1053.2
81	111	141	Jones Heward Canadian Balanced Fund (UA)	10.4	8.7	10.4	71.8
47	83	25	LaSalle Balanced Fund	21.1	11.7	11.8	3.8
89	85	78	Laurentian Canadian Balanced Fund	17.0	11.7	9.7	156.6
31	34	16	Leith Wheeler Balanced Fund (HH)	22.5	13.8	12.9	46.0
65	94	124	London Life Diversified (UA)	13.3	10.8	11.2	1665.0
43	96	81	Lotus (MKW) Balanced Fund	16.9	10.7	12.0	71.1

CANADIAN BALANCED FUNDS
RANKINGS/RETURNS *cont'd*

Rank			Name of Fund	Returns (%)			Assets
(99)	(119)	(156)		(16.6)	(12.5)	(12.1)	
5-Yr	3-Yr	1-Yr		1-Yr	3-Yr	5-Yr	($mns)
-	-	71	Lutheran Life Balanced Fund	17.5	-	-	8.2
90	107	145	Manulife Vistafund 1 Diversified (UA)	8.3	9.5	9.6	59.5
97	112	147	Manulife Vistafund 2 Diversified (UA)	7.5	8.7	8.7	483.0
71	64	97	Maritime Life Balanced - A & C	15.9	12.7	10.9	299.1
40	40	49	Mawer Cdn. Balanced RSP Fund (HH)	18.9	13.6	12.2	64.7
49	46	64	Mawer Cdn. Diversified Investment	17.9	13.4	11.7	24.0
25	51	45	Maxxum Canadian Balanced Fund (HH)	19.1	13.1	13.3	114.6
-	117	152	McDonald Canada Plus	3.4	6.9	-	1.3
29	19	23	McLean Budden Balanced Fund (HH)	21.1	15.1	12.9	14.6
16	11	21	McLean Budden Pooled Balanced Fund (HH)	21.6	15.8	14.3	198.7
13	5	18	McLean Budden Registered Balanced (HH)	22.0	16.6	14.7	47.4
-	28	55	MD Balanced Fund (RC)	18.4	14.1	-	657.2
95	104	120	Metlife MVP Balanced Fund (UA)	13.6	9.9	8.9	49.0
-	-	87	Millennia III Canadian Balanced 1	16.4	-	-	69.9
-	-	95	Millennia III Canadian Balanced 2	16.1	-	-	8.3
-	61	103	Millennium Diversified Fund	14.9	12.8	-	6.4
54	37	89	Mutual Diversifund 40	16.4	13.7	11.5	292.6
-	-	84	Mutual Premier Diversified Fund	16.6	-	-	351.0
-	-	30	NAL-Balanced Growth Fund	20.7	-	-	73.9
42	29	112	NAL-Canadian Diversified Fund	14.1	14.1	12.1	120.7
39	42	34	National Balanced Fund (HH)	20.1	13.5	12.2	104.2
48	31	31	National Trust Balanced Fund	20.6	14.0	11.8	208.9
36	39	60	NN Asset Allocation Fund (HH)	18.2	13.6	12.4	108.2
-	54	102	OHA Balanced Fund	15.2	13.0	-	2.5
30	48	44	Ontario Teachers Group Balanced (HH)	19.2	13.3	12.9	52.5
20	21	42	Phillips Hager & North Bal. Pens. Tr. (HH)	19.3	14.8	13.7	1420.8
23	27	52	Phillips Hager & North Balanced (HH)	18.7	14.2	13.3	349.8
44	93	114	Royal Balanced Fund (UA)	13.9	10.9	12.0	5414.9
64	62	46	Royal Life Balanced Fund	19.1	12.7	11.2	158.7
75	89	105	Royal Trust Advantage Balanced Fund (UA)	14.8	11.3	10.7	466.6
70	92	127	Royal Trust Advantage Growth Fund (UA)	13.2	11.0	11.0	192.6
88	97	117	Royal Trust Advantage Income Fund (UA)	13.8	10.6	9.8	160.0
2	12	63	Saxon Balanced Fund (HH)	18.1	15.8	17.6	9.3
11	6	32	Sceptre Balanced Growth Fund (HH)	20.2	16.5	14.9	154.3

CANADIAN BALANCED FUNDS
RANKINGS/RETURNS *cont'd*

Rank			Name of Fund	Returns (%)			Assets
(99)	(119)	(156)		(16.6)	(12.5)	(12.1)	
5-Yr	3-Yr	1-Yr		1-Yr	3-Yr	5-Yr	($mns)
55	87	128	Scotia Excelsior Balanced Fund (UA)	13.1	11.5	11.5	557.6
15	65	29	Scotia Excelsior Total Return Fund (HH)	20.7	12.6	14.5	576.9
-	90	99	Spectrum United Asset Alloc. Fund	15.8	11.2	-	468.6
24	57	119	Spectrum United Canadian Portfolio	13.7	13.0	13.3	371.1
76	74	54	Spectrum United Diversified Fund	18.6	12.2	10.7	178.7
-	24	39	Standard Life Balanced Mutual Fund (RC)	19.8	14.3	-	15.5
45	38	58	Standard Life Ideal Balanced Fund	18.3	13.6	11.8	250.1
-	-	85	STAR Cdn. Balanced Growth & Income	16.6	-	-	
-	-	110	STAR Reg. Balanced Growth & Income	14.3	-	-	
-	-	139	STAR Reg. Conserv. Income & Growth	10.8	-	-	
-	-	107	STAR Reg. Long-Term Growth	14.5	-	-	
67	84	92	Talvest Canadian Asset Allocation (UA)	16.2	11.7	11.1	209.7
34	43	13	Templeton Balanced Fund (HH)	22.9	13.5	12.6	39.8
-	-	65	Templeton Canadian Asset Allocation	17.8	-	-	45.0
6	68	1	Trans-Canada Pension Fund (Sagit)	39.9	12.4	16.1	2.2
80	95	126	Transamerica Balanced Inv. Growth (UA)	13.3	10.7	10.4	84.4
17	36	88	Trimark Income Growth Fund	16.4	13.7	14.2	623.2
19	30	51	Trimark Select Balanced Fund (HH)	18.8	14.0	14.1	3818.8
38	26	121	Trust Pret & Revenu Retirement Fund	13.6	14.2	12.3	70.6
73	49	28	Westbury Canadian Balanced Fund	20.9	13.2	10.8	30.0

( ) under Rank indicates total number of funds; ( ) under Returns (%) indicates average annual return; (HH) — Heavy Hitter; (UA) — Underachiever; (RC) — Rookie Camp member.

CANADIAN BALANCED FUNDS/SUMMARY

Name of Fund	MER	Load	RRSP	Vola-tility	Company Number (App. 3)
ABC Fully Managed Fund (R)	2.00	N	R	3	1
Acadia Balanced Fund (R)	2.29	N	R		2
Admax Asset Allocation Fund	2.65	Y	R	2	69
AGF Canadian Tactical Asset Alloc.	2.39	Y	R	3	3
AGF Growth & Income Fund	2.50	Y	R	3	3
Altamira Balanced Fund	2.00	N	R	3	6
Altamira Growth & Income Fund	1.40	N	R	4	6
AMI Private Capital Optimix	1.75	N	R	3	7
APEX Balanced Allocation Fund (R)	2.96	Y	R	2	126
APEX Growth & Income Fund (R)	2.55	Y	R		126
Atlas Canadian Balanced Fund	2.26	N	R	2	9
Azura Balanced RSP Pooled (R)	2.22	Y	R		127
Azura Conservative Pooled (R)	2.08	Y	R		127
Batirente - Section Diversifiee (R)	1.61	N	R	2	131
Beutel Goodman Balanced Fund	2.13	N	R	3	12
Beutel Goodman Private Balanced (R)	1.10	N	N	2	12
Bissett Retirement Fund (R)	0.44	Y	R	2	13
BPI Canadian Balanced Fund	2.47	Y	R	3	15
C.I. Canadian Balanced	2.35	Y	R	3	28
C.I. Canadian Income Fund	1.90	Y	R		28
Caldwell Securities Associate Fund	2.98	N	R	4	17
Cambridge Balanced Fund	2.89	Y	R	4	121
Canada Life Managed Fund S-35	2.25	Y	R	3	18
Canada Trust Everest Balanced Fund	2.13	N	R	2	19
Capstone Investment Trust	2.14	N	R	2	25
Cassels Blaikie Canadian Fund	1.04	Y	R	2	26
CCPE Diversified Growth Fund R (R)	1.35	N	R	2	21
CDA Balanced (R)	0.97	N	R	3	22
CIBC Balanced Fund	2.05	N	R	3	29
Clarington Canadian Balanced Fund	2.75	Y	R		30
Clarington Canadian Income Fund	1.90	Y	R		30
Clean Environment Balanced Fund (R)	3.00	Y	R	3	31
Co-operators Balanced Fund (R)	2.07	N	R	3	33
Colonia Strategic Balanced Fund	0.27	Y	R		32
Common Sense Asset Builder 1	2.10	Y	R		113

CANADIAN BALANCED FUNDS/SUMMARY *cont'd*

Name of Fund	MER	Load	RRSP	Vola-tility	Company Number (App. 3)
Common Sense Asset Builder 2	2.10	Y	R		113
Common Sense Asset Builder 3	2.10	Y	R		113
Common Sense Asset Builder 4	2.10	Y	R		113
Common Sense Asset Builder 5	2.10	Y	R		113
Concorde Balanced Fund (R)	1.95	Y	R		59
Cornerstone Balanced Fund	2.67	N	R	3	73
Dynamic Partners Fund	2.38	Y	R	2	40
Dynamic Team Fund	0.86	Y	R	3	40
Elliott & Page Balanced Fund	1.99	Y	R	3	41
Empire Asset Allocation Fund	2.57	Y	R		42
Empire Balanced Fund	2.57	Y	R	2	42
Equitable Life Asset Allocation	2.25	Y	R		43
Ethical Balanced Fund (R)	2.06	N	R	3	44
Ferique Balanced Fund (R)	0.44	N	R	3	109
Fidelity Canadian Asset Allocation	2.56	Y	R		46
First Cdn. Asset Allocation	2.09	N	R	3	11
Fonds de Professionnels Balanced (R)	0.75	N	R	2	50
Fonds de Professionnels Gr. & Inc. (R)	0.75	N	R		50
Fonds Desjardins Divers. Ambitieux (R)	1.75	N	R		37
Fonds Desjardins Divers. Audacieux (R)	1.97	N	R		37
Fonds Desjardins Divers. Modere (R)	1.82	N	R		37
Fonds Desjardins Divers. Secure (R)	1.72	N	R		37
Fonds Desjardins Equilibre (R)	1.94	N	R	3	37
Fonds Ficadre Equilibre	2.13	Y	R	2	128
Fonds Optimum Equilibre (R)	1.41	N	R	2	107
General Trust of Canada Balanced (R)	2.15	N	R	2	98
Global Strategy Income Plus Fund	2.63	Y	R	2	54
Green Line Balanced Growth	2.08	N	R	3	139
Green Line Balanced Income Fund	2.10	N	R	3	139
Greystone Managed Wealth Fund	2.50	N	R		58
Growsafe Canadian Balanced Fund	2.30	Y	R	2	141
GS Canadian Balanced Fund	2.80	Y	R		70
GT Global Canada Income Class	2.30	Y	R		60
Guardian Canadian Balanced Fund A	1.90	Y	R	2	61
Guardian Canadian Balanced Fund B	2.67	Y	R		61

CANADIAN BALANCED FUNDS/SUMMARY *cont'd*

Name of Fund	MER	Load	RRSP	Vola- tility	Company Number (App. 3)
Guardian Growth & Income Fund A	2.25	Y	R		61
Guardian Growth & Income Fund B	2.90	Y	R		61
GWL Advanced Portfolio (G) DSC	2.64	Y	R		57
GWL Advanced Portfolio (G) NL	2.88	N	R		57
GWL Balanced Fund (B) DSC	2.52	Y	R		57
GWL Balanced Fund (B) NL	2.76	N	R		57
GWL Balanced Fund (M) DSC	2.58	Y	R		57
GWL Balanced Fund (M) NL	2.82	N	R		57
GWL Balanced Fund (S) DSC	2.52	Y	R		57
GWL Balanced Fund (S) NL	2.76	N	R		57
GWL Balanced Portfolio (G) DSC	2.58	Y	R		57
GWL Balanced Portfolio (G) NL	2.82	N	R		57
GWL Conservative Portfolio (G) DSC	2.46	Y	R		57
GWL Conservative Portfolio (G) NL	2.70	N	R		57
GWL Diversified Fund (G) DSC (R)	2.41	Y	R		57
GWL Diversified Fund (G) NL (R)	2.65	N	R	2	57
GWL Equity/Bond Fund (G) DSC	2.40	Y	R		57
GWL Equity/Bond Fund (G) NL	2.65	N	R	3	57
GWL Growth & Income Fund (A) DSC	2.52	Y	R		57
GWL Growth & Income Fund (A) NL	2.76	N	R		57
GWL Growth & Income Fund (M) DSC	2.58	Y	R		57
GWL Growth & Income Fund (M) NL	2.82	N	R		57
GWL Moderate Portfolio (G) DSC	2.52	Y	R		57
GWL Moderate Portfolio (G) NL	2.76	N	R		57
Hongkong Bank Balanced Fund	1.92	N	R	2	63
HRL Balanced Fund	1.75	N	R	2	64
ICM Balanced Fund	0.30	N	R	2	68
IG Beutel Goodman Cdn. Balanced	2.99	Y	R		70
IG Sceptre Canadian Balanced Fund	2.95	Y	R		70
Imperial Growth Diversified Fund (C)	2.00	Y	R	2	65
Industrial Alliance Diversified (C)	1.58	N	R	3	66
Industrial Alliance Diversified - 2	2.94	N	R		66
Industrial Alliance Ecoflex Fund D	2.39	Y	R	2	66
Industrial Balanced Fund	2.37	Y	R	3	80
Industrial Income Fund	1.87	Y	R	3	80

CANADIAN BALANCED FUNDS/SUMMARY *cont'd*

Name of Fund	MER	Load	RRSP	Vola-tility	Company Number (App. 3)
Industrial Mortgage Securities	1.86	Y	R	2	80
Industrial Pension Fund	2.44	Y	R	3	80
InvesNat Retirement Balanced Fund (R)	2.14	N	R	2	98
Investors Asset Allocation Fund	2.73	Y	R		70
Investors Income Plus Portfolio	0.15	Y	R	2	70
Investors Mutual of Canada	2.34	Y	R	3	70
Investors Retirement Plus Portfolio	0.17	Y	R	2	70
Ivy Growth & Income Fund	2.13	Y	R	2	80
Jones Heward Canadian Balanced	2.40	Y	R	3	72
LaSalle Balanced Fund (R)	2.40	Y	R		151
Laurentian Canadian Balanced Fund	2.65	Y	R	2	135
Leith Wheeler Balanced Fund (R)	1.10	N	R	2	74
London Life Diversified	2.00	Y	R	3	76
Lotus (MKW) Balanced Fund (R)	2.10	N	R	3	79
Lutheran Life Balanced Fund (R)	2.50	N	R		78
Manulife Vistafund 1 Diversified	1.63	Y	R	3	83
Manulife Vistafund 2 Diversified	2.38	Y	R	3	83
Maritime Life Balanced - A & C	2.30	Y	R	2	85
Maritime Life Balanced - B	2.30	Y	R		85
Mawer Cdn. Balanced RSP Fund (R)	0.89	N	R	2	86
Mawer Cdn. Diversified Investment (R)	0.98	N	F	2	86
Maxxum Canadian Balanced Fund	2.15	Y	R	3	87
McDonald Canada Plus (R)	2.71	Y	R	4	88
McLean Budden Balanced Fund	1.75	N	R	3	89
McLean Budden Pooled Balanced Fund (R)	1.00	N	N	3	89
McLean Budden Registered Balanced (R)	1.00	N	R		89
MD Balanced Fund (R)	1.30	N	R	3	90
Members Mutual Fund (R)	2.00	N	R		91
Metlife MVP Balanced Fund	2.22	Y	R	3	92
Millennia III Canadian Balanced 1	2.71	Y	R		65
Millennia III Canadian Balanced 2	2.89	N	R		65
Millennium Diversified Fund	2.50	Y	R	3	96
Mutual Diversifund 40	1.77	Y	R	3	97
Mutual Premier Diversified Fund	2.30	N	F		97
NAL-Balanced Growth Fund	2.00	Y	R		83

CANADIAN BALANCED FUNDS/SUMMARY *cont'd*

Name of Fund	MER	Load	RRSP	Vola- tility	Company Number (App. 3)
NAL-Canadian Diversified Fund	1.75	Y	R	3	83
National Balanced Fund	2.00	Y	R	3	99
National Trust Balanced Fund (R)	1.81	N	R	3	100
NN Asset Allocation Fund	3.00	Y	R	3	102
North-West Life Ecoflex D	2.39	Y	R		103
O'Donnell Balanced Fund	2.40	Y	R		104
OHA Balanced Fund	0.90	N	R	2	105
Ontario Teachers Group Balanced (R)	1.00	N	R	3	106
Phillips Hager & North Bal. Pens. Tr. (R)	0.50	N	R	2	112
Phillips Hager & North Balanced (R)	0.91	N ·	R	2	112
Royal Balanced Fund	2.31	N	R	3	119
Royal Life Balanced Fund	2.34	Y	R	3	120
Royal Trust Advantage Balanced Fund	1.78	N	R	2	119
Royal Trust Advantage Growth Fund	1.92	N	R	2	119
Royal Trust Advantage Income Fund	1.65	N	R	2	119
Saxon Balanced Fund (R)	1.75	N	R	3	122
Sceptre Balanced Growth Fund	1.43	N	R	3	123
Scotia Excelsior Balanced Fund	2.01	N	R	3	124
Scotia Excelsior Total Return Fund	2.27	N	R	3	124
Spectrum United Asset Alloc. Fund	2.22	Y	R	3	129
Spectrum United Canadian Portfolio	2.20	Y	R	3	129
Spectrum United Diversified Fund	2.08	Y	R	3	129
Standard Life Balanced Mutual Fund (R)	2.00	Y	R	3	133
Standard Life Ideal Balanced Fund	2.00	Y	R	2	132
STAR Cdn. Balanced Growth & Income	N/A	Y	R		80
STAR Cdn. Conserv. Income & Growth	N/A	Y	R		80
STAR Cdn. Long-Term Growth	N/A	Y	R		80
STAR Reg. Balanced Growth & Income	N/A	Y	R		80
STAR Reg. Conserv. Income & Growth	N/A	Y	R		80
STAR Reg. Long-Term Growth	N/A	Y	R		80
Stone & Co. Growth & Inc. Fund	2.85	Y	R		134
Talvest Canadian Asset Allocation	2.42	Y	R	2	136
Templeton Balanced Fund	2.34	Y	R	3	137
Templeton Canadian Asset Allocation	2.15	Y	R		137
Trans-Canada Pension Fund	2.87	Y	R	5	121

CANADIAN BALANCED FUNDS/SUMMARY *cont'd*

Name of Fund	MER	Load	RRSP	Vola-tility	Company Number (App. 3)
Transamerica Balanced Inv. Growth	1.80	Y	R		141
Trimark Income Growth Fund	1.60	Y	R	3	143
Trimark Select Balanced Fund	2.20	Y	R	3	143
Trust Pret & Revenu Retirement Fund	1.93	N	R	3	145
Universal Canadian Balanced Fund	2.00	Y	R		80
Valorem Diversified (R)	2.00	Y	R		152
Westbury Canadian Balanced Fund (R)	2.42	N	R	3	148
Average	2.08			2.7	

(R) — Restricted; (C) — Closed to new investors; MER — Management Expense Ratio; Load — fee charged; RRSP: R = 100% eligible, F = eligible as foreign content only, N = not eligible; Volatility — measures swings in performance on a scale of 1 to 10 (1 = low, 10 = high). Blank space indicates that fund is less than three years old. Fund company addresses may be found by number in Appendix 3.

15

· ·

Canadian Bond Funds

BOND FUNDS TYPICALLY invest in medium- and long-term debt securities issued by governments and large corporations. These funds are designed to provide investors not only with regular interest payments but also with the potential for capital gains. The performance of these funds is tied to interest rates. When interest rates go down, bond prices go up, and when interest rates go up, bond prices fall. There are currently 141 Canadian bond funds on the market. Together these funds manage a total of $17.4 billion in assets.

Over the five calendar years from 1992 to 1996, the best year for Canadian bond funds was 1995, when returns averaged 17.8%. In contrast, the worst year was 1994, when returns averaged -5.3%. The average annual compound rate of return over the five-year period was 8.9%.

Canadian bond funds have an average volatility rating of 2.2, which is above the average of 1.9 for all fixed-income funds. The average fee for management expenses is $1.59 for every $100 in assets, which is up slightly from last year's average of $1.56. Ratings for bonds, given by the Canadian Bond Rating Service and Dominion Bond Rating Service, start at "AAA" (highest quality), followed by "AA" and "A."

The Heavy Hitters

There are 36 Canadian bond funds that have qualified for membership in the Heavy Hitters club this year. Each of these funds has consistently delivered *above*-average returns over the past one-, three-, and five-year periods. Collectively these Heavy Hitters manage a total of $9.4 billion in assets. Investors Government Bond Fund is the largest, with $1.5 billion in assets, and AMI's Private Capital Income Fund is the smallest, with $2.1 million in assets. Twenty-five of the 36 Heavy Hitters are no-load funds.

●●

Table 1

THE HEAVY HITTERS

CANADIAN BOND FUNDS

		Bench-mark*	Vola-tility	Performance Quartile 1	Quartile 2	Overall Rating
1	Batirente - Section Obligations (R) (N)	4	2	4	1	★★★
2	Fonds Optimum Obligations (R) (N)	3	3	4	1	★★1/2
3	Phillips Hager & North Bond Fund (R) (N)	2	2	5	0	★★1/2
4	AGF Canadian Bond Fund	2	3	4	1	★★1/2
5	Altamira Bond Fund (N)	3	3	3	0	★★
6	Altamira Income Fund (N)	3	3	3	0	★★
7	MD Bond Fund (R) (N)	1	2	4	1	★★
8	Bissett Bond Fund (R)	1	2	3	1	★★
9	Spectrum United Long-Term Bond Fund	1	3	4	0	★★
10	Beutel Goodman Income Fund (N)	1	3	4	0	★★
11	McLean Budden Pooled Fixed Income (R) (N)	4	2	4	1	★★
12	Industrial Bond Fund	1	3	3	1	★1/2
13	Equitable Life Segregated Accum. Inc.	1	2	2	2	★1/2
14	Maxxum Income Fund	2	3	2	1	★1/2
15	Ferique Bond Fund (R) (N)	1	2	1	4	★1/2
16	Hyperion High Yield Bond Fund	1	3	2	2	★1/2
17	GBC Canadian Bond Fund (R) (N)	0	3	3	2	★1/2
18	NN Bond Fund	1	3	1	3	★1/2
19	AMI Private Capital Income Fund (N)	0	2	2	2	★1/2
20	Co-operators Fixed Income Fund (R) (N)	1	3	2	1	★1/2
21	Ethical Income Fund (R) (N)	1	3	2	1	★1/2
22	Green Line Canadian Bond Fund (N)	2	3	2	3	★1/2
23	National Trust Canadian Bond Fund (R) (N)	1	3	2	1	★1/2
24	First Canadian Bond Fund (N)	0	2	1	3	★
25	Green Line Canadian Gov't Bond Fund (N)	0	2	1	3	★

Table 1

THE HEAVY HITTERS *continued*

CANADIAN BOND FUNDS

		Bench- mark*	Vola- tility	Performance Quartile 1	Quartile 2	Overall Rating
26	McLean Budden Fixed Income Fund (N)	0	3	3	0	★
27	National Fixed Income Fund	0	3	1	3	★
28	Talvest Bond Fund	0	2	1	2	★
29	Atlas Canadian Bond Fund (N)	0	2	0	4	★
30	Mawer Canadian Bond Fund (R) (N)	0	2	1	3	★
31	Royal Trust Bond Fund (N)	0	3	1	2	★
32	RoyFund Bond Fund (N)	0	2	0	3	★
33	Sceptre Bond Fund (N)	0	2	0	3	★
34	Investors Government Bond Fund	0	2	0	3	★
35	BNP (Canada) Bond Fund (N)	0	3	0	3	★
36	HRL Bond Fund (N)	0	2	0	2	★

* ScotiaMcLeod Universe Bond Index; (R) — Restricted; (C) — Closed to new members; (N) —No-load fund; Benchmark — number of times that a fund beat the benchmark from 1992 to 1996; Volatility — measures swings in fund returns on a scale of 1 to 10 (1 = low, 10 = high); Performance — number of times that a fund was in the first (top 25%) or second quartile (top 50%) from 1992 to 1996.

The benchmark used to compare Canadian bond fund returns is the ScotiaMcLeod Universe Bond Index. Over the past five calendar years, the index posted its highest return of 20.7% in 1995 and its lowest return of -4.3% in 1994.

Batirente - Section Obligations ★★★

This fund, the number-one Canadian bond fund for the second year in a row and the only one to receive three stars, is sponsored by the St-Laurent Financial Corporation of Montreal. The fund was launched in 1988 and has been managed by Carmand Normand since its inception. With $29 million in assets, the fund invests only in securities rated A or higher.

Its best year was 1995, when it posted a return of 22.2%, and its worst year was 1994, when its return was -4.6%. The fund's average

annual compound return over the past five years was 11.7%. A no-load fund, it charges management expenses of $1.61 for every $100 in assets, which is slightly higher than the group average of $1.59. The fund is available for sale only in Quebec.

Fonds Optimum Obligations ★★1/2

This bond fund, sponsored by Optimum Placement Inc. of Montreal, was launched in 1986 and is managed by Les Conseillers Financiers du St-Laurent Inc. The fund has $4 million in assets, with 63% of the portfolio invested in Government of Canada bonds and 32% in provincial bonds. The fund's investments are restricted to securities rated AA or higher.

In 1995, the fund's best year, it posted a return of 22.4%, and in 1994, its worst year, it returned -5.5%. Over the past five years, it yielded an average annual compound return of 11.2%. This no-load fund charges management expenses of $1.41 per $100 in assets, below the average. The fund is available for sale only in Quebec.

Phillips Hager & North Bond Fund ★★1/2

This fund was launched in 1970. It has been managed by the firm's fixed-income research team since its inception and its assets total $1.3 billion. Government of Canada bonds account for 53% of its portfolio, corporate bonds 16%, and provincial bonds 11%. Only securities with a rating of A or higher are considered for investment.

The fund posted its highest return, 20.4%, in 1995, and its lowest, -4.1%, in 1994. Over the past five years, its average annual compound return was 10.6%. This is a no-load fund which charges significantly below-average management expenses of $0.57 for every $100 in assets. The fund has a minimum initial investment requirement of $25,000 for non-RRSP accounts and $5,000 for RRSP accounts.

AGF Canadian Bond Fund ★★1/2

This fund was launched in 1962 and has been managed by Warren Goldring and Clive Coombes since January 1990. With $745 million in assets, 68% of the portfolio is invested in Canadian bonds and 18% in provincial bonds. The fund invests only in securities rated AAA.

Its best year was 1995, when it posted a return of 20.6%, and its worst year was 1994, when its return was -8.5%. The fund's average

annual compound return over the past five years was 10.1%. A load fund, it charges management expenses of $1.88 for every $100 in assets, which is higher than the group average of $1.59.

Altamira Bond Fund ★★

This fund, launched in 1987, has been managed by Robert Marcus since December 1993. The fund has $110 million in assets, with 60% of the portfolio invested in long-term Canadian bonds, 26% in short-term bonds, and 12% in mid-term bonds. The fund's investments are restricted to securities rated AAA.

In 1995, the fund's best year, it posted a return of 27.4%, and in 1994, its worst year, it returned -8.8%. Over the past five years, it yielded an average annual compound return of 12.1%. This no-load fund charges management expenses of $1.29 per $100 in assets, which is below the average.

Altamira Income Fund ★★

This fund was launched in 1970. It has been managed by Will Sutherland since September 1987 and its assets total $570 million. Eighty-four percent of its portfolio is invested in domestic bonds and 12% in foreign bonds. Only securities with a rating of AAA are considered for investment.

The fund posted its highest return, 22.8%, in 1995, and its lowest, -6.6%, in 1994. Over the past five years, its average annual compound return was 10.8%. This is a no-load fund which charges well-below-average management expenses of $1.00 for every $100 in assets.

MD Bond Fund ★★

This fund was launched in 1988 and has been managed by John Braive of the firm T.A.L. Investment Counsel Ltd. since its inception. With $366 million in assets, 56% of the portfolio is invested in Government of Canada bonds, 29% in corporate bonds, and 10% in provincial bonds.

Its best year was 1995, when it posted a return of 20.1%, and its worst year was 1994, when its return was -5.4%. The fund's average annual compound return over the past five years was 10.2%. A no-load fund, it charges management expenses of $1.03 for every $100 in assets, which is considerably lower than the group average of $1.59.

The fund is available for sale only to members of the Canadian Medical Association and their families.

Bissett Bond Fund ★★

This fund, launched in 1986, has been managed by Michael Quinn since its inception. The fund has $38 million in assets, with 29% of the portfolio invested in Government of Canada bonds, 31% in corporate bonds, and 25% in provincial bonds. The fund's investments are restricted to securities rated A or higher.

In 1995, the fund's best year, it posted a return of 20.6%, and in 1994, its worst year, it returned -3.8%. Over the past five years, it yielded an average annual compound return of 10.0%. A no-load fund if purchased directly from the sponsor, it charges management expenses of $0.75 per $100 in assets, well below the average. The fund is available for sale only in Alberta, British Columbia, and Ontario.

Spectrum United Long-Term Bond Fund ★★

This fund was launched in 1989. It is managed by Stuart Pomphrey and its assets total $115 million. Government of Canada bonds account for 40% of its portfolio and provincial bonds make up another 36%. Only securities with a rating of AAA are considered for investment.

The fund posted its highest return, 21.3%, in 1995, and its lowest, -9.1%, in 1994. Over the past five years, its average annual compound return was 9.5%. This is a load fund which charges slightly above-average management expenses of $1.66 for every $100 in assets.

Beutel Goodman Income Fund ★★

This fund was launched in 1990 and is managed by Bruce Corneil and David Gregoris. With $47 million in assets, 71% of the portfolio is invested in Government of Canada bonds and 29% in corporate bonds. The fund invests only in securities rated BBB or higher.

Its best year was 1995, when it posted a return of 20.6%, and its worst year was 1994, when its return was -7.2%. The fund's average annual compound return over the past five years was 9.7%. A no-load fund if purchased directly from the sponsor, it charges management expenses of $0.63 for every $100 in assets, which is considerably lower than the group average of $1.59.

McLean Budden Pooled Fixed Income ★★

This bond fund, launched in 1981, is managed by the firm's fixed-income team of Craig Barnard, Bill Giblin, and Peter Kotsopoulos. The fund has $272 million in assets, with 69% of the portfolio invested in Government of Canada bonds, 19% in corporate bonds, and 11% in provincial bonds. The fund's investments are restricted to securities rated A or higher.

In 1995, the fund's best year, it posted a return of 22.0%, and in 1994, its worst year, it returned -5.1%. Over the past five years, it yielded an average annual compound return of 11.3%. This no-load fund charges management expenses of $1.00 per $100 in assets, well below the average. The fund has a minimum initial investment requirement of $500,000.

Industrial Bond Fund ★1/2

This fund, sponsored by the Mackenzie Financial Corporation, was launched in 1989. It has been managed by Tim Gleeson since its inception and its assets total $419 million. Eighty-two percent of the fund's portfolio is invested in bonds and 18% in cash. Only securities with a rating of A or higher are considered for investment.

The fund posted its highest return, 21.7%, in 1995, and its lowest, -8.7%, in 1994. Over the past five years, its average annual compound return was 9.7%. This is a load fund which charges above-average management expenses of $1.98 for every $100 in assets.

Equitable Life Segregated Accumulative Income Fund ★1/2

This fund was launched in 1969 and has been managed by Robert Head since April 1995. With $15 million in assets, 42% of the portfolio is invested in Government of Canada bonds, 26% in corporate bonds, and 16% in provincial bonds. The fund invests only in securities rated BBB or higher.

Its best year was 1995, when it posted a return of 19.6%, and its worst year was 1994, when its return was -4.7%. The fund's average annual compound return over the past five years was 10.0%. A load fund, sold only on a front-end basis, it charges management expenses of $1.20 for every $100 in assets, which is lower than the group average of $1.59. This fund is available for sale only to existing contract holders.

Maxxum Income Fund ★1/2

This bond fund, launched in 1974, has been managed by Gerald Boychuk since October 1986. The fund has $79 million in assets, with 34% of the portfolio invested in Government of Canada bonds, 40% in corporate bonds, and 7% in provincial bonds. The fund's investments are restricted to securities rated A or higher.

In 1995, the fund's best year, it posted a return of 21.9%, and in 1994, its worst year, it returned -6.7%. Over the past five years, it yielded an average annual compound return of 9.8%. This load fund charges management expenses of $1.75 per $100 in assets, above the average.

Ferique Bond Fund ★1/2

This fund, sponsored by the Ordre des Ingenieurs du Quebec, a professional engineers' association, was launched in 1975. The fund is managed by Robert Ciamarro of the investment firm Canagex Inc. and its assets total $48 million. Government of Canada bonds account for 54% of its portfolio and provincial bonds make up another 23%. Only securities with a rating of AA or higher are considered for investment. The fund posted its highest return, 19.5%, in 1995, and its lowest, -4.0%, in 1994. Over the past five years, its average annual compound return was 9.9%. This is a no-load fund which charges well-below-average management expenses of $0.60 for every $100 in assets. The fund is available for sale only to the association's members.

Hyperion High Yield Bond Fund ★1/2

This fund, sponsored by Talvest Fund Management, was launched in 1989 and is managed by John Braive of the firm T.A.L. Investment Counsel Ltd. With $14 million in assets, 40% of the portfolio is invested in Government of Canada bonds, 25% in corporate bonds, and 22% in cash. The fund invests only in securities rated A or higher.

Its best year was 1995, when it posted a return of 23.1%, and its worst year was 1994, when its return was -10.0%. The fund's average annual compound return over the past five years was 9.7%. A load fund, it charges management expenses of $2.10 for every $100 in assets, which is higher than the group average of $1.59.

GBC Canadian Bond Fund ★1/2

This fund, launched in 1984, is co-managed by Jake Greydanus and Anthony Boeckh. The fund has $38 million in assets, with 77% of the portfolio invested in Government of Canada bonds and 21% in provincial bonds. The fund's investments are restricted to securities rated AAA.

In 1995, the fund's best year, it posted a return of 20.2%, and in 1994, its worst year, it returned -5.6%. Over the past five years, it yielded an average annual compound return of 10.1%. A no-load fund if purchased directly from the sponsor, it charges management expenses of $1.13 per $100 in assets, slightly below the average. The fund has a minimum initial investment requirement of $100,000.

NN Bond Fund ★

This segregated fund, sponsored by the NN Life Insurance Company of Canada, was launched in 1987. It has been managed by Michel Tremblay since July 1992 and its assets total $206 million. Government of Canada bonds account for 39% of its portfolio, provincial bonds 33%, and corporate bonds 26%. Only securities with a rating of A or higher are considered for investment.

The fund posted its highest return, 20.7%, in 1995, and its lowest, -4.8%, in 1994. Over the past five years, its average annual compound return was 9.4%. This is a load fund, sold only on a deferred basis, which charges above-average management expenses of $2.00 for every $100 in assets.

AMI Private Capital Income Fund ★1/2

This bond fund was launched in 1987 and is managed by AMI Partners Inc. With $2 million in assets, 97% of the portfolio is invested in fixed-income securities rated A or higher.

Its best year was 1993, when it posted a return of 17.2%, and its worst year was 1994, when its return was -5.5%. The fund's average annual compound return over the past five years was 9.4%. A no-load fund, it charges management expenses of $1.25 for every $100 in assets, which is lower than the group average of $1.59. The fund has a minimum initial investment requirement of $50,000.

Co-operators Fixed Income Fund ★1/2

This segregated bond fund, sponsored by the Co-operators Life Insurance Co. of Regina, was identified as a Rookie Camp member in last year's *World of Mutual Funds*. The fund was launched in 1992 and is managed by Jim Lorimer. The fund has $7 million in assets, with 39% of the portfolio invested in Government of Canada bonds, 20% in provincial bonds, and 16% in corporate bonds. The fund's investments are restricted to securities rated A or higher.

In 1995, the fund's best year, it posted a return of 21.7%, and in 1994, its worst year, it returned -6.1%. Over the past five years, it yielded an average annual compound return of 10.2%. This no-load fund charges management expenses of $2.37 per $100 in assets, above the average.

Ethical Income Fund ★1/2

This bond fund was launched in 1967. It is managed by Jim Lorimer of the firm Co-operators Investment Counselling Ltd. and its assets total $106 million. Government of Canada bonds account for 36% of its portfolio, provincial bonds 27%, and corporate bonds 22%. Only securities with a rating of A or higher are considered for investment.

The fund posted its highest return, 21.7%, in 1995, and its lowest, -6.2%, in 1994. Over the past five years, its average annual compound return was 8.9%. This is a no-load fund which charges slightly above-average management expenses of $1.62 for every $100 in assets.

Green Line Canadian Bond Fund ★1/2

This fund, sponsored by the Toronto-Dominion Bank, was launched in 1988 and is managed by TD Asset Management Inc. With $487 million in assets, 64% of the portfolio is invested in corporate bonds, 13% in provincial bonds, and 9% in Government of Canada bonds. The fund invests only in securities rated A or higher.

Its best year was 1995, when it posted a return of 21.5%, and its worst year was 1994, when its return was -5.6%. The fund's average annual compound return over the past five years was 10.6%. A no-load fund, it charges management expenses of $0.96 for every $100 in assets, which is lower than the group average of $1.59.

National Trust Canadian Bond Fund ★1/2

This fund, launched in 1957, is managed by Natrustco Investments Funds Ltd., a subsidiary of the National Trust Company. The fund has $127 million in assets, with 67% of the portfolio invested in Government of Canada bonds and 15% in provincial bonds. The fund's investments are restricted to securities rated A or higher.

In 1995, the fund's best year, it posted a return of 21.2%, and in 1994, its worst year, it returned -5.9%. Over the past five years, it yielded an average annual compound return of 10.0%. This no-load fund charges management expenses of $1.34 per $100 in assets, slightly below the average.

First Canadian Bond Fund ★

This fund, sponsored by the Bank of Montreal, was launched in 1987. It is managed by Mary Jane Yule and its assets total $784 million. Government of Canada bonds account for 50% of its portfolio, provincial bonds 18%, and cash and equivalents 25%. Only securities with a rating of AA or higher are considered for investment.

The fund posted its highest return, 20.2%, in 1995, and its lowest, -6.1%, in 1994. Over the past five years, its average annual compound return was 9.1%. This is a no-load fund which charges slightly below-average management expenses of $1.58 for every $100 in assets.

Green Line Canadian Government Bond Fund ★

This fund, TD's second Heavy Hitter bond fund, was launched in 1987 and is managed by TD Asset Management Inc. With $157 million in assets, 73% of the portfolio is invested in Government of Canada bonds and 22% in provincial bonds. The fund invests only in securities rated A or higher.

Its best year was 1995, when it posted a return of 19.7%, and its worst year was 1994, when its return was -5.2%. The fund's average annual compound return over the past five years was 9.8%. A no-load fund, it charges management expenses of $0.97 for every $100 in assets, which is lower than the group average of $1.59.

McLean Budden Fixed Income Fund ★

This fund, McLean Budden's second Heavy Hitter bond fund, launched in 1989, is managed by the firm's fixed-income team. The fund has $16 million in assets, with 66% of the portfolio invested in Government of Canada bonds, 18% in corporate bonds, and 15% in provincial bonds. The fund's investments are restricted to securities rated A or higher.

In 1995, the fund's best year, it posted a return of 20.1%, and in 1994, its worst year, it returned -6.2%. Over the past five years, it yielded an average annual compound return of 10.0%. This no-load fund charges management expenses of $1.00 per $100 in assets, below the average. The fund has a minimum initial investment requirement of $5,000.

National Fixed Income Fund ★

This segregated bond fund, sponsored by National Life of Canada, was launched in 1962. It has been managed by Nang Cheung since 1979 and its assets total $52 million. Government of Canada bonds account for 33% of its portfolio, provincial bonds 27%, and corporate bonds 25%. Only securities with a rating of A or higher are considered for investment.

The fund posted its highest return, 18.7%, in 1995, and its lowest, -6.1%, in 1994. Over the past five years, its average annual compound return was 9.2%. This is a load fund, sold only on a deferred basis, which charges above-average management expenses of $2.00 for every $100 in assets.

Talvest Bond Fund ★

This fund was launched in 1972 and is managed by John Braive of T.A.L. Investment Counsel Ltd. With $78 million in assets, 51% of the portfolio is invested in Government of Canada bonds and 29% in corporate bonds. The fund invests only in securities rated A or higher.

Its best year was 1995, when it posted a return of 19.3%, and its worst year was 1994, when its return was -6.1%. The fund's average annual compound return over the past five years was 9.1%. A load fund, it charges management expenses of $1.99 for every $100 in assets, which is higher than the group average of $1.59.

Atlas Canadian Bond Fund ★

This fund, launched in 1984 and sponsored by Atlas Asset Management Inc., a wholly owned subsidiary of Midland Walwyn, is managed by James Hymas of the investment firm Greydanus, Boeckh & Associates Inc. The fund has $23 million in assets, with 77% of the portfolio invested in Government of Canada bonds and 21% in provincial bonds. The fund's investments are restricted to securities rated AA or higher.

In 1995, the fund's best year, it posted a return of 18.9%, and in 1994, its worst year, it returned -5.1%. Over the past five years, it yielded an average annual compound return of 8.9%. This no-load fund charges management expenses of $1.97 per $100 in assets, above the average.

Mawer Canadian Bond Fund ★

This fund, identified as a Rookie Camp member in last year's *World of Mutual Funds*, was launched in 1991. It has been managed by Gary Feltham since February 1993 and its assets total $26 million. Government of Canada bonds account for 53% of its portfolio and corporate bonds make up another 35%. Only securities with a rating of A or higher are considered for investment.

The fund posted its highest return, 18.9%, in 1995, and its lowest, -5.5%, in 1994. Over the past five years, its average annual compound return was 9.3%. This is a no-load fund which charges well-below-average management expenses of $0.89 for every $100 in assets. The fund has a minimum initial investment requirement of $25,000.

Royal Trust Bond Fund ★

This fund, part of the Royal Bank's family of funds, was launched in 1966 and is managed by Tom Czitron. With $852 million in assets, 66% of the portfolio is invested in Government of Canada bonds and 25% in cash. The fund invests only in securities rated A or higher.

Its best year was 1995, when it posted a return of 20.2%, and its worst year was 1994, when its return was -6.5%. The fund's average annual compound return over the past five years was 9.3%. A no-load fund, it charges management expenses of $1.39 for every $100 in assets, which is lower than the group average of $1.59.

RoyFund Bond Fund ★

This fund, launched in 1973 and sponsored by the Royal Bank of Canada, is also managed by Tom Czitron. The fund has $773 million in assets, with 66% of the portfolio invested in Government of Canada bonds and 25% in cash. The fund's investments are restricted to securities rated A or higher.

In 1995, the fund's best year, it posted a return of 20.0%, and in 1994, its worst year, it returned -5.5%. Over the past five years, it yielded an average annual compound return of 9.1%. This no-load fund charges management expenses of $1.56 per $100 in assets, slightly below the average.

Sceptre Bond Fund ★

This fund was launched in 1987. It is managed by Ian Lee and its assets total $7 million. Government of Canada bonds account for 34% of its portfolio, corporate bonds 35%, and provincial bonds 29%. Only securities with a rating of A or higher are considered for investment.

The fund posted its highest return, 18.6%, in 1995, and its lowest, -4.4%, in 1994. Over the past five years, its average annual compound return was 9.3%. This is a no-load fund which charges below-average management expenses of $1.25 for every $100 in assets. The fund has a minimum initial investment requirement of $5,000.

Investors Government Bond Fund ★

This fund was launched in 1979 and has been managed by Allan Brownridge since 1984. With $1.5 billion in assets, 55% of the portfolio is invested in Government of Canada bonds, 16% in provincial bonds, 10% in corporate bonds, and 10% in municipal bonds. The fund invests only in securities rated AAA.

Its best year was 1995, when it posted a return of 19.3%, and its worst year was 1994, when its return was -5.2%. The fund's average annual compound return over the past five years was 9.1%. A load fund, sold only on a deferred basis, it charges management expenses of $1.90 for every $100 in assets, which is higher than the group average of $1.59.

BNP (Canada) Bond Fund ★

This fund, launched in 1991 and identified as a Rookie Camp member in last year's *World of Mutual Funds*, is managed by the investment firm RT Capital Management Inc. The fund has $5 billion in assets and restricts its investments to securities rated A or higher.

In 1995, the fund's best year, it posted a return of 19.2%, and in 1994, its worst year, it returned -5.8%. Over the past five years, it yielded an average annual compound return of 9.1%. This no-load fund charges management expenses of $1.69 per $100 in assets, slightly above the average. The fund has a minimum initial investment requirement of $3,000.

HRL Bond Fund ★

This fund, sponsored by HRL Funds Management Ltd. of Toronto, was launched in 1985. It is managed by Art Yeates and its assets total $5 million. Canadian bonds account for 94% of its portfolio and the fund invests only in securities with a rating of A or higher.

The fund posted its highest return, 18.9%, in 1995, and its lowest, -6.0%, in 1994. Over the past five years, its average annual compound return was 9.0%. This is a no-load fund which charges slightly below-average management expenses of $1.50 for every $100 in assets. The fund has a minimum initial investment requirement of $2,500.

The Rookie Camp

Six of the promising newer Canadian bond funds, each with at least a three-year track record, are in the Rookie Camp this year. Each of these funds, listed below, posted *above*-average returns over the past one-, two-, and three-year periods.

Beutel Goodman Private Bond Fund, sponsored by Beutel Goodman Managed Funds Inc., was launched in 1992 and has been managed by Greg Latremoille since August 1992. A no-load fund, it has $4 million in assets and charges well-below-average management expenses of $0.70 for every $100 in assets.

C.I. Canadian Bond Fund, sponsored by C.I. Mutual Funds, was launched in 1993 and is managed by John Zechner of J. Zechner Associates. A load fund, it has $40 million in assets and charges above-average management expenses of $1.65 for every $100 in assets.

Lotus Bond Fund, sponsored by M. K. Wong & Associates, was launched in 1994. The fund has been managed by Bob Deheart since its inception. A no-load fund, it has $1 million in assets and charges below-average management expenses of $1.25 for every $100 in assets.

Mawer Canadian Income Fund, sponsored by Mawer Investment Management of Calgary, was launched in 1992 and has been managed by Gary Feltham since February 1993. A no-load fund, it has $19 million in assets and charges well-below-average management expenses of $0.88 for every $100 in assets. The fund has a minimum initial investment requirement of $25,000 and is not RRSP eligible.

Optima Strategy Canadian Fixed Income Fund, sponsored by Loring Ward Investment Counsel Ltd. of Winnipeg, has $174 million in assets. It is a load fund and charges considerably below-average management expenses of $0.40 for every $100 in assets.

Standard Life Bond Fund, sponsored by Standard Life Mutual Funds Limited, was launched in 1992 and has $7 million in assets. A load fund, sold only on a deferred basis, it charges below-average management expenses of $1.50 for every $100 in assets.

The Underachievers

There are 20 Canadian bond funds that have failed to measure up to their peers. These Underachievers have consistently delivered *below-average* returns over the past one-, three-, and five-year periods. Collectively these Underachievers manage $1.2 billion in assets. The Green Line Short Term Income Fund is the largest, with $211.8 million in assets, and the Trans-Canada Bond Fund is the smallest, managing $0.8 million in assets. Five of the 20 Underachievers are no-load funds.

Table 2

THE UNDERACHIEVERS

CANADIAN BOND FUNDS

- BPI Canadian Bond Fund
- Concorde Revenu
- Elliott & Page Bond Fund
- Empire Bond Fund
- Fonds de Professionnels Bond*
- Green Line Short Term Income Fund*
- InvesNat Short Term Government Bond*
- Laurentian Government Bond Fund
- Laurentian Income Fund
- Manulife Vistafund 2 Bond Fund
- Maritime Life Bond - A & C
- Metlife MVP Bond Fund
- Mutual Bond Fund
- Pursuit Canadian Bond Fund
- Scotia Excelsior Defensive Income*
- Spectrum United Short-Term Bond
- Talvest Income Fund
- Templeton Canadian Bond Fund
- Trans-Canada Bond Fund
- Westbury Canadian Bond Fund*

* denotes a no-load fund

Heavy Hitters vs Underachievers

Table 3 shows the difference in returns, over three time periods, between the Heavy Hitters and Underachievers in this category. In dollar terms, for an initial investment of $10,000, the average Heavy Hitter Canadian bond fund would have returned a total of $16,032 over the past five years. For the same investment, the average Underachiever would have returned $14,223 — for a difference of $1,809 or 12.7%.

With respect to costs, the average Heavy Hitter charged management expenses of $1.40 for every $100 in assets, compared with $1.69 for the average Underachiever.

Table 3
HEAVY HITTERS vs UNDERACHIEVERS
CANADIAN BOND FUNDS
(Returns %)

	1-Year	3-Year*	5-Year*
• Heavy Hitters	13.7	11.7	9.9
• Underachievers	8.9	8.2	7.3

* annualized

CANADIAN BOND FUNDS
RANKINGS/RETURNS

Rank			Name of Fund	Returns (%)			Assets
(80)	(105)	(135)		(11.6)	(10.2)	(8.9)	
5-Yr	3-Yr	1-Yr		1-Yr	3-Yr	5-Yr	($mns)
-	-	65	Acadia Bond Fund	12.0	-	-	2.8
10	23	29	AGF Canadian Bond Fund (HH)	13.5	11.4	10.1	745.6
1	2	10	Altamira Bond Fund (HH)	15.4	13.6	12.1	110.0
5	25	67	Altamira Income Fund (HH)	11.9	11.4	10.8	569.4
-	-	124	Altamira Short Term Gov't Bond Fund	7.6	-	-	156.9
28	43	49	AMI Private Capital Income (HH)	12.4	10.7	9.4	2.1
-	79	60	APEX Fixed Income Fund	12.1	9.5	-	30.1
45	54	63	Atlas Canadian Bond Fund (HH)	12.0	10.5	8.9	23.0
-	-	9	Atlas Canadian High Yield Bond Fund	15.4	-	-	203.4
2	1	5	Batirente - Section Obligations (HH)	16.3	13.7	11.7	29.1
22	19	27	Beutel Goodman Income Fund (HH)	13.5	11.8	9.7	47.2
-	13	28	Beutel Goodman Private Bond (RC)	13.5	12.1	-	3.6
13	12	20	Bissett Bond Fund (HH)	14.2	12.2	10.0	37.7
38	36	32	BNP (Canada) Bond Fund (HH)	13.4	10.9	9.1	5.2
79	103	122	BPI Canadian Bond Fund (UA)	7.8	6.2	5.9	26.9
-	10	7	C.I. Canadian Bond Fund (RC)	15.9	12.3	-	40.3
54	57	68	Canada Life Fixed Income S-19	11.9	10.3	8.6	128.2
48	46	66	Canada Trust Everest Bond Fund	11.9	10.6	8.8	581.3
24	56	96	CCPE Fixed Income Fund	10.2	10.4	9.6	18.1
27	51	84	CDA Bond & Mortgage (Canagex)	11.1	10.5	9.4	42.7
51	32	41	CIBC Canadian Bond Fund	12.8	11.1	8.7	435.8
-	75	106	CIBC Canadian Short-Term Bond	9.6	9.7	-	138.6
-	104	117	Clean Environment Income Fund	8.5	5.9	-	2.6
9	8	23	Co-operators Fixed Income Fund (HH)	13.7	12.5	10.2	7.2
-	83	115	Colonia Bond Fund	8.7	9.1	-	12.2
66	73	89	Concorde Revenu (UA)	10.9	9.7	8.0	7.6
50	58	98	Cornerstone Bond Fund	10.1	10.3	8.8	40.3
-	68	86	Dynamic Government Income Fund	10.9	10.0	-	15.2
23	88	116	Dynamic Income Fund	8.5	8.6	9.7	415.1
75	90	101	Elliott & Page Bond Fund (UA)	9.9	8.1	6.7	17.7
65	74	87	Empire Bond Fund (UA)	10.9	9.7	8.0	54.7
-	65	59	Equitable Life Canadian Bond Fund	12.1	10.1	-	29.4
14	16	24	Equitable Life Segregated Accum. Inc. (HH)	13.6	11.9	10.0	14.6
44	20	37	Ethical Income Fund (HH)	13.0	11.6	8.9	105.7

CANADIAN BOND FUNDS
RANKINGS/RETURNS *cont'd*

Rank			Name of Fund	Returns (%)			Assets
(80)	(105)	(135)		(11.6)	(10.2)	(8.9)	
5-Yr	3-Yr	1-Yr		1-Yr	3-Yr	5-Yr	($mns)
17	30	50	Ferique Bond Fund (HH)	12.4	11.1	9.9	47.6
46	85	40	Fidelity Canadian Bond Fund	12.9	9.1	8.9	63.6
-	-	102	Fidelity Canadian Income Fund	9.7	-	-	38.7
35	34	70	First Canadian Bond Fund (HH)	11.8	11.0	9.1	784.2
58	67	109	Fonds de Professionnels Bond (UA)	9.2	10.0	8.3	62.5
37	45	74	Fonds Desjardins Obligations	11.6	10.7	9.1	64.5
59	52	80	Fonds Ficadre Obligations	11.3	10.5	8.3	10.4
4	5	12	Fonds Optimum Obligations (HH)	15.0	13.1	11.2	4.1
11	18	33	GBC Canadian Bond Fund (HH)	13.4	11.8	10.1	38.1
33	66	57	General Trust of Canada Bond Fund	12.3	10.0	9.2	45.2
-	94	126	Global Strategy Bond Fund	7.4	7.9	-	16.0
6	4	11	Green Line Canadian Bond Fund (HH)	15.0	13.2	10.6	487.2
19	21	43	Green Line Canadian Gov't Bond Fund (HH)	12.7	11.5	9.8	157.1
-	-	39	Green Line Real Return Bond Fund	13.0	-	-	19.9
78	93	129	Green Line Short Term Income Fund (UA)	7.0	8.0	6.2	211.8
-	100	112	Growsafe Canadian Bond Fund	8.8	7.0	-	5.6
-	-	130	Guardian Canadian Income Fund A	7.0	-	-	13.6
-	-	133	Guardian Canadian Income Fund B	6.4	-	-	6.0
-	-	56	GWL Bond Fund (B) DSC	12.3	-	-	2.2
-	-	64	GWL Bond Fund (B) NL	12.0	-	-	1.8
-	-	18	GWL Bond Fund (M) DSC	14.3	-	-	2.2
-	-	22	GWL Bond Fund (M) NL	14.1	-	-	2.3
-	-	72	GWL Bond Fund (S) DSC	11.8	-	-	3.6
-	-	78	GWL Bond Fund (S) NL	11.5	-	-	3.7
-	-	54	GWL Canadian Bond Fund (G) DSC	12.4	-	-	22.1
61	72	61	GWL Canadian Bond Fund (G) NL	12.1	9.8	8.2	47.4
-	-	111	GWL Government Bond Fund (G) DSC	9.1	-	-	5.9
-	-	113	GWL Government Bond Fund (G) NL	8.8	-	-	10.7
-	-	2	GWL Income Fund (G) DSC	17.3	-	-	14.2
-	-	3	GWL Income Fund (G) NL	17.0	-	-	19.6
-	-	31	Hongkong Bank Canadian Bond Fund	13.4	-	-	33.5
41	33	38	HRL Bond Fund (HH)	13.0	11.0	9.0	5.0
20	6	1	Hyperion High Yield Bond Fund (HH)	17.9	12.8	9.7	13.9
12	40	92	ICM Bond Fund	10.6	10.8	10.0	50.0

CANADIAN BOND FUNDS
RANKINGS/RETURNS *cont'd*

Rank			Name of Fund	Returns (%)			Assets
(80)	(105)	(135)		(11.6)	(10.2)	(8.9)	
5-Yr	3-Yr	1-Yr		1-Yr	3-Yr	5-Yr	($mns)
55	61	97	Industrial Alliance Bond Fund	10.2	10.2	8.4	23.9
-	77	103	Industrial Alliance Ecoflex Fund B	9.7	9.7	-	33.3
21	14	6	Industrial Bond Fund (HH)	16.3	12.1	9.7	418.9
-	80	69	InvesNat Canadian Bond Fund	11.8	9.3	-	33.0
70	91	121	InvesNat Short Term Government Bond (UA)	8.1	8.1	7.3	112.8
-	64	52	Investors Corporate Bond Fund	12.4	10.1	-	803.0
34	28	45	Investors Government Bond Fund (HH)	12.6	11.2	9.1	1516.0
60	69	73	Jones Heward Bond Fund	11.6	9.9	8.3	4.1
76	98	131	Laurentian Government Bond Fund (UA)	6.6	7.5	6.6	71.9
57	76	95	Laurentian Income Fund (UA)	10.4	9.7	8.3	149.9
-	50	77	Leith Wheeler Fixed Income Fund	11.5	10.6	-	5.7
49	59	88	London Life Bond	10.9	10.2	8.8	735.2
-	27	36	Lotus (MKW) Bond Fund (RC)	13.2	11.3	-	1.3
-	-	75	Lutheran Life Canadian Bond Fund	11.6	-	-	1.7
-	102	135	Manulife Cabot Diversified Bond	6.0	6.6	-	6.2
63	86	76	Manulife Vistafund 1 Bond Fund	11.6	8.9	8.1	16.3
69	92	91	Manulife Vistafund 2 Bond Fund (UA)	10.8	8.1	7.3	120.5
56	70	94	Maritime Life Bond - A & C (UA)	10.5	9.9	8.4	38.7
29	35	55	Mawer Canadian Bond Fund (HH)	12.4	11.0	9.3	26.2
-	31	17	Mawer Canadian Income Fund (RC)	14.5	11.1	-	19.1
-	-	93	Mawer High Yield Bond Fund	10.5	-	-	6.2
18	15	13	Maxxum Income Fund (HH)	14.9	12.0	9.8	79.0
-	-	127	McDonald Enhanced Bond	7.4	-	-	0.6
16	17	26	McLean Budden Fixed Income Fund (HH)	13.5	11.9	10.0	16.4
3	3	15	McLean Budden Pooled Fixed Income (HH)	14.8	13.3	11.3	272.0
-	-	125	MD Bond and Mortgage Fund	7.5	-	-	88.5
8	22	30	MD Bond Fund (HH)	13.5	11.5	10.2	365.8
73	95	110	Metlife MVP Bond Fund (UA)	9.1	7.8	6.8	22.7
-	-	104	Millennia III Income Fund 1	9.7	-	-	20.7
-	-	107	Millennia III Income Fund 2	9.5	-	-	2.4
62	81	99	Mutual Bond Fund (UA)	10.1	9.3	8.1	18.7
-	71	81	Mutual Premier Bond Fund	11.3	9.9	-	111.3
42	55	79	NAL-Canadian Bond Fund	11.4	10.5	9.0	23.4
32	42	48	National Fixed Income Fund (HH)	12.5	10.8	9.2	51.6

CANADIAN BOND FUNDS
RANKINGS/RETURNS *cont'd*

Rank			Name of Fund	Returns (%)			Assets
(80)	(105)	(135)		(11.6)	(10.2)	(8.9)	
5-Yr	3-Yr	1-Yr		1-Yr	3-Yr	5-Yr	($mns)
15	9	8	National Trust Canadian Bond Fund (HH)	15.7	12.4	10.0	127.5
-	-	19	Navigator Canadian Income Fund	14.3	-	-	11.3
26	29	46	NN Bond Fund (HH)	12.6	11.1	9.4	205.6
-	-	21	O'Donnell High Income Fund	14.2	-	-	165.1
-	47	90	OHA Bond Fund	10.9	10.6	-	31.6
-	7	4	Optima Strategy Cdn. Fixed Income (RC)	16.4	12.7	-	173.5
-	97	128	Optima Strategy Short Term Income	7.3	7.5	-	87.1
-	63	100	PH&N Short Term Bond & Mortgage	9.9	10.2	-	158.8
7	11	34	Phillips Hager & North Bond Fund (HH)	13.3	12.3	10.6	1263.9
72	105	123	Pursuit Canadian Bond Fund (UA)	7.7	4.9	7.0	15.7
52	44	25	Royal Life Income Fund	13.6	10.7	8.7	29.9
30	37	44	Royal Trust Bond Fund (HH)	12.7	10.9	9.3	852.0
36	48	47	RoyFund Bond Fund (HH)	12.5	10.6	9.1	772.9
31	41	35	Sceptre Bond Fund (HH)	13.3	10.8	9.3	7.4
71	89	134	Scotia Excelsior Defensive Income (UA)	6.3	8.2	7.2	137.2
47	53	105	Scotia Excelsior Income Fund	9.7	10.5	8.8	314.2
-	-	114	Scudder Canadian Short Term Bond	8.7	-	-	10.9
25	26	16	Spectrum United Long-Term Bond Fund (HH)	14.8	11.3	9.5	114.6
53	60	83	Spectrum United Mid-Term Bond Fund	11.2	10.2	8.6	452.6
77	96	132	Spectrum United Short-Term Bond (UA)	6.6	7.6	6.6	25.2
-	38	62	Standard Life Bond Mutual Fund (RC)	12.1	10.9	-	7.4
40	62	71	Standard Life Ideal Bond Fund	11.8	10.2	9.0	24.8
39	39	58	Talvest Bond Fund (HH)	12.2	10.8	9.1	77.5
64	82	108	Talvest Income Fund (UA)	9.5	9.2	8.1	103.3
74	101	120	Templeton Canadian Bond Fund (UA)	8.3	6.8	6.8	19.0
68	78	53	Tradex Bond Fund	12.4	9.6	7.7	10.6
80	99	118	Trans-Canada Bond Fund (Sagit) (UA)	8.4	7.1	5.8	0.8
-	-	14	Trimark Advantage Bond Fund	14.8	-	-	152.0
-	-	51	Trimark Canadian Bond Fund	12.4	-	-	60.2
-	87	119	Trimark Government Income Fund	8.4	8.9	-	227.0
43	49	82	Trust Pret & Revenu Bond Fund	11.3	10.6	9.0	49.5
-	24	42	University Avenue Bond Fund	12.8	11.4	-	1.8
67	84	85	Westbury Canadian Bond Fund (UA)	11.0	9.1	7.9	12.5

( ) under Rank indicates total number of funds; ( ) under Returns (%) indicates average annual return; (HH) — Heavy Hitter; (UA) — Underachiever; (RC) — Rookie Camp member.

CANADIAN BOND FUNDS/SUMMARY

Name of Fund	MER	Load	RRSP	Vola-tility	Company Number (App. 3)
Acadia Bond Fund (R)	1.99	N	R		2
AGF Canadian Bond Fund	1.88	Y	R	3	3
Altamira Bond Fund	1.29	N	R	3	6
Altamira Income Fund	1.00	N	R	3	6
Altamira Short Term Gov't Bond Fund	1.26	N	R		6
AMI Private Capital Income	1.25	N	R	2	7
APEX Fixed Income Fund (R)	2.27	Y	R	2	126
Atlas Canadian Bond Fund	1.97	N	R	2	9
Atlas Canadian High Yield Bond Fund	1.88	N	R		9
Batirente - Section Obligations (R)	1.61	N	R	2	131
Beutel Goodman Income Fund	0.63	N	R	3	12
Beutel Goodman Private Bond	0.70	N	R	2	12
Bissett Bond Fund (R)	0.75	Y	R	2	13
BNP (Canada) Bond Fund	1.69	N	R	3	14
BPI Canadian Bond Fund	1.50	Y	R	3	15
C.I. Canadian Bond Fund	1.65	Y	R	2	28
Canada Life Fixed Income S-19	2.00	Y	R	2	18
Canada Trust Everest Bond Fund	1.36	N	R	2	19
Canada Trust Everest S/T Bond	1.31	N	R		19
CCPE Fixed Income Fund (R)	1.35	N	R	2	21
CDA Bond & Mortgage (R)	0.91	N	R	2	22
CIBC Canadian Bond Fund	1.50	N	R	3	29
CIBC Canadian Short-Term Bond	1.25	N	R	2	29
Clean Environment Income Fund (R)	2.59	Y	R	2	31
Co-operators Fixed Income Fund (R)	2.07	N	R	3	33
Colonia Bond Fund	1.74	Y	R	2	32
Concorde Revenu (R)	1.96	Y	R	2	59
Cornerstone Bond Fund	1.60	N	R	2	73
Dynamic Government Income Fund	0.85	Y	R		40
Dynamic Income Fund	1.68	Y	R	1	40
Elliott & Page Bond Fund	1.71	Y	R	2	41
Empire Bond Fund	2.18	Y	R	2	42
Equitable Life Canadian Bond Fund	2.00	Y	R	2	43
Equitable Life Segregated Accum. Inc.	1.20	Y	R	2	43
Ethical Income Fund (R)	1.62	N	R	3	44

CANADIAN BOND FUNDS/SUMMARY *cont'd*

Name of Fund	MER	Load	RRSP	Vola-tility	Company Number (App. 3)
Ferique Bond Fund (R)	0.60	N	R	2	109
Fidelity Canadian Bond Fund	1.34	Y	R	3	46
Fidelity Canadian Income Fund	1.25	Y	R		46
First Canadian Bond Fund	1.58	N	R	2	11
Fonds de Professionnels Bond (R)	0.75	N	R	2	50
Fonds Desjardins Obligations (R)	1.63	N	R	2	37
Fonds Ficadre Obligations	1.63	Y	R	2	128
Fonds Optimum Obligations (R)	1.41	N	R	3	107
GBC Canadian Bond Fund (R)	1.13	N	R	3	52
General Trust of Canada Bond Fund (R)	1.58	N	R	2	98
Global Strategy Bond Fund	1.50	Y	R		54
Green Line Canadian Bond Fund	0.96	N	R	3	139
Green Line Canadian Gov't Bond Fund	0.97	N	R	2	139
Green Line Real Return Bond Fund	1.61	N	R		139
Green Line Short Term Income Fund	1.14	N	R	1	139
Growsafe Canadian Bond Fund	2.10	Y	R	2	141
Guardian Canadian Income Fund A	1.25	Y	R		61
Guardian Canadian Income Fund B	1.87	Y	R		61
GWL Bond Fund (B) DSC	2.04	Y	R		57
GWL Bond Fund (B) NL	2.28	N	R		57
GWL Bond Fund (M) DSC	2.07	Y	R		57
GWL Bond Fund (M) NL	2.31	N	R		57
GWL Bond Fund (S) DSC	2.04	Y	R		57
GWL Bond Fund (S) NL	2.28	N	R		57
GWL Canadian Bond Fund (G) DSC	1.92	Y	R		57
GWL Canadian Bond Fund (G) NL	2.17	N	R	2	57
GWL Government Bond Fund (G) DSC	1.95	Y	R		57
GWL Government Bond Fund (G) NL	2.20	N	R		57
GWL Income Fund (G) DSC	1.95	Y	R		57
GWL Income Fund (G) NL	2.19	N	R		57
Hongkong Bank Canadian Bond Fund	1.24	N	R		63
HRL Bond Fund	1.50	N	R	2	64
Hyperion High Yield Bond Fund	2.10	Y	R	3	136
ICM Bond Fund	0.14	N	R		68
IG Sceptre Canadian Bond Fund	2.64	Y	R		70

CANADIAN BOND FUNDS/SUMMARY *cont'd*

Name of Fund	MER	Load	RRSP	Vola-tility	Company Number (App. 3)
Industrial Alliance Bond Fund (C)	1.50	N	R	2	66
Industrial Alliance Bond Fund - 2	1.65	N	R		66
Industrial Alliance Ecoflex Fund B	1.76	Y	R	2	66
Industrial Bond Fund	1.98	Y	R	3	80
InvesNat Canadian Bond Fund (R)	1.46	N	R	2	98
InvesNat Short Term Gov't Bond (R)	1.35	N	R	1	98
Investors Corporate Bond Fund	1.89	Y	R		70
Investors Government Bond Fund	1.90	Y	R	2	70
Jones Heward Bond Fund	1.75	Y	R	2	72
Laurentian Government Bond Fund	2.15	Y	R	1	135
Laurentian Income Fund	2.15	Y	R	2	135
Leith Wheeler Fixed Income Fund (R)	0.75	N	R		74
London Life Bond	2.00	Y	R	3	76
Lotus (MKW) Bond Fund (R)	1.25	N	R		79
Lutheran Life Canadian Bond Fund (R)	2.25	N	R		78
Manulife Cabot Diversified Bond	2.00	N	R		84
Manulife Vistafund 1 Bond Fund	1.63	Y	R	3	83
Manulife Vistafund 2 Bond Fund	1.63	Y	R	3	83
Maritime Life Bond - A & C	1.90	Y	R	2	85
Maritime Life Bond - B	1.90	Y	R		85
Mawer Canadian Bond Fund (R)	0.89	N	R	2	86
Mawer Canadian Income Fund (R)	0.88	N	F	2	86
Mawer High Yield Bond Fund	1.16	N	F		86
Maxxum Income Fund	1.75	Y	R	3	87
McDonald Enhanced Bond (R)	2.50	Y	R		88
McLean Budden Fixed Income Fund	1.00	N	R	3	89
McLean Budden Pooled Fixed Income (R)	1.00	N	R	2	89
MD Bond and Mortgage Fund (R)	1.06	N	R		90
MD Bond Fund (R)	1.03	N	R	2	90
Metlife MVP Bond Fund	2.22	Y	R	2	92
Millennia III Income Fund 1	2.19	Y	R		65
Millennia III Income Fund 2	2.37	N	R		65
Mutual Bond Fund	1.87	Y	R	2	97
Mutual Premier Bond Fund	1.90	N	R	2	97

CANADIAN BOND FUNDS/SUMMARY *cont'd*

Name of Fund	MER	Load	RRSP	Vola-tility	Company Number (App. 3)
NAL-Canadian Bond Fund	1.75	Y	R	2	83
National Fixed Income Fund	2.00	Y	R	3	99
National Trust Canadian Bond Fund (R)	1.34	N	R	3	100
Navigator Canadian Income Fund (R)	3.15	Y	R		101
NN Bond Fund	2.00	Y	R	3	102
North-West Life Ecoflex B	1.76	Y	R		103
O'Donnell High Income Fund	2.00	Y	R		104
OHA Bond Fund	0.90	N	R	2	105
Optima Strategy Cdn. Fixed Income (R)	0.40	Y	R	3	77
Optima Strategy Short Term Income (R)	0.28	Y	R	1	77
PH&N Short Term Bond & Mortgage (R)	0.64	N	R		112
Phillips Hager & North Bond Fund (R)	0.57	N	R	2	112
Pursuit Canadian Bond Fund	0.80	Y	R	2	117
Royal Life Income Fund	1.88	Y	R	2	120
Royal Trust Bond Fund	1.39	N	R	3	119
RoyFund Bond Fund	1.56	N	R	2	119
Sceptre Bond Fund	1.25	N	R	2	123
Scotia Excelsior Defensive Income	1.37	N	R	2	124
Scotia Excelsior Income Fund	1.37	N	R	2	124
Scudder Canadian Short Term Bond (R)	0.50	N	R		125
Spectrum United Long-Term Bond Fund	1.66	Y	R	3	129
Spectrum United Mid-Term Bond Fund	1.59	Y	R	3	129
Spectrum United Short-Term Bond	1.45	Y	R	2	129
Standard Life Bond Mutual Fund (R)	1.50	Y	R	3	133
Standard Life Ideal Bond Fund	2.00	Y	R	3	132
Talvest Bond Fund	1.99	Y	R	2	136
Talvest Income Fund	1.50	Y	R	2	136
Templeton Canadian Bond Fund	1.65	Y	R	2	137
Tradex Bond Fund (R)	1.68	N	R	2	140
Trans-Canada Bond Fund	2.38	Y	R	2	121
Trimark Advantage Bond Fund	1.25	Y	R		143
Trimark Canadian Bond Fund	1.25	Y	R		143
Trimark Government Income Fund	1.25	Y	R	1	143
Trust Pret & Revenu Bond Fund	1.57	N	R	2	145

CANADIAN BOND FUNDS/SUMMARY *cont'd*

Name of Fund	MER	Load	RRSP	Vola-tility	Company Number (App. 3)
University Avenue Bond Fund	1.99	Y	R	2	146
Valorem Canadian Bond-Value (R)	1.60	Y	R		152
Westbury Canadian Bond Fund (R)	2.08	N	R	2	148
Average	1.59			2.2	

(R) — Restricted; (C) — Closed to new investors; MER — Management Expense Ratio; Load — fee charged; RRSP: R = 100% eligible, F = eligible as foreign content only, N = not eligible; Volatility — measures swings in performance on a scale of 1 to 10 (1 = low, 10 = high). Blank space indicates that fund is less than three years old. Fund company addresses may be found by number in Appendix 3.

16

• •

Canadian Mortgage Funds

MOST MORTGAGE FUNDS invest in conventional and insured first mortgages on prime residential properties located in major cities across Canada. Some funds also include commercial properties in their portfolios. These funds typically produce a rate of income that is in line with mortgage interest rates. There are currently 32 Canadian mortgage funds on the market. These funds manage close to $13.5 billion in assets. Next to money-market funds, these funds are the least risky type of mutual fund.

Over the five calendar years from 1992 to 1996, the best year for Canadian mortgage funds was 1995, when returns averaged 11.4%. In contrast, the worst year was 1994, when returns averaged 0.1%. The average annual compound rate of return over the five-year period was 7.7%.

Canadian mortgage funds have an average volatility rating of 1.4, which is below the average of 1.9 for all fixed-income funds. The average fee for management expenses is $1.64 for every $100 in assets, which is up from last year's average of $1.60.

The Heavy Hitters

There are five Canadian mortgage funds that have qualified for membership in the Heavy Hitters club this year. Each of these funds has consistently delivered *above*-average returns over the past one-, three-, and five-year periods. Collectively these Heavy Hitters manage a total of $4.7 billion in assets. The Bank of Montreal's First Canadian Mortgage Fund is the largest, with $2 billion in assets, and the Ontario Teachers Group Mortgage Income Fund is the smallest, with $105.8 million in assets. Four of the five Heavy Hitters are no-load funds.

Table 1

THE HEAVY HITTERS

CANADIAN MORTGAGE FUNDS

		Bench-mark*	Vola-tility	Performance Quartile 1	Quartile 2	Overall Rating
1	Ontario Teachers Group Mortgage Inc. (R) (N)	2	1	4	1	★★1/2
2	Investors Income Portfolio Fund	2	2	3	0	★★
3	CIBC Mortgage Fund (N)	1	2	2	2	★1/2
4	First Canadian Mortgage Fund (N)	1	2	2	2	★1/2
5	GWL Mortgage Fund (G) NL (N)	0	2	2	1	★

* ScotiaMcLeod Conventional Mortgage Index; (R) — Restricted; (C) — Closed to new members; (N) — No-load fund; Benchmark — number of times that a fund beat the benchmark from 1992 to 1996; Volatility — measures swings in fund returns on a scale of 1 to 10 (1 = low, 10 = high); Performance — number of times that a fund was in the first (top 25%) or second quartile (top 50%) from 1992 to 1996.

The benchmark used to compare Canadian mortgage fund returns is the ScotiaMcLeod Conventional Mortgage Index. Over the past five calendar years, the index posted its highest return of 15.3% in 1995 and its lowest return of -0.9% in 1994.

Ontario Teachers Group Mortgage Income Fund ★★1/2

This fund, the number-one Heavy Hitter mortgage fund for the second year in a row, was launched in 1975 and has been managed by the Toronto investment firm AMI Partners Inc. since its inception. With $106 million in assets, 60% of the portfolio is invested in Government of Canada bonds rated A or higher and 27% in mortgages.

Its best year was 1995, when it posted a return of 13.1%, and its worst year was 1994, when its return was 2.2%. Its average annual compound return over the past five years was 8.7%. A no-load fund, it charges management expenses of $0.75 for every $100 in assets, which is considerably lower than the group average of $1.64. The fund is available only to members of the Ontario Teachers Group.

Investors Income Portfolio Fund ★★

Launched in 1989, this fund is managed by Bob Darling and invests in a number of the Investors group of funds. With $840 million in assets, 34% is invested in the firm's Corporate Bond Fund, 33% in the Mortgage Fund, and 33% in the Bond Fund.

In 1995, its best year, the fund posted a return of 16.1%, and in 1994, its worst year, it returned -3.6%. Over the past five years, it yielded an average annual compound return of 8.0%. This load fund charges below-average management expenses of only $0.16 for every $100 in assets. This low figure is, however, over and above the management fees that are levied by the individual funds in the portfolio and represents an additional charge for administrative purposes.

CIBC Mortgage Fund ★1/2

This fund was launched in 1975 and is managed by Bert Pearsoll of T.A.L. Investment Counsel Ltd., which is partially owned by the CIBC. With $1.7 billion in assets, 86% of the portfolio is invested in residential mortgages insured under the National Housing Act and 14% in cash.

The fund posted its highest return, 12.0%, in 1995, and its lowest, 0.0%, in 1994. Over the past five years, its average annual compound return was 7.9%. This is a no-load fund which charges management expenses of $1.60 for every $100 in assets, slightly lower than the group average of $1.64.

First Canadian Mortgage Fund ★1/2

This fund was launched in 1974 and is managed by Mary Jane Yule. With $2 billion in assets, 94% of the portfolio is invested in mortgages and 6% in Canadian T-bills.

Its best year was 1995, when it posted a return of 12.9%, and its worst year was 1994, when its return was -0.5%. The fund's average annual compound return over the past five years was 7.9%. A no-load fund, it charges management expenses of $1.47 for every $100 in assets, which is below the group average.

Great-West Life Mortgage Fund (G) NL ★

Launched in 1966, this fund has been managed by Harv Andres since 1987. With $118 million in assets, 47% of the portfolio is invested in residential mortgages, 37% in commercial mortgages, and 10% in industrial mortgages.

In 1995, its best year, the fund posted a return of 14.1%, and in 1994, its worst year, it returned -2.8%. Over the past five years, it yielded an average annual compound return of 7.7%. This no-load fund charges significantly above-average management expenses of $2.41 for every $100 in assets.

The Rookie Camp

Four of the promising newer Canadian mortgage funds, each with at least a three-year track record, are in the Rookie Camp this year. Each of these funds, listed below, posted *above*-average returns over the past one-, two-, and three-year periods.

Hongkong Bank Mortgage Fund, sponsored by the Hongkong Bank of Canada, was launched in 1992 and is managed by Jim Gilliland of the investment firm M. K. Wong & Associates Ltd. A no-load fund, it has $293 million in assets and charges below-average management expenses of $1.47 for every $100 in assets.

Ivy Mortgage Fund, sponsored by the Mackenzie Financial Corporation, was launched in 1994. A load fund, it has $214 million in assets and charges above-average management expenses of $1.90 for every $100 in assets.

National Trust Mortgage Fund, sponsored by the National Trust Company, was launched in 1992 and is managed by the investment firm Cassels Blaikie Investment Management Ltd. A no-load fund, it has $74 million in assets and charges below-average management expenses of $1.52 for every $100 in assets.

Scotia Excelsior Mortgage Fund, sponsored by Scotia Securities Inc., a wholly owned subsidiary of the Bank of Nova Scotia, was launched in 1992. A no-load fund, it has $532 million in assets and charges below-average management expenses of $1.56 for every $100 in assets.

The Underachievers

There are six Canadian mortgage funds that have failed to measure up to their peers. These Underachievers have consistently delivered *below*-average returns over the past one-, three-, and five-year periods. Collectively these Underachievers manage $2 billion in assets. Toronto-Dominion's Green Line Mortgage Fund is the largest, with $891 million in assets, and the Concorde Hypotheques Fund is the smallest, with $4.8 million. Five of the six Underachievers are no-load funds.

Table 2

THE UNDERACHIEVERS

CANADIAN MORTGAGE FUNDS

- Concorde Hypotheques
- Fonds Desjardins Hypotheques*
- General Trust of Canada Mortgage*
- Green Line Mortgage Fund*
- Industrial Alliance Mortgage Fund*
- Royal Trust Mortgage Fund*

---

* denotes a no-load fund

Heavy Hitters vs Underachievers

Table 3 shows the difference in returns, over three time periods, between the Heavy Hitters and Underachievers in this category. In dollar terms, for an initial investment of $10,000, the average Heavy Hitter Canadian mortgage fund would have returned a total of $14,693 over the past five years. For the same investment, the average Underachiever would have returned $13,830 — for a difference of $863 or 6.2%.

With respect to costs, the average Heavy Hitter charged management expenses of $1.28 for every $100 in assets, compared with $1.66 for the average Underachiever.

Table 3
HEAVY HITTERS vs UNDERACHIEVERS
CANADIAN MORTGAGE FUNDS
(Returns %)

	1-Year	3-Year*	5-Year*
• Heavy Hitters	9.0	8.8	8.0
• Underachievers	5.7	6.8	6.7

* annualized

CANADIAN MORTGAGE FUNDS
RANKINGS/RETURNS

Rank			Name of Fund	Returns (%)			Assets
(19)	(26)	(30)		(6.9)	(7.7)	(7.4)	
5-Yr	3-Yr	1-Yr		1-Yr	3-Yr	5-Yr	($mns)
-	-	31	Acadia Mortgage Fund	2.6	-	-	7.6
-	-	29	APEX Mortgage Fund	4.8	-	-	6.6
10	20	21	Canada Trust Everest Mortgage Fund	6.4	7.3	7.5	644.0
5	7	6	CIBC Mortgage Fund (HH)	8.2	8.2	7.9	1695.6
-	14	25	Colonia Mortgage Fund	5.7	7.6	-	4.1
15	24	17	Concorde Hypotheques (UA)	6.6	6.5	6.8	4.8
-	-	22	Equitable Life Mortgage Fund	6.3	-	-	1.7
6	5	11	First Canadian Mortgage Fund (HH)	7.5	8.3	7.9	1989.5
13	21	27	Fonds Desjardins Hypotheques (UA)	5.1	7.0	6.9	216.3
-	-	13	Fonds Ficadre Hypotheques	7.1	-	-	0.9
18	26	30	General Trust of Canada Mortgage (UA)	4.8	6.1	6.5	57.7
12	19	18	Green Line Mortgage Fund (UA)	6.5	7.3	7.2	891.1
14	18	15	Green Line Mortgage-Backed Fund	7.0	7.4	6.9	94.8
-	-	2	GWL Mortgage Fund (G) DSC	10.1	-	-	48.2
7	3	3	GWL Mortgage Fund (G) NL (HH)	9.8	8.9	7.7	117.6
-	4	4	Hongkong Bank Mortgage Fund (RC)	9.2	8.9	-	292.9
-	25	28	Industrial Alliance Ecoflex Fund H	5.1	6.4	-	11.8
17	22	26	Industrial Alliance Mortgage Fund (UA)	5.5	7.0	6.6	6.2
9	13	19	InvesNat Mortgage Fund	6.4	7.6	7.6	293.2
4	1	1	Investors Income Portfolio Fund (HH)	10.3	9.5	8.0	839.5
16	16	14	Investors Mortgage Fund	7.1	7.5	6.6	2764.4
-	9	8	Ivy Mortgage Fund (RC)	8.0	8.1	-	214.1
8	12	12	London Life Mortgage	7.2	7.7	7.6	409.1
2	10	23	Mandate National Mortgage Corp.	6.2	8.1	8.3	10.5
-	17	20	Mutual Premier Mortgage Fund	6.4	7.5	-	188.8
-	8	7	National Trust Mortgage Fund (RC)	8.1	8.2	-	73.8
1	2	5	Ontario Teachers Group Mortgage Inc. (HH)	9.1	9.0	8.7	105.8
19	23	24	Royal Trust Mortgage Fund (UA)	5.9	6.9	6.3	841.2
3	15	9	RoyFund Mortgage Fund	7.8	7.5	8.0	993.7
-	6	10	Scotia Excelsior Mortgage Fund (RC)	7.6	8.2	-	531.8
11	11	16	Trust Pret & Revenu H Fund	6.7	7.9	7.3	93.3

( ) under Rank indicates total number of funds; ( ) under Returns (%) indicates average annual return; (HH) — Heavy Hitter; (UA) — Underachiever; (RC) — Rookie Camp member.

CANADIAN MORTGAGE FUNDS/SUMMARY

Name of Fund	MER	Load	RRSP	Vola-tility	Company Number (App. 3)
Acadia Mortgage Fund (R)	2.05	N	R		2
APEX Mortgage Fund (R)	2.00	Y	R		126
Canada Trust Everest Mortgage Fund	1.60	N	R	1	19
CIBC Mortgage Fund	1.60	N	R	2	29
Colonia Mortgage Fund	2.01	Y	R	1	32
Concorde Hypotheques (R)	1.92	Y	R	2	59
Equitable Life Mortgage Fund	2.25	Y	R		43
First Canadian Mortgage Fund	1.47	N	R	2	11
Fonds Desjardins Hypotheques (R)	1.62	N	R	1	37
Fonds Ficadre Hypotheques	1.66	Y	R		128
General Trust of Canada Mortgage (R)	1.56	N	R	1	98
Green Line Mortgage Fund	1.62	N	R	2	139
Green Line Mortgage-Backed Fund	1.56	N	R	1	139
GWL Mortgage Fund (G) DSC	2.16	Y	R		57
GWL Mortgage Fund (G) NL	2.41	N	R	2	57
Hongkong Bank Mortgage Fund	1.47	N	R	1	63
Industrial Alliance Ecoflex Fund H	1.76	Y	R	1	66
Industrial Alliance Mortgage Fund (C)	1.50	N	R	1	66
InvesNat Mortgage Fund (R)	1.55	N	R	1	98
Investors Income Portfolio Fund	0.16	Y	R	2	70
Investors Mortgage Fund	1.89	Y	R	1	70
Ivy Mortgage Fund	1.90	Y	R		80
London Life Mortgage	2.00	Y	R	1	76
Mandate National Mortgage Corp.	0.30	N	R		82
Mutual Premier Mortgage Fund	1.58	N	R	1	97
National Trust Mortgage Fund (R)	1.52	N	R	2	100
North-West Life Ecoflex H	1.76	Y	R		103
Ontario Teachers Group Mortgage Inc. (R)	0.75	N	R	1	106
Royal Trust Mortgage Fund	1.73	N	R	1	119
RoyFund Mortgage Fund	1.79	N	R	2	119
Scotia Excelsior Mortgage Fund	1.56	N	R	2	124
Trust Pret & Revenu H Fund	1.67	N	R	1	145
Average	1.64			1.4	

(R) — Restricted; (C) — Closed to new investors; MER — Management Expense Ratio; Load — fee charged; RRSP: R = 100% eligible, F = eligible as foreign content only, N = not eligible; Volatility — measures swings in performance on a scale of 1 to 10 (1 = low, 10 = high). Blank space indicates that fund is less than three years old. Fund company addresses may be found by number in Appendix 3.

17

• •

Canadian Dividend Funds

MANY CANADIAN CORPORATIONS pay a portion of their annual profits to shareholders in the form of dividend income. Canadian dividend funds invest in dividend-paying preferred shares of corporations, and in common shares that are expected to yield a high level of dividend income. Investors who purchase dividend funds receive a regular stream of income. There is also the potential for long-term capital growth through higher share prices of the fund's holdings. As a general rule, dividend funds are less volatile than equity funds. They have the added advantage that dividend income is taxed at a substantially lower rate of return than other types of investment income.

There are currently 42 dividend funds on the market. These funds manage a total of $11.5 billion in assets. Over the five calendar years from 1992 to 1996, the best year for Canadian dividend funds was 1996, when returns averaged 24.8%. In contrast, the worst year was 1994, when returns averaged -1.3%. The average annual compound rate of return over the five-year period was 11.7%.

Canadian dividend funds have an average volatility rating of 2.5, which is below the average of 4.1 for all equity funds. The average fee for management expenses is $1.84 for every $100 in assets, which is up slightly from last year's average of $1.82.

The Heavy Hitters

There are seven Canadian dividend funds that have qualified for membership in the Heavy Hitters club this year. Each of these funds has consistently delivered *above*-average returns over the past one-, three-, and five-year periods. Collectively these Heavy Hitters manage a total of $2.5 billion in assets. The AGF Dividend Fund is the largest, with $859 million in assets, and the Maxxum Dividend Fund is the smallest, with $159 million in assets. Three of the seven Heavy Hitters are no-load funds.

Table 1

THE HEAVY HITTERS

CANADIAN DIVIDEND FUNDS

		Bench-mark*	Vola-tility	Performance Quartile 1	Quartile 2	Overall Rating
1	Maxxum Dividend Fund	4	3	4	1	★★★
2	AGF Dividend Fund	4	3	3	1	★★1/2
3	Phillips Hager & North Div. Income (R) (N)	3	3	3	1	★★1/2
4	Industrial Dividend Growth Fund Ltd.	3	3	3	0	★★
5	Scotia Excelsior Dividend Fund (N)	2	2	1	2	★1/2
6	Dynamic Dividend Growth Fund	2	2	1	1	★1/2
7	Royal Trust Growth and Income Fund (N)	2	3	1	1	★1/2

* TSE 300 Total Return Index; (R) — Restricted; (C) — Closed to new members; (N) — No-load fund; Benchmark — number of times that a fund beat the benchmark from 1992 to 1996; Volatility — measures swings in fund returns on a scale of 1 to 10 (1 = low, 10 = high); Performance — number of times that a fund was in the first (top 25%) or second quartile (top 50%) from 1992 to 1996.

The benchmark used to compare Canadian dividend fund returns is the TSE 300 Total Return Index. Over the past five calendar years, the index posted its highest return of 32.6% in 1993 and its lowest return of -1.4% in 1992. Returns were also negative in 1994, when the index dipped by 0.2%.

Maxxum Dividend Fund ★★★

This fund is the number-one Heavy Hitter fund in this category for the second year in a row and the only dividend fund to receive a three-star rating. The fund was launched in 1986 and is managed by Jackee Pratt. With $159 million in assets, it follows a bottom-up/value investment strategy. Investments in financial services, utilities, industrial products, and metals and minerals account for about 50% of the fund's assets.

Its best year was 1993, when it posted a return of 35.2%, and its worst year was 1994, when its return was 2.4%. The fund's average annual compound return over the past five years was 21.6%. A load fund, it charges management expenses of $1.75 for every $100 in assets, which is lower than the group average of $1.84.

AGF Dividend Fund ★★1/2

This fund, formerly the 20/20 Dividend Fund, was started in 1986 and is managed by Gordon MacDougall and Martin Gerger of the investment firm Connor, Clarke & Lumm Investment Management Inc. The fund has $860 million in assets and follows a top-down/blend investment strategy. Investments in financial services, industrial products, oil and gas, and transportation account for about 60% of the fund's assets.

In 1993, its best year, the fund posted a return of 26.3%, and in 1994, its worst year, it returned 0.4%. Over the past five years, it yielded an average annual compound return of 16.8%. This load fund charges slightly above-average management expenses of $1.91 for every $100 in assets.

Phillips Hager & North Dividend Income Fund ★★1/2

This fund was launched in 1977 and is managed by the firm's Canadian equity research team. With $202 million in assets, it follows a value/ growth/sector investment strategy. Seventy percent of the fund's assets are made up of investments in pipelines and utilities and financial services.

The fund posted its highest return, 33.3%, in 1996, and its lowest, -1.0%, in 1992. Over the past five years, its average annual compound return was 18.3%. This is a no-load fund which charges management expenses of $1.21 for every $100 in assets, lower than the group average of $1.84. The fund has a minimum initial investment requirement of $25,000 for non-RRSP accounts and $5,000 for RRSP accounts.

Industrial Dividend Growth Fund Ltd. ★★

This fund, formerly the Industrial Dividend Fund, is sponsored by the Mackenzie Financial Corporation. The fund was launched in 1975 and is managed by William Proctor. With $569 million in assets, it follows a top-down/value investment strategy. Investments in financial services, industrial products, and natural resources account for close to 70% of the fund's assets.

Its best year was 1993, when it posted a return of 58.4%, and its worst year was 1992, when its return was -2.9%. The fund's average annual compound return over the past five years was 19.5%. A load fund, it charges management expenses of $2.39 for every $100 in assets, which is higher than the group average of $1.84.

Scotia Excelsior Dividend Fund ★1/2

This fund was started in 1986 and is managed by Montrusco Associates Inc. The fund has $319 million in assets and follows a top-down/value investment strategy. Investments in financial services, utilities, pipelines, and communications account for over 50% of the fund's assets.

In 1996, its best year, the fund posted a return of 24.6%, and in 1994, its worst year, it returned -2.9%. Over the past five years, it yielded an average annual compound return of 13.6%. This no-load fund charges well-below-average management expenses of $1.07 for every $100 in assets.

Dynamic Dividend Growth Fund ★1/2

This fund was launched in 1985 and is managed by the firm's investment team. With $236 million in assets, it follows a bottom-up/value investment strategy. Sixty-three percent of the fund's assets are made up of investments in Canadian equities and 25% in cash.

The fund posted its highest return, 28.8%, in 1996, and its lowest, -1.4%, in 1994. Over the past five years, its average annual compound return was 15.3%. This is a load fund which charges management expenses of $1.83 for every $100 in assets, marginally lower than the group average of $1.84.

Royal Trust Growth & Income Fund ★1/2

This fund, part of the Royal Bank's family of funds, was launched in 1986 and has been managed by John Kellett since June 1994. With $188 million in assets, it follows a bottom-up/value investment strategy. Investments in financial services, utilities, and pipelines account for 65% of the fund's assets.

Its best year was 1996, when it posted a return of 33.2%, and its worst year was 1994, when its return was -3.7%. The fund's average annual compound return over the past five years was 14.2%. A no-load fund, it charges below-average management expenses of $1.77 for every $100 in assets.

The Rookie Camp

Two of the promising newer Canadian dividend funds, each with at least a three-year track record, are in the Rookie Camp this year. Each of these funds, listed below, posted *above*-average returns over the past one-, two-, and three-year periods.

Bissett Dividend Income Fund, sponsored by Bissett & Associates Investment Management Ltd. of Calgary, is managed by Fred Pynn. With $22 million in assets, the fund follows a blend/bottom-up investment strategy. A no-load fund when purchased directly from the sponsor, it charges below-average management expenses of $1.50 for every $100 in assets. The fund is available for sale only in Alberta, British Columbia, and Ontario and has a minimum initial investment requirement of $10,000.

RoyFund Dividend Fund, sponsored by the Royal Bank, was launched in 1993 and follows a bottom-up/value investment strategy. The fund has been managed by John Kellett since its inception. A no-load fund, it has $809 million in assets and charges average management expenses of $1.84 for every $100 in assets.

The Underachievers

There are eight Canadian dividend funds that have failed to measure up to their peers. These Underachievers have consistently delivered *below*-average returns over the past one-, three-, and five-year periods.

165

Collectively these Underachievers manage $5.3 billion in assets. Investors Dividend Fund is the largest, with $3.4 billion in assets, and the Trans-Canada Dividend Fund is the smallest, with $6.4 million. Seven of the eight Underachievers are load funds.

Table 2

THE UNDERACHIEVERS

CANADIAN DIVIDEND FUNDS

- AGF High Income Fund
- CIBC Dividend Fund*
- Dynamic Dividend Fund
- Guardian Monthly Dividend Fund A
- Investors Dividend Fund
- Laurentian Dividend Fund Ltd.
- Spectrum United Dividend Fund
- Trans-Canada Dividend Fund

---

*denotes a no-load fund

Heavy Hitters vs Underachievers

Table 3 shows the difference in returns, over three time periods, between the Heavy Hitters and Underachievers in this category. As can be seen, the Heavy Hitters posted returns that were, on average, significantly higher than the Underachievers'. In dollar terms, for an initial investment of $10,000, the average Heavy Hitter Canadian dividend fund would have returned a total of $21,924 over the past five years. For the same investment, the average Underachiever would have returned $16,549 — for a difference of $5,375 or 32.5%.

With respect to costs, the average Heavy Hitter charged management expenses of $1.70 for every $100 in assets, compared with $2.01 for the average Underachiever.

Table 3

HEAVY HITTERS vs UNDERACHIEVERS

CANADIAN DIVIDEND FUNDS

(Returns %)

	1-Year	3-Year*	5-Year*
• Heavy Hitters	32.2	18.1	17.0
• Underachievers	18.0	11.5	10.6

* annualized

CANADIAN DIVIDEND FUNDS
RANKINGS/RETURNS

Rank			Name of Fund	Returns (%)			Assets
(17)	(24)	(34)		(26.0)	(14.6)	(13.5)	
5-Yr	3-Yr	1-Yr		1-Yr	3-Yr	5-Yr	($mns)
4	2	9	AGF Dividend Fund (HH)	33.4	20.0	16.8	859.3
17	23	34	AGF High Income Fund (UA)	11.7	9.7	8.6	443.6
-	-	22	Altamira Dividend Fund	22.4	-	-	161.9
-	3	13	Bissett Dividend Income Fund (RC)	28.4	19.5	-	22.4
9	10	20	BPI Dividend Income Fund	23.4	15.4	12.1	218.4
-	-	17	Canada Trust Everest Div. Income	25.2	-	-	291.2
11	20	25	CIBC Dividend Fund (UA)	20.4	11.2	11.6	447.3
-	-	2	Concorde Dividend Fund	40.1	-	-	11.2
10	18	27	Dynamic Dividend Fund (UA)	18.5	12.2	11.9	304.5
5	7	15	Dynamic Dividend Growth Fund (HH)	27.1	16.6	15.3	236.2
-	-	7	First Canadian Dividend Income Fund	35.0	-	-	420.0
-	11	18	Fonds Desjardins Dividendes	24.8	15.3	-	88.8
8	15	8	Green Line Dividend Fund	33.8	13.0	12.9	215.1
16	24	31	Guardian Monthly Dividend Fund A (UA)	14.3	9.6	9.1	143.9
-	-	32	Guardian Monthly Dividend Fund B	13.9	-	-	395.5
-	-	14	Hongkong Bank Dividend Income Fund	28.2	-	-	115.5
2	8	11	Industrial Dividend Growth Fund Ltd. (HH)	29.7	16.4	19.5	569.1
-	22	33	InvesNat Dividend Fund	13.4	10.4	-	36.8
12	16	19	Investors Dividend Fund (UA)	24.1	12.8	11.4	3439.2
13	17	23	Laurentian Dividend Fund Ltd. (UA)	22.1	12.2	10.9	396.7
-	-	21	Maritime Life Dividend Inc. - A & C	22.5	-	-	57.2
1	5	12	Maxxum Dividend Fund (HH)	28.8	18.9	21.6	159.1
-	19	29	MD Dividend Fund	16.4	11.3	-	103.8
-	13	10	National Trust Dividend Fund	30.4	13.8	-	54.5
-	12	24	NN Dividend Fund	21.2	15.0	-	140.8
3	1	1	Phillips Hager & North Div. Income (HH)	41.9	20.6	18.3	202.4
6	6	5	Royal Trust Growth and Income Fund (HH)	38.3	18.6	14.2	188.3
-	4	6	RoyFund Dividend Fund (RC)	37.9	19.3	-	809.1
7	9	16	Scotia Excelsior Dividend Fund (HH)	26.6	15.5	13.6	319.2
15	21	28	Spectrum United Dividend Fund (UA)	18.0	11.1	10.3	123.8
-	-	4	Standard Life Canadian Dividend	39.5	-	-	12.5
-	-	26	Talvest Dividend Fund	19.6	-	-	110.6

CANADIAN DIVIDEND FUNDS
RANKINGS/RETURNS *cont'd*

Rank			Name of Fund	Returns (%)			Assets
(17)	(24)	(34)		(26.0)	(14.6)	(13.5)	
5-Yr	3-Yr	1-Yr		1-Yr	3-Yr	5-Yr	($mns)
14	14	30	Trans-Canada Dividend Fund (Sagit) (UA)	14.8	13.3	10.8	6.4
-	-	3	Trust Pret & Revenu Dividend Fund	39.6	-	-	17.4

( ) under Rank indicates total number of funds; ( ) under Returns (%) indicates average annual return;

(HH) — Heavy Hitter; (UA) — Underachiever; (RC) — Rookie Camp member.

CANADIAN DIVIDEND FUNDS/SUMMARY

Name of Fund	MER	Load	RRSP	Vola-tility	Company Number (App. 3)
AGF Dividend Fund	1.91	Y	R	3	3
AGF High Income Fund	1.92	Y	R	2	3
Altamira Dividend Fund	1.55	N	R		6
Atlas Cdn. Dividend Growth Fund	2.50	N	R		9
Bissett Dividend Income Fund (R)	1.50	Y	F	3	13
BPI Dividend Income Fund	1.00	Y	R	2	15
BPI High Income Fund	1.25	Y	R		15
Canada Trust Everest Div. Income	1.96	N	R		19
CIBC Dividend Fund	1.80	N	R	3	29
Concorde Dividend Fund (R)	1.90	Y	R		59
Dynamic Dividend Fund (C)	1.60	Y	R	2	40
Dynamic Dividend Growth Fund	1.83	Y	R	2	40
First Canadian Dividend Income Fund	1.66	N	F		11
Fonds Desjardins Dividendes (R)	1.94	N	R		37
Green Line Dividend Fund	2.02	N	R	3	139
Guardian Monthly Dividend Fund A (C)	1.25	Y	R	2	61
Guardian Monthly Dividend Fund B (C)	1.85	Y	R		61
Guardian Monthly High Income A (C)	1.46	Y	R		61
Guardian Monthly High Income B (C)	2.07	Y	R		61
Hongkong Bank Dividend Income Fund	1.96	N	R		63
Industrial Dividend Growth Fund Ltd.	2.39	Y	R	3	80
Infinity Income Fund	2.24	Y	R		67
InvesNat Dividend Fund (R)	1.70	N	R	2	98
Investors Dividend Fund	2.34	Y	R	2	70
Laurentian Dividend Fund Ltd.	2.65	Y	R	2	135
Maritime Life Dividend Inc. - B	2.05	Y	R		85
Maritime Life Dividend Inc. - A & C	2.05	Y	R		85
Maxxum Dividend Fund	1.75	Y	R	3	87
MD Dividend Fund (R)	1.30	N	R	2	90
Millennium Income Fund (R)	2.50	Y	R		96
Monarch Dividend Fund	1.91	Y	R		28
National Trust Dividend Fund (R)	1.84	N	R	3	100
NN Dividend Fund	2.00	Y	R		102
Phillips Hager & North Div. Income (R)	1.21	N	R	3	112
Royal Trust Growth and Income Fund	1.77	N	R	3	119

CANADIAN DIVIDEND FUNDS/SUMMARY *cont'd*

Name of Fund	MER	Load	RRSP	Vola-tility	Company Number (App. 3)
RoyFund Dividend Fund	1.84	N	R	3	119
Scotia Excelsior Dividend Fund	1.07	N	R	2	124
Spectrum United Dividend Fund	1.61	Y	R	2	129
Standard Life Canadian Dividend	1.50	Y	R		133
Talvest Dividend Fund	1.99	Y	R		136
Trans-Canada Dividend Fund	2.88	Y	R	3	121
Trust Pret & Revenu Dividend Fund	1.63	N	R		145
Average	1.84			2.5	

(R) — Restricted; (C) — Closed to new investors; MER — Management Expense Ratio; Load — fee charged; RRSP: R = 100% eligible, F = eligible as foreign content only, N = not eligible; Volatility — measures swings in performance on a scale of 1 to 10 (1 = low, 10 = high). Blank space indicates that fund is less than three years old. Fund company addresses may be found by number in Appendix 3.

18

• •

Canadian Money-Market Funds

THERE ARE CURRENTLY 119 money-market funds available. Together they manage about $33.6 billion in assets. Banks and trust companies dominate the money-market fund business in Canada and account for two-thirds of the total assets. The primary objectives of these funds are to provide income based on general interest rates and maximum protection of the capital invested. Money-market funds typically invest in high-grade, short-term money-market instruments that are issued or guaranteed by the Government of Canada or a province, and short-term securities that are issued by Canadian corporations and financial institutions.

Most money-market funds maintain a constant net asset value or share price of $10 per unit. Investors earn income by receiving interest on the fund's investments in short-term securities. A hallmark of money-market funds is their safety. To date, no money-market fund has posted a negative return. Moreover, these funds typically pay one or two percentage points above bank savings rates.

Over the five calendar years from 1992 to 1996, the best year for Canadian money-market funds was 1995, when returns averaged 6.2%. In contrast, the worst year was 1996, when returns averaged 3.9%. The average annual compound rate of return over the five-year period was 4.9%. The average fee for management expenses is $1.02 for every $100 in assets, which is slightly up from last year's average of $1.01.

The Heavy Hitters

There are 33 Canadian money-market funds that have qualified for membership in the Heavy Hitters club this year. Each of these funds has consistently delivered *above*-average returns over the past one-, three-, and five-year periods. Collectively these Heavy Hitters manage a total of $12.3 billion in assets. TD's Green Line Canadian Money Market Fund is the largest, with $5.3 billion in assets, and the AMI's Private Capital Money Market Fund is the smallest, with $1.5 million in assets. Twenty-four of the 33 Heavy Hitters are no-load funds.

The performance of money-market funds tends to cluster in a fairly narrow band. Clearly, the consistent performers that have the lowest expenses and do not charge sales fees will have the edge. To help you narrow down your choices, Table 1 and each Heavy Hitter entry provide the following information: load/no-load, asset size, how often the fund has beaten the benchmark, quartile performance, and management expenses. Because of their short-term nature, all money-market funds have a volatility rating of 1, the lowest on the scale of 1 to 10.

Table 1

THE HEAVY HITTERS

CANADIAN MONEY-MARKET FUNDS

		Bench-mark*	Vola-tility	Performance Quartile 1	Quartile 2	Overall Rating
1	Ontario Teachers Grp. Fixed Value (R) (N)	3	1	5	0	★★★
2	Fonds de Professionnels Short Term (R) (N)	3	1	4	1	★★★
3	Ferique Short Term Income Fund (R) (N)	2	1	5	0	★★★
4	Pursuit Money Market Fund (N)	2	1	4	1	★★1/2
5	Bissett Money Market Fund (R)	1	1	5	0	★★1/2
6	Beutel Goodman Money Market Fund (N)	1	1	5	0	★★1/2
7	Capstone Cash Management Fund (N)	1	1	4	1	★★1/2
8	Talvest Money Fund	0	1	4	1	★★
9	AMI Private Capital Money Market (N)	0	1	4	1	★★
10	CDA Money Market Fund (R) (N)	0	1	4	1	★★
11	Maxxum Money Market Fund (N)	0	1	4	1	★★
12	NN Money Market Fund (N)	0	1	4	1	★★
13	PH&N Canadian Money Market (R) (N)	0	1	4	1	★★
14	Elliott & Page Money Fund	0	1	3	2	★★

● ●

Table 1

THE HEAVY HITTERS *continued*

CANADIAN MONEY-MARKET FUNDS

		Bench-mark*	Vola-tility	Performance Quartile 1	Quartile 2	Overall Rating
15	C.I. Money Market Fund	0	1	3	2	★★
16	Industrial Cash Management Fund	0	1	3	2	★★
17	Green Line Cdn. Money Market (N)	0	1	3	2	★★
18	HRL Instant $$ Fund (N)	0	1	3	2	★★
19	MD Money Fund (R) (N)	0	1	4	0	★★
20	BPI T-Bill Fund	0	1	2	3	★1/2
21	Trans-Canada Money Market Fund	0	1	2	3	★1/2
22	Sceptre Money Market Fund (N)	0	1	3	1	★1/2
23	InvesNat Treasury Bill Plus Fund (R) (N)	0	1	1	4	★1/2
24	Lotus (MKW) Income Fund (R) (N)	0	1	1	4	★1/2
25	Trimark Interest Fund	0	1	0	5	★1/2
26	Manulife Vistafund 1 Short Term Sec.	0	1	2	1	★1/2
27	CIBC Premium T-Bill Fund (N)	0	1	1	3	★1/2
28	General Trust of Canada Money Mkt. (R) (N)	0	1	1	3	★1/2
29	Fonds Ficadre Money Market (N)	0	1	1	2	★
30	Mawer Canadian Money Market Fund (R) (N)	0	1	0	4	★
31	McLean Budden Money Market Fund (N)	0	1	1	2	★
32	Green Line Canadian T-Bill Fund (N)	0	1	0	3	★
33	Hongkong Bank Money Market Fund (N)	0	1	1	1	★

* Three-month Treasury Bill; (R) — Restricted; (C) — Closed to new members; (N) — No-load fund; Benchmark — number of times that a fund beat the benchmark from 1992 to 1996; Volatility — measures swings in fund returns on a scale of 1 to 10 (1 = low, 10 = high); Performance — number of times that a fund was in the first (top 25%) or second quartile (top 50%) from 1992 to 1996.

The benchmark used to compare Canadian money-market fund returns is the three-month treasury-bill rate. Over the past five calendar years, T-bill yields ranged from a high of 7.6% in 1995 to a low of 4.8% in 1996.

Ontario Teachers Group Fixed Value Fund ★★★

This no-load fund is sponsored by the Ontario Teachers Group of Toronto. It has $27 million in assets and charges below-average management expenses of $0.50 for every $100 in assets. The fund is available for sale only in Ontario.

Fonds de Professionnels Short-Term ★★★

This no-load fund, sponsored by the Federation of Medical Specialists of Quebec, has $27 million in assets and charges below-average management expenses of $0.40 for every $100 in assets. The fund is restricted to members of the association and their families.

Ferique Short Term Income Fund ★★★

Sponsored by the Ordre des Ingenieurs du Quebec, a professional engineers' association, this no-load fund has $44 million in assets and charges below-average management expenses of $0.41 for every $100 in assets. The fund is restricted to members of the association.

Pursuit Money Market Fund ★★1/2

This no-load fund is sponsored by Pursuit Financial Management Corporation of Toronto. It has $6 million in assets and charges below-average management expenses of $0.50 for every $100 in assets. The fund has a minimum initial investment requirement of $10,000.

Bissett Money Market Fund ★★1/2

This no-load fund, sponsored by Bissett & Associates Investment Management Ltd. of Calgary, has $23 million in assets and charges below-average management expenses of $0.50 for every $100 in assets. The fund has a minimum initial investment requirement of $10,000 and is available for sale only in Alberta, British Columbia, and Ontario.

Beutel Goodman Money Market Fund ★★1/2

Sponsored by Beutel Goodman Managed Fund Inc. of Toronto, this no-load fund has $94 million in assets and charges below-average management expenses of $0.63 for every $100 in assets.

Capstone Cash Management Fund ★★1/2

This no-load fund is sponsored by Hughes King & Co. Ltd. of Toronto. It has $3 million in assets and charges below-average management expenses of $0.60 for every $100 in assets.

Talvest Money Fund ★★

This front-end load fund, sponsored by Talvest Fund Management Inc., has $100 million in assets and charges below-average management expenses of $0.75 for every $100 in assets.

AMI Private Capital Money Market Fund ★★

Sponsored by AMI Partners Inc. of Montreal, this no-load fund has $2 million in assets and charges below-average management expenses of $0.75 for every $100 in assets. The fund has a minimum initial investment requirement of $50,000.

CDA Money Market Fund ★★

This no-load fund is sponsored by the Canadian Dental Association. It has $26 million in assets and charges below-average management expenses of $0.55 for every $100 in assets. The fund is available for sale only to members of the Canadian Dental Association.

Maxxum Money Market Fund ★★

This no-load fund, sponsored by London Fund Management Ltd., has $65 million in assets and charges below-average management expenses of $0.85 for every $100 in assets.

NN Money Market Fund ★★

Sponsored by the NN Life Insurance Company of Canada, this no-load segregated fund has $18 million in assets and charges below-average management expenses of $0.75 for every $100 in assets.

PH&N Canadian Money Market Fund ★★

This no-load fund is sponsored by the investment firm Phillips Hager & North of Vancouver. It has $523 million in assets and charges below-average management expenses of $0.48 for every $100 in assets. The fund has a minimum initial investment requirement of $25,000 for non-RRSP accounts and $5,000 for RRSP accounts.

Elliott & Page Money Fund ★★

This front-end load fund, sponsored by Elliott & Page Ltd. of Toronto, has $511 million in assets and charges below-average management expenses of $0.26 for every $100 in assets.

C.I. Money Market Fund ★★

Sponsored by C.I. Mutual Funds of Toronto, this load fund has $259 million in assets and charges below-average management expenses of $0.75 for every $100 in assets.

Industrial Cash Management Fund ★★

This front-end load fund is sponsored by the Mackenzie Financial Corporation. It has $355 million in assets and charges below-average management expenses of $0.50 for every $100 in assets.

Green Line Canadian Money Market Fund ★★

This no-load fund, sponsored by the Toronto-Dominion Bank, has $5.3 billion in assets and charges below-average management expenses of $0.83 for every $100 in assets.

HRL Instant $$ Fund ★★

Sponsored by HRL Funds Management Limited of Toronto, this no-load fund has $17 million in assets and charges below-average management expenses of $0.50 for every $100 in assets.

MD Money Fund ★★

This no-load fund is sponsored by MD Management Ltd. of Ottawa. It has $313 million in assets and charges below-average management expenses of $0.54 for every $100 in assets. The fund is available for sale only to members of the Canadian Medical Association and their families.

BPI T-Bill Fund ★1/2

This load fund, sponsored by BPI Mutual Funds of Toronto, has $186 million in assets and charges below-average management expenses of $0.65 for every $100 in assets.

Trans-Canada Money Market Fund ★1/2

Sponsored by Sagit Investment Management Limited of Vancouver, this load fund has $34 million in assets and charges below-average management expenses of $0.59 for every $100 in assets.

Sceptre Money Market Fund ★1/2

This no-load fund is sponsored by Sceptre Investment Counsel Ltd. of Toronto. It has $38 million in assets and charges below-average management expenses of $0.75 for every $100 in assets. The fund has a minimum initial investment requirement of $5,000.

InvesNat Treasury Bill Plus Fund ★1/2

This no-load fund, sponsored by the National Bank of Canada, has $401 million in assets and charges below-average management expenses of $0.77 for every $100 in assets.

Lotus Income Fund ★1/2

Sponsored by M. K. Wong Management Ltd. of Toronto, this no-load fund has $5 million in assets and charges below-average management expenses of $0.75 for every $100 in assets.

Trimark Interest Fund ★1/2

This front-end load fund is sponsored by Trimark Investment Management Inc. It has $661 million in assets and charges below-average management expenses of $0.75 for every $100 in assets.

Manulife Vistafund 1 Short Term Securities ★1/2

This front-end load segregated fund, sponsored by Manulife Financial, has $7 million in assets and charges above-average management expenses of $1.63 for every $100 in assets.

CIBC Premium T-Bill Fund ★1/2

Sponsored by the Canadian Imperial Bank of Commerce, this no-load fund has $1.9 billion in assets and charges below-average management expenses of $0.50 for every $100 in assets.

General Trust of Canada Money Market Fund ★1/2

This no-load fund is sponsored by the National Bank of Canada. It has $43 million in assets and charges above-average management expenses of $1.09 for every $100 in assets.

Fonds Ficadre Money Market Fund ★

This no-load fund, sponsored by Sogefonds MFQ Inc. of Quebec City, has $5 million in assets and charges above-average management expenses of $1.07 for every $100 in assets.

Mawer Canadian Money Market Fund ★

Sponsored by Mawer Investment Management of Calgary, this no-load fund has $41 million in assets and charges below-average management expenses of $0.57 for every $100 in assets. The fund has a minimum initial investment requirement of $25,000.

McLean Budden Money Market Fund ★

This no-load fund is sponsored by McLean Budden Limited of Toronto. It has $9 million in assets and charges below-average management expenses of $0.75 for every $100 in assets. The fund has a minimum initial investment requirement of $5,000.

Green Line Canadian T-Bill Fund ★

This no-load fund, sponsored by the Toronto-Dominion Bank, has $677 million in assets and charges below-average management expenses of $0.83 for every $100 in assets.

Hongkong Bank Money Market Fund ★

Sponsored by the Hongkong Bank of Canada, this no-load fund has $568 million in assets and charges below-average management expenses of $0.92 for every $100 in assets.

The Underachievers

There are 30 Canadian money-market funds that have failed to measure up to their peers. These Underachievers have consistently delivered *below*-average returns over the past one-, three-, and five-year periods. Collectively these Underachievers manage $8.8 billion in assets. The CIBC's Money Market Fund is the largest, with $1.7 billion in assets, and the Imperial Growth Money Market Fund is the smallest, with $2.3 million. Seventeen of the 30 Underachievers are no-load funds.

Table 2

THE UNDERACHIEVERS

CANADIAN MONEY-MARKET FUNDS

- AGF Money Market Account
- Atlas Canadian Money Market Fund*
- Atlas Canadian T-Bill Fund*
- BNP (Canada) Canadian Money Market*

Table 2

THE UNDERACHIEVERS *continued*
CANADIAN MONEY-MARKET FUNDS

- C.I. Short-Term Sector Shares
- Canada Trust Everest Money Market*
- CIBC Canadian T-Bill Fund*
- CIBC Money Market Fund*
- Cornerstone Gov't Money*
- Empire Money Market Fund*
- Fidelity Cdn. Short Term Asset Fund*
- Fonds Desjardins Monetaire
- GWL Money Market Fund (G) NL*
- Imperial Growth Money Market Fund
- Industrial Alliance Ecoflex Fund M
- Industrial Alliance Money Mkt. Fund*
- Industrial Short-Term Fund
- Investors Money Market Fund*
- Laurentian Money Market Fund*
- Manulife Vistafund 2 Short Term Sec.
- Maritime Life Money Market - A & C
- Metlife MVP Money Market Fund
- NAL-Canadian Money Market Fund
- National Life Money Market Fund
- NN T-Bill Fund
- Royal Trust Canadian Money Market*
- RoyFund Canadian Money Market Fund*
- Scotia Excelsior Money Market Fund*
- Scotia Excelsior T-Bill Fund*
- Spectrum United Canadian T-Bill

* denotes a no-load fund

Heavy Hitters vs Underachievers

Table 3 shows the difference in returns, over three time periods, between the Heavy Hitters and Underachievers in this category. Although money-market returns tend to cluster in a fairly narrow

181

range, the Heavy Hitters nevertheless posted returns that were, on average, about a full percentage point higher than the Underachievers'. In dollar terms, for an initial investment of $10,000, the average Heavy Hitter Canadian money-market fund would have returned a total of $12,824 over the past five years. For the same investment, the average Underachiever would have returned $12,224 — for a difference of $599 or 4.9%.

With respect to costs, the average Heavy Hitter charged management expenses of $0.69 for every $100 in assets, compared with $1.25 for the average Underachiever.

Table 3

HEAVY HITTERS vs UNDERACHIEVERS

CANADIAN MONEY-MARKET FUNDS

(Returns %)

	1-Year	3-Year*	5-Year*
• Heavy Hitters	3.5	5.1	5.1
• Underachievers	2.6	4.2	4.2

* annualized

CANADIAN MONEY-MARKET FUNDS
RANKINGS/RETURNS

Rank			Name of Fund	Returns (%)			Assets
(83)	(97)	(110)		(3.0)	(4.7)	(4.6)	
5-Yr	3-Yr	1-Yr		1-Yr	3-Yr	5-Yr	($mns)
-	-	68	Acadia Money Market Fund	2.9	-	-	0.7
-	81	39	Admax Cash Performance Fund	3.2	4.3	-	10.3
56	73	89	AGF Money Market Account (UA)	2.5	4.4	4.5	801.8
-	-	81	AIC Money Market Fund	2.7	-	-	65.7
48	4	1	Allstar Money Market Fund	8.3	5.7	4.6	3.7
17	36	41	AMI Private Capital Money Market (HH)	3.1	4.9	5.0	1.5
-	70	92	APEX Money Market Fund	2.5	4.5	-	11.1
50	55	69	Atlas Canadian Money Market Fund (UA)	2.9	4.6	4.5	300.0
66	78	90	Atlas Canadian T-Bill Fund (UA)	2.5	4.3	4.3	389.0
39	54	62	Batirente - Sec. Marche Monetaire	2.9	4.6	4.6	1.6
6	20	24	Beutel Goodman Money Market Fund (HH)	3.5	5.2	5.3	94.3
5	7	9	Bissett Money Market Fund (HH)	4.0	5.5	5.4	22.5
61	67	60	BNP (Canada) Canadian Money Market (UA)	2.9	4.5	4.4	6.0
20	22	16	BPI T-Bill Fund (HH)	3.5	5.1	5.0	185.9
15	24	28	C.I. Money Market Fund (HH)	3.4	5.1	5.0	259.4
83	97	91	C.I. Short-Term Sector Shares (UA)	2.5	2.9	2.9	38.4
59	53	43	Canada Life Money Market S-29	3.1	4.6	4.4	135.9
64	75	78	Canada Trust Everest Money Market (UA)	2.8	4.4	4.3	1027.1
7	11	29	Capstone Cash Management Fund (HH)	3.4	5.4	5.3	2.7
-	-	61	CCPE Money Market Fund	2.9	-	-	41.0
8	10	19	CDA Money Market (Canagex) (HH)	3.5	5.4	5.2	26.0
69	74	63	CIBC Canadian T-Bill Fund (UA)	2.9	4.4	4.2	668.4
67	69	57	CIBC Money Market Fund (UA)	2.9	4.5	4.3	1733.0
26	31	33	CIBC Premium T-Bill Fund (HH)	3.3	5.0	4.8	1933.4
-	30	27	Colonia Money Market Fund	3.4	5.0	-	3.9
44	46	53	Concorde Monetaire	3.0	4.7	4.6	7.3
58	71	93	Cornerstone Gov't Money (UA)	2.5	4.5	4.5	53.8
45	51	86	Dynamic Money Market Fund	2.6	4.6	4.6	235.6
22	33	35	Elliott & Page Money Fund (HH)	3.2	4.9	4.9	510.8
-	95	108	Elliott & Page T-Bill Fund	2.0	3.5	-	17.6
72	88	96	Empire Money Market Fund (UA)	2.4	4.1	4.0	40.6
-	-	104	Equitable Life Money Market Fund	2.2	-	-	6.9
52	66	47	Ethical Money Market Fund	3.0	4.5	4.5	101.2
4	5	8	Ferique Short Term Income Fund (HH)	4.1	5.7	5.6	44.0

CANADIAN MONEY-MARKET FUNDS
RANKINGS/RETURNS *cont'd*

Rank			Name of Fund	Returns (%)			Assets
(83)	(97)	(110)		(3.0)	(4.7)	(4.6)	
5-Yr	3-Yr	1-Yr		1-Yr	3-Yr	5-Yr	($mns)
70	84	97	Fidelity Cdn. Short Term Asset Fund (UA)	2.4	4.2	4.2	252.5
53	62	56	First Canadian Money Market	3.0	4.6	4.5	1863.3
-	63	59	First Cdn. T-Bill Fund	2.9	4.6	-	964.8
2	1	6	Fonds de Professionnels Short Term (HH)	4.1	5.9	5.6	27.0
51	82	70	Fonds Desjardins Monetaire (UA)	2.8	4.3	4.5	104.4
35	41	42	Fonds Ficadre Money Market (HH)	3.1	4.8	4.7	5.2
27	44	67	Fonds Optimum Epargne	2.9	4.7	4.8	2.0
30	45	74	GBC Money Market Fund	2.8	4.7	4.8	13.9
32	40	49	General Trust of Canada Money Mkt. (HH)	3.0	4.9	4.7	43.0
37	68	75	Global Strategy Money Market Fund	2.8	4.5	4.7	118.8
21	32	22	Green Line Canadian Money Mkt. (HH)	3.5	5.0	5.0	5257.8
34	38	25	Green Line Canadian T-Bill Fund (HH)	3.4	4.9	4.7	677.3
-	96	54	Growsafe Canadian Money Market	3.0	3.5	-	11.0
40	57	76	Guardian Canadian Money Market A	2.8	4.6	4.6	38.7
-	-	106	Guardian Canadian Money Market B	2.1	-	-	20.8
-	-	98	GWL Money Market Fund (G) DSC	2.4	-	-	36.6
80	93	107	GWL Money Market Fund (G) NL (UA)	2.1	3.8	3.9	118.1
38	37	30	Hongkong Bank Money Market Fund (HH)	3.3	4.9	4.7	568.1
18	18	23	HRL Instant $$ Fund (HH)	3.5	5.2	5.0	16.9
-	2	5	ICM Short Term Investment Fund	4.1	5.8	-	184.2
78	92	109	Imperial Growth Money Market Fund (UA)	2.0	3.9	3.9	2.3
74	86	84	Industrial Alliance Ecoflex Fund M (UA)	2.6	4.1	4.0	14.1
75	87	87	Industrial Alliance Money Mkt. Fund (UA)	2.5	4.1	4.0	10.4
19	26	36	Industrial Cash Management (HH)	3.2	5.0	5.0	354.8
73	85	101	Industrial Short-Term Fund (UA)	2.4	4.2	4.0	240.0
-	-	12	InvesNat Corporate Cash Mgmt. Fund	3.7	-	-	436.9
41	48	40	InvesNat Money Market Fund	3.2	4.7	4.6	529.0
24	34	26	InvesNat Treasury Bill Plus Fund (HH)	3.4	4.9	4.8	401.3
55	61	82	Investors Money Market Fund (UA)	2.7	4.6	4.5	533.5
-	-	48	Jones Heward Money Market Fund	3.0	-	-	2.7
62	72	85	Laurentian Money Market Fund (UA)	2.6	4.4	4.4	39.8
-	35	45	Leith Wheeler Money Market Fund	3.1	4.9	-	4.9
28	27	58	London Life Money Market	2.9	5.0	4.8	97.4
23	29	17	Lotus (MKW) Income Fund (HH)	3.5	5.0	4.9	4.8

CANADIAN MONEY-MARKET FUNDS
RANKINGS/RETURNS *cont'd*

Rank			Name of Fund	Returns (%)			Assets
(83)	(97)	(110)		(3.0)	(4.7)	(4.6)	
5-Yr	3-Yr	1-Yr		1-Yr	3-Yr	5-Yr	($mns)
-	-	102	Lutheran Life Money Market Fund	2.3	-	-	0.3
-	59	88	Manulife Cabot Money Market Fund	2.5	4.6	-	8.0
33	21	38	Manulife Vistafund 1 Short Term Sec. (HH)	3.2	5.1	4.7	7.1
76	79	94	Manulife Vistafund 2 Short Term Sec. (UA)	2.5	4.3	3.9	94.5
81	94	99	Maritime Life Money Market - A & C (UA)	2.4	3.7	3.8	54.8
31	39	44	Mawer Canadian Money Market Fund (HH)	3.1	4.9	4.7	41.4
10	16	14	Maxxum Money Market Fund (HH)	3.7	5.2	5.2	64.8
25	23	11	McLean Budden Money Market Fund (HH)	3.8	5.1	4.8	8.9
14	14	20	MD Money Fund (HH)	3.5	5.3	5.0	312.7
82	91	110	Metlife MVP Money Market Fund (UA)	1.9	3.9	3.8	13.6
-	-	100	Millennia III Money Market Fund 1	2.4	-	-	5.2
-	-	105	Millennia III Money Market Fund 2	2.2	-	-	6.8
47	56	80	Mutual Money Market	2.7	4.6	4.6	333.3
68	83	95	NAL-Canadian Money Market Fund (UA)	2.5	4.2	4.2	41.0
79	90	103	National Life Money Market Fund (UA)	2.3	4.0	3.9	10.1
49	52	32	National Trust Money Market Fund	3.3	4.6	4.6	189.0
12	19	18	NN Money Market Fund (HH)	3.5	5.2	5.1	18.4
71	89	79	NN T-Bill Fund (UA)	2.7	4.1	4.1	38.8
-	-	37	O'Donnell Money Market Fund	3.2	-	-	10.4
-	-	83	O'Donnell Short Term Fund	2.7	-	-	8.1
-	43	64	OHA Short Term Fund	2.9	4.7	-	62.1
1	9	13	Ontario Teachers Group Fixed Value (HH)	3.7	5.5	5.9	27.1
16	25	34	PH&N Canadian Money Market (HH)	3.2	5.0	5.0	522.8
3	8	4	Pursuit Money Market Fund (HH)	4.2	5.5	5.6	5.7
-	6	10	Royal Life Money Market Fund	3.9	5.6	-	36.4
65	76	65	Royal Trust Canadian Money Market (UA)	2.9	4.4	4.3	539.7
77	80	51	Royal Trust Canadian T-Bill Fund	3.0	4.3	3.9	529.4
63	77	71	RoyFund Canadian Money Market Fund (UA)	2.8	4.3	4.4	404.2
42	50	52	RoyFund Canadian T-Bill Fund	3.0	4.6	4.6	3899.4
13	17	15	Sceptre Money Market Fund (HH)	3.6	5.2	5.0	38.4
60	60	73	Scotia Excelsior Money Market Fund (UA)	2.8	4.6	4.4	496.6
-	28	31	Scotia Excelsior Premium T-Bill	3.3	5.0	-	1166.9
57	58	77	Scotia Excelsior T-Bill Fund (UA)	2.8	4.6	4.5	462.4
54	64	66	Spectrum United Canadian T-Bill (UA)	2.9	4.6	4.5	245.6

CANADIAN MONEY-MARKET FUNDS
RANKINGS/RETURNS *cont'd*

Rank			Name of Fund	Returns (%)			Assets
(83)	(97)	(110)		(3.0)	(4.7)	(4.6)	
5-Yr	3-Yr	1-Yr		1-Yr	3-Yr	5-Yr	($mns)
46	47	55	Spectrum United Savings Fund	3.0	4.7	4.6	13.7
-	3	2	Standard Life Ideal Money Market	4.2	5.8	-	40.8
-	12	3	Standard Life Money Market Fund	4.2	5.3	-	7.7
9	15	21	Talvest Money Fund (HH)	3.5	5.2	5.2	99.5
43	65	72	Templeton Treasury Bill Fund	2.8	4.6	4.6	167.4
11	13	7	Trans-Canada Money Market (Sagit) (HH)	4.1	5.3	5.1	33.8
29	42	46	Trimark Interest Fund (HH)	3.1	4.8	4.8	660.9
36	49	50	Trust Pret & Revenu Money Market	3.0	4.7	4.7	78.5

( ) under Rank indicates total number of funds; ( ) under Returns (%) indicates average annual return; (HH) — Heavy Hitter; (UA) — Underachiever; (RC) — Rookie Camp member.

CANADIAN MONEY-MARKET FUNDS/SUMMARY

Name of Fund	MER	Load	RRSP	Vola-tility	Company Number (App. 3)
Acadia Money Market Fund (R)	1.41	N	R		?
Admax Cash Performance Fund	1.12	Y	R	1	69
AGF Money Market Account	1.41	Y	R	1	3
AIC Money Market Fund	1.00	Y	R		4
Allstar Money Market Fund	2.58	Y	R		5
AMI Private Capital Money Market	0.75	N	R	1	7
APEX Money Market Fund (R)	1.55	Y	R		126
Atlas Canadian Money Market Fund	1.10	N	R	1	9
Atlas Canadian T-Bill Fund	1.30	N	R	1	9
Batirente - Sec. Marche Monetaire (R)	1.61	N	R	1	131
Beutel Goodman Money Market Fund	0.63	N	R	1	12
Bissett Money Market Fund (R)	0.50	Y	R	1	13
BNP (Canada) Cdn. Money Market	1.26	N	R	1	14
BPI T-Bill Fund	0.65	Y	R	1	15
C.I. Money Market Fund	0.75	Y	R	1	28
C.I. Short-Term Sector Shares	0.05	Y	F	1	28
Canada Life Money Market S-29	1.25	Y	R	1	18
Canada Trust Everest Money Market	1.09	N	R	1	19
Canada Trust Everest Premium Mon. (R)	0.30	N	R		19
Capstone Cash Management Fund	0.60	N	R	1	25
CCPE Money Market Fund (R)	1.75	N	R		21
CDA Money Market (R)	0.55	N	R	1	22
CIBC Canadian T-Bill Fund	0.95	N	R	1	29
CIBC Money Market Fund	0.95	N	R	1	29
CIBC Premium T-Bill Fund	0.50	N	R	1	29
Clarington Money Market Fund	0.75	Y	R		30
Colonia Money Market Fund	1.07	N	R	1	32
Concorde Monetaire (R)	1.17	Y	R	1	59
Cornerstone Gov't Money	1.30	N	R	1	73
Dynamic Money Market Fund	0.79	Y	R	1	40
Elliott & Page Money Fund	0.26	Y	R	1	41
Elliott & Page T-Bill Fund	1.95	Y	R		41
Empire Money Market Fund	1.54	N	R		42
Equitable Life Money Market Fund	1.75	Y	R		43
Ethical Money Market Fund (R)	1.24	N	R	1	44

CANADIAN MONEY-MARKET FUNDS/SUMMARY *cont'd*

Name of Fund	MER	Load	RRSP	Vola-tility	Company Number (App. 3)
Ferique Short Term Income Fund (R)	0.41	N	R	1	109
Fidelity Cdn. Short Term Asset Fund	1.25	Y	R	1	46
First Canadian Money Market	1.13	N	R	1	11
First Cdn. T-Bill Fund	1.06	N	R	1	11
Fonds de Professionnels Short Term (R)	0.40	N	R	1	50
Fonds Desjardins Monetaire (R)	1.11	N	R	1	37
Fonds Ficadre Money Market	1.07	N	R	1	128
Fonds Optimum Epargne (R)	0.75	N	R	1	107
GBC Money Market Fund (R)	0.75	N	R	1	52
General Trust of Canada Money Mkt. (R)	1.09	N	R	1	98
Global Strategy Money Market Fund	0.85	Y	R	1	54
Green Line Cdn. Money Market	0.83	N	R	1	139
Green Line Canadian T-Bill Fund	0.83	N	R	1	139
Growsafe Canadian Money Market	0.90	Y	R	1	141
GT Global Canada Money Market	0.80	Y	R		60
Guardian Canadian Money Market A	0.85	Y	R	1	61
Guardian Canadian Money Market B	1.57	Y	R		61
GWL Money Market Fund (G) DSC	1.51	Y	R		57
GWL Money Market Fund (G) NL	1.75	N	R	1	57
Hongkong Bank Money Market Fund	0.92	N	R	1	63
HRL Instant $$ Fund	0.50	N	R	1	64
ICM Short Term Investment Fund	0.12	N	R	1	68
Imperial Growth Money Market (C)	1.50	Y	R	1	65
Industrial Alliance Ecoflex Fund M	1.26	Y	R	1	66
Industrial Alliance Money Mkt. Fund (C)	1.50	N	R	1	66
Industrial Cash Management	0.50	Y	R	1	80
Industrial Short-Term Fund	1.23	Y	R	1	80
Infinity T-Bill Fund	1.00	Y	R		67
InvesNat Corporate Cash Mgmt. Fund (R)	0.52	N	R		98
InvesNat Money Market Fund (R)	1.05	N	R	1	98
InvesNat Treasury Bill Plus Fund (R)	0.77	N	R	1	98
Investors Money Market Fund	1.07	N	R	1	70
Jones Heward Money Market Fund	1.00	Y	R		72
Laurentian Money Market Fund	1.15	N	R	1	135
Leith Wheeler Money Market Fund (R)	0.60	N	R		74

CANADIAN MONEY-MARKET FUNDS/SUMMARY *cont'd*

Name of Fund	MER	Load	RRSP	Vola-tility	Company Number (App. 3)
London Life Money Market	1.30	Y	R	1	76
Lotus (MKW) Income Fund (R)	0.75	N	R	1	79
Lutheran Life Money Market Fund (R)	2.00	N	R		78
Manulife Cabot Money Market Fund	1.25	N	R		84
Manulife Vistafund 1 Short Term Sec.	1.63	Y	R	1	83
Manulife Vistafund 2 Short Term Sec.	2.38	Y	R	1	83
Maritime Life Money Market - B	1.50	Y	R		85
Maritime Life Money Market - A & C	1.50	Y	R		85
Mawer Cdn. Money Market Fund (R)	0.57	N	R	1	86
Maxxum Money Market Fund	0.85	N	R	1	87
McLean Budden Money Market Fund	0.75	N	R	1	89
MD Money Fund (R)	0.54	N	R	1	90
Metlife MVP Money Market Fund	1.72	Y	R	1	92
Middlefield Money Market Fund (R)	0.54	Y	R		93
Millennia III Money Market Fund 1	1.38	Y	R		65
Millennia III Money Market Fund 2	1.56	N	R		65
Mutual Money Market	1.03	N	R	1	97
NAL-Canadian Money Market Fund	1.25	Y	R	1	83
National Money Market Fund	1.60	Y	R	1	99
National Trust Money Market Fund (R)	1.16	N	R	1	100
NN Money Market Fund	0.75	N	R	1	102
NN T-Bill Fund	1.25	Y	R	1	102
North-West Life Ecoflex M	1.26	Y	R		103
O'Donnell Money Market Fund	1.10	Y	R		104
O'Donnell Short Term Fund	1.35	Y	R		104
OHA Short Term Fund	0.70	N	R	1	105
Ontario Teachers Group Fixed Value (R)	0.50	N	R	1	106
PH&N Canadian Money Market (R)	0.48	N	R	1	112
Pursuit Money Market Fund	0.50	N	R	1	117
Royal Life Money Market Fund	1.00	Y	R	1	120
Royal Premium Money Market Fund (R)	0.35	N	R		119
Royal Trust Canadian Money Market	1.00	N	R	1	119
Royal Trust Canadian T-Bill Fund	0.93	N	R	1	119
RoyFund Canadian Money Market Fund	1.00	N	R	1	119
RoyFund Canadian T-Bill Fund	0.93	N	R	1	119

CANADIAN MONEY-MARKET FUNDS/SUMMARY *cont'd*

Name of Fund	MER	Load	RRSP	Vola-tility	Company Number (App. 3)
Sceptre Money Market Fund	0.75	N	R	1	123
Scotia Excelsior Money Market Fund	1.00	N	R	1	124
Scotia Excelsior Premium T-Bill	0.52	N	R	1	124
Scotia Excelsior T-Bill Fund	1.00	N	R	1	124
Spectrum United Canadian T-Bill	0.92	Y	R	1	129
Spectrum United Savings Fund	1.00	N	R	1	129
Standard Life Ideal Money Market	1.00	Y	R	1	132
Standard Life Money Market Fund (R)	0.90	Y	R	1	133
Stone & Co. Flagship Mon. Mkt.	1.00	Y	R		134
Talvest Money Fund	0.75	Y	R	1	136
Templeton Treasury Bill Fund	0.75	N	R	1	137
Trans-Canada Money Market	0.59	Y	R	1	121
Trimark Interest Fund	0.75	Y	R	1	143
Trust Pret & Revenu Money Market	1.10	N	R	1	145
Average	1.02			1	

(R) — Restricted; (C) — Closed to new investors; MER — Management Expense Ratio; Load — fee charged; RRSP: R = 100% eligible, F = eligible as foreign content only, N = not eligible; Volatility — measures swings in performance on a scale of 1 to 10 (1 = low, 10 = high). Blank space indicates that fund is less than three years old. Fund company addresses may be found by number in Appendix 3.

19

● ●

Special Equity Funds

SOME MUTUAL FUNDS focus exclusively on specific industries and sectors of the economy. These funds invest only in companies in specialized areas such as real estate, resources, precious metals, or technology. Due to the cyclical nature of these industries and their narrow focus, these special equity funds are among the most volatile of all mutual funds. Although they offer investors the potential of substantial gains, there is also the possibility of considerable loss.

There are currently 92 special equity funds on the market. These funds manage $10.4 billion in assets. Over the five calendar years from 1992 to 1996, the best year for special equity funds was 1993, when returns averaged 48.1%. In contrast, the worst year was 1994, when returns averaged -2.8%. The average annual compound rate of return over the five-year period was 11.5%.

Special equity funds have an average volatility rating of 5.3, which is significantly above the average of 4.1 for all equity funds. The average fee for management expenses is $2.97 for every $100 in assets, which is well below last year's average of $3.32.

The Heavy Hitters

There are three Canadian special equity funds that have qualified for membership in the Heavy Hitters club this year. Each of these funds has consistently delivered *above*-average returns over the past one-, three-, and five-year periods. Collectively these Heavy Hitters manage a total of $916 million in assets. The 20/20 Canadian Resources Fund is the largest, with $347 million in assets, and the Universal Canadian Resource Fund is the smallest, with $280 million in assets. Two of the three Heavy Hitters are load funds.

• •

Table 1

THE HEAVY HITTERS

SPECIAL EQUITY FUNDS

		Bench- mark*	Vola- tility	Performance Quartile 1	Quartile 2	Overall Rating
1	20/20 Canadian Resources Fund	3	6	1	3	★1/2
2	Royal Energy Fund (N)	3	5	2	1	★1/2
3	Universal Canadian Resource Fund	3	6	3	0	★1/2

* TSE 300 Total Return Index; (R) — Restricted; (C) — Closed to new members; (N) — No-load fund; Benchmark — number of times that a fund beat the benchmark from 1992 to 1996; Volatility — measures swings in fund returns on a scale of 1 to 10 (1 = low, 10 = high); Performance — number of times that a fund was in the first (top 25%) or second quartile (top 50%) from 1992 to 1996.

The benchmark used to compare Canadian special equity fund returns is the TSE 300 Total Return Index. Over the past five calendar years, the index posted its highest return of 32.6% in 1993 and its lowest return of -1.4% in 1992. Returns were also negative in 1994, when the index dipped by 0.2%.

Universal Canadian Resource Fund ★1/2

This fund, sponsored by the Mackenzie Financial Corporation, was launched in 1978 and is managed by Fred Sturn. With $280 million in assets, it follows a top-down/value investment strategy. Investments in oil and gas, gold and precious metals, and paper and paper products account for over 65% of the fund's assets.

Its best year was 1993, when it posted a return of 89.2%, and its worst year was 1994, when its return was -8.4%. The fund's average annual compound return over the past five years was 29.0%. A load fund, it charges management expenses of $2.40 for every $100 in assets, which is lower than the group average of $2.97.

Royal Energy Fund ★1/2

This fund was started in 1980 and has been managed by Gordon Zive since 1994. The fund has $289 million in assets and follows a bottom-up/blend investment strategy. Investments in oil and gas account for over 90% of the fund's assets.

In 1993, its best year, the fund posted a return of 45.6%, and in 1994, its worst year, it returned -7.1%. Over the past five years, it yielded an average annual compound return of 23.1%. This no-load fund charges below-average management expenses of $2.32 for every $100 in assets.

20/20 Canadian Resources Fund ★1/2

This fund was launched in 1960 and has been managed by Robert Farquharson since 1975. With $347 million in assets, it follows a top-down/blend investment strategy. Close to 95% of the fund's assets are made up of investments in oil and gas, gold and precious metals, resource services, and metals and minerals.

The fund posted its highest return, 67.7%, in 1993, and its lowest, -12.1%, in 1994. Over the past five years, its average annual compound return was 25.0%. This is a load fund which charges management expenses of $2.88 for every $100 in assets, lower than the group average of $2.97.

The Rookie Camp

Four of the promising newer special equity funds, each with at least a three-year track record, are in the Rookie Camp this year. Each of these funds, listed below, posted *above*-average returns over the past one-, two-, and three-year periods.

Admax Global Health Sciences Fund follows a bottom-up/growth/sector investment strategy and has been managed by John Schroer since January 1996. A load fund, it has $156 million in assets and charges below-average management expenses of $2.58 for every $100 in assets.

First Canadian Resource Fund, sponsored by the Bank of Montreal, was launched in 1993 and is managed by Margot Naudie. With $82 million in assets, the fund follows a bottom-up/sector investment strategy. It is

193

a no-load fund and charges below-average management expenses of $2.20 for every $100 in assets.

Green Line Resource Fund, sponsored by the Toronto-Dominion Bank, was launched in 1993 and follows a sector investment strategy. A no-load fund, it has $160 million in assets and charges below-average management expenses of $2.12 for every $100 in assets.

Green Line Science & Technology Fund, also sponsored by the TD Bank, was launched in 1993 and is managed by the U.S. investment firm T. Rowe Price Investment Services Inc. With $177 million in assets, the fund follows a top-down/growth investment strategy. It is a no-load fund and charges below-average management expenses of $2.59 for every $100 in assets.

The Underachievers

There are five Canadian special equity funds that have failed to measure up to their peers. These Underachievers have consistently delivered *below*-average returns over the past one-, three-, and five-year periods. Collectively these Underachievers manage $840 million in assets. The Working Ventures Canadian Fund is the largest, with $820 million in assets, and the Allstar Adrian Day Gold Plus Fund is the smallest, with $0.4 million in assets. All five Underachievers are load funds.

Table 2

THE UNDERACHIEVERS

SPECIAL EQUITY FUNDS

- All-Canadian Resources Corporation
- Allstar Adrian Day Gold Plus Fund
- Goldfund Ltd. (CSA Mgmt.)
- Goldtrust (CSA Mgmt.)
- Working Ventures Canadian Fund Inc.

Heavy Hitters vs Underachievers

Table 3 shows the difference in returns, over three time periods, between the Heavy Hitters and Underachievers in this category. As can be seen, the Heavy Hitters posted returns that, on average, far outstripped the Underachievers'. In dollar terms, for an initial investment of $10,000, the average Heavy Hitter Canadian special equity fund would have returned a total of $31,382 over the past five years. For the same investment, the average Underachiever would have returned $14,898 — for a difference of $16,483 or 110.6%.

With respect to costs, the average Heavy Hitter charged management expenses of $2.53 for every $100 in assets, compared with $2.68 for the average Underachiever.

Table 3

HEAVY HITTERS vs UNDERACHIEVERS
SPECIAL EQUITY FUNDS
(Returns %)

	1-Year	3-Year*	5-Year*
• Heavy Hitters	20.0	11.3	25.7
• Underachievers	-19.4	-3.5	8.3

* annualized

SPECIAL EQUITY FUNDS
RANKINGS/RETURNS

Rank			Name of Fund	Returns (%)			Assets
(23)	(34)	(67)		(-1.8)	(6.8)	(14.5)	
5-Yr	3-Yr	1-Yr		1-Yr	3-Yr	5-Yr	($mns)
4	6	13	20/20 Canadian Resources Fund (HH)	10.3	12.9	25.0	347.0
-	-	10	20/20 Managed Futures Value Fund	11.7	-	-	101.1
-	1	38	Admax Global Health Sciences Fund (RC)	-0.6	30.9	-	155.8
16	29	55	All-Canadian Resources Corporation (UA)	-22.6	-1.8	11.2	3.9
20	30	52	Allstar Adrian Day Gold Plus Fund (UA)	-15.8	-2.0	3.6	0.4
-	-	64	Altamira Precious and Strategic Metals	-32.8	-	-	90.4
10	24	40	Altamira Resource Fund	-1.0	2.5	18.2	379.1
-	-	46	Altamira Science & Technology Fund	-3.9	-	-	73.3
11	27	61	BPI Canadian Resource Fund Inc.	-27.3	0.5	15.6	57.6
-	-	15	C.I. Covington Labour-Sponsored	9.9	-	-	102.2
-	-	62	Cambridge Precious Metals Fund	-28.3	-	-	5.3
9	26	67	Cambridge Resource Fund (Sagit)	-48.9	0.8	18.8	23.5
-	-	39	Canadian Medical Discoveries Fund	-0.6	-	-	250.0
-	34	32	Canadian Venture Opportunities Fund	2.2	-12.3	-	15.8
-	-	37	Capital Alliance Ventures Inc.	0.1	-	-	40.6
-	-	35	CIBC Canadian Resource Fund	1.0	-	-	104.3
-	-	29	CIBC Global Technology Fund	2.8	-	-	61.6
-	28	48	Contrarian Strategy Futures L.P.	-7.7	-1.3	-	0.4
-	-	49	Contrarian Strategy RRSP Futures	-11.2	-	-	2.1
-	-	8	DGC Entertainment Ventures Corp.	15.3	-	-	7.6
7	21	5	Dominion Equity Resource Fund Inc.	22.5	3.5	20.3	20.5
-	-	20	Dynamic Global Precious Metals Fund	7.9	-	-	37.4
-	-	22	Dynamic Global Resources Fund	6.9	-	-	109.5
8	25	60	Dynamic Precious Metals Fund	-26.8	1.6	18.9	320.3
-	-	3	Dynamic Real Estate Equity Fund	37.7	-	-	140.5
-	-	23	FESA Enterprise Venture Capital	6.4	-	-	8.4
-	10	30	First Canadian Resource Fund (RC)	2.8	9.5	-	81.6
13	19	34	First Heritage Fund	1.5	6.0	14.0	5.4
-	-	31	First Ontario LSIF Ltd.	2.7	-	-	22.3
18	16	24	Fonds de Sold. des Trav. du Quebec	5.0	7.2	5.3	1902.0
-	-	4	Friedberg Currency Fund	29.4	-	-	47.0
17	31	21	Friedberg Double Gold Plus Fund	7.1	-2.2	7.1	1.1
-	-	51	Global Manager - Gold Index Fund	-14.7	-	-	0.0
-	13	66	Global Strategy Gold Plus Fund	-36.5	9.2	-	116.6
15	33	63	Goldfund Ltd. (CSA Mgmt.) (UA)	-29.4	-9.9	12.0	4.8

SPECIAL EQUITY FUNDS
RANKINGS/RETURNS *cont'd*

Rank			Name of Fund	Returns (%)			Assets
(23)	(34)	(67)		(-1.8)	(6.8)	(14.5)	
5-Yr	3-Yr	1-Yr		1-Yr	3-Yr	5-Yr	($mns)
14	32	58	Goldtrust (CSA Mgmt.) (UA)	-25.8	-6.4	12.3	11.0
-	-	2	Green Line Energy Fund	37.7	-	-	114.8
-	-	56	Green Line Precious Metals Fund	-23.7	-	-	137.6
-	12	26	Green Line Resource Fund (RC)	3.9	9.3	-	160.1
-	2	36	Green Line Science & Tech. Fund (RC)	0.2	30.3	-	176.9
-	-	7	GT Global Health Care Class	15.4	-	-	319.0
-	-	18	GT Global Infrastructure Class	9.0	-	-	68.1
-	-	42	GT Global Natural Resources Class	-1.5	-	-	31.3
-	-	50	GT Global Telecommunication Class	-11.9	-	-	380.8
-	-	17	GWL Cdn. Resource Fund (A) DSC	9.0	-	-	18.9
-	-	19	GWL Cdn. Resource Fund (A) NL	8.7	-	-	26.4
-	17	11	Horizons 1 Multi-Asset Fund Inc.	11.4	6.2	-	22.0
12	4	9	Hyperion Global Science & Tech.	12.0	16.3	14.1	10.0
22	22	27	Investors Real Property Fund	3.8	3.5	1.6	424.2
2	5	54	Maxxum Natural Resource Fund	-19.9	15.7	28.5	89.7
5	9	65	Maxxum Precious Metals Fund	-33.2	11.6	23.7	18.2
-	-	33	Retrocom Growth Fund Inc.	1.6	-	-	33.7
6	8	1	Royal Energy Fund (HH)	39.2	11.7	23.1	289.1
23	20	41	Royal LePage Commercial Real Estate	-1.0	4.0	0.6	16.3
-	-	14	Royal Life Science & Technology	9.9	-	-	258.9
3	3	59	Royal Precious Metals Fund	-26.6	26.4	25.3	352.4
-	15	53	Scotia Excelsior Prec. Metals Fund	-19.7	7.7	-	61.9
-	7	44	Spectrum United Global Telecom.	-2.5	11.8	-	76.0
-	-	6	Sportfund Inc.	17.4	-	-	13.2
-	-	28	Standard Life Natural Resources	3.7	-	-	7.7
-	-	43	Triax Growth Fund Inc.	-1.6	-	-	161.5
-	-	47	Trillium Growth Capital Inc.	-5.6	-	-	8.4
1	14	12	Universal Canadian Resource Fund (HH)	10.5	9.1	29.0	279.9
-	11	57	Universal Precious Metals Fund	-24.1	9.4	-	116.7
-	-	16	VenGrowth Investment Fund Inc.	9.8	-	-	136.2
19	18	25	Working Opportunity Fund	5.0	6.1	4.2	158.6
21	23	45	Working Ventures Canadian Fund Inc. (UA)	-3.6	2.8	2.6	819.7

( ) under Rank indicates total number of funds; ( ) under Returns (%) indicates average annual return;
(HH) — Heavy Hitter; (UA) — Underachiever; (RC) — Rookie Camp member.

SPECIAL EQUITY FUNDS/SUMMARY

Name of Fund	MER	Load	RRSP	Vola-tility	Company Number (App. 3)
20/20 Canadian Resources Fund	2.88	Y	R	6	3
20/20 Managed Futures Value Fund	3.94	Y	R		3
Admax Global Health Sciences Fund	2.58	Y	F	5	69
Admax Global Technology Fund	2.60	Y	F		69
All-Canadian Resources Corporation (R)	2.00	Y	R	5	138
Allstar Adrian Day Gold Plus Fund	3.34	Y	F		5
Altamira Prec. and Strategic Metals	2.30	N	R		6
Altamira Resource Fund	2.28	N	R	5	6
Altamira Science & Technology Fund	2.31	N	F		6
B.E.S.T. Discoveries Fund	1.50	Y	R		154
BPI Canadian Resource Fund Inc.	2.90	Y	R	7	15
C.I. Covington Labour-Sponsored	4.49	Y	R		23
C.I. Global Financial Serv. Sector	2.47	Y	F		28
C.I. Global Health Sciences Sector	2.46	Y	F		28
C.I. Global Resource Sector Shares	2.45	Y	F		28
C.I. Global Tech. Sector Shares	2.49	Y	F		28
C.I. Global Telecom. Sector Shares	2.52	Y	F		28
Cambridge Precious Metals Fund	2.81	Y	R		121
Cambridge Resource Fund	2.92	Y	R	10	121
Canadian Medical Discoveries Fund	5.00	Y	R		115
Canadian Sci. & Tech. Growth Fund	3.50	Y	R		136
Canadian Venture Opportunities Fund	9.11	Y	R		24
Capital Alliance Ventures Inc.	4.87	Y	R		114
Centerfire Growth Fund Inc.	1.80	Y	R		153
CIBC Canadian Resource Fund	2.15	N	R		29
CIBC Energy Fund	2.00	N	R		29
CIBC Global Technology Fund	2.25	N	F		29
CIBC North American Demographics	2.50	N	F		29
CIBC Precious Metals Fund	2.00	N	R		29
Clarington Global Communications	2.95	Y	F		30
Contrarian Strategy Futures L.P.	2.00	Y	N	5	47
Contrarian Strategy RRSP Futures	1.21	Y	R		47
DGC Entertainment Ventures Corp.	4.90	Y	R		38
Dominion Equity Resource Fund Inc.	2.10	N	R	6	39
Dynamic Canadian Real Estate Fund	2.00	Y	R		40

SPECIAL EQUITY FUNDS/SUMMARY *cont'd*

Name of Fund	MER	Load	RRSP	Vola-tility	Company Number (App. 3)
Dynamic Global Precious Metals Fund	2.97	Y	F		40
Dynamic Global Resources Fund	2.80	Y	F		40
Dynamic Precious Metals Fund	2.49	Y	R	6	40
Dynamic Real Estate Equity Fund	3.24	Y	F		40
FESA Enterprise Venture Capital	6.20	Y	R		45
First Canadian Global Sci. & Tech.	2.01	N	F		11
First Canadian Precious Metals Fund	2.07	N	N		11
First Canadian Resource Fund	2.20	N	R	5	11
First Heritage Fund	4.10	Y	R	5	56
First Ontario LSIF Ltd.	3.86	Y	R		49
Fonds de Sold. des Trav. du Quebec	1.60	N	R		155
Friedberg Currency Fund	5.38	N	N		51
Friedberg Diversified Fund ($US)	4.30	N	N		51
Friedberg Double Gold Plus Fund	0.00	Y	R	4	51
Global Manager - Gold Index Fund (R)	1.00	Y	N		10
Global Strategy Gold Plus Fund	2.89	Y	R	9	10
Goldfund Ltd. (CSA Mgmt.)	2.96	Y	F	7	35
Goldtrust (CSA Mgmt.)	2.42	Y	R	6	35
Green Line Energy Fund	2.13	N	R		139
Green Line Health Sciences Fund	2.64	N	F		139
Green Line Precious Metals Fund	2.13	N	R		139
Green Line Resource Fund	2.12	N	R	5	139
Green Line Science & Tech. Fund	2.59	N	F	6	139
GT Global Health Care Class	2.88	Y	F		60
GT Global Infrastructure Class	2.90	Y	F		60
GT Global Natural Resources Class	2.95	Y	F		60
GT Global Telecommunication Class	2.86	Y	F		60
GWL Cdn. Resource Fund (A) DSC	3.00	Y	R		57
GWL Cdn. Resource Fund (A) NL	3.24	N	R		57
Horizons 1 Multi-Asset Fund Inc.	10.00	Y	N	3	47
Hyperion Global Science & Tech.	2.25	Y	F	3	136
Investors Cdn. Natural Resource	2.85	Y	R		70
Investors Real Property Fund	2.39	Y	R	1	70
Marathon Resource Fund	2.50	Y	R		48
Maxxum Natural Resource Fund	2.25	Y	R	6	87

SPECIAL EQUITY FUNDS/SUMMARY *cont'd*

Name of Fund	MER	Load	RRSP	Vola-tility	Company Number (App. 3)
Maxxum Precious Metals Fund	2.25	Y	R	9	87
Middlefield Global Technology Fund	2.75	Y	F		93
O'Donnell World Prec. Metals Fund	2.90	Y	F		104
Retrocom Growth Fund Inc.	5.04	Y	R		118
Royal Energy Fund	2.32	N	R	5	119
Royal LePage Commercial Real Estate	3.40	N	R	2	119
Royal Life Science & Technology	2.81	N	F		120
Royal Precious Metals Fund	2.21	N	R	8	119
Scotia Excelsior Prec. Metals Fund	2.19	N	R	7	124
Spectrum United Cdn. Resource Fund	2.35	Y	R		129
Spectrum United Global Telecom.	2.55	Y	F		129
Sportfund Inc.	5.54	Y	R		130
Standard Life Natural Resources	2.00	Y	R		133
Triax Growth Fund Inc.	4.62	Y	R		142
Trillium Growth Capital Inc.	5.60	Y	R		16
Universal Canadian Resource Fund	2.40	Y	R	6	80
Universal Precious Metals Fund	2.41	Y	R		80
Universal World Science & Tech.	2.00	Y	F		80
Valorem Demographic Trends Fund	2.00	Y	F		152
VenGrowth Investment Fund Inc.	4.00	Y	R		8
Working Opportunity Fund	3.30	N	R	1	149
Working Ventures Canadian Fund Inc.	2.67	Y	R	1	150
Average	2.97			5.3	

(R) — Restricted; (C) — Closed to new investors; MER — Management Expense Ratio; Load — fee charged; RRSP: R = 100% eligible, F = eligible as foreign content only, N = not eligible; Volatility — measures swings in performance on a scale of 1 to 10 (1 = low, 10 = high). Blank space indicates that fund is less than three years old. Fund company addresses may be found by number in Appendix 3.

PART FOUR

· ·

HOW INTERNATIONAL MUTUAL FUNDS RATE

20

● ●

International Equity Funds

INTERNATIONAL EQUITY FUNDS invest primarily in a diversified portfolio of stocks of companies from around the world, with the basic objective of achieving long-term capital appreciation. International funds spread their risk by diversifying investments on a worldwide basis. This way they are able to take advantage of high-growth regions as well as exploit the timing of stock-market cycles in different countries. As a result, international equity funds tend to be less volatile than funds that invest in a particular country or region of the world.

There are 145 international equity funds currently on the market. These funds manage a total of $40.2 billion in assets. Over the five calendar years from 1992 to 1996, the best year for international equity funds was 1993, when returns averaged 31.3%. In contrast, the worst year was 1994, when returns averaged 2.3%. The average annual compound rate of return over the five-year period was 12.1%.

International equity funds have an average volatility rating of 3.3, which is below the average of 4.1 for all equity funds. The average fee for management expenses is $2.29 for every $100 in assets, which is up slightly from last year's average of $2.26.

The Heavy Hitters

There are 16 international equity funds that have qualified for membership in the Heavy Hitters club this year. Each of these funds has consistently delivered *above*-average returns over the past one-, three-, and five-year periods. Collectively these Heavy Hitters manage a total of $26.6 billion in assets. The Templeton Growth Fund is the largest, with $7.6 billion in assets, and the Special Opportunities Fund is the smallest, with $7.5 million in assets. Thirteen of the 16 Heavy Hitters are load funds.

●●

Table 1

THE HEAVY HITTERS

INTERNATIONAL EQUITY FUNDS

		Bench-mark*	Vola-tility	Performance Quartile 1	Performance Quartile 2	Overall Rating
1	Templeton Growth Fund Ltd.	3	3	3	2	★★1/2
2	Templeton International Stock Fund	3	3	3	2	★★1/2
3	Trimark Fund	3	3	3	2	★★1/2
4	MD Growth Fund (R) (N)	3	3	3	1	★★1/2
5	Trimark Select Growth Fund	2	3	3	1	★★
6	Empire International Fund	3	3	1	3	★★
7	Canada Life U.S. & Int'l Equity S-34	2	3	3	0	★★
8	Investors Growth Portfolio Fund	2	3	2	1	★1/2
9	Investors North American Growth	2	3	2	1	★1/2
10	Investors Special Fund	2	3	2	1	★1/2
11	Dynamic International Fund	3	4	1	2	★1/2
12	Fidelity International Portfolio	2	3	1	3	★1/2
13	Special Opportunities Fund (R)	3	5	2	1	★1/2
14	National Global Equities Fund	2	3	1	2	★1/2
15	Cornerstone Global Fund (N)	1	3	2	2	★1/2
16	Mawer World Investment Fund (R) (N)	2	3	1	2	★1/2

* Morgan Stanley World Index; (R) — Restricted; (C) — Closed to new members; (N) — No-load fund; Benchmark — number of times that a fund beat the benchmark from 1992 to 1996; Volatility — measures swings in fund returns on a scale of 1 to 10 (1 = low, 10 = high); Performance — number of times that a fund was in the first (top 25%) or second quartile (top 50%) from 1992 to 1996.

The benchmark used to compare international equity fund returns is the Morgan Stanley World Index, measured in Canadian dollars. Over the past five calendar years, the index posted its highest return of 28.1% in 1993 and its lowest return of 4.9% in 1992.

Templeton Growth Fund Ltd. ★★1/2

This fund was launched in 1954 and has been managed by Mark Holowesko since 1985. With $7.6 billion in assets, it follows a bottom-up/value investment strategy. About 34% of the fund's portfolio is invested in Europe, 33% in North America, and 8% in Asia.

Its best year was 1993, when it posted a return of 36.3%, and its worst year was 1994, when its return was 3.8%. The fund's average annual compound return over the past five years was 16.2%. A load fund, it charges management expenses of $2.00 for every $100 in assets, which is lower than the group average of $2.29.

Templeton International Stock Fund ★★1/2

This fund, Templeton's second international Heavy Hitter, was started in 1989 and is managed by Don Reed. The fund has $3.4 billion in assets and follows a bottom-up/value investment strategy. Investments in Europe account for 57% of the fund's assets, with Australia and New Zealand accounting for another 10% and Asia 8%.

In 1993, its best year, the fund posted a return of 48.2%, and in 1994, its worst year, it returned 5.2%. Over the past five years, it yielded an average annual compound return of 19.3%. This load fund charges above-average management expenses of $2.51 for every $100 in assets.

Trimark Fund ★★1/2

This fund was launched in 1981 and is managed by the investment team of Robert Krembil, Angela Eaton, and Richard Jenkins. With $2.7 billion in assets, it follows a bottom-up/growth investment strategy. Investments in the United States account for 62% of the fund's portfolio and Japan 7%.

The fund posted its highest return, 31.6%, in 1993, and its lowest, 14.7%, in 1996. Over the past five years, its average annual compound return was 19.8%. This is a load fund, sold only on a front-end basis, which charges management expenses of $1.52 for every $100 in assets, lower than the group average of $2.29.

MD Growth Fund ★★1/2

This fund was launched in 1969 and is managed by Marvin & Palmer Associates Inc. and Templeton International. With $2.7 billion in assets, it follows a top-down/blend investment strategy. About 28% of the fund's portfolio is invested in the United States, 7% in France, and 6% in the United Kingdom.

Its best year was 1993, when it posted a return of 44.9%, and its worst year was 1994, when its return was -1.1%. The fund's average annual compound return over the past five years was 16.4%. A no-load fund, it charges management expenses of $1.29 for every $100 in assets, which is considerably lower than the group average of $2.29. The fund is available only to members of the Canadian Medical Association and their families.

Trimark Select Growth Fund ★★

This fund was started in 1989 and is similar to the Trimark Fund except that the Select Growth Fund can be purchased on a back-end load. This fund is also managed by the investment team of Robert Krembil, Angela Eaton, and Richard Jenkins. The fund has $1.5 billion in assets and follows a bottom-up/growth investment strategy. Investments in the United States account for 62% of the fund's portfolio and Japan 7%.

In 1992, its best year, the fund posted a return of 27.8%, and in 1994, its worst year, it returned 13.5%. Over the past five years, it yielded an average annual compound return of 17.6%. This load fund charges slightly below-average management expenses of $2.25 for every $100 in assets.

Empire International Fund ★★

This segregated fund, sponsored by the Empire Life Insurance Company, was launched in 1989 and has been managed by Catharina van Berkel since 1993. With $86 million in assets, it follows a bottom-up/value investment strategy. About 60% of the fund's portfolio is invested in North America, 9% in Australia, and 8% in Japan.

The fund posted its highest return, 31.8%, in 1993, and its lowest, -1.5%, in 1994. Over the past five years, its average annual compound return was 14.7%. This is a load fund which charges management expenses of $2.56 for every $100 in assets, higher than the group average of $2.29.

Canada Life U.S. & International Equity S-34 Fund ★★

This segregated fund was launched in 1984 and is managed by Diana Haflidson, Tom Tibbles, and Gary Kondrat. With $450 million in assets, it follows a bottom-up/blend investment strategy. Investments in the United States account for 44% of the fund's assets, with another 13% in Japan and 5% in the United Kingdom.

Its best year was 1993, when it posted a return of 27.3%, and its worst year was 1994, when its return was 2%. The fund's average annual compound return over the past five years was 16.9%. A load fund, sold only on a deferred basis, it charges management expenses of $2.40 for every $100 in assets, which is slightly higher than the group average of $2.29.

Investors Growth Portfolio Fund ★1/2

This fund, which was launched in 1989, invests in a number of the Investors group of funds and has $550 million in assets. Forty percent of the fund's portfolio is invested in the Global Fund, 20% each in the Canadian Equity Fund and the U.S. Growth Fund, and 10% each in the Special Fund and the North American Fund.

In 1993, its best year, the fund posted a return of 26.4%, and in 1992, its worst year, it returned 5.3%. Over the past five years, it yielded an average annual compound return of 16.0%. A load fund, it charges management expenses of only $0.18 for every $100 in assets. This low figure is, however, over and above the management fees levied by the individual funds in the portfolio and represents an additional charge for administration purposes.

Investors North American Growth Fund ★1/2

This fund, Investors' second international Heavy Hitter, was launched in 1957 and has been managed by Bill Chornous since January 1995. With $1.6 billion in assets, it follows a bottom-up/growth investment strategy. About 44% of the fund's portfolio is invested in foreign equities, with another 47% in domestic equities.

The fund posted its highest return, 18.0%, in 1993, and its lowest,

4.8%, in 1994. Over the past five years, its average annual compound return was 15.3%. This is a load fund which charges management expenses of $2.38 for every $100 in assets, slightly higher than the group average of $2.29.

Investors Special Fund ★1/2

This fund, Investors' third international Heavy Hitter, was launched in 1967 and has been managed by Bill Chornous since January 1994. With $480 million in assets, it follows a bottom-up/growth investment strategy. Over 38% of the fund's portfolio is invested in foreign equities and 56% in domestic equities.

Its best year was 1993, when it posted a return of 22.3%, and its worst year was 1994, when its return was -1.2%. The fund's average annual compound return over the past five years was 15.1%. A load fund, it charges management expenses of $2.39 for every $100 in assets, which is slightly higher than the group average of $2.29.

Dynamic International Fund ★1/2

This fund was started in 1985 and is managed by the firm's investment team. The fund has $61 million in assets and follows a bottom-up/value investment strategy. About 85% of the fund's portfolio is invested in foreign equities, with another 9% in cash.

In 1993, its best year, the fund posted a return of 34.1%, and in 1994, its worst year, it returned -2.8%. Over the past five years, it yielded an average annual compound return of 14.6%. This load fund charges above-average management expenses of $2.78 for every $100 in assets.

Fidelity International Portfolio ★1/2

This fund was launched in 1987 and has been managed by Dick Habermann since March 1993. With $1.6 billion in assets, it follows a bottom-up/growth investment strategy. About 45% of the fund's port-folio is invested in the United States, 11% in Japan, and 7% in the United Kingdom.

The fund posted its highest return, 35.1%, in 1993, and its lowest, 2.9%, in 1992. Over the past five years, its average annual compound return was 16.6%. This is a load fund which charges management expenses of $2.76 for every $100 in assets, higher than the group average of $2.29.

Special Opportunities Fund ★1/2

This fund, sponsored by the investment firm MOF Management Ltd. of Vancouver, was launched in 1990 and has been managed by Channing Buckland since its inception. With $8 million in assets, it follows a growth investment strategy. About 52% of the fund's portfolio is invested in common stocks and 48% in cash and short-term securities. Its best year was 1993, when it posted a return of 33.2%, and its worst year was 1994, when its return was -13.7%. The fund's average annual compound return over the past five years was 19.9%. A load fund, sold only on a front-end basis, it charges management expenses of $2.14 for every $100 in assets, which is lower than the group average of $2.29.

National Global Equities Fund ★1/2

This segregated fund was started in 1993 and has been co-managed by James Fairweather of the Scottish investment firm Martin Currie Inc. and Thomas Dea of National Life since 1989. The fund has $53 million in assets and follows a top-down/growth investment strategy. About 29% of the fund's portfolio is invested in Europe, 17% in North America, 14% in Asia, and 12% in Latin America.

In 1993, its best year, the fund posted a return of 37.8%, and in 1994, its worst year, it returned 2.1%. Over the past five years, it yielded an average annual compound return of 13.0%. This load fund, sold only on a deferred basis, charges slightly above-average management expenses of $2.40 for every $100 in assets.

Cornerstone Global Fund ★1/2

This fund, sponsored by the Laurentian Bank of Canada, was launched in 1985 and has been managed since April 1993 by James Shakin of the Boston-based investment firm Wellington Management Company. With $16 million in assets, it follows a bottom-up/growth investment strategy. About 37% of the fund's portfolio is invested in the United States, 18% in Japan, 8% in the United Kingdom, and 7% in France.

The fund posted its highest return, 17.9%, in 1995, and its lowest, 3.9%, in 1994. Over the past five years, its average annual compound return was 14.2%. This is a no-load fund which charges management expenses of $2.75 for every $100 in assets, higher than the group average of $2.29.

Mawer World Investment Fund ★1/2

This fund was launched in 1987 and has been managed by Gerald Cooper-Key since its inception. With $41 million in assets, it follows a bottom-up/blend investment strategy. About 55% of the fund's portfolio is invested in Europe, 21% in Asia, and 11% in Latin America.

Its best year was 1993, when it posted a return of 36.7%, and its worst year was 1994, when its return was 4.1%. The fund's average annual compound return over the past five years was 14.3%. A no-load fund, it charges management expenses of $1.29 for every $100 in assets, which is considerably lower than the group average of $2.29. The fund has a minimum initial investment requirement of $25,000.

The Rookie Camp

Nine of the promising newer international equity funds, each with at least a three-year track record, are in the Rookie Camp this year. Each of these funds, listed below, posted *above*-average returns over the past one-, two-, and three-year periods.

Clean Environment International Equity Fund, sponsored by Clean Environment Mutual Fund Ltd. of Toronto, was launched in 1993 and follows a bottom-up/value investment strategy. The fund has been managed by Ian Ihnatowycz since its inception. A load fund, it has $7 million in assets and charges above-average management expenses of $3.25 for every $100 in assets.

Fonds de Professionnels International Equity Fund, sponsored by the Quebec Federation of Medical Specialists, was launched in 1992 and is co-managed by the investment firms Ark Asset Management, Lopresti Gabbay & Associates, and Les Conseillers Financiers du St-Laurent. With $70 million in assets, the fund follows a top-down/growth investment strategy. It is a no-load fund and charges well-below-average management expenses of $0.75 for every $100 in assets. The fund is available for sale only to members of the association.

Greystone Managed Global Fund, sponsored by Greystone Capital Management Inc. of Regina, is managed by Mark Schoenhals and David McCaslin of the investment firm Vontobel U.S.A. Inc. The fund has $43 million in assets and follows a bottom-up/value investment strategy. A no-load fund, it charges above-average management expenses of $2.46 for every $100 in assets. The fund is available for sale only in Alberta, British Columbia, and Ontario and has a minimum initial investment requirement of $10,000.

ICM International Equity Fund, sponsored by Integra Capital Management Corporation of Toronto, was launched in 1993 and follows a top-down/ blend investment strategy. The fund is managed by the investment firms Brinson Partners Inc. and UBS International Investment London Ltd. A no-load fund, it has $49 million in assets and charges well-below-average management expenses of $0.35 for every $100 in assets. The fund has a minimum initial investment requirement of $10,000.

Ivy Foreign Equity Fund, sponsored by the Mackenzie Financial Corporation, was launched in 1992 and has been managed by Bill Kanko since May 1997. With $332 million in assets, the fund follows a bottom-up/blend investment strategy. It is a load fund and charges slightly above-average management expenses of $2.40 for every $100 in assets.

OHA Foreign Equity Fund, sponsored by OHA Investment Management Ltd., a wholly owned subsidiary of the Ontario Hospital Association, is managed by Rick Hutcheon. The fund has $2 million in assets and follows a bottom-up/value investment strategy. A no-load fund, it charges below-average management expenses of $1.70 for every $100 in assets. The fund is available for sale only in Ontario.

Optima Strategy International Equity Fund, sponsored by Loring Ward Investment Counsel Ltd. of Winnipeg, was launched in 1994 and follows a top-down/blend investment strategy. The fund is managed by the investment firm CS First Boston Investment Management Limited. A load fund, it has $93 million in assets and charges considerably below-average management expenses of $0.47 for every $100 in assets.

PH&N North American Equity Fund, sponsored by the investment firm Phillips Hager & North of Vancouver, was launched in 1992 and is managed by the firm's equity research team. With $64 million in assets, the fund follows a bottom-up/growth investment strategy. It is a no-load fund and charges well-below-average management expenses of $1.18 for every $100 in assets. The fund has a minimum initial investment requirement of $25,000 for non-RRSP accounts and $5,000 for RRSP accounts.

Trimark - The Americas Fund, sponsored by Trimark Investment Management Inc., is co-managed by Patricia Perez-Coutts and Richard Whiting. The fund has $369 million in assets and follows a bottom-up/growth investment strategy. A load fund, it charges above-average management expenses of $2.53 for every $100 in assets.

The Underachievers

There are 14 international equity funds that have failed to measure up to their peers. These Underachievers have consistently delivered *below-average* returns over the past one-, three-, and five-year periods. Collectively these Underachievers manage $1.3 billion in assets. The Laurentian Commonwealth Fund is the largest, with $293 million in assets, and the Cambridge Global Fund is the smallest, with $1.5 million in assets. Six of the 14 Underachievers are load funds.

Table 2

THE UNDERACHIEVERS

INTERNATIONAL EQUITY FUNDS

- Altamira Global Diversified Fund*
- Cambridge Global Fund
- Canada Trust Everest Int'l Equity*
- Capstone Int'l Investment Trust*
- Fonds Desjardins International*
- GBC International Growth Fund*
- General Trust of Canada Int'l*
- Laurentian Commonwealth Fund Ltd.
- Laurentian International Fund Ltd.
- Mackenzie Sentinel Global Fund*
- McLean Budden Pooled Offshore Eq.*
- Spectrum United Global Equity Fund

Table 2

THE UNDERACHIEVERS *continued*
INTERNATIONAL EQUITY FUNDS

- Spectrum United Global Growth Fund
- Universal World Equity Fund

---

* denotes a no-load fund

Heavy Hitters vs Underachievers

Table 3 shows the difference in returns, over three time periods, between the Heavy Hitters and Underachievers in this category. As can be seen, the Heavy Hitters posted returns that were, on average, significantly higher than the Underachievers'. In dollar terms, for an initial investment of $10,000, the average Heavy Hitter international equity fund would have returned a total of $21,185 over the past five years. For the same investment, the average Underachiever would have returned $15,386 — for a difference of $5,799 or 37.7%.

With respect to costs, the average international equity Heavy Hitter charged management expenses of $2.10 for every $100 in assets, compared with $2.16 for the average Underachiever.

Table 3

HEAVY HITTERS vs UNDERACHIEVERS
INTERNATIONAL EQUITY FUNDS
(Returns %)

	1-Year	3-Year*	5-Year*
• Heavy Hitters	19.6	14.5	16.2
• Underachievers	1.4	4.2	9.0

---

* annualized

INTERNATIONAL EQUITY FUNDS
RANKINGS/RETURNS

Rank			Name of Fund	Returns (%)			Assets
(50)	(74)	(118)		(12.9)	(9.7)	(12.8)	
5-Yr	3-Yr	1-Yr		1-Yr	3-Yr	5-Yr	($mns)
-	-	115	20/20 Aggressive Global Stock Fund	-1.9	-	-	53.7
20	68	36	Admax International Fund	16.4	4.9	13.3	20.6
-	-	5	AGF International Value Fund	25.1	-	-	809.3
-	34	66	AGF RSP Int'l Equity Allocation	12.2	10.7	-	272.0
-	-	59	AGF World Equity Fund	13.3	-	-	70.8
-	51	21	AIC World Equity Fund	19.4	8.2	-	43.7
44	43	108	Altamira Global Diversified Fund (UA)	5.7	9.0	9.8	49.8
28	52	58	Atlas Global Value Fund	13.4	7.9	12.3	16.3
-	-	83	Azura Growth Pooled	10.5	-	-	24.1
-	63	71	Beutel Goodman International Equity	11.4	5.7	-	20.7
-	-	1	Bissett Multinational Growth Fund	31.9	-	-	16.7
25	27	32	BPI Global Equity Value Fund	16.9	11.4	12.4	315.7
-	-	4	BPI Global Opportunities Fund	27.1	-	-	30.9
-	53	50	BPI Global Small Companies Fund	14.4	7.8	-	108.7
-	56	69	C.I. Global Equity RSP Fund	12.0	7.5	-	284.5
36	48	40	C.I. Global Fund	15.6	8.3	11.2	788.7
38	54	52	C.I. Global Sector Shares	14.2	7.6	10.8	168.5
45	49	20	Cambridge Americas Fund (Sagit)	19.5	8.3	8.9	1.8
50	74	118	Cambridge Global Fund (Sagit) (UA)	-46.5	-15.1	-3.9	1.5
6	3	7	Canada Life U.S. & Int'l Equity S-34 (HH)	23.2	17.2	16.9	449.4
43	62	81	Canada Trust Everest Int'l Equity (UA)	10.9	5.9	10.0	202.7
27	36	9	Canada Trust Everest North American	21.6˙	10.6	12.3	37.6
30	45	116	Capstone Int'l Investment Trust (UA)	-4.0	8.9	12.2	2.0
-	-	94	CCPE Global Equity	8.7	-	-	58.4
-	-	91	CDA International Equity (KBSH)	9.5	-	-	5.4
40	41	35	CIBC Global Equity Fund	16.8	9.1	10.7	186.3
-	16	39	Clean Environment Int'l Equity Fund (RC)	15.7	13.0	-	7.0
-	-	112	Concorde International Fund	3.7	-	-	4.0
19	15	48	Cornerstone Global Fund (HH)	14.9	13.2	14.2	16.1
10	28	77	Cundill Value Fund	11.0	11.4	16.3	458.3
35	22	30	Dynamic Global Millennia Fund	17.1	12.6	11.3	16.6
17	18	34	Dynamic International Fund (HH)	16.9	12.9	14.6	60.7
-	-	56	Elliott & Page Global Equity Fund	13.6	-	-	43.4
16	17	15	Empire International Fund (HH)	20.2	13.0	14.7	85.7

INTERNATIONAL EQUITY FUNDS
RANKINGS/RETURNS *cont'd*

Rank			Name of Fund	Returns (%)			Assets
(50)	(74)	(118)		(12.9)	(9.7)	(12.8)	
5-Yr	3-Yr	1-Yr		1-Yr	3-Yr	5-Yr	($mns)
-	-	49	Equitable Life International Fund	14.5	-	-	19.7
-	65	82	Ferique International Fund	10.6	5.4	-	20.5
7	10	16	Fidelity International Portfolio (HH)	20.1	13.7	16.6	1592.8
-	69	111	First Canadian International Growth	4.1	4.8	-	177.2
-	24	54	Fonds de Professionnels Int'l Equity (RC)	14.0	12.1	-	70.0
23	46	95	Fonds Desjardins International (UA)	8.6	8.8	12.7	46.7
-	-	84	Fonds Optimum Internationales	10.5	-	-	3.1
49	72	110	GBC International Growth Fund (UA)	5.1	1.2	4.6	21.7
46	70	100	General Trust of Canada Int'l (UA)	7.3	3.6	8.8	5.8
-	-	51	Global Strategy Divers. World Equity	14.4	-	-	43.6
-	-	99	Global Strategy World Emerging Co.	7.7	-	-	137.1
-	-	80	Global Strategy World Equity	10.9	-	-	122.4
-	23	89	Green Line Global Select Fund	10.0	12.3	-	143.9
-	67	96	Green Line International Equity	8.2	5.0	-	114.6
-	32	45	Greystone Managed Global Fund (RC)	15.2	11.1	-	43.2
-	-	78	GS International Equity Fund	11.0	-	-	203.9
33	37	90	Guardian Global Equity Fund A	10.0	9.9	11.7	8.5
-	-	92	Guardian Global Equity Fund B	9.5	-	-	7.6
-	-	38	GWL Int'l Equity Fund (P) DSC	15.9	-	-	44.0
-	-	41	GWL Int'l Equity Fund (P) NL	15.6	-	-	65.4
-	-	3	Hongkong Bank Americas Fund	27.2	-	-	22.9
-	61	75	HRL Overseas Growth Fund	11.3	6.1	-	77.5
-	30	43	ICM International Equity Fund (RC)	15.4	11.2	-	49.0
-	-	27	Industrial Alliance Ecoflex Fund I	18.4	-	-	64.5
-	-	24	Industrial Alliance Int'l Fund	19.1	-	-	6.8
26	29	68	Investors Global Fund	12.1	11.3	12.3	1348.5
13	9	22	Investors Growth Portfolio Fund (HH)	19.2	14.0	16.0	550.0
14	6	13	Investors North American Growth (HH)	20.2	15.5	15.3	1604.9
15	11	17	Investors Special Fund (HH)	19.7	13.7	15.1	480.7
-	38	86	Investors World Growth Portfolio	10.4	9.8	-	993.0
-	5	23	Ivy Foreign Equity Fund (RC)	19.2	16.1	-	332.3
42	58	103	Laurentian Commonwealth Fund Ltd. (UA)	6.8	6.9	10.0	293.2
39	57	105	Laurentian International Fund Ltd. (UA)	6.3	7.1	10.8	169.4
-	-	114	London Life International Equity	-1.2	-	-	154.8

215

INTERNATIONAL EQUITY FUNDS
RANKINGS/RETURNS *cont'd*

Rank (50) (74) (118) 5-Yr 3-Yr 1-Yr	Name of Fund	Returns (%) (12.9) (9.7) (12.8) 1-Yr 3-Yr 5-Yr	Assets ($mns)

5-Yr	3-Yr	1-Yr	Name of Fund	1-Yr	3-Yr	5-Yr	($mns)
-	-	8	Lutheran Life Int'l Equity Fund	22.9	-	-	4.4
34	64	109	Mackenzie Sentinel Global Fund (UA)	5.5	5.7	11.3	7.0
-	35	61	Manulife Cabot Global Equity Fund	13.1	10.7	-	31.5
-	-	67	Manulife Vistafund 1 Global Equity	12.2	-	-	14.4
-	-	73	Manulife Vistafund 2 Global Equity	11.4	-	-	89.1
-	-	85	Maritime Life Global Equity - A & C	10.4	-	-	10.1
18	20	6	Mawer World Investment Fund (HH)	24.7	12.7	14.3	41.1
-	-	93	Maxxum Global Equity Fund	9.2	-	-	14.0
-	-	29	McLean Budden Global Equity Fund	17.7	-	-	6.0
37	66	102	McLean Budden Pooled Offshore Eq. (UA)	7.1	5.1	11.1	148.7
9	14	12	MD Growth Fund (HH)	20.3	13.3	16.4	2733.8
-	-	106	Millennia III Int'l Equity 1	6.2	-	-	33.8
-	-	107	Millennia III Int'l Equity 2	6.0	-	-	2.3
-	44	76	Mutual Premier International Fund	11.1	8.9	-	54.7
22	59	98	NAL-Global Equity Fund	8.0	6.8	12.8	58.4
21	26	28	National Global Equities Fund (HH)	18.0	11.7	13.0	52.9
-	-	113	National Trust Int'l Equity Fund	1.8	-	-	15.9
-	7	26	OHA Foreign Equity Fund (RC)	18.6	15.5	-	1.6
31	25	31	Ontario Teachers Group Global	17.0	11.9	12.2	9.1
-	21	57	Optima Strategy Int'l Equity (RC)	13.6	12.7	-	92.8
-	-	11	Orbit North American Equity Fund	21.1	-	-	2.3
47	71	33	Orbit World Fund	16.9	2.9	7.8	4.7
-	-	87	PH&N International Equity Fund	10.4	-	-	360.6
-	33	25	PH&N North American Equity Fund (RC)	18.7	11.0	-	64.2
-	-	62	Pursuit Global Equity Fund	13.1	-	-	8.1
-	39	46	Royal International Equity Fund	15.1	9.5	-	169.2
-	-	101	Royal Life Int'l Equity Fund	7.1	-	-	11.5
3	2	97	Saxon World Growth	8.2	17.9	19.3	45.3
8	42	44	Sceptre International Fund	15.4	9.0	16.5	166.3
32	50	63	Scotia Excelsior International Fund	13.0	8.3	11.8	158.4
-	-	37	Scudder Global Fund	16.1	-	-	15.7
1	1	2	Special Opportunities Fund (HH)	27.5	22.1	19.9	7.5
41	47	79	Spectrum United Global Equity Fund (UA)	11.0	8.4	10.3	56.5
48	73	117	Spectrum United Global Growth Fund (UA)	-11.1	-2.3	6.8	14.2

INTERNATIONAL EQUITY FUNDS
RANKINGS/RETURNS *cont'd*

Rank			Name of Fund	Returns (%)			Assets
(50)	(74)	(118)		(12.9)	(9.7)	(12.8)	
5-Yr	3-Yr	1-Yr		1-Yr	3-Yr	5-Yr	($mns)
-	-	53	Standard Life International Equity	14.1	-	-	7.0
-	-	88	STAR For. Maximum Equity Growth	10.1	-	-	-
-	-	74	Strategic Value Fund	11.3	-	-	6.6
-	55	64	Talvest Global RRSP Fund Inc.	12.9	7.5	-	20.2
12	19	70	Templeton Global Smaller Companies	11.9	12.7	16.1	335.3
11	12	14	Templeton Growth Fund Ltd. (HH)	20.2	13.7	16.2	7614.2
4	13	18	Templeton International Stock Fund (HH)	19.7	13.4	19.3	3407.4
-	31	55	Trimark - The Americas Fund (RC)	14.0	11.2	-	368.9
-	-	72	Trimark Discovery Fund	11.4	-	-	284.9
2	4	42	Trimark Fund (HH)	15.6	17.1	19.8	2738.9
5	8	60	Trimark Select Growth Fund (HH)	13.3	15.1	17.6	5137.4
-	-	65	Trust Pret & Revenu International	12.6	-	-	17.0
24	40	10	Universal Americas Fund	21.3	9.2	12.5	86.9
-	-	47	Universal Growth Fund	15.0	-	-	255.0
29	60	104	Universal World Equity Fund (UA)	6.4	6.4	12.3	244.2
-	-	19	Universal World Growth RRSP Fund	19.6	-	-	331.9

( ) under Rank indicates total number of funds; ( ) under Returns (%) indicates average annual return; (HH) — Heavy Hitter; (UA) — Underachiever; (RC) — Rookie Camp member.

INTERNATIONAL EQUITY FUNDS/SUMMARY

Name of Fund	MER	Load	RRSP	Vola-tility	Company Number (App. 3)
20/20 Aggressive Global Stock Fund	2.88	Y	F		3
Admax Global RRSP Index Fund	2.25	Y	R		69
Admax International Fund	2.90	Y	F	4	69
AGF International Value Fund	2.78	Y	F		3
AGF RSP Int'l Equity Allocation	2.44	Y	R	3	3
AGF World Equity Fund	3.03	Y	F		3
AIC World Equity Fund	2.74	Y	F	3	4
Altamira Global Diversified Fund	2.00	N	F	3	6
Altamira Global Small Co. Fund	3.02	N	F		6
APEX Global Equity Fund (R)	2.80	Y	F		126
Atlas Global Value Fund	2.73	N	F	3	9
Atlas Int'l Large-Cap Growth Fund	3.00	N	F		9
Atlas Int'l R.S.P. Index Fund	2.06	N	R		9
Azura Growth Pooled (R)	2.28	Y	F		127
Beutel Goodman International Equity	2.58	N	F	3	12
Bissett Multinational Growth Fund (R)	1.50	Y	N		13
BPI Global Equity Value Fund	2.63	Y	F	3	15
BPI Global Opportunities Fund (R)	2.50	Y	F		15
BPI Global Small Companies Fund	2.83	Y	F	4	15
C.I. Global Equity RSP Fund	2.52	Y	R	3	28
C.I. Global Fund	2.55	Y	F	3	28
C.I. Global Sector Shares	2.60	Y	F	3	28
Cambridge Americas Fund	2.88	Y	F	7	121
Cambridge Global Fund	2.91	Y	F	10	121
Canada Life U.S. & Int'l Equity S-34	2.40	Y	F	3	18
Canada Trust Everest Global Growth	2.57	N	R		19
Canada Trust Everest Int'l Equity	2.72	N	F	3	19
Canada Trust Everest North American	2.42	N	F	3	19
Capstone Int'l Investment Trust	2.14	N	F	4	25
CCPE Global Equity (R)	1.75	N	F		21
CDA Global (R)	1.59	N	F		22
CDA International Equity (R)	1.45	N	F		22
CIBC Global Equity Fund	2.40	N	F	3	29
CIBC Int'l Index RRSP Fund	1.75	N	R		29
Clarington Global Opportunities	2.95	Y	F		30

INTERNATIONAL EQUITY FUNDS/SUMMARY *cont'd*

Name of Fund	MER	Load	RRSP	Vola- tility	Company Number (App. 3)
Clean Environment Int'l Equity Fund (R)	3.25	Y	F	4	31
Concorde International Fund (R)	2.38	Y	F		59
Cornerstone Global Fund	2.75	N	F	3	73
Cundill Value Fund	2.02	Y	F	2	111
Dynamic Global Millennia Fund	2.65	Y	F	5	40
Dynamic International Fund	2.78	Y	F	4	40
Elliott & Page Global Equity Fund	1.51	Y	F		41
Empire International Fund	2.57	Y	F	3	42
Equitable Life International Fund	2.75	Y	R		43
Ferique International Fund (R)	0.95	N	R	3	109
Fidelity International Portfolio	2.76	Y	F	3	46
First Canadian International Growth	2.15	N	F	3	11
Fonds de Professionnels Int'l Equity (R)	0.75	N	N	2	50
Fonds Desjardins International (R)	2.37	N	F	3	37
Fonds Optimum Internationales (R)	1.90	N	F		107
GBC International Growth Fund (R)	1.76	N	F	3	52
General Trust of Canada Int'l (R)	2.47	N	F	3	98
Global Strategy Divers. World Eq.	2.40	Y	R		54
Global Strategy World Emerging Co.	2.98	Y	F		54
Global Strategy World Equity	2.87	Y	F		54
Green Line Global Select Fund	2.36	N	F	3	139
Green Line International Equity	2.35	N	F	3	139
Greystone Managed Global Fund	2.46	N	F		58
GS International Equity Fund	2.89	Y	F		70
GT Global - Global Theme Class	2.95	Y	F		60
Guardian Global Equity Fund A	1.28	Y	F	3	61
Guardian Global Equity Fund B	2.95	Y	F		61
GWL Int'l Equity Fund (P) DSC	2.80	Y	F		57
GWL Int'l Equity Fund (P) NL	3.10	N	F		57
Hansberger Global Small-Cap Fund	2.95	Y	F		28
Hansberger Global Small-Cap Sector	2.97	Y	F		28
Hansberger Int'l Sector Shares	2.65	Y	F		28
Hansberger International Fund	2.60	Y	F		28
Hansberger Value Fund	2.53	Y	F		28
Hansberger Value Sector Shares	2.58	Y	F		28

INTERNATIONAL EQUITY FUNDS/SUMMARY *cont'd*

Name of Fund	MER	Load	RRSP	Vola-tility	Company Number (App. 3)
Hongkong Bank Americas Fund	2.34	N	F		63
HRL Overseas Growth Fund	1.75	N	N	3	64
ICM International Equity Fund	0.35	N	F		68
Industrial Alliance Ecoflex Fund E	3.66	Y	F		66
Industrial Alliance Ecoflex Fund I	2.96	Y	F		66
Industrial Alliance Int'l Fund	2.30	N	F		66
Infinity International Fund	2.95	Y	F		67
Investors Global Fund	2.46	Y	F	3	70
Investors Growth Portfolio Fund	0.18	Y	F	3	70
Investors North American Growth	2.38	Y	F	3	70
Investors Special Fund	2.39	Y	F	3	70
Investors World Growth Portfolio	0.18	Y	F	3	70
Ivy Foreign Equity Fund	2.40	Y	F	2	80
Laurentian Commonwealth Fund Ltd.	2.65	Y	F	3	135
Laurentian International Fund Ltd.	2.65	Y	F	3	135
London Life International Equity	2.50	Y	F		76
Lutheran Life Int'l Equity Fund (R)	2.60	N	F		78
Mackenzie Sentinel Global Fund (C)	0.51	N	F	3	80
Manulife Cabot Global Equity Fund	2.50	N	F		84
Manulife Vistafund 1 Global Equity	1.63	Y	F		83
Manulife Vistafund 2 Global Equity	2.38	Y	F		83
Maritime Life Eurasia - A & C	2.30	Y	R		85
Maritime Life Eurasia - B	2.30	Y	R		85
Maritime Life Global Equity - B	2.55	Y	F		85
Maritime Life Global Equity - A & C	2.55	Y	F		85
Mawer World Investment Fund (R)	1.29	N	F	3	86
Maxxum Global Equity Fund	2.50	Y	F		87
McLean Budden Global Equity Fund (R)	1.00	N	N		89
McLean Budden Pooled Offshore Eq. (R)	1.00	N	N	3	89
MD Growth Fund (R)	1.29	N	F	3	90
Metlife MVP Global Equity Fund	2.90	Y	F		92
Millennia III Int'l Equity 1	2.90	Y	F		65
Millennia III Int'l Equity 2	3.08	N	F		65
Mutual Premier International Fund	2.38	N	F	3	97
NAL-Global Equity Fund	2.50	Y	F	3	83

INTERNATIONAL EQUITY FUNDS/SUMMARY *cont'd*

Name of Fund	MER	Load	RRSP	Vola-tility	Company Number (App. 3)
National Global Equities Fund	2.40	Y	F	3	99
National Trust Int'l Equity Fund (R)	2.79	N	F		100
North-West Life Ecoflex E	3.66	Y	F		103
North-West Life Ecoflex I	2.96	Y	F		103
O'Donnell World Equity Fund	2.75	Y	F		104
OHA Foreign Equity Fund	1.70	N	F	3	105
Ontario Teachers Group Global (R)	1.00	N	F	3	106
Optima Strategy Int'l Equity (R)	0.47	Y	F		77
Orbit North American Equity Fund (R)	2.50	Y	F		108
Orbit World Fund (R)	2.50	Y	F	3	108
PH&N International Equity Fund (R)	1.49	N	F		112
PH&N North American Equity Fund (R)	1.18	N	F	5	112
Pursuit Global Equity Fund (R)	1.75	Y	F		117
Pursuit Growth Fund	1.75	Y	F	4	117
Royal International Equity Fund	2.49	N	F	3	119
Royal Life Int'l Equity Fund	2.25	Y	F		120
Saxon World Growth (R)	1.75	N	F	3	122
Sceptre International Fund	2.10	N	F	3	123
Scotia Excelsior International Fund	2.20	N	F	3	124
Scudder Global Fund (R)	1.75	N	F		125
Special Opportunities Fund (R)	2.14	Y	F	5	94
Spectrum United Global Equity Fund	2.30	Y	F	3	129
Spectrum United Global Growth Fund	2.30	Y	F	3	129
Standard Life International Equity	2.00	Y	F		133
STAR For. Maximum Equity Growth	0.00	Y	F		80
Strategic Value Fund (R)	3.00	Y	F		135
Strategic Value Global Equity Fund	2.75	Y	F		135
Talvest Global RRSP Fund Inc.	2.50	Y	R	3	136
Templeton Global Smaller Companies	2.55	Y	F	3	137
Templeton Growth Fund Ltd.	2.00	Y	F	3	137
Templeton International Stock Fund	2.51	Y	F	3	137
Trimark - The Americas Fund	2.53	Y	F	4	143
Trimark Discovery Fund	2.50	Y	F		143
Trimark Fund	1.52	Y	F	3	143
Trimark Select Growth Fund	2.25	Y	F	3	143

INTERNATIONAL EQUITY FUNDS/SUMMARY *cont'd*

Name of Fund	MER	Load	RRSP	Vola-tility	Company Number (App. 3)
Trust Pret & Revenu International	2.13	N	F		145
Universal Americas Fund	2.53	Y	F	4	80
Universal Growth Fund	2.39	Y	F		80
Universal World Equity Fund	2.45	Y	F	4	80
Universal World Growth RRSP Fund	2.44	Y	R		80
Average	2.29			3.3	

(R) — Restricted; (C) — Closed to new investors; MER — Management Expense Ratio; Load — fee charged; RRSP: R = 100% eligible, F = eligible as foreign content only, N = not eligible; Volatility — measures swings in performance on a scale of 1 to 10 (1 = low, 10 = high). Blank space indicates that fund is less than three years old. Fund company addresses may be found by number in Appendix 3.

21

●●●●●●●●●●●●●●●●●●●●●●●●●●●●●●

Asian Funds

THE OVERRIDING INVESTMENT objective of Asian equity funds is to achieve long-term capital growth by investing in Asian stock markets. There are now 69 Asian funds on the market that manage $8.3 billion in assets. Because of the wide swings in the region's stock markets, Asian funds are considerably more volatile than both international and Canadian equity funds. Nevertheless, with Asia's continued bullish economic and corporate outlook, there is little question that investing in this region holds the potential for superior returns over the longer term.

Over the five calendar years from 1992 to 1996, the best year for Asian funds was 1993, when returns averaged 60.5%. In contrast, the worst year was 1994, when returns averaged -3.7%. Returns were also negative in 1995, declining by 2.2%. The average annual compound rate of return over the five-year period was 10.7%.

Asian funds have an average volatility rating of 5.5, which is significantly higher than the average of 4.1 for all equity funds. The average fee for management expenses is $2.57 for every $100 in assets, which is down from last year's average of $2.66.

The Heavy Hitters

There are five Asian funds that have qualified for membership in the Heavy Hitters club this year. Each of these funds has consistently delivered *above*-average returns over the past one-, three-, and five-year periods. Collectively these Heavy Hitters manage a total of $4.4 billion in assets. The Fidelity Far East Fund is the largest, with $1.9 billion in assets, and Talvest's Hyperion Asian Fund is the smallest, with $156 million in assets. All five Heavy Hitters are load funds.

• •

Table 1

THE HEAVY HITTERS

ASIAN FUNDS

		Bench-mark*	Vola-tility	Performance Quartile 1	Quartile 2	Overall Rating
1	Fidelity Far East Fund	4	6	3	1	★★
2	Investors Pacific International	4	5	1	4	★★
3	C.I. Pacific Fund	3	5	2	1	★1/2
4	C.I. Pacific Sector Shares	3	5	2	0	★1/2
5	Hyperion Asian Fund	3	7	2	2	★1/2

* Morgan Stanley Far East Index; (R) — Restricted; (C) — Closed to new members; (N) — No-load fund; Benchmark — number of times that a fund beat the benchmark from 1992 to 1996; Volatility — measures swings in fund returns on a scale of 1 to 10 (1 = low, 10 = high); Performance — number of times that a fund was in the first (top 25%) or second quartile (top 50%) from 1992 to 1996.

The benchmark used to compare Asian fund returns is the Morgan Stanley Far East Index, measured in Canadian dollars. Over the past five calendar years, the index posted its highest return of 41.6% in 1993 and its lowest return of -10.7% in 1992. Returns were also negative in 1995 and 1996.

Fidelity Far East Fund ★★

This fund, identified as a Rookie Camp member in last year's *World of Mutual Funds*, was launched in 1991 and has been managed by K. P. Lee since its inception. With $1.9 billion in assets, it follows a bottom-up/value/growth investment strategy. Investments in Hong Kong account for about 63% of the fund's portfolio, with another 6% invested in Malaysia and 6% in Korea.

Its best year was 1993, when it posted a return of 86.4%, and its worst year was 1994, when its return was -16.7%. The fund's average

annual compound return over the past five years was 20.4%. A load fund, it charges management expenses of $2.83 for every $100 in assets, which is higher than the group average of $2.57.

Investors Pacific International Fund ★★

This fund was started in 1990 and is managed by Jeremy Higgs. The fund has $1.2 billion in assets and follows a bottom-up/value investment strategy. About 27% of the fund's portfolio is invested in Hong Kong, 13% each in Malaysia and the Philippines, and 10% in Indonesia.

In 1993, its best year, the fund posted a return of 88.1%, and in 1994, its worst year, it returned -6.7%. Over the past five years, it yielded an average annual compound return of 13.9%. This load fund charges slightly below-average management expenses of $2.56 for every $100 in assets.

C.I. Pacific Fund ★1/2

This fund was launched in 1981 and has been managed by Shaun Chan of the investment firm TCW Asia since October 1990. With $990 million in assets, it follows a top-down/blend investment strategy. About 34% of the fund's portfolio is invested in Hong Kong, 22% in Malaysia, 11% in Singapore, and 9% in Taiwan.

The fund posted its highest return, 91.7%, in 1993, and its lowest, -12.3%, in 1994. Over the past five years, its average annual compound return was 13.8%. This is a load fund which charges management expenses of $2.61 for every $100 in assets, slightly higher than the group average.

C.I. Pacific Sector Shares ★1/2

This fund, launched in 1987, invests in the shares of the C.I. Pacific Fund only. This allows investors to switch between eligible C.I. funds without incurring any immediate tax liabilities. The returns of this fund and the C.I. Pacific Fund differ slightly because of the lag in timing. For example, the average annual compound return over the past five years was 13.4% for this fund, compared with 13.8% for the C.I. Pacific Fund. The fund has $197 million in assets and charges management expenses of $2.66 for every $100 in assets, slightly higher than those for the C.I. Pacific Fund.

Hyperion Asian Fund ★1/2

This fund, sponsored by Talvest Fund Management Inc., was started in 1989 and is managed by Duncan Mount of the Hong Kong–based firm CEF Investment Management Limited. The fund has $156 million in assets and follows a bottom-up/growth investment strategy. Investments in Hong Kong account for 34% of the fund's portfolio, with another 18% in Malaysia, 16% in Japan, and 10% in Thailand.

In 1993, its best year, the fund posted a return of 117.0%, and in 1994, its worst year, it returned -20.1%. Over the past five years, it yielded an average annual compound return of 13.3%. This load fund charges above-average management expenses of $3.25 for every $100 in assets.

The Rookie Camp

Five of the promising newer Asian equity funds, each with at least a three-year track record, are in the Rookie Camp this year. Each of these funds, listed below, posted *above*-average returns over the past one-, two-, and three-year periods.

AGF China Focus Fund, sponsored by AGF Management Limited, was launched in 1994 and follows a bottom-up/growth investment strategy. The fund is managed by Stephen Way and Yuki Aiga. A load fund, it has $22 million in assets and charges above-average management expenses of $3.49 for every $100 in assets.

Dynamic Far East Fund, sponsored by Dynamic Mutual Funds, was launched in 1994 and is managed by the firm's investment team. It is a load fund with $13 million in assets and charges above-average management expenses of $3.57 for every $100 in assets.

Green Line Asian Growth Fund, sponsored by the Toronto-Dominion Bank, is managed by the Hong Kong–based investment firm Peregrine Asset Management. The fund has $70 million in assets and follows a blend investment strategy. A no-load fund, it charges above-average management expenses of $2.70 for every $100 in assets.

NN Can-Asian Fund, a segregated fund sponsored by NN Life Insurance Company of Canada, was launched in 1993 and follows a top-down/

blend investment strategy. The fund is managed by David Patterson. A load fund, sold only on a deferred basis, it has $111 million in assets and charges above-average management expenses of $3.00 for every $100 in assets.

Sceptre Asian Growth Fund, sponsored by Sceptre Investment Counsel Limited of Toronto, was launched in 1993 and is managed by Tariq Ahmed. With $20 million in assets, the fund follows a value/sector investment strategy. It is a no-load fund and charges below-average management expenses of $2.40 for every $100 in assets. The fund has a minimum initial investment requirement of $5,000.

The Underachievers

There are four Asian funds that have failed to measure up to their peers. These Underachievers have consistently delivered *below*-average returns over the past one-, three-, and five-year periods. Collectively these Underachievers manage $766 million in assets. Investors Japanese Growth Fund is the largest, with $668 million in assets, and the Cambridge Pacific Fund is the smallest, with $2 million. Three of the four Underachievers are load funds.

Table 2
THE UNDERACHIEVERS
ASIAN FUNDS

- Admax Korea Fund
- Cambridge Pacific Fund
- Investors Japanese Growth Fund
- Royal Japanese Stock Fund*

---

* denotes a no-load fund

Heavy Hitters vs Underachievers

Table 3 shows the substantial difference in returns over three time periods between the Heavy Hitters and the Underachievers for Asian funds. In dollar terms, for an initial investment of $10,000, the average Heavy

Hitter Asian fund would have returned a total of $20,114 over the past five years. For the same investment, the average Underachiever would have returned $10,720 — for a difference of $9,394 or 87.6%.

With respect to costs, the average Asian Heavy Hitter charged management expenses of $2.78 for every $100 in assets, compared with $2.90 for the average Underachiever.

Table 3
HEAVY HITTERS vs UNDERACHIEVERS
ASIAN FUNDS

(Returns %)

	1-Year	3-Year*	5-Year*
• Heavy Hitters	7.2	4.8	15.0
• Underachievers	-18.6	-10.3	1.4

* annualized

ASIAN FUNDS
RANKINGS/RETURNS

Rank			Name of Fund	Returns (%)			Assets
(12)	(35)	(64)		(0.1)	(-0.8)	(9.4)	
5-Yr	3-Yr	1-Yr		1-Yr	3-Yr	5-Yr	($mns)
-	-	60	20/20 India Fund	-19.4	-	-	31.4
-	22	22	Admax Dragon 888 Fund	5.7	-1.4	-	2.8
12	35	63	Admax Korea Fund (UA)	-28.1	-13.7	-3.5	29.7
-	19	38	Admax Nippon Fund	-2.6	-0.4	-	22.0
9	27	19	Admax Tiger Fund	7.1	-5.2	6.0	51.2
2	7	37	AGF Asian Growth Class	-2.0	3.9	15.9	617.1
-	3	4	AGF China Focus Fund (RC)	24.8	6.0	-	22.3
7	23	18	AGF Japan Class	7.1	-1.5	7.0	144.9
-	33	54	Altamira Asia Pacific Fund	-13.3	-10.1	-	179.7
-	-	49	Altamira Japanese Opportunity Fund	-8.3	-	-	24.1
-	14	40	APEX Asian Pacific Fund	-3.4	1.9	-	19.6
-	29	53	Atlas Pacific Basin Value Fund	-12.4	-6.1	-	9.8
4	9	15	C.I. Pacific Fund (HH)	8.2	3.0	13.8	990.9
5	10	16	C.I. Pacific Sector Shares (HH)	7.3	2.6	13.4	179.3
-	25	64	Cambridge China Fund (Sagit)	-31.7	-4.6	-	1.3
11	34	61	Cambridge Pacific Fund (Sagit) (UA)	-26.0	-13.4	-0.9	2.0
-	-	35	Canada Life Asia Pacific S-38	-1.2	-	-	19.5
-	18	46	Canada Trust Everest AsiaGrowth	-5.1	0.0	-	156.1
-	-	11	CDA Pacific Basin (KBSH)	11.1	-	-	1.9
-	12	31	CIBC Far East Prosperity Fund	-0.8	2.4	-	186.9
-	-	13	CIBC Japanese Equity Fund	9.1	-	-	28.5
-	2	7	Dynamic Far East Fund (RC)	17.8	9.2	-	12.8
-	-	28	Elliott & Page Asian Growth Fund	1.0	-	-	27.8
-	-	5	Ethical Pacific Rim Fund	21.5	-	-	29.6
1	1	6	Fidelity Far East Fund (HH)	18.3	13.0	20.4	1894.4
-	28	45	Fidelity Japanese Growth Fund	-5.1	-6.0	-	199.1
-	-	12	First Canadian Far East Growth Fund	9.7	-	-	25.3
-	-	55	First Canadian Japanese Growth Fund	-14.2	-	-	25.6
-	-	1	Global Manager - HK Geared Fund	45.4	-	-	0.3
-	-	3	Global Manager - HK Index Fund	28.6	-	-	0.9
-	-	62	Global Manager - Japan Geared Fund	-27.9	-	-	0.5
-	-	56	Global Manager - Japan Index Fund	-15.9	-	-	0.9
-	13	30	Global Strategy Asia Fund	-0.4	2.2	-	42.6
-	32	58	Global Strategy Div. Japan Plus	-17.4	-9.8	-	15.2

ASIAN FUNDS
RANKINGS/RETURNS cont'd

Rank			Name of Fund	Returns (%)			Assets
(12)	(35)	(64)		(0.1)	(-0.8)	(9.4)	
5-Yr	3-Yr	1-Yr		1-Yr	3-Yr	5-Yr	($mns)
-	21	47	Global Strategy Diversified Asia	-5.4	-1.3	-	21.8
-	-	59	Global Strategy Japan Fund	-18.0	-	-	22.6
-	5	23	Green Line Asian Growth Fund (RC)	3.9	4.0	-	69.5
-	-	48	Green Line Japanese Growth Fund	-6.0	-	-	45.8
-	-	8	GT Global Pacific Growth Class	15.6	-	-	29.0
-	-	32	Guardian Asia Pacific Fund A	-0.9	-	-	4.3
-	-	36	Guardian Asia Pacific Fund B	-1.6	-	-	2.3
-	24	41	Hansberger Asian Fund	-3.8	-2.7	-	82.5
-	-	42	Hansberger Asian Sector Shares	-4.4	-	-	12.7
-	6	34	Hongkong Bank Asian Growth Fund	-1.1	3.9	-	50.9
6	11	27	Hyperion Asian Fund (HH)	1.0	2.4	13.3	155.5
-	-	20	InvesNat Far East Equity Fund	7.0	-	-	24.0
-	-	57	InvesNat Japanese Equity Fund	-17.1	-	-	20.8
8	30	52	Investors Japanese Growth Fund (UA)	-11.2	-6.2	6.1	667.5
3	8	26	Investors Pacific International (HH)	1.1	3.2	13.9	1221.2
-	-	39	Laurentian Asia Pacific Fund	-2.7	-	-	11.3
-	-	25	Maritime Life Pacific Basin - A & C	1.7	-	-	14.8
-	-	21	McDonald Asia Plus	6.7	-	-	0.5
-	-	51	McDonald New Japan	-9.8	-	-	1.0
-	-	2	Navigator Asia Pacific Fund	35.6	-	-	6.5
-	4	17	NN Can-Asian Fund (RC)	7.2	5.9	-	110.6
-	16	43	Royal Asian Growth Fund	-4.5	0.7	-	153.2
10	31	50	Royal Japanese Stock Fund (UA)	-9.1	-7.9	3.8	67.1
-	20	29	Sceptre Asian Growth Fund (RC)	0.4	-0.4	-	20.3
-	-	9	Scotia Excelsior Pacific Rim Fund	14.2	-	-	38.4
-	-	14	Scudder Pacific Fund	8.7	-	-	2.3
-	17	44	Spectrum United Asian Dynasty Fund	-4.8	0.3	-	22.0
-	-	10	Trimark Indo-Pacific Fund	12.4	-	-	295.5
-	15	24	Universal Far East Fund	2.5	1.8	-	94.9
-	26	33	Universal Japan Fund	-1.0	-5.0	-	30.7

( ) under Rank indicates total number of funds; ( ) under Returns (%) indicates average annual return; (HH) — Heavy Hitter; (UA) — Underachiever; (RC) — Rookie Camp member.

ASIAN FUNDS/SUMMARY

Name of Fund	MER	Load	RRSP	Vola-tility	Company Number (App. 3)
20/20 India Fund	3.91	Y	F		3
Admax Dragon 888 Fund	2.94	Y	F		69
Admax Korea Fund	3.20	Y	F	6	69
Admax Nippon Fund	3.08	Y	F	5	69
Admax Tiger Fund	3.20	Y	F	4	69
AGF Asian Growth Class	2.90	Y	F	6	3
AGF China Focus Fund	3.49	Y	F		3
AGF Japan Class	2.97	Y	F	5	3
Allstar AIG Asian Fund (R)	2.35	Y	F		5
Altamira Asia Pacific Fund	2.37	N	F	4	6
Altamira Japanese Opportunity Fund	2.36	N	F		6
APEX Asian Pacific Fund (R)	2.76	Y	F		126
Atlas Pacific Basin Value Fund	2.88	N	F	5	9
BPI Asia Pacific Fund	2.80	Y	F		15
C.I. Pacific Fund	2.61	Y	F	5	28
C.I. Pacific Sector Shares	2.66	Y	F	5	28
Cambridge China Fund	2.87	Y	F		121
Cambridge Pacific Fund	2.98	Y	F	7	121
Canada Life Asia Pacific S-38	2.40	Y	F		18
Canada Trust Everest AsiaGrowth	2.46	N	R		19
CDA Pacific Basin (R)	1.45	N	F		22
CIBC Far East Prosperity Fund	2.60	N	F	7	29
CIBC Japanese Equity Fund	2.60	N	F		29
Dynamic Far East Fund	3.57	Y	N		40
Elliott & Page Asian Growth Fund	1.36	Y	F		41
Ethical Pacific Rim Fund (R)	3.22	N	F		44
Fidelity Far East Fund	2.83	Y	F	6	46
Fidelity Japanese Growth Fund	3.13	Y	F	6	46
First Canadian Far East Growth Fund	2.17	N	F		11
First Canadian Japanese Growth Fund	2.06	N	F		11
Global Manager - HK Geared Fund (R)	1.00	Y	N		10
Global Manager - HK Index Fund (R)	1.00	Y	N		10
Global Manager - Japan Geared (R)	1.00	Y	N		10
Global Manager - Japan Index Fund (R)	1.00	Y	N		10

ASIAN FUNDS/SUMMARY *cont'd*

Name of Fund	MER	Load	RRSP	Vola-tility	Company Number (App. 3)
Global Strategy Asia Fund	2.89	Y	F	6	54
Global Strategy Div. Japan Plus	2.54	Y	R		54
Global Strategy Diversified Asia	2.69	Y	R		54
Global Strategy Japan Fund	2.89	Y	F		54
Green Line Asian Growth Fund	2.70	N	F	6	139
Green Line Japanese Growth Fund	2.63	N	F		139
Growsafe Japanese 225 Index Fund	1.99	Y	R		141
GT Global Pacific Growth Class	2.95	Y	F		60
Guardian Asia Pacific Fund A	1.84	Y	F		61
Guardian Asia Pacific Fund B	2.98	Y	F		61
Hansberger Asian Fund	2.88	Y	F	5	28
Hansberger Asian Sector Shares	2.93	Y	F		28
Hongkong Bank Asian Growth Fund	2.29	N	F	5	63
Hyperion Asian Fund	3.25	Y	F	7	136
InvesNat Far East Equity Fund (R)	2.45	N	F		98
InvesNat Japanese Equity Fund (R)	2.43	N	F		98
Investors Japanese Growth Fund	2.46	Y	F	5	70
Investors Pacific International	2.56	Y	F	5	70
Laurentian Asia Pacific Fund	2.65	Y	F		135
Maritime Life Pacific Basin - A & C	2.55	Y	F		85
Maritime Life Pacific Basin - B	2.55	Y	F		85
McDonald Asia Plus (R)	2.80	Y	N		88
McDonald New Japan (R)	2.50	Y	N		88
Metlife MVP Asian-Pacific RSP Eq.	2.90	Y	F		92
Navigator Asia Pacific Fund (R)	2.39	Y	F		101
NN Can-Asian Fund	3.00	Y	R	5	102
Royal Asian Growth Fund	2.84	N	F	5	119
Royal Japanese Stock Fund	2.95	N	F	6	119
Sceptre Asian Growth Fund	2.40	N	F	5	123
Scotia Excelsior Pacific Rim Fund	2.36	N	F		124
Scudder Pacific Fund (R)	1.75	N	F		125
Spectrum United Asian Dynasty Fund	2.58	Y	F	5	129
Trimark Indo-Pacific Fund	2.74	Y	F		143

ASIAN FUNDS/SUMMARY *cont'd*

Name of Fund	MER	Load	RRSP	Vola-tility	Company Number (App. 3)
Universal Far East Fund	2.60	Y	F	6	80
Universal Japan Fund	2.54	Y	F		80
Average	2.57			5.5	

(R) — Restricted; (C) — Closed to new investors; MER — Management Expense Ratio; Load — fee charged; RRSP: R = 100% eligible, F = eligible as foreign content only, N = not eligible; Volatility — measures swings in performance on a scale of 1 to 10 (1 = low, 10 = high). Blank space indicates that fund is less than three years old. Fund company addresses may be found by number in Appendix 3.

22

• •

European Funds

THE PRIMARY OBJECTIVE of European equity funds is to achieve long-term capital growth by investing in the stocks of companies located in various European countries. There are currently 38 European funds on the market. These funds manage a total of $4.4 billion in assets.

Over the five calendar years from 1992 to 1996, the best year for European funds was 1996, when returns averaged 23.8%. In contrast, the worst year was 1992, when returns averaged 0.2%. The average annual compound rate of return over the five-year period was 12.0%.

European funds have an average volatility rating of 3.3, which is below the average of 4.1 for all equity funds. The average fee for management expenses is $2.25 for every $100 in assets, which is down from last year's average of $2.56.

The Heavy Hitters

There are two European funds that have qualified for membership in the Heavy Hitters club this year. Each of these funds has consistently delivered *above*-average returns over the past one-, three-, and five-year periods. Collectively these Heavy Hitters manage a total of $155 million in assets. The Dynamic Europe Fund is the largest, with $126 million in assets, and the Vision Europe Fund is the smallest, with $29 million in assets. Both of these Heavy Hitters are load funds.

Table 1
THE HEAVY HITTERS
EUROPEAN FUNDS

		Bench-mark*	Vola-tility	Performance Quartile 1	Performance Quartile 2	Overall Rating
1	Dynamic Europe Fund	1	4	1	1	★
2	Vision Europe Fund	1	3	1	0	★

* Morgan Stanley European Index; (R) — Restricted; (C) — Closed to new members; (N) — No-load fund; Benchmark — number of times that a fund beat the benchmark from 1992 to 1996; Volatility — measures swings in fund returns on a scale of 1 to 10 (1 = low, 10 = high); Performance — number of times that a fund was in the first (top 25%) or second quartile (top 50%) from 1992 to 1996.

The benchmark used to compare European fund returns is the Morgan Stanley European Index, measured in Canadian dollars. Over the past five calendar years, the index posted its highest return of 33.3% in 1993 and its lowest return of 5.2% in 1992.

Dynamic Europe Fund ★

This fund was launched in 1989 and is managed by the firm's investment team. With $126 million in assets, it follows a bottom-up/value investment strategy. About 15% of the fund's portfolio is invested in Sweden, 12% in Italy, 10% in Russia, and 9% each in France and Finland.

Its best year was 1996, when it posted a return of 34.7%, and its worst year was 1992, when its return was -0.6%. The fund's average annual compound return over the past five years was 15.3%. A load fund, it charges management expenses of $2.64 for every $100 in assets, which is higher than the group average of $2.25.

Vision Europe Fund ★

This fund, sponsored by Trust General du Canada of Montreal, was started in 1989 and is managed by Didier LeConte of the investment firm Indosuez Asset Management. The fund has $29 million in assets and follows a bottom-up/sector investment strategy. About 26% of the fund's portfolio is invested in the United Kingdom, 20% in France, 14% in Germany, and 12% in Switzerland.

In 1996, its best year, the fund posted a return of 22.8%, and in 1994, its worst year, it returned 3.1%. Over the past five years, it yielded an average annual compound return of 12.6%. This load fund, sold only on a deferred basis, charges slightly below-average management expenses of $2.23 for every $100 in assets.

The Rookie Camp

Atlas European Value Fund, sponsored by Atlas Asset Management Inc., a wholly owned subsidiary of Midland Walwyn, is the only one of the newer European equity funds to make it into the Rookie Camp category this year. This fund, which posted *above*-average returns over the past one-, two-, and three-year periods, was launched in 1993 and is managed by Nils Franke of the U.K.-based firm Pictet International Management Ltd. The fund follows a bottom-up/value investment strategy. A no-load fund, it has $22 million in assets and charges above-average management expenses of $2.84 for every $100 in assets.

The Underachievers

Talvest's Hyperion European Fund is the only Underachiever in this category. It has consistently delivered *below*-average returns over the past one-, three-, and five-year periods. A load fund with $34 million in assets, it charges above-average management expenses of $3.00 for every $100 in assets.

Table 2
THE UNDERACHIEVERS
EUROPEAN FUNDS

• Hyperion European Fund

Heavy Hitters vs Underachievers

Table 3 shows the difference in returns over three time periods between the Heavy Hitters and the Underachievers for European funds. In dollar terms, for an initial investment of $10,000, the average Heavy Hitter

European fund would have returned a total of $19,170 over the past five years. For the same investment, the average Underachiever would have returned $17,389 — for a difference of $1,781 or 10.2%.

With respect to costs, the average European Heavy Hitter charged management expenses of $2.44 for every $100 in assets, compared with $3.00 for the average Underachiever.

Table 3

HEAVY HITTERS vs UNDERACHIEVERS

EUROPEAN FUNDS

(Returns %)

	1-Year	3-Year*	5-Year*
• Heavy Hitters	28.2	17.8	13.9
• Underachievers	20.5	13.5	11.7

* annualized

EUROPEAN FUNDS
RANKINGS/RETURNS

Rank			Name of Fund	Returns (%)			Assets
(6)	(15)	(36)		(23.0)	(14.1)	(12.1)	
5-Yr	3-Yr	1-Yr		1-Yr	3-Yr	5-Yr	($mns)
-	13	7	Admax Europa Performance Fund	28.5	11.4	-	4.1
-	7	34	AGF European Growth Fund	11.0	14.5	-	104.8
-	-	3	AGF Germany Class M	33.8	-	-	42.2
-	-	6	AGF Germany Fund	31.8	-	-	27.2
-	6	26	Altamira European Equity Fund	18.6	14.8	-	181.5
-	4	15	Atlas European Value Fund (RC)	23.3	15.9	-	22.1
-	-	17	Canada Life European Equity S-37	22.2	-	-	42.9
-	9	10	Canada Trust Everest EuroGrowth	25.2	13.8	-	141.6
-	-	32	CDA European (KBSH)	13.1	-	-	2.3
-	-	35	CIBC European Equity Fund	9.7	-	-	21.7
1	1	4	Dynamic Europe Fund (HH)	33.3	18.8	15.3	125.8
-	3	21	Fidelity European Growth Fund	20.4	16.6	-	1196.3
-	-	28	First Canadian European Growth Fund	17.8	-	-	26.5
-	-	36	Global Manager - German Bund Index	-2.1	-	-	0.1
-	-	1	Global Manager - German Geared Fund	60.5	-	-	0.2
-	-	12	Global Manager - German Index Fund	24.2	-	-	1.0
-	-	2	Global Manager - U.K. Geared Fund	51.8	-	-	0.2
-	-	27	Global Manager - U.K. Gilt Index Fund	18.1	-	-	0.1
-	-	5	Global Manager - U.K. Index Fund	32.3	-	-	2.0
-	8	13	Global Strategy Diversified Europe	23.7	13.8	-	77.0
-	-	22	Global Strategy Europe Plus	19.8	-	-	89.8
-	-	19	Green Line European Growth Fund	22.0	-	-	81.5
6	14	11	Hansberger European Fund	24.3	11.0	7.8	75.8
-	15	14	Hansberger European Sector Shares	23.5	10.6	-	33.6
-	-	18	Hongkong Bank European Growth Fund	22.1	-	-	35.5
5	10	20	Hyperion European Fund (UA)	20.5	13.5	11.7	33.7
-	12	30	InvesNat European Equity Fund	16.9	12.0	-	20.9
4	5	23	Investors European Growth Fund	19.0	15.0	11.8	1104.2
-	-	25	Laurentian Europe Fund	18.8	-	-	23.6
-	-	33	McDonald Euro Plus	11.6	-	-	2.1
-	-	8	NN Can-Euro Fund	28.4	-	-	77.0
2	11	31	Royal European Growth Fund	16.9	13.0	13.3	225.3
-	-	24	Scudder Greater Europe Fund	18.9	-	-	6.7
-	-	29	Spectrum United European Growth	17.6	-	-	79.7

EUROPEAN FUNDS
RANKINGS/RETURNS *cont'd*

Rank			Name of Fund	Returns (%)			Assets
(6)	(15)	(36)		(23.0)	(14.1)	(12.1)	
5-Yr	3-Yr	1-Yr		1-Yr	3-Yr	5-Yr	($mns)
-	-	9	Universal European Opportunities	28.0	-	-	411.6
3	2	16	Vision Europe Fund (HH)	23.2	16.7	12.6	28.9

( ) under Rank indicates total number of funds; ( ) under Returns (%) indicates average annual return; (HH) — Heavy Hitter; (UA) — Underachiever; (RC) — Rookie Camp member.

EUROPEAN FUNDS/SUMMARY

Name of Fund	MER	Load	RRSP	Vola-tility	Company Number (App. 3)
Admax Europa Performance Fund	3.48	Y	F	3	69
AGF European Growth Fund	3.01	Y	F		3
AGF Germany Class M (C)	1.36	Y	F		3
AGF Germany Fund	3.12	Y	F		3
Altamira European Equity Fund	2.33	N	F	3	6
Atlas European Value Fund	2.84	N	F	3	9
Canada Life European Equity S-37	2.40	R	F		18
Canada Trust Everest EuroGrowth	2.30	N	R		19
CDA European (R)	1.45	N	F		22
CIBC European Equity Fund	2.50	N	F		29
Dynamic Europe Fund	2.64	Y	F	4	40
Fidelity European Growth Fund	2.80	Y	F	3	46
First Canadian European Growth Fund	2.19	N	F		11
Global Manager - German Bund Index (R)	1.00	Y	N		10
Global Manager - German Geared (R)	1.00	Y	N		10
Global Manager - German Index Fund (R)	1.00	Y	N		10
Global Manager - U.K. Geared Fund (R)	1.00	Y	N		10
Global Manager - U.K. Gilt Index Fund (R)	1.00	Y	N		10
Global Manager - U.K. Index Fund (R)	1.00	Y	N		10
Global Strategy Diversified Europe	2.52	Y	R	3	54
Global Strategy Europe Plus	2.88	Y	F		54
Green Line European Growth Fund	2.62	N	F		139
Growsafe European 100 Index Fund	1.99	Y	R		141
Hansberger European Fund	2.56	Y	F	4	28
Hansberger European Sector Shares	2.61	Y	F	4	28
Hongkong Bank European Growth	2.31	N	F		63
Hyperion European Fund	3.00	Y	F	3	136
InvesNat European Equity Fund (R)	2.31	N	F	3	98
Investors European Growth Fund	2.45	Y	F	3	70
Laurentian Europe Fund	2.65	Y	F		135
McDonald Euro Plus (R)	2.50	Y	N		88
NN Can-Euro Fund	2.85	Y	R		103
Royal European Growth Fund	2.66	N	F	3	119
Scotia Excelsior European Growth	2.17	N	F		124
Scudder Greater Europe Fund (R)	1.75	N	F		125

EUROPEAN FUNDS/SUMMARY *cont'd*

Name of Fund	MER	Load	RRSP	Vola-tility	Company Number (App. 3)
Spectrum United European Growth	2.60	Y	F		129
Universal European Opportunities	2.48	Y	F		80
Vision Europe Fund	2.23	Y	F	3	144
Average	2.25			3.3	

(R) — Restricted; (C) — Closed to new investors; MER — Management Expense Ratio; Load — fee charged; RRSP: R = 100% eligible, F = eligible as foreign content only, N = not eligible; Volatility — measures swings in performance on a scale of 1 to 10 (1 = low, 10 = high). Blank space indicates that fund is less than three years old. Fund company addresses may be found by number in Appendix 3.

23

• •

U.S. Equity Funds

U.S. EQUITY FUNDS have been a part of the Canadian mutual fund scene for a long time, with several dating back to the 1960s. The primary objective of U.S. equity funds is to achieve long-term capital growth by investing in the stocks of U.S. corporations. There are currently 126 U.S. and North American equity funds available to investors. These funds manage $10.2 billion in assets.

Over the five calendar years from 1992 to 1996, the best year for U.S. equity funds was 1995, when returns averaged 24.8%. In contrast, the worst year was 1994, when returns averaged 0.9%. The average annual compound rate of return over the five-year period was 14.0%.

U.S. equity funds have an average volatility rating of 3.5, which is below the average of 4.1 for all equity funds. The average fee for management expenses is $2.21 for every $100 in assets, which is slightly down from last year's average of $2.28.

The Heavy Hitters

There are 18 U.S. equity funds that have qualified for membership in the Heavy Hitters club this year. Each of these funds has consistently delivered *above*-average returns over the past one-, three-, and five-year periods. Collectively these Heavy Hitters manage a total of $4.0 billion in assets. Fidelity Growth America Fund is the largest, with $1.1 billion in assets, and the Mutual Amerifund is the smallest, with $6.6 million in assets. Nine of the 18 Heavy Hitters are load funds.

Table 1
THE HEAVY HITTERS
U.S. EQUITY FUNDS

		Bench-mark*	Vola-tility	Performance Quartile 1	Performance Quartile 2	Overall Rating
1	Phillips Hager & North U.S. Equity (R) (N)	3	3	2	3	★★1/2
2	Chou Associates Fund	2	3	3	1	★★
3	RoyFund U.S. Equity Fund (N)	2	3	3	1	★★
4	Fidelity Growth America Fund	2	4	2	3	★★
5	AIC Value Fund	2	4	3	0	★1/2
6	Investors U.S. Growth Fund	1	3	1	3	★1/2
7	AGF American Growth Fund	1	4	1	3	★
8	Green Line U.S. Index Fund ($US) (N)	1	3	2	0	★
9	McLean Budden Pooled American Eq. (R) (N)	1	4	2	1	★
10	Hyperion Value Line U.S. Equity	1	4	1	2	★
11	Ethical North American Equity Fund (N)	1	4	1	2	★
12	Royal Trust American Stock Fund (N)	1	3	0	3	★
13	Dynamic Americas Fund	1	4	1	1	★
14	Cornerstone U.S. Fund (N)	0	3	1	2	★
15	McLean Budden American Gr. Fund (N)	0	4	2	1	★
16	Mutual Amerifund	0	3	1	1	★
17	Atlas Amer. Large Cap Growth Fund (N)	0	3	0	3	★
18	BPI American Equity Value Fund	0	3	0	2	★

* S&P 500 Total Return Index; (R) — Restricted; (C) — Closed to new members; (N) — No-load fund; Benchmark — number of times that a fund beat the benchmark from 1992 to 1996; Volatility — measures swings in fund returns on a scale of 1 to 10 (1 = low, 10 = high); Performance — number of times that a fund was in the first (top 25%) or second quartile (top 50%) from 1992 to 1996.

The benchmark used to compare U.S. equity fund returns is the Standard & Poor's Total Return Index (S&P 500), measured in Canadian dollars. Over the past five calendar years, the index posted its highest return of 33.8% in 1995 and its lowest return of 7.4% in 1994.

Phillips Hager & North U.S. Equity Fund ★★1/2

This fund was launched in 1964 and is managed by the firm's U.S. equity team. With $459 million in assets, it follows a bottom-up/

growth investment strategy. Investments in financial services, consumer products, health care, and capital goods account for about 45% of the fund's assets.

Its best year was 1995, when it posted a return of 25.9%, and its worst year was 1994, when its return was 2.4%. The fund's average annual compound return over the past five years was 19.3%. A no-load fund, it charges management expenses of $1.10 for every $100 in assets, which is considerably lower than the group average of $2.21. The fund has a minimum initial investment requirement of $25,000 for non-RRSP accounts and $5,000 for RRSP accounts.

Chou Associates Fund ★★

This fund, sponsored by Chou Associates Management, was started in 1986 and has been managed by Francis Chou since its inception. The fund has $8 million in assets and follows a bottom-up/value investment strategy.

In 1995, its best year, the fund posted a return of 31.0%, and in 1994, its worst year, it returned -2.6%. Over the past five years, it yielded an average annual compound return of 18.8%. This load fund, sold only on a front-end basis, charges slightly above-average management expenses of $2.24 for every $100 in assets.

RoyFund U.S. Equity Fund ★★

This fund, sponsored by the Royal Bank of Canada, was launched in 1991 and has been managed by James Young since its inception. With $131 million in assets, it follows a bottom-up/blend investment strategy. About 90% of the fund's portfolio is invested in U.S. equities and 10% in cash.

The fund posted its highest return, 30.6%, in 1995, and its lowest, 3.4%, in 1994. Over the past five years, its average annual compound return was 19.7%. This is a no-load fund which charges management expenses of $2.12 for every $100 in assets, slightly lower than the group average of $2.21.

Fidelity Growth America Fund ★★

This fund was launched in 1990 and has been managed by Brad Lewis since its inception. With $1.1 billion in assets, it follows a bottom-up/

growth investment strategy. Investments in energy, financial services, technology, and utilities account for over 60% of the fund's assets.

Its best year was 1995, when it posted a return of 29.3%, and its worst year was 1994, when its return was 6.2%. The fund's average annual compound return over the past five years was 19.0%. A load fund, it charges management expenses of $2.33 for every $100 in assets, which is higher than the group average of $2.21.

AIC Value Fund ★1/2

This fund was started in 1990 and is managed by the investment team of Michael Lee-Chin, Jonathan Wellum, and Neil Murdoch. The fund has $437 million in assets and follows a bottom-up/blend investment strategy. Investments in financial services, mutual fund companies, and consumer products account for over 70% of the fund's portfolio.

In 1993, its best year, the fund posted a return of 35.9%, and in 1994, its worst year, it returned -4.2%. Over the past five years, it yielded an average annual compound return of 25.7%. This load fund charges above-average management expenses of $2.55 for every $100 in assets.

Investors U.S. Growth Fund ★1/2

This fund was launched in 1961 and has been managed by Larry Sarbit since September 1987. With $910 million in assets, it follows a bottom-up/value investment strategy. Investments in financial services, consumer products, and communications account for over 80% of the fund's portfolio.

The fund posted its highest return, 24.8%, in 1995, and its lowest, 7.0%, in 1994. Over the past five years, its average annual compound return was 18.9%. This is a load fund which charges management expenses of $2.35 for every $100 in assets, higher than the group average of $2.21.

AGF American Growth Fund ★

This fund was launched in 1957 and has been managed by Stephen Rogers since March 1993. With $259 million in assets, it follows a bottom-up/growth investment strategy. Investments in technology stocks account for about 33% of the fund's assets, with another 30% in consumer products.

Its best year was 1995, when it posted a return of 28.8%, and its worst year was 1994, when its return was 3.5%. The fund's average annual compound return over the past five years was 20.1%. A load fund, it charges above-average management expenses of $2.79 for every $100 in assets.

Green Line U.S. Index Fund ★

This index fund, sponsored by the Toronto-Dominion Bank, was started in 1986. The fund has $101 million in assets and tracks the S&P 500 Index, which consists of stocks of major U.S. companies.

In 1995, its best year, the fund posted a return of 35.3%, and in 1994, its worst year, it returned 0.5%. Over the past five years, it yielded an average annual compound return of 16.8%. This no-load fund charges well-below-average management expenses of $0.72 for every $100 in assets.

McLean Budden Pooled American Equity Fund ★

This fund was launched in 1983 and is managed by the firm's U.S. equities team of Bill Giblin, Mary Hallward, and Bruce Murray. With $146 million in assets, it follows a bottom-up/growth investment strategy. Investments in consumer products, capital goods and technology, and financial services account for close to 70% of the fund's assets.

The fund posted its highest return, 29.2%, in 1995, and its lowest, 6.7%, in 1994. Over the past five years, its average annual compound return was 19.2%. This is a no-load fund which charges management expenses of $1.00 for every $100 in assets, considerably lower than the group average of $2.21. The fund has a minimum initial investment requirement of $500,000 and is not RRSP eligible.

Hyperion Value Line U.S. Equity Fund ★

This fund, sponsored by Talvest Fund Management Inc., was identified as a Rookie Camp member in last year's *World of Mutual Funds*. The fund was launched in 1991 and has been managed by Nancy Bendig of the New York–based firm Value Line Inc. since October 1995. With $72 million in assets, it follows a bottom-up/growth investment strategy. Investments in financial services, oil and gas, technology, and health care account for over 70% of the fund's assets.

Its best year was 1995, when it posted a return of 37.4%, and its worst year was 1994, when its return was 0.6%. The fund's average annual compound return over the past five years was 19.5%. A load fund, it charges management expenses of $3.00 for every $100 in assets, which is higher than the group average of $2.21.

Ethical North American Equity Fund ★

This fund was started in 1968 and has been managed by Cynthia Frick of the U.S.-based investment firm Alliance Capital Management since June 1993. The fund has $72 million in assets and follows a bottom-up/growth investment strategy. Investments in financial services, pharmaceuticals, computer technology, and telecommunications account for close to 70% of the fund's portfolio.

In 1995, its best year, the fund posted a return of 29.8%, and in 1994, its worst year, it returned -4.2%. Over the past five years, it yielded an average annual compound return of 17.9%. This no-load fund charges above-average management expenses of $2.49 for every $100 in assets. The fund is not available for sale in Quebec.

Royal Trust American Stock Fund ★

This fund, part of the Royal Bank's family of funds, was launched in 1966 and has been managed by James Young since January 1994. With $176 million in assets, it follows a bottom-up/blend investment strategy. About 50% of the fund's assets are made up of investments in technology, capital goods, consumer products, and energy.

The fund posted its highest return, 28.0%, in 1995, and its lowest, 2.6%, in 1994. Over the past five years, its average annual compound return was 16.9%. This is a no-load fund which charges management expenses of $2.18 for every $100 in assets, slightly lower than the group average of $2.21.

Dynamic Americas Fund ★

This fund, formerly the Dynamic American Fund, was launched in 1979 and is managed by the firm's investment team. With $70 million in assets, it follows a bottom-up/value investment strategy. Investments in consumer products, industrial products, and interest-sensitive sectors account for close to 70% of the fund's assets.

Its best year was 1996, when it posted a return of 26.9%, and its worst year was 1994, when its return was -4.0%. The fund's average annual compound return over the past five years was 16.2%. A load fund, it charges management expenses of $2.48 for every $100 in assets, which is higher than the group average of $2.21.

Cornerstone U.S. Fund ★

This fund, sponsored by the Laurentian Bank of Canada, was started in 1963 and is managed by Matthew Megargel of the Boston-based investment firm Wellington Management Company. The fund has $32 million in assets and follows a bottom-up/growth investment strategy. Investments in consumer products, industrial products, and financial services account for close to 60% of the fund's portfolio.

In 1995, its best year, the fund posted a return of 24.9%, and in 1994, its worst year, it returned 5.6%. Over the past five years, it yielded an average annual compound return of 16.0%. This no-load fund charges above-average management expenses of $2.84 for every $100 in assets.

McLean Budden American Growth Fund ★

This fund, McLean Budden's second U.S. equity Heavy Hitter, was launched in 1989 and is managed by the U.S. equities team of Bill Giblin, Mary Hallward, and Bruce Murray. With $16 million in assets, it follows a bottom-up/growth investment strategy. Close to 70% of the fund's assets are made up of investments in consumer products, capital goods, and financial services.

The fund posted its highest return, 26.6%, in 1995, and its lowest, 2.8%, in 1993. Over the past five years, its average annual compound return was 16.6%. This is a no-load fund which charges management expenses of $1.75 for every $100 in assets, lower than the group average of $2.21. The fund has a minimum initial investment requirement of $5,000.

Mutual Amerifund ★

This segregated fund, sponsored by Mutual Life of Canada, was launched in 1986 and has $7 million in assets. The fund's investment objective is to provide long-term capital appreciation through investment in U.S. equity securities.

Its best year was 1996, when it posted a return of 22.6%, and its worst year was 1994, when its return was 0.4%. The fund's average annual compound return over the past five years was 15.8%. A load fund, sold only on a front-end basis, it charges management expenses of $2.07 for every $100 in assets, which is lower than the group average of $2.21.

Atlas American Large Cap Growth Fund ★

This fund, sponsored by Atlas Asset Management Inc., a wholly owned subsidiary of Midland Walwyn, was started in 1985 and is managed by Len Racioppo of the investment firm Jarislowsky Fraser & Co. Ltd. The fund has $15 million in assets and follows a top-down/growth investment strategy. Investments in health care, electronics, oil and gas, and financial services account for 50% of the fund's assets.

In 1995, its best year, the fund posted a return of 29.6%, and in 1994, its worst year, it returned 2.8%. Over the past five years, it yielded an average annual compound return of 16.2%. This no-load fund charges above-average management expenses of $2.67 for every $100 in assets.

BPI American Equity Value Fund ★

This fund was launched in 1989 and has been managed by Paul Holland and Noah Blackstein since April 1997. With $63 million in assets, it follows a bottom-up/value investment strategy. Close to 60% of the fund's assets are made up of investments in consumer products, financial services, industrial products, and technology.

The fund posted its highest return, 26.4%, in 1995, and its lowest, 3.5%, in 1994. Over the past five years, its average annual compound return was 15.5%. This is a load fund which charges management expenses of $2.62 for every $100 in assets, higher than the group average of $2.21.

The Rookie Camp

Nine of the promising newer U.S. equity funds, each with at least a three-year track record, are in the Rookie Camp this year. Each of these funds, listed below, posted *above*-average returns over the past one-, two-, and three-year periods.

Canada Trust Everest AmeriGrowth Fund, sponsored by Canada Trust, was launched in 1993 and follows a top-down investment strategy. A no-load fund, it has $421 million in assets and charges well-below-average management expenses of $1.48 for every $100 in assets.

Co-operators U.S. Equity Fund, a segregated fund sponsored by the Co-operators Life Insurance Company of Regina, was launched in 1994 and is managed by Milton Burns. With $5 million in assets, the fund follows a bottom-up/value investment strategy. It is a no-load fund and charges below-average management expenses of $2.07 for every $100 in assets.

Mawer U.S. Equity Fund, sponsored by Mawer Investment Management of Calgary, has been managed by Darrell Anderson since November 1994. The fund has $19 million in assets and follows a bottom-up/blend investment strategy. A no-load fund, it charges well-below-average management expenses of $1.18 for every $100 in assets. The fund has a minimum initial investment requirement of $25,000.

MD U.S. Equity Fund, sponsored by MD Management Limited, was launched in 1992 and follows a bottom-up/growth investment strategy. The fund is managed by the U.S. investment firm Alliance Capital Management of Delaware. A no-load fund, it has $178 million in assets and charges below-average management expenses of $1.31 for every $100 in assets. The fund is available only to members of the Canadian Medical Association and their families.

Metlife MVP U.S. Equity Fund, a segregated fund sponsored by the Metropolitan Life Insurance Company of Canada, was launched in 1993 and is managed by the Boston-based investment firm State Street Research & Management Company. With $20 million in assets, the fund follows a bottom-up/blend investment strategy. It is a load fund, sold only on a deferred basis, and charges slightly above-average management expenses of $2.23 for every $100 in assets.

NAL-U.S. Equity Fund, sponsored by Manulife Financial, is co-managed by the investment firms Elliott & Page Ltd. and Goldman Sachs Asset Management. The fund has $23 million in assets and follows a bottom-up/value investment strategy. A load fund, sold only on a deferred basis, it charges slightly above-average management expenses of $2.25 for every $100 in assets.

NN Can-Am Fund, a segregated fund sponsored by NN Life Insurance Company of Canada, was launched in 1992 and follows a top-down/blend investment strategy. The fund is managed by David Patterson of the investment firm Newcastle Capital Management Inc. A load fund, sold only on a deferred basis, it has $164 million in assets and charges above-average management expenses of $2.85 for every $100 in assets.

Optima Strategy U.S. Equity Fund, sponsored by Loring Ward Investment Counsel Limited of Winnipeg, was launched in 1994 and is managed by the investment firm Dreman Value Management. With $112 million in assets, the fund follows a bottom-up/value investment strategy. It is a load fund and charges considerably below-average management expenses of $0.42 for every $100 in assets.

Scotia CanAm Growth Fund, sponsored by the Bank of Nova Scotia, is designed to track closely the performance of the S&P 500 Index. A no-load fund, it has $130 million in assets and charges below-average management expenses of $1.34 for every $100 in assets.

The Underachievers

There are 13 U.S. equity funds that have failed to measure up to their peers. These Underachievers have consistently delivered *below*-average returns over the past one-, three-, and five-year periods. Collectively these Underachievers manage just under $1 billion in assets. The Industrial American Fund, sponsored by Mackenzie Financial Corporation, is the largest, with $280 million in assets, and the Century DJ Fund is the smallest, with $0.3 million in assets. Eight of the 13 Underachievers are load funds.

Table 2

THE UNDERACHIEVERS

U.S. EQUITY FUNDS

- AGF Special U.S. Class
- Bissett American Equity Fund
- Cambridge American Growth
- Century DJ Fund
- CIBC U.S. Equity Fund*

Table 2

THE UNDERACHIEVERS *continued*

U.S. EQUITY FUNDS

- First American (Guardian Timing)
- General Trust of Canada U.S. Equity*
- Industrial American Fund
- Laurentian American Equity Fund Ltd.
- Scotia Excelsior American Growth*
- Trust Pret & Revenu American Fund*
- University Avenue Growth Fund
- Zweig Strategic Growth*

* denotes a no-load fund

Heavy Hitters vs Underachievers

Table 3 shows the difference in returns, over three time periods, between the Heavy Hitters and Underachievers in this category. As can be seen, the Heavy Hitters posted returns that were, on average, significantly higher than the Underachievers'. In dollar terms, for an initial investment of $10,000, the average Heavy Hitter U.S. equity fund would have returned a total of $23,072 over the past five years. For the same investment, the average Underachiever would have returned $16,474 — for a difference of $6,598 or 40%.

With respect to costs, the average U.S. equity Heavy Hitter charged management expenses of $2.18 for every $100 in assets, compared with $2.39 for the the average Underachiever.

Table 3

HEAVY HITTERS vs UNDERACHIEVERS

U.S. EQUITY FUNDS

(Returns %)

	1-Year	3-Year*	5-Year*
• Heavy Hitters	27.6	21.7	18.2
• Underachievers	6.3	10.7	10.5

* annualized

U.S. EQUITY FUNDS
RANKINGS/RETURNS

Rank			Name of Fund	Returns (%)			Assets
(47)	(68)	(97)		(17.2)	(17.7)	(15.4)	
5-Yr	3-Yr	1-Yr		1-Yr	3-Yr	5-Yr	($mns)
-	53	94	20/20 Aggressive Growth Fund	-6.7	14.4	-	274.0
-	-	30	ABC American-Value Fund	23.9	-	-	11.1
43	61	46	Admax American Growth Fund	19.4	10.6	8.5	1.9
4	11	9	AGF American Growth Fund (HH)	30.0	22.8	20.1	258.7
42	65	95	AGF Special U.S. Class (UA)	-6.8	8.5	11.0	151.9
2	2	1	AIC Value Fund (HH)	48.7	28.5	25.7	437.4
8	56	90	Altamira Select American Fund	-1.1	13.5	19.3	221.1
-	28	80	Altamira U.S. Larger Company Fund	8.4	19.4	-	88.3
19	7	6	Atlas Amer. Large Cap Growth Fund (HH)	31.0	23.3	16.2	15.2
15	44	43	Beutel Goodman American Equity	19.7	16.1	17.2	6.5
29	37	60	Bissett American Equity Fund (UA)	15.1	17.6	14.6	10.3
26	35	47	BPI American Equity Value Fund (HH)	18.6	18.2	15.5	63.2
1	18	59	BPI American Small Companies Fund	15.6	21.0	26.1	118.7
-	36	66	C.I. American Fund	13.2	17.7	-	183.9
-	-	50	C.I. American RSP Fund	18.3	-	-	24.4
-	39	73	C.I. American Sector Shares	12.2	17.1	-	53.1
47	67	86	Cambridge American Growth (Sagit) (UA)	3.6	2.4	3.2	0.4
-	6	25	Canada Trust Everest AmeriGrowth (RC)	25.0	23.5	-	420.8
38	46	41	Canada Trust Everest U.S. Equity	20.4	15.8	13.0	133.9
35	17	57	Cassels Blaikie American Fund ($US)	15.7	21.3	13.4	11.3
-	-	20	CCPE U.S. Equity	26.1	-	-	23.2
46	66	84	Century DJ Fund (UA)	5.0	4.4	4.5	0.3
13	12	4	Chou Associates Fund (HH)	33.3	22.7	18.8	7.7
34	43	63	CIBC U.S. Equity Fund (UA)	14.8	16.3	14.2	150.7
-	-	92	CIBC U.S. Opportunities Fund	-5.0	-	-	12.2
-	1	52	Co-operators U.S. Equity Fund (RC)	17.5	33.4	-	4.8
21	26	17	Cornerstone U.S. Fund (HH)	26.6	19.7	16.0	31.9
20	19	19	Dynamic Americas Fund (HH)	26.4	20.9	16.2	69.7
28	31	21	Elliott & Page American Growth Fund	26.1	18.6	15.4	96.5
14	16	8	Ethical North American Equity Fund (HH)	30.6	22.4	17.9	71.6
-	-	14	Ferique American Fund	27.2	-	-	4.2
11	29	48	Fidelity Growth America Fund (HH)	18.5	19.4	19.0	1055.6
-	45	75	Fidelity Small-Cap America Fund	11.5	16.0	-	56.1
44	68	93	First American (Guardian Timing) (UA)	-5.8	1.3	4.6	10.3

U.S. EQUITY FUNDS
RANKINGS/RETURNS cont'd

Rank			Name of Fund	Returns (%)			Assets
(47)	(68)	(97)		(17.2)	(17.7)	(15.4)	
5-Yr	3-Yr	1-Yr		1-Yr	3-Yr	5-Yr	($mns)
-	-	56	First Canadian NAFTA Advantage Fund	16.3	-	-	23.4
-	54	18	First Cdn. U.S. Growth Fund	26.5	14.2	-	128.7
-	-	39	Fonds Desjardins Marche Americain	21.4	-	-	8.9
23	55	89	GBC North American Growth Fund Inc.	1.7	13.6	15.9	93.5
37	58	62	General Trust of Canada U.S. Equity (UA)	14.9	12.9	13.3	5.6
-	-	2	Global Manager - U.S. Geared Fund	38.6	-	-	0.2
-	-	37	Global Manager - U.S. Index Fund	22.0	-	-	1.6
-	-	61	Global Strategy U.S. Equity	15.1	-	-	11.5
-	24	79	Green Line North Amer. Growth A	9.1	20.1	-	133.7
17	5	11	Green Line U.S. Index Fund ($US) (HH)	28.4	24.5	16.8	101.0
-	-	13	Growsafe U.S. 500 Index Fund	27.5	-	-	21.5
-	-	22	GS American Equity Fund	26.0	-	-	16.8
-	-	91	GT Global America Growth Class	-3.5	-	-	18.1
22	50	76	Guardian American Equity Fund A	10.8	15.5	16.0	37.8
-	-	77	Guardian American Equity Fund B	10.1	-	-	14.4
-	-	53	GWL U.S. Equity Fund (G) DSC	17.3	-	-	14.2
-	-	54	GWL U.S. Equity Fund (G) NL	17.0	-	-	24.0
7	13	49	Hyperion Value Line U.S. Equity (HH)	18.4	22.5	19.5	72.2
25	48	58	Imperial Growth North American Equity	15.7	15.6	15.5	3.4
36	59	64	Industrial American Fund (UA)	13.7	12.7	13.4	280.2
-	62	69	InvesNat Blue Chip Amer. Equity ($US)	12.9	10.3	-	4.5
12	22	7	Investors U.S. Growth Fund (HH)	30.7	20.4	18.9	909.7
41	63	35	Jones Heward American Fund	22.6	10.2	11.7	16.2
33	52	67	Laurentian American Equity Fund Ltd. (UA)	12.9	15.0	14.2	123.7
-	40	72	Leith Wheeler U.S. Equity Fund	12.6	16.7	-	2.9
31	41	12	London Life U.S. Equity	27.6	16.7	14.4	182.5
-	-	81	Manulife Vistafund 1 Amer. Stock	8.2	-	-	13.8
-	-	82	Manulife Vistafund 2 Amer. Stock	7.4	-	-	85.0
32	42	38	Margin of Safety Fund (Hillery Inv.)	21.8	16.6	14.2	5.3
-	-	45	Maritime Life Amer. Gr. & Inc. - A & C	19.4	-	-	94.2
-	-	26	Maritime Life S&P 500 - A & C	24.5	-	-	148.7
-	23	36	Mawer U.S. Equity Fund (RC)	22.1	20.1	-	18.6
-	-	51	Maxxum American Equity Fund	17.9	-	-	17.4
-	-	74	McDonald New America	12.0	-	-	0.7

U.S. EQUITY FUNDS
RANKINGS/RETURNS *cont'd*

Rank			Name of Fund	Returns (%)			Assets
(47)	(68)	(97)		(17.2)	(17.7)	(15.4)	
5-Yr	3-Yr	1-Yr		1-Yr	3-Yr	5-Yr	($mns)
18	14	10	McLean Budden American Growth Fund (HH)	28.6	22.5	16.6	16.2
10	4	5	McLean Budden Pooled American Eq. (HH)	31.9	25.2	19.2	146.2
-	9	15	MD U.S. Equity Fund (RC)	26.9	23.0	-	177.8
-	32	27	Metlife MVP U.S. Equity Fund (RC)	24.4	18.4	-	19.9
-	-	68	Millennia III American Equity 1	12.9	-	-	16.1
-	-	70	Millennia III American Equity 2	12.7	-	-	3.0
24	34	28	Mutual Amerifund (HH)	24.3	18.3	15.8	6.6
-	38	32	Mutual Premier American Fund	23.7	17.3	-	36.7
-	33	23	NAL-U.S. Equity Fund (RC)	25.7	18.4	-	23.2
-	47	42	National Trust American Equity Fund	20.0	15.7	-	21.2
-	-	44	Navigator American Value Inv.	19.6	-	-	1.0
-	15	34	NN Can-Am Fund (RC)	23.6	22.4	-	163.9
-	-	88	O'Donnell American Sector Growth	1.8	-	-	21.0
-	-	78	O'Donnell U.S. Mid-Cap Fund	9.8	-	-	10.0
-	3	3	Optima Strategy U.S. Equity (RC)	33.9	25.9	-	111.9
9	21	31	Phillips Hager & North U.S. Equity (HH)	23.8	20.5	19.3	458.8
-	-	40	Royal Life U.S. Equity Fund	20.7	-	-	11.3
16	30	29	Royal Trust American Stock Fund (HH)	24.2	19.0	16.9	176.2
6	25	33	RoyFund U.S. Equity Fund (HH)	23.7	20.0	19.7	131.3
-	8	24	Scotia CanAm Growth Fund (RC)	25.0	23.3	-	129.6
39	57	71	Scotia Excelsior American Growth (UA)	12.7	13.2	12.9	62.5
27	20	55	Spectrum United American Equity	16.8	20.7	15.4	291.2
5	10	87	Spectrum United American Growth	3.3	23.0	19.7	442.0
-	49	65	Spectrum United Optimax U.S.A. Fund	13.4	15.5	-	14.6
-	-	16	Standard Life U.S. Equity Fund	26.9	-	-	3.6
40	51	96	Trust Pret & Revenu American Fund (UA)	-8.9	15.4	11.9	5.7
3	27	97	Universal U.S. Emerging Growth Fund	-16.1	19.6	21.3	308.2
45	64	85	University Avenue Growth Fund (UA)	3.6	8.5	4.5	0.7
30	60	83	Zweig Strategic Growth (UA)	6.4	11.5	14.6	163.8

( ) under Rank indicates total number of funds; ( ) under Returns (%) indicates average annual return; (HH) — Heavy Hitter; (UA) — Underachiever; (RC) — Rookie Camp member.

U.S. EQUITY FUNDS/SUMMARY

Name of Fund	MER	Load	RRSP	Vola-tility	Company Number (App. 3)
20/20 Aggressive Growth Fund	2.45	Y	F	6	3
ABC American-Value Fund (R)	2.00	N	F		1
Admax American Growth Fund	2.75	Y	F	4	69
AGF American Growth Fund	2.79	Y	F	4	3
AGF Special U.S. Class	2.81	Y	F	5	3
AIC Value Fund	2.55	Y	F	4	4
Altamira Select American Fund	2.28	N	F	4	6
Altamira U.S. Larger Company Fund	2.30	N	F	4	6
APEX U.S. Equity Fund (R)	2.80	Y	F		126
Atlas Amer. Large Cap Growth Fund	2.67	N	F	3	9
Atlas American R.S.P. Index Fund	1.61	N	R		9
Beutel Goodman American Equity	2.78	N	F	3	12
Bissett American Equity Fund (R)	1.50	Y	F	3	13
BPI American Equity Value Fund	2.62	Y	F	3	15
BPI American Small Companies Fund	2.92	Y	F	4	15
C.I. American Fund	2.46	Y	F	3	28
C.I. American RSP Fund	2.46	Y	R		28
C.I. American Sector Shares	2.51	Y	F	3	28
Cambridge American Growth	2.91	Y	F	6	121
Canada Trust Everest AmeriGrowth	1.48	N	R	3	19
Canada Trust Everest U.S. Equity	2.43	N	F	3	19
Cassels Blaikie American Fund ($US)	1.13	Y	F	4	26
CCPE U.S. Equity (R)	1.75	N	F		21
CDA U.S. Equity (R)	1.20	N	F		22
Century DJ Fund	1.80	Y	F	1	81
Chou Associates Fund	2.24	Y	F	3	27
CIBC U.S. Equity Fund	2.25	N	F	3	29
CIBC U.S. Index RRSP Fund	1.00	N	R		29
CIBC U.S. Opportunities Fund	2.45	N	F		29
Clarington U.S. Equity Fund	2.95	Y	F		30
Clarington U.S. Smaller Co. Growth	2.95	Y	F		30
Co-operators U.S. Equity Fund (R)	2.07	N	F		33
Cornerstone U.S. Fund	2.83	N	F	3	73
Cote 100 U.S. (R)	0.41	Y	F	4	34
Dynamic Americas Fund	2.48	Y	F	4	40

U.S. EQUITY FUNDS/SUMMARY *cont'd*

Name of Fund	MER	Load	RRSP	Vola-tility	Company Number (App. 3)
Elliott & Page American Growth Fund	1.16	Y	F	3	41
Ethical North American Equity Fund (R)	2.49	N	F	4	44
Ferique American Fund (R)	0.65	N	R		109
Fidelity Growth America Fund	2.33	Y	F	4	46
Fidelity Small-Cap America Fund	2.66	Y	F		46
First American (Guardian Timing) (R)	2.80	Y	R	2	62
First Canadian NAFTA Advantage Fund	2.00	N	F		11
First Canadian U.S. Equity Index	1.16	N	R		11
First Canadian U.S. Special Growth	1.72	N	F		11
First Canadian U.S. Value Fund	1.75	N	F		11
First Canadian U.S. Growth Fund	2.21	N	F	4	11
Fonds Desjardins Marche Americain (R)	2.25	●N	R		37
Franklin U.S. Small-Cap Growth Fund	2.00	Y	F		137
GBC North American Gr. Fund Inc. (R)	1.83	N	F	4	52
General Trust of Canada U.S. Eq. (R)	2.15	N	F	4	98
Global Manager - U.S. Geared (R)	1.00	Y	N		10
Global Manager - U.S. Index Fund (R)	1.00	Y	N		10
Global Strategy U.S. Equity	2.75	Y	F		54
Green Line North Amer. Growth A	2.34	N	F	4	139
Green Line U.S. Blue Chip Equity	2.44	N	F		139
Green Line U.S. Index Fund ($US)	0.72	N	F	3	139
Growsafe U.S. 21st Century Index	1.99	Y	R		141
Growsafe U.S. 500 Index Fund	1.99	Y	R		141
GS American Equity Fund	3.24	Y	F		70
GT Global America Growth Class	2.95	Y	F		60
Guardian American Equity Fund A	2.37	Y	F	4	61
Guardian American Equity Fund B	2.97	Y	F		61
GWL U.S. Equity Fund (G) DSC	2.60	Y	F		57
GWL U.S. Equity Fund (G) NL	2.85	N	F		57
Hyperion Global Health Care Fund	3.30	Y	F		136
Hyperion Value Line U.S. Equity	3.00	Y	F	4	136
Imperial Growth N. A. Equity (C)	1.60	Y	F	3	65
Industrial Alliance Ecoflex Fund S	3.65	Y	F		66
Industrial Alliance U.S. Stock Fund	2.99	N	F		66
Industrial American Fund	2.38	Y	F	4	80

U.S. EQUITY FUNDS/SUMMARY *cont'd*

Name of Fund	MER	Load	RRSP	Vola-tility	Company Number (App. 3)
InvesNat Blue Chip Amer. Eq. ($US) (R)	2.33	N	F	3	98
Investors U.S. Growth Fund	2.35	Y	F	3	70
Investors U.S. Opportunities Fund	2.61	Y	F		70
Jones Heward American Fund	2.50	Y	F	4	72
Laurentian American Equity Fund Ltd.	2.65	Y	F	3	135
Leith Wheeler U.S. Equity Fund (R)	1.25	N	F		74
London Life U.S. Equity	2.00	Y	F	3	76
Manulife Vistafund 1 Amer. Stock	1.63	Y	F		83
Manulife Vistafund 2 Amer. Stock	2.38	Y	F		83
Margin of Safety Fund (Hillery Inv.) (R)	1.87	N	N	2	71
Maritime Life Amer. Gr. & Inc. - A & C	2.30	Y	F		85
Maritime Life Amer. Gr. & Inc. - B	2.30	Y	F		85
Maritime Life Discovery - A & C	2.30	Y	F		85
Maritime Life Discovery - B	2.30	Y	F		85
Maritime Life S&P 500 - A & C	2.05	Y	R		85
Maritime Life S&P 500 - B	2.05	Y	R		85
Mawer U.S. Equity Fund (R)	1.18	N	F	3	86
Maxxum American Equity Fund	2.50	Y	F		87
McDonald New America (R)	2.50	Y	N		88
McLean Budden American Growth Fund	1.75	N	F	4	89
McLean Budden Pooled American Eq. (R)	1.00	N	N	4	89
MD U.S. Equity Fund (R)	1.31	N	F	4	90
Metlife MVP U.S. Equity Fund	2.23	Y	N	3	92
Millennia III American Equity 1	2.77	Y	F		65
Millennia III American Equity 2	2.95	N	F		65
Mutual Amerifund	2.07	Y	F	3	97
Mutual Premier American Fund	2.34	N	F	3	97
NAL-U.S. Equity Fund	2.25	Y	F	3	83
National Trust American Equity Fund (R)	2.59	N	F	3	100
National Trust U.S. Index Fund (R)	0.80	N	F		100
Navigator American Growth Fund (R)	3.05	Y	F		101
Navigator American Value Inv. (R)	2.95	Y	F		101
NN Can-Am Fund	2.85	Y	R	3	102
NN Can-Daq 100 Fund	2.85	Y	R		102
North-West Life Ecoflex S	3.65	Y	F		103

U.S. EQUITY FUNDS/SUMMARY *cont'd*

Name of Fund	MER	Load	RRSP	Vola-tility	Company Number (App. 3)
O'Donnell American Sector Growth	2.90	Y	F		104
O'Donnell U.S. Mid-Cap Fund	2.90	Y	F		104
Optima Strategy U.S. Equity (R)	0.42	Y	F		77
Phillips Hager & North U.S. Equity (R)	1.10	N	F	3	112
Royal Life U.S. Equity Fund	2.25	Y	F		120
Royal Trust American Stock Fund	2.18	N	F	3	119
RoyFund U.S. Equity Fund	2.12	N	F	3	119
Scotia CanAm Growth Fund	1.34	N	R	3	124
Scotia Excelsior American Growth	2.19	N	F	4	124
Scudder U.S. Gr. & Income Fund (R)	1.25	N	F		125
Spectrum United American Equity	2.30	Y	F	4	129
Spectrum United American Growth	2.35	Y	F	4	129
Spectrum United Optimax U.S.A. Fund	2.35	Y	F	3	129
Standard Life U.S. Equity Fund	2.00	Y	F		133
Strategic Value American Equity	2.75	Y	F		135
Templeton Mutual Beacon Fund	2.00	Y	F		137
Trust Pret & Revenu American Fund	2.09	N	F	5	145
Universal U.S. Emerging Growth Fund	2.40	Y	F	6	80
University Avenue Growth Fund	2.99	Y	F	3	146
Valorem U.S. Equity-Value (R)	2.25	Y	F		152
Zweig Strategic Growth	2.59	N	F	2	119
Average	2.21			3.5	

(R) — Restricted; (C) — Closed to new investors; MER — Management Expense Ratio; Load — fee charged; RRSP: R = 100% eligible, F = eligible as foreign content only, N = not eligible; Volatility — measures swings in performance on a scale of 1 to 10 (1 = low, 10 = high). Blank space indicates that fund is less than three years old. Fund company addresses may be found by number in Appendix 3.

24

● ●

Emerging-Market Funds

THE PRIMARY OBJECTIVE of emerging-market funds is to invest in the stocks of companies that are located in the developing countries of the world, including Latin America, Southeast Asia, the Indian subcontinent, Eastern Europe, the Middle East, and Africa. There are currently 48 emerging-market funds. These funds manage a total of $3.9 billion in assets.

Over the five calendar years from 1992 to 1996, the best year for emerging-market funds was 1993, when returns averaged 70.3%. In contrast, the worst year was 1995, when returns averaged -10.8%. Returns were also negative in 1994, -9.7%. The average annual compound rate of return over the five-year period was 10.3%.

Emerging-market funds have an average volatility rating of 5.5, which is significantly higher than the average of 4.1 for all equity funds. These funds are some of the most volatile of those in any fund category. The average fee for management expenses is $2.82 for every $100 in assets, which is the highest for any international fund group.

The Heavy Hitters

The Templeton Emerging Markets Fund is the only fund in this category to qualify for membership in the Heavy Hitters club this year. This fund has consistently delivered *above*-average returns over the past one-, three-, and five-year periods.

Table 1

THE HEAVY HITTERS

EMERGING-MARKET FUNDS

		Bench-mark*	Vola-tility	Performance Quartile 1	Quartile 2	Overall Rating
1	Templeton Emerging Markets Fund	3	4	2	2	★★

* Morgan Stanley Emerging Markets Index; (R) — Restricted; (C) — Closed to new members; (N) — No-load fund; Benchmark — number of times that a fund beat the benchmark from 1992 to 1996; Volatility — measures swings in fund returns on a scale of 1 to 10 (1 = low, 10 = high); Performance — number of times that a fund was in the first (top 25%) or second quartile (top 50%) from 1992 to 1996.

The benchmark used to compare emerging-market fund returns is the Morgan Stanley Emerging Markets Index, measured in Canadian dollars. Over the past five calendar years, the index posted its highest return of 82.3% in 1993 and its lowest return of -7.8% in 1995. Returns were also negative in 1994.

Templeton Emerging Markets Fund ★★

This fund, the only Heavy Hitter in this category, was launched in 1991 and has been managed by Mark Mobius since its inception. With $1.3 billion in assets, it follows a bottom-up/value investment strategy. Investments in Asia, Europe, and Latin America account for over 75% of the fund's assets.

Its best year was 1993, when it posted a return of 82.8%, and its worst year was 1995, when its return was -4.4%. Returns were also negative in 1994. The fund's average annual compound return over the past five years was 16.2%. A load fund, it charges management expenses of $3.30 for every $100 in assets, which is higher than the group average of $2.82.

The Rookie Camp

Four of the promising newer emerging-market funds, each with at least a three-year track record, are in the Rookie Camp this year. Each of these funds, listed below, posted *above*-average returns over the past one-, two-, and three-year periods.

20/20 Latin America Fund, sponsored by AGF Management Ltd., was launched in 1994 and follows a bottom-up/value investment strategy. The fund is managed by Peter Gruber of the U.S. investment firm Globalvest Management Corporation. A load fund, it has $305 million in assets and charges above-average management expenses of $3.20 for every $100 in assets.

Global Strategy Latin America Fund, sponsored by Global Strategy Financial Inc. of Toronto, was launched in 1994 and is co-managed by the investment firms Rothschild, Schroeder Capital Management and Platinum Asset Management. With $11 million in assets, the fund follows a blend investment strategy. It is a load fund and charges above-average management expenses of $2.95 for every $100 in assets.

Global Strategy Diversified Latin America Fund, sponsored by Global Strategy Financial Inc. of Toronto, is co-managed by the investment firms Rothschild, Schroeder Capital Management and Platinum Asset Management. A load fund with $24 million in assets, it charges above-average management expenses of $2.95 for every $100 in assets. Unlike the Latin America Fund, by investing in derivatives this fund is 100% RRSP eligible.

Spectrum United Emerging Markets Fund, sponsored by Spectrum United Mutual Funds Inc., was launched in 1993 and follows a growth investment strategy. The fund is managed by Ewen Cameron Watt of the U.K. investment firm Mercury Investment Management International Limited. A load fund, it has $47 million in assets and charges below-average management expenses of $2.66 for every $100 in assets.

The Underachievers

C.I. Emerging Markets Fund is the only Underachiever in this category. It has consistently delivered *below*-average returns over the past one-, three-, and five-year periods. A load fund with $343 million in assets, it charges above-average management expenses of $2.93 for every $100 in assets.

Table 2

THE UNDERACHIEVERS

EMERGING-MARKET FUNDS

- C.I. Emerging Markets Fund

Heavy Hitters vs Underachievers

Table 3 shows the difference in returns over three time periods between the Heavy Hitters and the Underachievers for emerging-market funds. In dollar terms, for an initial investment of $10,000, the Templeton Emerging Markets Fund would have returned a total of $21,185 over the past five years. For the same investment, the C.I. Emerging Markets Fund would have returned $13,637 — for a difference of $7,548 or 55.4%.

With respect to costs, the Templeton Emerging Markets Fund charged management expenses of $3.30 for every $100 in assets, compared with $2.93 for the C.I. Emerging Markets Fund.

Table 3

HEAVY HITTERS vs UNDERACHIEVERS

EMERGING-MARKET FUNDS

(Returns %)

	1-Year	3-Year*	5-Year*
• Heavy Hitters	26.2	11.1	16.2
• Underachievers	8.0	-1.2	6.4

---

* annualized

EMERGING-MARKET FUNDS
RANKINGS/RETURNS

	Rank		Name of Fund	Returns (%)			Assets
(2)	(13)	(40)		(16.3)	(5.2)	(11.3)	
5-Yr	3-Yr	1-Yr		1-Yr	3-Yr	5-Yr	($mns)
-	13	26	20/20 Emerging Markets Value Fund	10.1	-1.8	-	23.1
-	1	1	20/20 Latin America Fund (RC)	52.0	18.6	-	305.4
-	-	38	AIC Emerging Markets Fund	2.6	-	-	4.8
-	-	14	Altamira Global Discovery Fund	20.1	-	-	34.1
-	7	10	Atlas Latin American Value Fund	25.0	3.3	-	17.9
-	-	9	BPI Emerging Markets Fund	25.4	-	-	9.5
2	11	30	C.I. Emerging Markets Fund (UA)	8.0	-1.2	6.4	343.2
-	12	31	C.I. Emerging Markets Sector Shares	7.3	-1.5	-	58.0
-	10	15	C.I. Latin American Fund	17.3	1.0	-	341.7
-	-	17	C.I. Latin American Sector Shares	16.7	-	-	33.8
-	-	25	Canada Trust Everest Emerging Mkts.	10.3	-	-	68.4
-	-	40	CDA Emerging Markets (KBSH)	-8.1	-	-	0.6
-	-	20	CIBC Emerging Economies Fund	13.9	-	-	12.5
-	-	19	Elliott & Page Emerging Markets	14.1	-	-	24.2
-	-	39	Fidelity Emerging Markets Portfolio	-5.6	-	-	97.3
-	8	4	Fidelity Latin American Growth Fund	34.4	3.3	-	179.8
-	-	21	First Canadian Emerging Mkts. Fund	12.1	-	-	58.9
-	-	18	GFM Emerging Markets Country ($US)	15.4	-	-	57.8
-	5	2	Global Strategy Diversified Latin (RC)	38.7	7.4	-	24.0
-	4	5	Global Strategy Latin America Fund (RC)	33.3	10.7	-	11.3
-	-	29	Globelnvest Emerg. Markets Country	9.1	-	-	14.8
-	9	34	Green Line Emerging Markets	5.8	1.2	-	153.9
-	-	11	Green Line Latin Amer. Growth Fund	24.2	-	-	47.5
-	-	3	GT Global Latin America Class	36.7	-	-	31.6
-	-	35	Guardian Emerging Markets Fund A	5.8	-	-	3.6
-	-	36	Guardian Emerging Markets Fund B	5.5	-	-	6.4
-	-	32	Hongkong Bank Emerging Markets Fund	6.9	-	-	12.8
-	-	28	Laurentian Emerging Markets Fund	9.7	-	-	4.7
-	-	33	McDonald Emerging Economies	6.4	-	-	0.6
-	-	16	MD Emerging Markets Fund	16.8	-	-	68.8
-	-	22	Merrill Lynch Emerging Markets Fund	11.4	-	-	93.5
-	-	37	Mutual Premier Emerging Markets	3.9	-	-	26.4
-	-	27	National Trust Emerging Markets	10.0	-	-	13.0
-	-	13	Royal Latin American Fund	21.7	-	-	35.5

EMERGING-MARKET FUNDS
RANKINGS/RETURNS *cont'd*

Rank			Name of Fund	Returns (%)			Assets
(2)	(13)	(40)		(16.3)	(5.2)	(11.3)	
5-Yr	3-Yr	1-Yr		1-Yr	3-Yr	5-Yr	($mns)
-	-	6	Scotia Excelsior Latin American	32.4	-	-	46.3
-	-	7	Scudder Emerging Markets Fund	31.6	-	-	22.9
-	2	12	Spectrum United Emerging Markets (RC)	22.9	11.2	-	47.3
1	3	8	Templeton Emerging Markets Fund (HH)	26.2	11.1	16.2	1279.4
-	-	24	Tradex Emerging Mkts. Country Fund	11.0	-	-	3.1
-	6	23	Universal World Emerging Growth	11.2	4.0	-	157.1

( ) under Rank indicates total number of funds; ( ) under Returns (%) indicates average annual return;

(HH) — Heavy Hitter; (UA) — Underachiever; (RC) — Rookie Camp member.

● ●

EMERGING-MARKET FUNDS/SUMMARY

Name of Fund	MER	Load	RRSP	Vola-tility	Company Number (App. 3)
20/20 Emerging Markets Value Fund	3.80	Y	F		3
20/20 Latin America Fund	3.20	Y	F		3
AIC Emerging Markets Fund	2.78	Y	F		4
Altamira Global Discovery Fund	2.98	N	F		6
Atlas Int'l Emerging Mkts. Growth	3.50	N	F		9
Atlas Latin American Value Fund	2.94	N	F	8	9
BPI Emerging Markets Fund	2.99	Y	F		15
C.I. Emerging Markets Fund	2.93	Y	F	5	28
C.I. Emerging Markets Sector Shares	2.97	Y	F	5	28
C.I. Latin American Fund	2.98	Y	F	7	28
C.I. Latin American Sector Shares	3.03	Y	F		28
Canada Trust Everest Emerging Mkts.	3.53	N	F		19
CDA Emerging Markets (R)	1.45	N	F		22
CIBC Emerging Economies Fund	2.70	N	F		29
CIBC Latin American Fund	2.50	N	F		29
Elliott & Page Emerging Markets	1.61	Y	F		41
Fidelity Emerging Markets Portfolio	3.44	Y	F		46
Fidelity Latin American Growth Fund	3.50	Y	F		46
First Canadian Emerging Mkts. Fund	2.07	N	F		11
First Canadian Latin American Fund	1.88	N	F		11
GFM Emerging Markets Country ($US) (R)	1.50	N	N		55
Global Strategy Diversified Latin	2.95	Y	R		54
Global Strategy Latin America Fund	2.95	Y	F		54
GlobeInvest Emerg. Markets Country (R)	2.72	Y	F		55
Green Line Emerging Markets	2.69	N	F	6	139
Green Line Latin Amer. Growth Fund	2.67	N	F		139
GT Global Latin America Class	2.95	Y	F		60
Guardian Emerging Markets Fund A	1.51	Y	F		61
Guardian Emerging Markets Fund B	2.97	Y	F		61
Hansberger Developing Markets Fund	2.95	Y	F		28
Hansberger Developing Mkts. Sector	3.00	Y	F		28
Hongkong Bank Emerging Mkts. Fund	2.72	N	F		63
Industrial Alliance Emerging Market	3.00	N	F		66
Investors Latin American Growth	3.00	Y	F		70
Laurentian Emerging Markets Fund	2.95	Y	F		135

EMERGING-MARKET FUNDS/SUMMARY *cont'd*

Name of Fund	MER	Load	RRSP	Vola-tility	Company Number (App. 3)
McDonald Emerging Economies (R)	3.00	Y	N		88
MD Emerging Markets Fund (R)	2.46	N	F		90
Merrill Lynch Emerging Markets Fund	3.21	Y	F		70
Mutual Premier Emerging Markets	3.76	N	N		
National Trust Emerging Markets (R)	3.08	N	F		100
NN Can-Emerge Fund	2.85	Y	R		102
Royal Latin American Fund	3.00	N	F		119
Scotia Excelsior Latin American	2.31	N	F		124
Scudder Emerging Markets Fund (R)	2.00	Y	F		125
Spectrum United Emerging Markets	2.66	Y	F	5	129
Templeton Emerging Markets Fund	3.30	Y	F	4	137
Tradex Emerging Mkts. Country Fund (R)	3.72	N	F		140
Universal World Emerging Growth	2.56	Y	F	4	80
Average	2.82			5.5	

(R) — Restricted; (C) — Closed to new investors; MER — Management Expense Ratio; Load — fee charged; RRSP: R = 100% eligible, F = eligible as foreign content only, N = not eligible; Volatility — measures swings in performance on a scale of 1 to 10 (1 = low, 10 = high). Blank space indicates that fund is less than three years old. Fund company addresses may be found by number in Appendix 3.

25

• •

International Balanced Funds

THE **INVESTMENT OBJECTIVE** of international balanced funds is to provide long-term capital growth plus regular income by investing in a combination of stocks, bonds, and short-term securities in different countries and industries around the world. Proportions will, of course, vary depending on market conditions and the preferences of the portfolio managers. There are currently 38 international balanced funds on the market and they manage a total of $2.5 billion in assets.

Over the five calendar years from 1992 to 1996, the best year for international balanced funds was 1993, when returns averaged 26.5%. In contrast, the worst year was 1994, when returns averaged -0.5%. The average annual compound rate of return over the five-year period was 11.0%.

International balanced funds have an average volatility rating of 2.7, which is below the average of 4.1 for all equity funds but above the 1.9 rating for all fixed-income funds. The average fee for management expenses is $2.52 for every $100 in assets, which is up slightly from last year's average of $2.50.

The Heavy Hitters

There are two international balanced funds that have qualified for membership in the Heavy Hitters club this year. Both of these funds have consistently delivered *above*-average returns over the past one-, three-, and five-year periods. Together these Heavy Hitters manage a total of $616 million in assets, with each fund managing $308 million. Both of these Heavy Hitters are load funds.

● ●

Table 1
THE HEAVY HITTERS
INTERNATIONAL BALANCED FUNDS

		Bench-mark*	Vola-tility	Performance Quartile 1	Quartile 2	Overall Rating
1	AGF American Tactical Asset Allocation	3	3	2	1	★1/2
2	Investors Growth Plus Portfolio	1	2	1	2	★1/2

* Morgan Stanley World Index/Salomon Brothers World Bond Index (equally weighted); (R) — Restricted; (C) — Closed to new members; (N) — No-load fund; Benchmark — number of times that a fund beat the benchmark from 1992 to 1996; Volatility — measures swings in fund returns on a scale of 1 to 10 (1 = low, 10 = high); Performance — number of times that a fund was in the first (top 25%) or second quartile (top 50%) from 1992 to 1996.

The benchmark used to compare international balanced fund returns is the Morgan Stanley World Index/Salomon Brothers World Bond Index (equally weighted), measured in Canadian dollars. Over the past five calendar years, the index posted its highest return of 22.9% in 1993 and its lowest return of 9.3% in 1996.

Investors Growth Plus Portfolio ★1/2

This fund was launched in 1989 and invests in a number of the Investors group of funds, including its Global Fund, Bond Fund, Canadian Equity Fund, and U.S. Growth Fund. With $308 million in assets, close to 70% of the fund's portfolio is invested in the equity funds and 30% in fixed-income funds.

Its best year was 1993, when it posted a return of 18.6%, and its worst year was 1994, when its return was 3.4%. The fund's average annual compound return over the past five years was 12.4%. A load fund, it charges management expenses of only $0.17 for every $100 in assets. This low figure is, however, over and above the management fees levied by the individual funds in the portfolio and represents an additional charge for administration purposes.

AGF American Tactical Asset Allocation Fund ★1/2

This fund was started in 1988 and is managed by Kathy Taylor of the San Francisco–based investment firm Barclays Global Investors. The fund has $308 million in assets, with 56% invested in fixed-income securities and 42% in equities.

In 1995, its best year, the fund posted a return of 22.9%, and in 1994, its worst year, it returned 0.6%. Over the past five years, it yielded an average annual compound return of 13.8%. This load fund charges average management expenses of $2.52 for every $100 in assets.

The Rookie Camp

Four of the promising newer international balanced funds, each with at least a three-year track record, are in the Rookie Camp this year. Each of these funds, listed below, posted *above*-average returns over the past one-, two-, and three-year periods.

AGF European Asset Allocation Fund, sponsored by AGF Management Limited, was launched in 1993 and has been managed by Warren Walker of the Boston-based firm Oechsle International Advisors since February 1996. A load fund, it has $47 million in assets and charges slightly above-average management expenses of $2.62 for every $100 in assets.

Dynamic Global Partners Fund, sponsored by Dynamic Mutual Funds, was launched in 1994 and is managed by the firm's investment team. It is a load fund and charges slightly above-average management expenses of $2.60 for every $100 in assets.

Fidelity Asset Manager Fund, sponsored by Fidelity Investments Canada Limited, was launched in 1993 and is managed by the investment team of Richard Habermann, George Vanderheiden, and Charles Morrison. A no-load fund with $263 million in assets, it charges above-average management expenses of $2.69 for every $100 in assets.

Universal World Balanced RRSP Fund, sponsored by Mackenzie Financial Corporation, was launched in 1994 and is managed by Michael Landry and Barbara Trebbi. A load fund, it has $233 million in assets and charges slightly below-average management expenses of $2.43 for every $100 in assets.

The Underachievers

There are four international balanced funds that have failed to measure up to their peers. These Underachievers have consistently delivered *below*-average returns over the past one-, three-, and five-year periods. Together these Underachievers manage $92 million in assets. The Talvest Global Asset Allocation Fund is the largest, with $60 million in assets, and the Protected American Fund is the smallest, with about $1.4 million in assets. All four Underachievers are load funds.

Table 2

THE UNDERACHIEVERS

INTERNATIONAL BALANCED FUNDS

- Caldwell Securities International
- Laurentian Global Balanced Fund
- Protected American Fund
- Talvest Global Asset Allocation

Heavy Hitters vs Underachievers

Table 3 shows the difference in returns, over three time periods, between the Heavy Hitters and Underachievers in this category. In dollar terms, for an initial investment of $10,000, the average Heavy Hitter international balanced fund would have returned a total of $18,506 over the past five years. For the same investment, the average Underachiever would have returned $15,176 — for a difference of $3,330 or 21.9%.

With respect to costs, the average international balanced Heavy Hitter charged management expenses of $1.35 for every $100 in assets, compared with $2.79 for the average Underachiever.

Table 3
HEAVY HITTERS vs UNDERACHIEVERS
INTERNATIONAL BALANCED FUNDS
(Returns %)

	1-Year	3-Year*	5-Year*
• Heavy Hitters	15.0	12.6	13.1
• Underachievers	3.9	5.5	8.7

* annualized

INTERNATIONAL BALANCED FUNDS
RANKINGS/RETURNS

Rank			Name of Fund	Returns (%)			Assets
(9)	(16)	(37)		(11.0)	(8.2)	(10.4)	
5-Yr	3-Yr	1-Yr		1-Yr	3-Yr	5-Yr	($mns)
1	1	10	AGF American Tactical Asset Alloc. (HH)	14.4	13.3	13.8	307.6
-	5	4	AGF European Asset Allocation (RC)	16.4	11.0	-	47.4
6	14	17	AGF World Balanced Fund	12.5	3.8	9.7	130.6
-	-	1	Atlas American Advantage Value	20.6	-	-	25.1
-	-	21	Azura Balanced Pooled	10.6	-	-	16.0
2	12	28	BPI Global Balanced RSP Fund	8.1	6.7	12.8	187.1
-	-	13	C.I. International Balanced Fund	13.9	-	-	90.4
-	-	16	C.I. International Balanced RSP	12.9	-	-	145.0
5	11	33	Caldwell Securities International (UA)	5.7	7.4	9.9	4.5
-	6	11	Dynamic Global Partners Fund (RC)	14.1	10.1	-	62.1
-	-	26	Elliott & Page Global Balanced Fund	8.3	-	-	11.0
-	4	2	Fidelity Asset Manager Fund (RC)	20.3	11.6	-	262.8
-	-	25	Fonds Desjardins Mondial Equilibre	9.5	-	-	27.6
-	-	31	Global Strategy World Balanced	6.5	-	-	11.7
-	9	18	Growsafe International Balanced	11.1	8.1	-	22.1
-	-	14	GT Global Growth & Income Fund	13.3	-	-	17.3
-	8	19	Guardian International Balanced A	10.9	8.3	-	7.5
-	-	24	Guardian International Balanced B	10.0	-	-	69.8
3	3	7	Investors Growth Plus Portfolio (HH)	15.5	12.0	12.4	307.9
8	10	27	Laurentian Global Balanced Fund (UA)	8.2	7.4	9.0	25.8
-	-	5	Merrill Lynch Capital Asset Fund	15.9	-	-	21.2
-	-	12	Merrill Lynch World Allocation Fund	14.0	-	-	81.4
9	16	37	Protected American Fund (UA)	-5.6	1.4	6.4	1.4
4	7	32	Spectrum United Global Diversified	5.8	9.6	10.4	30.2
-	-	35	STAR For. Balanced Growth & Income	5.2	-	-	-
-	-	34	STAR For. Maximum Long-Term Growth	5.5	-	-	-
-	-	15	STAR Inv. Balanced Growth & Income	13.0	-	-	-
-	-	20	STAR Inv. Conserv. Income & Growth	10.7	-	-	-
-	-	8	STAR Inv. Long-Term Growth	15.0	-	-	-
-	-	30	STAR Inv. Maximum Long-Term Growth	6.5	-	-	-
-	-	22	STAR Reg. Maximum Long-Term Growth	10.6	-	-	-
7	13	29	Talvest Global Asset Allocation (UA)	7.5	5.8	9.6	60.1
-	-	6	Templeton Global Balanced Fund	15.6	-	-	20.3
-	-	9	Templeton Int'l Balanced Fund	14.5	-	-	19.3

INTERNATIONAL BALANCED FUNDS
RANKINGS/RETURNS *cont'd*

Rank			Name of Fund	Returns (%)			Assets
(9)	(16)	(37)		(11.0)	(8.2)	(10.4)	
5-Yr	3-Yr	1-Yr		1-Yr	3-Yr	5-Yr	($mns)
-	15	36	Universal World Asset Allocation	0.2	1.9	-	179.0
-	2	3	Universal World Balanced RRSP (RC)	18.5	12.6	-	233.4
-	-	23	Zweig Global Managed Assets	10.0	-	-	32.1

( ) under Rank indicates total number of funds; ( ) under Returns (%) indicates average annual return; (HH) — Heavy Hitter; (UA) — Underachiever; (RC) — Rookie Camp member.

INTERNATIONAL BALANCED FUNDS/SUMMARY

Name of Fund	MER	Load	RRSP	Vola-tility	Company Number (App. 3)
AGF American Tactical Asset Alloc.	2.52	Y	F	3	3
AGF European Asset Allocation	2.62	Y	F	4	3
AGF World Balanced Fund	2.35	Y	F	3	3
Atlas American Advantage Value	2.60	N	F		9
Azura Balanced Pooled (R)	2.30	Y	F		127
BPI Global Balanced RSP Fund	2.52	Y	R	3	15
C.I. International Balanced Fund	2.63	Y	F		28
C.I. International Balanced RSP	2.53	Y	R		28
Caldwell Securities International	3.45	Y	F	4	17
Dynamic Global Partners Fund	2.60	Y	F		40
Elliott & Page Global Balanced Fund	1.96	Y	F		41
Fidelity Asset Manager Fund	2.69	Y	F	3	46
Fonds Desjardins Mondial Equilibre (R)	2.18	N	R		37
Global Strategy World Balanced	2.41	Y	F		54
Growsafe International Balanced	2.60	Y	R	2	141
GT Global Growth & Income Fund	2.95	Y	F		60
Guardian International Balanced A	2.35	Y	R	2	61
Guardian International Balanced B	2.95	Y	R		61
Investors Growth Plus Portfolio	0.17	Y	F	2	70
Laurentian Global Balanced Fund	2.65	Y	F	2	135
Merrill Lynch Capital Asset Fund	3.05	Y	F		70
Merrill Lynch World Allocation Fund	2.97	Y	F		70
Protected American Fund (R)	2.30	Y	R	2	62
Spectrum United Global Diversified	2.30	Y	F	2	129
STAR For. Balanced Growth & Income	N/A	Y	F		80
STAR For. Maximum Long-Term Growth	N/A	Y	F		80
STAR Inv. Balanced Growth & Income	N/A	Y	N		80
STAR Inv. Conserv. Income & Growth	N/A	Y	N		80
STAR Inv. Long-Term Growth	N/A	Y	N		80
STAR Inv. Maximum Long-Term Growth	N/A	Y	N		80
STAR Reg. Maximum Long-Term Growth	N/A	Y	R		80
Strategic Value Global Balanced RSP	2.75	Y	R		135
Talvest Global Asset Allocation	2.75	Y	F	3	136
Templeton Global Balanced Fund	2.55	Y	F		137
Templeton Int'l Balanced Fund	2.55	Y	F		137

INTERNATIONAL BALANCED FUNDS/SUMMARY *cont'd*

Name of Fund	MER	Load	RRSP	Vola-tility	Company Number (App. 3)
Universal World Asset Allocation	2.45	Y	F	3	80
Universal World Balanced RRSP	2.43	Y	R		80
Zweig Global Managed Assets	2.99	N	F		119
Average	2.52			2.7	

(R) — Restricted; (C) — Closed to new investors; MER — Management Expense Ratio; Load — fee charged; RRSP: R = 100% eligible, F = eligible as foreign content only, N = not eligible; Volatility — measures swings in performance on a scale of 1 to 10 (1 = low, 10 = high). Blank space indicates that fund is less than three years old. Fund company addresses may be found by number in Appendix 3.

26

●●●●●●●●●●●●●●●●●●●●●●●●●●●●●●●●●●●●

International Bond Funds

THE PRIMARY OBJECTIVE of international bond funds is to provide a combination of income and the opportunity for capital appreciation by investing selectively in government and corporate bonds worldwide. International bond funds seek opportunities around the world by investing in countries where interest rates are high and in those where there is the prospect of capital appreciation due to falling interest rates. There are currently 70 international bond funds on the market that manage assets of $4.3 billion.

Unlike their domestic counterparts, international bond funds are subject to currency risk. This means that if the Canadian dollar drops against the other currencies contained in the portfolio, the value of foreign bonds rises in terms of the dollar. As a result, the fund will realize a capital gain which will boost its total rate of return. If the dollar strengthens, however, the value of the foreign bonds in the portfolio falls in terms of the Canadian dollar, and the funds will experience a capital loss.

By investing in foreign-currency bonds of Canadian issuers, about half of the bond funds are 100% RRSP-eligible, with the rest subject to the 20% foreign-content rule.

Over the five calendar years from 1992 to 1996, the best year for international bond funds was 1993, when returns averaged 14.3%. In contrast, the worst year was 1994, when returns averaged -1.6%. The average annual compound rate of return over the five-year period was 8.9%.

International bond funds have an average volatility rating of 2.0, which is slightly above the average of 1.9 for all fixed-income funds. The average fee for management expenses is $2.05 for every $100 in assets, which is up marginally from last year's average of $2.04.

The Heavy Hitters

There are three international bond funds that have qualified for membership in the Heavy Hitters club this year. Each of these funds has consistently delivered *above*-average returns over the past one-, three-, and five-year periods. Collectively they manage $480 million in assets. Dynamic's Global Bond Fund is the largest, with $413 million in assets, and the Admax World Income Fund is the smallest, with $19 million in assets. All of the Heavy Hitters are load funds.

● ●

Table 1

THE HEAVY HITTERS

INTERNATIONAL BOND FUNDS

		Bench-mark*	Vola-tility	Performance Quartile 1	Quartile 2	Overall Rating
1	Guardian International Income A	3	2	3	1	★★1/2
2	Dynamic Global Bond Fund	1	2	2	1	★★
3	Admax World Income Fund	1	2	2	0	★1/2

* Salomon Brothers World Bond Index; (R) — Restricted; (C) — Closed to new members; (N) — No-load fund; Benchmark — number of times that a fund beat the benchmark from 1992 to 1996; Volatility — measures swings in fund returns on a scale of 1 to 10 (1 = low, 10 = high); Performance — number of times that a fund was in the first (top 25%) or second quartile (top 50%) from 1992 to 1996.

The benchmark used to compare international bond fund returns is the Salomon Brothers World Bond Index, measured in Canadian dollars. Over the past five calendar years, the index posted its highest return of 17.8% in 1993 and its lowest return of 4.1% in 1996.

Guardian International Income Fund A ★★1/2

This fund, the number-one Heavy Hitter international bond fund for the second year in a row, was launched in 1986 and has been managed by Laurence Linklater of the investment firm Kleinwort Benson Investment Management since February 1993. With $47 million in assets, 49% of the portfolio is invested in fixed-income securities in the United States, 19% in Germany, 13% in the United Kingdom, and 9% in the Netherlands. The fund invests only in securities rated A or higher.

The fund's best year was 1995, when it posted a return of 17.8%, and its worst year was 1994, when its return was -6.3%. The fund's average annual compound return over the past five years was 9.0%. A load fund, sold only on a front-end basis, it charges management expenses of $2.10 for every $100 in assets, which is slightly higher than the group average of $2.05.

Dynamic Global Bond Fund ★★

This fund was started in 1988 and is managed by the firm's investment team. The fund has $413 million in assets, with about 46% of the portfolio invested in short-term securities, 38% in foreign bonds, and 16% in Canadian bonds.

In 1995, its best year, the fund posted a return of 19.8%, and in 1996, its worst year, it returned 3.9%. Over the past five years, it yielded an average annual compound return of 10.0%. This load fund charges below-average management expenses of $1.88 for every $100 in assets.

Admax World Income Fund ★1/2

This fund, sponsored by the Invesco Funds Group (Canada) Inc., was launched in 1992 and is managed by the firm's investment team. With $19 million in assets, about 41% of the fund's portfolio is invested in medium-term bonds, 10% in short-term bonds, and 6% in common stocks. The fund invests only in fixed-income securities rated AAA.

The fund posted its highest return, 12.9%, in 1996, and its lowest, 3.1%, in 1994. Over the past five years, its average annual compound return was 10.4%. This is a load fund which charges management expenses of $2.33 for every $100 in assets, higher than the group average of $2.05.

The Rookie Camp

Four of the promising newer international bond funds, each with at least a three-year track record, are in the Rookie Camp this year. Each of these funds, listed below, posted *above*-average returns over the past one-, two-, and three-year periods.

C.I. Global Bond RSP Fund, sponsored by C.I. Mutual Funds, was launched in 1993 and is managed by Greg Diliberto of the New York–based investment firm BEA Associates. A load fund, it has $91 million in assets and charges slightly above-average management expenses of $2.07 for every $100 in assets.

C.I. World Bond Fund, sponsored by C.I. Mutual Funds, was launched in 1992 and is managed by Greg Diliberto. A load fund, it has $96 million in assets and charges slightly above-average management expenses of $2.06 for every $100 in assets.

Fidelity Emerging Markets Bond Fund, sponsored by Fidelity Investments Canada Ltd., is managed by John Carlson. A load fund with $49 million in assets, it charges above-average management expenses of $2.35 for every $100 in assets.

Green Line Global RSP Bond Fund, sponsored by the Toronto-Dominion Bank, was launched in 1993. A no-load fund, it has $141 million in assets and charges slightly below-average management expenses of $2.03 for every $100 in assets.

The Underachievers

There are three international bond funds that have failed to measure up to their peers. These Underachievers have consistently delivered *below*-average returns over the past one-, three-, and five-year periods. Collectively these Underachievers manage $665 million in assets. The Global Strategy Diversified Bond Fund is the largest, with $369 million in assets, and the Scotia CanAm Income Fund is the smallest, with $25 million in assets. Two of the three Underachievers are load funds.

Table 2
THE UNDERACHIEVERS
INTERNATIONAL BOND FUNDS

- Global Strategy Diversified Bond
- Global Strategy World Bond Fund
- Scotia CanAm Income Fund*

* denotes a no-load fund

Heavy Hitters vs Underachievers

Table 3 shows the difference in returns over three time periods between the Heavy Hitters and the Underachievers for international bond funds. In dollar terms, for an initial investment of $10,000, the average Heavy Hitter international bond fund would have returned a total of $15,959 over the past five years. For the same investment, the average Underachiever would have returned $14,157 — for a difference of $1,802 or 12.7%.

With respect to costs, the average international bond Heavy Hitter charged somewhat higher management expenses of $2.10 for every $100 in assets, compared with $2.02 for the average Underachiever.

Table 3
HEAVY HITTERS vs UNDERACHIEVERS
INTERNATIONAL BOND FUNDS
(Returns %)

	1-Year	3-Year*	5-Year*
• Heavy Hitters	9.0	8.1	9.8
• Underachievers	6.0	5.9	7.2

* annualized

INTERNATIONAL BOND FUNDS
RANKINGS/RETURNS

Rank			Name of Fund	Returns (%)			Assets
(9)	(28)	(64)		(6.4)	(6.7)	(8.4)	
5-Yr	3-Yr	1-Yr		1-Yr	3-Yr	5-Yr	($mns)
1	5	5	Admax World Income Fund (HH)	12.3	8.3	10.4	19.3
7	12	23	AGF Global Government Bond Fund	6.6	6.4	7.2	168.6
-	23	28	AGF RSP Global Bond Fund	5.9	5.3	-	89.9
-	26	47	AGF U.S. Income Fund	3.9	3.5	-	9.8
-	-	8	AGF U.S. Short-Term High Yield	9.0	-	-	19.0
-	17	40	Altamira Global Bond Fund	4.8	6.1	-	40.2
-	-	3	Altamira Spec. High Yield Bond	17.2	-	-	7.0
-	4	26	Atlas World Bond Fund	6.1	8.4	-	34.2
-	-	11	BPI Global RSP Bond Fund	8.5	-	-	3.6
-	3	20	C.I. Global Bond RSP Fund (RC)	7.1	8.5	-	91.0
-	-	2	C.I. Global High Yield Fund	17.8	-	-	8.9
-	9	21	C.I. World Bond Fund (RC)	7.0	7.0	-	95.8
-	11	42	Canada Life International Bond S-36	4.5	6.5	-	40.6
-	-	62	Canada Trust Everest Int'l Bond	1.9	-	-	79.4
-	-	33	CIBC Global Bond Fund	5.7	-	-	49.7
2	6	15	Dynamic Global Bond Fund (HH)	7.6	8.3	10.0	412.9
-	-	51	Elliott & Page Global Bond Fund	3.2	-	-	13.5
-	-	50	Empire Foreign Curr. Cdn. Bond Fund	3.5	-	-	3.1
-	-	12	Ethical Global Bond Fund	8.4	-	-	11.2
-	1	1	Fidelity Emerging Markets Bond Fund (RC)	35.2	19.8	-	49.2
-	28	30	Fidelity North American Income Fund	5.9	1.6	-	117.0
-	27	61	Fidelity RSP Global Bond Fund	2.3	3.1	-	43.0
-	14	64	First Cdn. International Bond Fund	1.3	6.3	-	148.2
-	-	41	Global Manager - U.S. Bond Index Fund	4.6	-	-	0.2
-	-	32	Global Strategy Div. Foreign Bond	5.7	-	-	7.9
9	19	25	Global Strategy Diversified Bond (UA)	6.2	6.0	6.5	368.7
8	21	27	Global Strategy World Bond Fund (UA)	6.0	5.8	7.0	270.4
-	24	53	Green Line Global Government Bond	3.1	5.1	-	113.8
-	2	7	Green Line Global RSP Bond Fund (RC)	10.9	8.7	-	141.1
-	-	60	GS International Bond Fund	2.4	-	-	9.5
-	-	16	GT Global World Bond Fund	7.5	-	-	5.0
-	-	10	Guardian Foreign Income Fund A	8.6	-	-	2.7
-	-	14	Guardian Foreign Income Fund B	7.7	-	-	1.5
4	7	18	Guardian International Income A (HH)	7.3	7.7	9.0	47.1

INTERNATIONAL BOND FUNDS
RANKINGS/RETURNS *cont'd*

Rank			Name of Fund	Returns (%)			Assets
(9)	(28)	(64)		(6.4)	(6.7)	(8.4)	
5-Yr	3-Yr	1-Yr		1-Yr	3-Yr	5-Yr	($mns)
-	-	24	Guardian International Income B	6.4	-	-	135.6
-	-	46	GWL Global Inc. Fund (A) DSC	3.9	-	-	3.8
-	-	49	GWL Global Inc. Fund (A) NL	3.7	-	-	4.7
-	-	55	GWL International Bond Fund (P) DSC	3.0	-	-	5.0
-	-	56	GWL International Bond Fund (P) NL	2.7	-	-	8.1
-	-	45	Hongkong Bank Global Bond Fund	4.1	-	-	8.9
-	-	34	InvesNat International RSP Bond	5.4	-	-	5.3
-	25	59	Investors Global Bond Fund	2.4	4.3	-	236.8
-	-	48	Lutheran Life Int'l Bond Fund	3.7	-	-	0.4
-	-	54	Manulife Vistafund 1 Global Bond	3.0	-	-	2.4
-	-	63	Manulife Vistafund 2 Global Bond	1.3	-	-	25.5
-	-	6	McLean Budden Int'l Fixed Income	11.8	-	-	21.6
-	-	58	MD Global Bond Fund	2.6	-	-	47.0
-	-	35	Merrill Lynch World Bond Fund	5.3	-	-	26.2
-	-	4	National Trust Int'l RSP Bond Fund	13.3	-	-	12.0
-	-	13	NN Can-Global Bond Fund	7.7	-	-	10.4
-	8	38	Optima Strategy Global Fixed Income	5.0	7.0	-	95.4
-	-	39	Pursuit Global Bond Fund	5.0	-	-	9.6
3	16	31	Royal Trust International Bond Fund	5.8	6.2	9.7	177.8
-	15	36	RoyFund International Income Fund	5.2	6.2	-	119.2
5	20	29	Scotia CanAm Income Fund (UA)	5.9	6.0	8.1	25.4
-	-	44	Scotia Excelsior Global Bond Fund	4.1	-	-	13.2
-	13	43	Spectrum United Global Bond Fund	4.2	6.3	-	14.6
-	22	57	Spectrum United RRSP Int'l Bond	2.6	5.6	-	81.6
-	-	37	Standard Life International Bond	5.1	-	-	5.6
-	18	17	Talvest Foreign Pay Canadian Bond	7.5	6.1	-	82.1
6	10	19	Templeton Global Bond Fund	7.1	6.9	7.6	46.1
-	-	52	Trust Pret & Revenu World Bond Fund	3.2	-	-	0.9
-	-	9	Universal World Income RRSP Fund	9.0	-	-	418.0
-	-	22	Universal World Tactical Bond Fund	6.7	-	-	31.0

( ) under Rank indicates total number of funds; ( ) under Returns (%) indicates average annual return; (HH) — Heavy Hitter; (UA) — Underachiever; (RC) — Rookie Camp member.

INTERNATIONAL BOND FUNDS/SUMMARY

Name of Fund	MER	Load	RRSP	Vola-tility	Company Number (App. 3)
Admax World Income Fund	2.33	Y	R	2	69
AGF Global Government Bond Fund	1.79	Y	F	2	3
AGF RSP Global Bond Fund	1.96	Y	R	2	3
AGF U.S. Income Fund	2.50	Y	F	2	3
AGF U.S. Short-Term High Yield	2.50	Y	F		3
Altamira Global Bond Fund	1.81	N	R	2	6
Altamira Spec. High Yield Bond	2.31	N	F		6
Atlas World Bond Fund	2.04	N	R	2	9
BPI Global RSP Bond Fund	1.50	Y	R		15
C.I. Global Bond RSP Fund	2.07	Y	R	2	28
C.I. Global High Yield Fund	2.17	Y	F		28
C.I. World Bond Fund	2.06	Y	F	2	28
Canada Life International Bond S-36	2.00	Y	R		18
Canada Trust Everest Int'l Bond	2.10	N	R		19
CIBC Global Bond Fund	1.90	N	F		29
Dynamic Global Bond Fund	1.88	Y	R	2	40
Dynamic Income & Growth Fund	1.75	Y	F		40
Elliott & Page Global Bond Fund	1.60	Y	F		41
Empire Foreign Curr. Cdn. Bond Fund	2.18	Y	R		42
Ethical Global Bond Fund (R)	2.39	N	R		44
Fidelity Emerging Markets Bond Fund	2.35	Y	F		46
Fidelity North American Income Fund	1.75	Y	F	3	46
Fidelity RSP Global Bond Fund	2.51	Y	R	2	46
First Cdn. International Bond Fund	1.97	N	F	2	11
Friedberg Foreign Bond Fund	0.93	N	F		51
Global Manager - U.S. Bond Index (R)	1.00	Y	N		10
Global Strategy Div. Foreign Bond	2.24	Y	R		54
Global Strategy Diversified Bond	2.24	Y	R	2	54
Global Strategy World Bond Fund	2.21	Y	F	2	54
Green Line Global Government Bond	2.10	N	F	2	139
Green Line Global RSP Bond Fund	2.03	N	R	2	139
GS International Bond Fund	2.70	Y	R		70
GT Global World Bond Fund	2.45	Y	F		60
Guardian Foreign Income Fund A	2.05	Y	R		61
Guardian Foreign Income Fund B	2.95	Y	R		61

INTERNATIONAL BOND FUNDS/SUMMARY *cont'd*

Name of Fund	MER	Load	RRSP	Vola-tility	Company Number (App. 3)
Guardian International Income A	2.10	Y	R	2	61
Guardian International Income B	2.94	Y	R		61
GWL Global Inc. Fund (A) DSC	2.46	Y	F		57
GWL Global Inc. Fund (A) NL	2.70	N	F		57
GWL International Bond Fund (P) DSC	2.69	Y	F		57
GWL International Bond Fund (P) NL	2.95	N	F		57
Hongkong Bank Global Bond Fund	2.07	N	F		63
Industrial Alliance Ecoflex Fund G	1.76	Y	F		66
Industrial Alliance Global Bond Fund	1.65	N	F		66
InvesNat International RSP Bond (R)	2.12	N	R		98
Investors Global Bond Fund	2.18	Y	F	2	70
Investors N.A. High-Yield Bond	2.21	Y	F		70
Lutheran Life Int'l Bond Fund (R)	2.25	N	R		78
Manulife Vistafund 1 Global Bond	1.63	Y	F		83
Manulife Vistafund 2 Global Bond	2.38	Y	F		83
McLean Budden Int'l Fixed Income (R)	1.00	N	N		89
MD Global Bond Fund (R)	1.11	N	F		90
Merrill Lynch World Bond Fund	2.28	Y	R		70
National Trust Int'l RSP Bond Fund (R)	2.15	N	R		100
NN Can-Global Bond Fund	2.50	Y	R		102
North-West Life Ecoflex G	1.76	Y	F		103
Optima Strategy Global Fixed Income (R)	0.48	Y	F		77
Pursuit Global Bond Fund (R)	1.25	Y	F		117
Royal Trust International Bond Fund	1.87	N	R	2	119
RoyFund International Income Fund	2.06	N	R	2	119
Scotia CanAm Income Fund	1.60	N	R	2	124
Scotia Excelsior Global Bond Fund	1.86	N	F		124
Spectrum United Global Bond Fund	2.03	Y	F	2	129
Spectrum United RRSP Int'l Bond	1.98	Y	R	2	129
Standard Life International Bond	2.00	Y	R		133
Talvest Foreign Pay Canadian Bond	2.15	Y	R	2	136
Templeton Global Bond Fund	2.25	Y	F	2	137
Trust Pret & Revenu World Bond Fund	1.90	N	F		144
Universal World Income RRSP Fund	2.16	Y	R		80

INTERNATIONAL BOND FUNDS/SUMMARY *cont'd*

Name of Fund	MER	Load	RRSP	Vola-tility	Company Number (App.3)
Universal World Tactical Bond Fund	2.62	Y	F		80
Average	2.05			2.0	

(R) — Restricted; (C) — Closed to new investors; MER — Management Expense Ratio; Load — fee charged; RRSP: R = 100% eligible, F = eligible as foreign content only, N = not eligible; Volatility — measures swings in performance on a scale of 1 to 10 (1 = low, 10 = high). Blank space indicates that fund is less than three years old. Fund company addresses may be found by number in Appendix 3.

27

● ●

International Money-Market Funds

INTERNATIONAL MONEY-MARKET FUNDS invest primarily in high-quality and highly liquid short-term (less than a year) money-market securities issued by governments, banks, and "blue-chip" corporations. These funds form the least risky international fund category and are designed to maximize monthly income while preserving capital. Although international money-market funds are subject to currency fluctuations, like their domestic counterparts not a single international fund lost money last year. Because of their short-term nature, virtually all international money-market funds have a volatility rating of 1, the lowest on the scale of 1 to 10.

Investor interest in international money-market funds has continued to grow in recent years, partly as a hedge against a faltering Canadian dollar, partly because of the opportunity this market provides to take advantage of higher interest rates elsewhere. There are currently 21 international money-market funds on the market. Together these funds manage close to $1 billion in assets. While the majority focus on the U.S. money markets, a few spread their wings and invest in short-term securities globally. By investing in Canadian short-term debt that is denominated in foreign currencies, several international money-market funds are also 100% RRSP-eligible.

Over the five calendar years from 1992 to 1996, the best year for international money-market funds was 1996, when returns averaged 4.8%. In contrast, the worst year was 1993, when returns averaged 2.9%. The average annual compound rate of return over the five-year period was 3.8%.

The average fee for management expenses is $1.21 for every $100 in assets, which is significantly below last year's average of $1.52.

The Heavy Hitters

There are two international money-market funds that have qualified for membership in the Heavy Hitters club this year, one load and one no-load. Each of these funds has consistently delivered *above*-average returns over the past one-, three-, and five-year periods. Collectively, these Heavy Hitters manage $65.2 million.

• •

Table 1

THE HEAVY HITTERS

INTERNATIONAL MONEY-MARKET FUNDS

		Bench-mark*	Vola-tility	Performance Quartile 1	Performance Quartile 2	Overall Rating
1	PH&N $US Money Market (R) (N)	0	1	4	1	★★
2	AGF U.S. Dollar Money Market ($US)	0	1	1	4	★1/2

* U.S. 91-Day Treasury Bill (R) — Restricted; (C) — Closed to new members; (N) — No-load fund; Benchmark — number of times that a fund beat the benchmark from 1992 to 1996; Volatility — measures swings in fund returns on a scale of 1 to 10 (1 = low, 10 = high); Performance — number of times that a fund was in the first (top 25%) or second quartile (top 50%) from 1992 to 1996.

The benchmark used to compare international money-market fund returns is the U.S. 91-day treasury-bill rate. Over the past five calendar years, T-bill yields ranged from a high of 5.8% in 1995 to a low of 3.1% in 1993.

Phillips Hager & North $US Money Market Fund ★★

This fund, the number-one Heavy Hitter international money-market fund for the second year in a row, was launched in 1990 and has $40 million in assets. The fund is managed by the firm's fixed-income research team.

Its best year was 1995, when it posted a return of 5.5%, and its worst year was 1993, when it returned 2.7%. The fund's average annual compound return over the past five years was 4.2%. A no-load fund, it charges management expenses of $0.52 for every $100 in assets, which is considerably below the group average of $1.21. The fund has a minimum initial investment requirement of $25,000 for non-RRSP accounts and $5,000 for RRSP accounts.

AGF U.S. Dollar Money Market ($US) Fund ★1/2

This fund, with $25 million in assets, was launched in 1988 and is managed by Warren Goldring and Clive Coombes.

Its best year was 1995, when it posted a return of 4.9%, and its worst year was 1993, when it returned 2.7%. The fund's average annual compound return over the past five years was 3.8%. A load fund, it charges below-average management expenses of $0.85 for every $100 in assets.

The Underachievers

No international money-market fund qualified for membership in the Underachievers club this year.

A Final Word

There is little to choose from among the international money-market funds that specialize in the U.S. money markets. Returns tend to cluster within a narrow band, with at most a one-percentage-point spread between the fund with the highest return and the one with the lowest return. As in the case of Canadian money-market funds, those funds that have the lowest management expenses and do not charge sales fees will have the edge.

INTERNATIONAL MONEY-MARKET FUNDS
RANKINGS/RETURNS

Rank			Name of Fund	Returns (%)			Assets
(11)	(11)	(20)		(3.7)	(4.2)	(3.8)	
5-Yr	3-Yr	1-Yr		1-Yr	3-Yr	5-Yr	($mns)
-	-	20	AGF Int'l Short Term Income Fund	-0.7	-	-	7.2
3	2	3	AGF U.S. Dollar Money Market ($US) (HH)	4.5	4.5	3.8	25.2
1	11	19	Altamira Short Term Global Income	1.1	1.8	5.4	40.3
6	5	5	Atlas American Money Market ($US)	4.4	4.4	3.6	52.9
-	-	10	BPI U.S. Money Market ($US)	4.3	-	-	1.8
-	-	2	C.I. U.S. Money Market Fund ($US)	4.8	-	-	26.2
7	7	7	CIBC U.S. Dollar Money Market ($US)	4.3	4.4	3.5	121.3
-	-	11	Fidelity U.S. Money Market ($US)	4.2	-	-	29.5
-	-	18	Global Manager - U.S. Dollar Cash	3.0	-	-	0.4
8	8	9	Green Line U.S. Money Mkt. ($US)	4.3	4.3	3.5	303.8
-	-	16	GT Global Short-term Income A	3.6	-	-	7.8
-	-	17	GT Global Short-term Income B	3.0	-	-	9.1
4	3	4	Guardian U.S. Money Market ($US) A	4.4	4.5	3.8	12.8
-	-	15	Guardian U.S. Money Market ($US) B	3.7	-	-	0.2
11	10	8	InvesNat U.S. Money Market ($US)	4.3	4.3	3.4	21.5
2	1	1	PH&N $US Money Market (HH)	5.0	5.0	4.2	40.0
9	6	6	Royal Trust U.S. Money Market ($US)	4.4	4.4	3.5	107.7
10	9	12	RoyFund U.S. Dollar Money ($US)	4.2	4.3	3.5	82.4
5	4	13	Spectrum United U.S. Dollar Money	4.0	4.5	3.7	4.8
-	-	14	Universal U.S. Money Market ($US)	3.7	-	-	4.9

( ) under Rank indicates total number of funds; ( ) under Returns (%) indicates average annual return; (HH) — Heavy Hitter; (UA) — Underachiever; (RC) — Rookie Camp member.

INTERNATIONAL MONEY-MARKET FUNDS/SUMMARY

Name of Fund	MER	Load	RRSP	Vola-tility	Company Number (App. 3)
AGF Int'l Short Term Income Fund	2.51	Y	F		3
AGF U.S. Dollar Money Market ($US)	0.85	Y	F	1	3
Altamira Short Term Global Income	1.21	N	R	2	6
Atlas American Money Market ($US)	1.19	N	F	1	9
BPI U.S. Money Market ($US)	0.65	Y	R		15
C.I. U.S. Money Market Fund ($US)	0.51	Y	F		28
CIBC U.S. Dollar Money Market ($US)	0.95	N	F	1	29
Fidelity U.S. Money Market ($US)	1.25	Y	F		46
Global Manager - U.S. Dollar Cash (R)	1.00	Y	N		10
Green Line U.S. Money Mkt. ($US)	1.27	N	R	1	139
GT Global Short-term Income A	1.76	Y	F		60
GT Global Short-term Income B	2.25	Y	F		60
Guardian U.S. Money Market ($US) A	0.97	Y	R	1	61
Guardian U.S. Money Market ($US) B	1.66	Y	R		61
InvesNat U.S. Money Market ($US) (R)	1.11	N	R	1	98
PH&N $US Money Market (R)	0.52	N	R	1	112
Royal Trust U.S. Money Market ($US)	1.12	N	F	1	119
RoyFund U.S. Dollar Money ($US)	1.20	N	R	1	119
Scotia CanAm Money Market Fund	1.00	N	R		124
Spectrum United U.S. Dollar Money	1.20	Y	F	1	129
Universal U.S. Money Market ($US)	1.25	Y	F		80
Average	1.21			1.1	

(R) — Restricted; (C) — Closed to new investors; MER — Management Expense Ratio; Load — fee charged; RRSP: R = 100% eligible, F = eligible as foreign content only, N = not eligible; Volatility — measures swings in performance on a scale of 1 to 10 (1 = low, 10 = high). Blank space indicates that fund is less than three years old. Fund company addresses may be found by number in Appendix 3.

PART FIVE

••••••••••••••••••••••••••••••••

THE ESSENTIALS OF MUTUAL FUND INVESTING

28

● ●

How Much Will It Cost?

THERE ARE COSTS involved if you decide to invest in mutual funds. Before you buy, weigh these various costs against any potential return.

Obviously it costs less to invest in mutual funds that do not charge loads. However, basing your selection criteria solely on whether or not you pay a sales commission can eliminate many excellent load funds. Although a sales charge is something we would all rather not pay, it should be only one factor among many in determining our final selection. A better starting point is to zero in on all Heavy Hitter funds in the category of your choice. Then, after careful consideration of factors such as risk, investment objectives, fund philosophy, and management expenses, turn your attention to sales fees.

Before you purchase any fund, make sure you fully understand what fees are payable, both directly and indirectly. If it is a load fund, negotiate the rate where possible and don't hesitate to shop around.

Management Fees

All mutual funds charge a non-negotiable management fee based on the funds' total assets. If they say 2%, they mean 2%. These fees range between 0.5% and 2.5% of the total assets, and include the wages and bonuses of fund managers. Management fees are deducted from the asset value of a fund before the unit or share value is calculated, and these fees are levied annually.

You should compare management fees between similar funds before making a final choice. The difference between 1.75% and 2% may not seem like much at the beginning, but over a long investment period that additional 0.25% will take more of a bite out of your total return.

Management Expense Ratio

For a better measure of the up-front cost to the investor, check the management expense ratio (MER) as well. This charge, which includes the management fee and all other operating expenses, such as office administration and trading and advertising costs, is calculated by dividing the value of a fund's assets by its total expenses. If a fund with $1 billion of assets has total yearly expenses of $20 million, its expense ratio is 2% ($20 million divided by $1 billion). This means that out of every $100 you have invested, $2 goes to management expenses.

The impact of the MER on a fund's return warrants more investor attention. For example, if your equity fund delivers a compound annual return of 7.5%, with a MER of (say) 2.5%, it has a gross return of roughly 10%. This means that the MER, expressed as a percentage of returns, is 25% of the return (the MER (2.5%) divided by the gross return (10%), multiplied by 100). In years when the market is returning 30% or more, many investors tend to focus on the high returns and not on the accompanying high costs. However, in down markets, or if a fund is a poor performer, high MERs can only exacerbate the situation. A fund's simplified prospectus will show the management fee and the expense ratio. To compare the expense ratios of similar funds, look at the summary table in the appropriate chapter.

Trailer Fees

A trailer fee is an annual commission paid to the person who sold you the mutual fund, and continues to be paid as long as you hold the fund. These fees generally range between 0.25% and 1% and are intended as compensation for ongoing services that sales representatives provide to clients, such as answering questions about accounts, tax information, the performance of an investor's fund, and other related matters. These practices came under fire from Ontario Securities Commissioner Glorianne Stromberg in her 1995 report. The reasons given: "no one monitors whether in fact the services have been provided," and "these fees may also be a factor in a sales representative not recommending a change in the client's portfolio when it would be in the client's interests to make such change." The Stromberg Report recommended that the mutual fund industry voluntarily end the payment of these fees.

In response, the Investment Funds Institute of Canada (IFIC) recommended, and is still pushing for, the adoption of a Code of Sales Practices that would include restrictions on the payment of trailer fees, for "voluntary" compliance by institute members. IFIC is the lobbying and educative association of the Canadian investment funds industry. Its membership is made up of mutual fund management companies, retail distributors (such as brokers and financial planners), and members of the legal, accounting, and other professions.

Sales Commissions

Mutual funds that are sold on a commission basis either at the time of purchase (front-end load) or at redemption (back-end load or deferred sales charge (DSC)) are generally not purchased directly from the sponsoring mutual fund company. Instead, these companies rely on independent sales representatives such as brokers, discount brokers, and most financial planners to promote their products. The commission, which is split between the salesperson and the parent company, compensates the salesperson for his or her advice and time.

Front-End Load

A front-end load is a sales charge paid at the time of purchase. It can be as high as 9%, although most companies charge a maximum of around 5%. This sales charge is deducted from the amount being invested. Therefore, if you have $5,000 to invest and you pay a 5% front-end load, the actual amount of money invested will be $4,750. This charge is negotiable with your salesperson and you should not hesitate to shop around to get the best rate.

Back-End Load

A back-end load is a fee charged to investors upon redemption. It is usually staggered, but basically the earlier the redemption the higher the fee. It is designed to discourage early withdrawals. A typical range starts at 5% or 6% for redemptions during the first two years, and decreases to 0% after 7 to 10 years. The redemption fee schedule shown below is typical of many funds.

During the 1st year	6.0%
During the 2nd year	5.5%
During the 3rd year	5.0%
During the 4th year	4.5%
During the 5th year	3.0%
During the 6th year	1.5%
Thereafter	Nil

Opting for a back-end load, instead of the front-end load, allows your entire investment amount to go to work for you immediately. Some funds base this fee on the original purchase price (better for you, assuming your investment increases in value), while others assess it at the market value of the units when you sell. Unlike the front-end load, the back-end load is usually not negotiable. A few companies offer some room to manoeuvre, so do ask. Some funds offer privileges such as cashing in up to 10% of your holdings annually without charging the redemption fee and switching within their family of funds at no cost or for a substantially reduced fee. This could be an important consideration if your fund is not performing as well as expected.

Before choosing the back-end load option, as an investor you should also be aware that although you won't pay a fee directly to your sales representative at the time of purchase, the mutual fund company will, usually around 5% of the invested amount. This, of course, increases its costs. As a result, you may be paying higher annual management fees by around 0.25% to 0.5%. Before choosing the deferred sales charge option, you should ensure that you have set aside an adequate emergency fund. If not, and unforeseen circumstances arise, you may have to redeem some or all of your units. To be hit by a high redemption charge at such a time could only make matters worse.

No-Load Option

Some load companies now offer a no-load option. However, don't be fooled by the name. Instead of paying a fee at the time of either purchase or redemption, the investor in most cases pays a higher annual management fee. Some companies offer the no-load option only on higher minimum initial investments. Get the salesperson to calculate which option — front-end, back-end, or no-load — would be best, given your investment time frame.

Distribution Fees

These fees may apply if you buy a back-end load fund. Distribution fees (usually between 0.25% and 0.5%) are calculated on the net asset value of your holdings and would typically increase along with their value for a predetermined time period (normally seven to nine years). Due to investor resistance many companies have dropped this charge.

Other Costs

Switching Fees. Most banks and trust companies, and some mutual fund groups, allow you to switch within their family of funds at no cost or for a small fee of around $25. Don't assume, however, that your chosen fund falls into this category. A few companies charge anywhere from 2% to a maximum of 9% of the amount being transferred!

Set-Up and Closing Fees. Some companies charge a nominal amount (around $50) when you open or close an account.

Handling Fees. If you purchase no-load funds through a broker or sales representative, you may be charged a handling fee of around $50 on amounts under $100,000 and $100 for amounts over $100,000.

RRSP/RRIF Fees. An annual administration fee (between $25 and $75) and a termination fee (typically $15) may be charged. Also, switching fees of up to 2% of your holdings may apply with some funds.

29

● ●

The Prospectus

AFTER TWO YEARS of study by Canada's securities regulators, the "simplified prospectus" is about to be revamped. The proposed new document for mutual fund buyers has been released for public comment by the Canadian Securities Administrators, a national umbrella group of provincial securities commissions. The proposed Summary Information Statement would include a short (five-to-eight-page), easy-to-read summary on the fund's objectives, fees, risks, and performance and would list income and capital gains distributions by the fund and the portfolio turnover. Unlike current prospectuses, the statement would give a fund's performance numbers on a calendar year basis as well as compound annual returns over the past ten years. The fund company would also have to compare its fund's performance with a benchmark or index. As in current prospectuses, the section on costs and fees would include compensation and payments to dealers. A new addition would be a bar chart or graph showing the impact of fees under different purchase options on a hypothetical investment of $1,000.

However, a "base disclosure document" and the equally important latest "financial statement" would not be released to investors unless specifically requested. The base disclosure document contains important and sensitive information on how unitholders are protected from abuses and a description of any potential conflicts of interest involving providers of services to the fund, such as personal trading by fund managers. The financial statements would include an analysis of the fund's performance, a discussion of changes in the portfolio, and details on any unusually large redemptions on net sales. Under the current prospectus system, investors have to specifically request a copy of a fund's latest financial statement and statement of portfolio transactions. These important documents are not sent automatically with the simplified prospectus.

Implementation of the above proposals is likely to take some time; meanwhile, the important points of the current prospectus are as follows:

Date. Make sure the prospectus you receive is for the current year. The date is usually given on the front cover.

Summary of Fund Expenses. This section lists the management fees and management expense ratio for each fund included in the prospectus. Fees vary according to the type of fund being managed, but generally speaking a 2% annual management fee is at the top end. Most management fees are calculated daily and paid monthly. The management expense ratio is the actual amount paid by each fund for management fees and all other operating expenses, expressed as a percentage of the average net asset value.

Summary of Investors' Expenses. This section gives details on the fees payable, if any, on the purchase of a fund's units. It is important to remember that when a prospectus states "up to 9%" or "to a maximum of 2%" this means these fees are negotiable.

Sales-Charge Option (or Front-End Load). Gives the fee payable at time of purchase and will also list any early redemption fees, if applicable.

Deferred Option (or Back-End Load). Gives the fee payable at the time of redemption and is usually on a sliding scale. Distribution fees may also be included in this section.

Exchange or Switching Fee. The fee charged, if any, for the privilege of switching from one fund to another.

RRSP Fees. This section will tell you the fee payable each year for fund units held in an RRSP.

The Funds. All the funds included in the prospectus are listed in this section, along with the date they were established.

Investment Objectives. This section gives the objectives of each fund, including a general description of the type of assets held, and may also give risk factors relative to the different types of funds. For more specific details on the assets held, however, you should consult the fund's current annual report. This will give you a better understanding of whether or not the fund is appropriate for your investment objectives and comfort level.

Pricing or Valuation of Securities. This paragraph tells you how the Net Asset Value of a unit is calculated, and when (usually after 4 p.m. Toronto time on any business day).

Distribution of Income and Capital Gains. This section tells you what income and capital gains, if any, are paid, and when. Most funds offer a choice between payment by cheque or automatic reinvestment in additional units of the fund. Some funds, however, automatically reinvest any income or capital gains unless they receive a written request specifying otherwise, so do ask, to be on the safe side.

How to Buy. Included in this section are details on how to purchase units of a fund (usually through a bank, mutual fund company, dealer, broker, mutual fund representative, or by mail) and how payment must be made (cash, cheque, wire transfer, or money order).

Redemption. This gives details on how to request a redemption of fund units, how long it will take, and how it will be paid. Requests for redemption are usually required in writing with the signature of the unitholder guaranteed by a bank, trust company, broker, or mutual fund representative. Some fund companies, however, allow redemption by telephone or fax, provided the investor has signed such an agreement. If this service would be important to you, make sure you sign the necessary papers at the time of purchase.

Income-Tax Information. This section gives information on the type of tax payable by unitholders and advises what documentation the fund will provide.

Special Services and Information. Any special services, such as pre-authorized payment plans, automatic withdrawal plans, or deferred income plans, are listed in this section. It may also give information on statements, confirmations, financial reports, or newsletters.

30

....

How to Minimize the Risks

RISK IS, SIMPLY PUT, the possibility that an investment may not perform as well as anticipated. We would all like the high returns without putting our investment dollars at risk. The fact is that, hard though it may be to accept, no investment, whether domestic or international, is risk free. Even money in a seemingly "risk-free" savings account is at risk from the bite of inflation and taxes. Some common risk factors include:

Credit Risk. The possibility that the company holding your money will not pay the interest or dividend due, or the principal amount when it matures.

Inflation Risk. The risk that the dollar you get on redemption will buy less than the dollar you originally invested.

Interest-Rate Risk. The possibility that a fixed debt instrument, such as a bond, will decline in value due to a rise in interest rates. Rising interest rates can also affect stocks, by making it more difficult for companies to grow and increase their profits. Rising rates also take investors' money out of the stock market and into bonds.

Market Risk. The risk that the overall stock market will fall and the unit price, or value, of your investment will decrease. Fund managers may try to deal with this risk by moving a larger percentage of their portfolios into cash.

Risk of Principal. The possibility that the invested capital will decrease in value.

To a certain extent, by investing in mutual funds we relieve ourselves of the time-consuming and almost impossible task of researching each investment opportunity and its possible risk. Instead we rely on the knowledge and expertise of a fund manager, or team of professionals, to buy and sell the best investments at the right time. In order to capitalize on this, however, you must ensure that the fund's objectives and risk level closely match your own. If you don't take the time to figure out your investment objectives and comfort level, you run the risk of investing in unsuitable funds.

The following will give you a quick overview of the various funds' possible risks.

Money-Market Funds are the safest of all mutual funds. They provide a good rate of return when interest rates are high — but low income when interest rates are low. Funds that invest in Government of Canada treasury bills are the safest, followed by funds holding provincial treasury bills and debentures issued by major corporations. The shorter the investment term of the securities held, the less risky the fund. Money-market funds are a good low-risk, short-term parking place but over the long term provide the lowest real rates of return.

Bond Funds are sensitive to interest-rate fluctuations. When interest rates fall, bond prices go up, and conversely when interest rates rise, bond prices fall. However, the interest income will keep coming. Funds that invest in Government of Canada securities have the least risk, followed by those holding provincial government bonds and high-quality corporate bonds. Funds that hold short-term bonds (one to five years) are less volatile than those with intermediate- and long-term bonds.

Dividend Funds are sensitive to stock-market fluctuations. For the highest degree of safety in dividend funds, look for funds that invest the majority of their assets in high-quality preferred shares that carry a P1 or P2 rating issued by the Canadian Bond Rating Service and Dominion Bond Rating Service.

Equity Funds are considered the riskiest of all funds. You can choose from funds that concentrate on "moderate growth" by investing in more established companies, or on "aggressive growth" by investing in smaller, rapidly growing companies, which are usually more volatile. Because all equity funds are susceptible to stock-market fluctuations, a longer-term approach is generally recommended.

Balanced Funds are, as their name suggests, a balance of bonds and equities. They are less risky than equity funds due to their built-in diversification. If, for example, the stock market falls, bond prices may continue to do well.

International Funds are affected by the same risks as their domestic counterparts and, in addition, are also sensitive to currency exchange factors. The investor wins if the Canadian dollar weakens against the currency of the invested country and loses if the Canadian dollar strengthens. A strengthening Canadian dollar will cut into your returns. If your overseas fund gained 15%, and the Canadian dollar appreciated against that currency by 10%, your actual gain would be (very roughly speaking) reduced to 5%. Many international fund managers use hedging techniques to limit the impact of these exchange-rate fluctuations, thereby reducing this risk. Investing internationally may also involve additional risks based on political and social factors, volatile markets, or lack of liquidity. International funds that place a significant portion of their assets in one issue or country may be more susceptible to risk than funds that invest in several countries.

Volatility Ratings

Before you invest in any fund it is also a good idea to reflect on your own feelings towards risk. Many mutual funds have a high volatility rating, indicating wide swings in returns. Even if it is a fund with an excellent track record, the bumpy ride may be too nerve-wracking for some investors to stomach. This could influence you to sell at the wrong time, thereby increasing your risk level. It is therefore very important to check out a fund's volatility rating before you invest. Moreover, don't make the mistake of thinking that because a fund has a high volatility rating, it will over time automatically provide equally high returns. While many do, others do not.

All mutual funds with at least a three-year history are given a volatility rating ranging from a low of 1 to a high of 10. To arrive at this rating a fund's standard deviation, the degree to which a fund's monthly return fluctuates around its average, is compared with all other funds' returns and classified into one of ten deciles. A low volatility rating of 1 would indicate a fund with a more stable monthly rate of return. Money-market funds would fit into this category. The higher the volatility rating, the wider the swings in return. Ask your sales representative to provide you with a fund's annual returns over, if possible, the last five or ten years. This way, if you decide to invest, you have a better idea of what to expect. Asian and special equity funds, with average volatility ratings of 6.2 and 5 respectively, are at the high end. To compare the volatility ratings of similar funds, look at the Summary table in the appropriate chapter.

Minimizing Risk

Investing only in funds with a low volatility rating will certainly reduce risk in the short term. The flip side, however, is that generally they will provide little or no real growth over the long term. As an investor you must decide how much growth you require in order to achieve your financial objectives and how much risk you are willing to take to get there. However, it need not be an either/or situation. One of the best and easiest ways for any investor to minimize risk and still achieve his or her financial goals is through diversification. Dividing your investment dollars between income and growth, domestic and international markets, and different fund companies effectively decreases the level of risk and, over time, increases the potential for higher returns. Many financial planners also recommend diversifying by management style if you are investing in several funds within the same category. Also, the longer your investment time frame, the more aggressive you can be with your investments. Those with a shorter investment time frame should favour a more conservative approach because they will have far less time to recoup any losses. Individuals with smaller amounts of money available for investment should also adopt a more conservative approach.

Finally, keep in mind that there are many investment options that are less secure than mutual funds. The single-issue aspect of investing in a bond, stock, or real estate — as many of us have discovered in recent years — may make these investments more vulnerable than even some of the more volatile mutual funds.

31

●●●●●●●●●●●●●●●●●●●●●●●●●●●●●●

Monitoring Your Fund's Performance

IF YOU INVEST in mutual funds, you should be prepared to spend some time monitoring their performance. This book gives you an opportunity to *independently* review your fund's performance on an annual basis. To illustrate how quickly and easily this is done, let's assume you own units in the Templeton Global Smaller Companies Fund.

Annual Performance Review — How It's Done

First, turn to the Rankings/Returns table in the appropriate chapter; in this example, "International Equity Funds," Chapter 20. Funds are listed alphabetically in the Rankings/Returns table, and the Templeton Global Smaller Companies Fund can be found on page 217. Looking at its one-year return, to the right of the fund's name, you will see that the fund delivered 11.9%, slightly below the average of 12.9% for all international equity funds. The average return is given in parentheses at the top of the page. Next, compare the three- and five-year returns in the same manner. In both time periods the fund delivered above-average returns: 12.7% compared to an average of 9.7% over the past three-year period, and 16.1% compared to an average of 12.8% over the past five years. Now turn your attention to how the Templeton Global Smaller Companies Fund ranked compared to its peers. To the left of the fund's name you will see that this fund ranked 12th out of a total of 50 international equity funds that were in existence over the five-year period,

19th out of 74 over the three-year period, and 70th out of 118 over the latest one-year period.

From the above information you can now clearly see that the Templeton Global Smaller Companies Fund delivered above-average returns over two of the three time periods. However, its return, and consequently its ranking, has dipped slightly over the latest one-year period. This is quite normal. *All* funds have temporary periods of underperformance, and these lapses are not necessarily an indication to redeem your units. Monitoring a fund's performance on a regular basis will ensure that you won't be caught off guard.

The final step in your annual check-up is to review the sponsoring company's overall performance; in this case, Templeton Management Limited. To do this, turn to Appendix 3, the "Mutual Fund Company Scorecard," company number 137. (Company numbers for all funds are given in the Summary tables at the end of the fund chapters.) Here you will see that Templeton Management Limited has nine qualifying funds (mutual funds with a five-year history), of which four are Heavy Hitters and one is an Underachiever. This overview will help you with any future investment decisions within this fund family.

Regular Check-Ups — How It's Done

It's a good habit to review the performance of your funds on a regular basis throughout the year. The business section of most newspapers will allow you to compare your fund's return against the average for its category. Make a note of these figures, along with the date, in your investment file. Over time, any prolonged periods of underperformance — when your fund delivers below-average returns every month over, for example, a 12-to-18-month period — will clearly stand out. This record will help you make more informed investment decisions, such as whether or not to put any new money into the fund, or redeem some or all of your units.

What to Read

The Globe and Mail's Report on Business. The *Globe and Mail* publishes a special mutual funds section on the third Thursday of each month. This section gives monthly performance figures, and includes numerous articles on the mutual fund industry. The *Globe* also publishes the net asset values for all mutual funds on a daily basis.

The Financial Post. Like the *Globe*, the *Post* publishes daily net asset values for all mutual funds. The *Post* also publishes a monthly fund survey, which includes a measure of volatility, in the weekend issue dated the third Monday of each month.

In addition, *The Economist* and *Financial Times* of London are particularly good for international political and economic developments.

Mutual Fund Company Financial Report. This report typically gives information on your fund's rate of return and any shifts in portfolio asset allocation. It also includes a detailed "Statement of Investment Portfolio" with the amount and type of assets owned by the fund. Any proposed changes in objectives, management fees, or responsibilities should also be included in this report. You may not automatically receive a copy of this report, so make sure you ask for one.

Mutual Fund Company Statement of Account. Usually sent quarterly, this shows all transactions in your account, including income and/or capital-gains information, and gives the total value of your account as of that date. Read this carefully; mistakes do happen. If you don't understand the format, give your salesperson a call and get him or her to go over it with you. You should also keep these statements in a safe place, because you may require them for tax purposes.

Although the following reference materials are geared towards financial-industry professionals, they will be of specific interest to investors who want the most comprehensive, up-to-date information available on mutual funds. The computerized software also allows investors to perform a variety of calculations.

Mutual Fund SourceBook, published by Southam Inc.: $350 per year + shipping and GST, with quarterly updates. Also available, the *Mutual Fund SourceDisk*. The cost (excluding taxes and shipping) for 12 monthly disks is $399, four quarterly disks $179, or one single disk $44.95. For more information call 1-800-268-7742, ext. 2205.

Globe HySales. This powerful, easy-to-use software has the added bonus of a number of financial planning calculators, including a college tuition planner, as well as a retirement planner. With a few clicks of a mouse you can easily project how much you will have to save each month to meet your desired goals under different scenarios. Although it is aimed at financial planners, individual investors will find Globe HySales a powerful tool in making informed investment decisions. The cost (excluding taxes and shipping) for 12 monthly disks is $495, four quarterly disks $289. For more information call Globe Information Services, a division of Thomson Newspapers Company Limited, at 416-585-5677 or 1-800-268-9128.

PALTrack. The wealth of information contained in this program is a researcher's delight. The cost (excluding taxes and shipping) for 12 monthly disks is $399, four quarterly disks $139, or one single disk $39. For more information call Portfolio Analytics Limited at 416-489-7074 or 1-800-531-4725.

BellCharts on Disk. This program is another mainstay in the industry. The cost (including taxes and shipping) for 12 monthly disks is $369.95, four quarterly disks $129.95, or one single disk $34.95. For more information call BellCharts Inc. at 416-515-4757.

Other Sources of Information

Whenever the opportunity presents itself, you should endeavour to increase your investment knowledge. Many financial institutions and brokerage houses give free seminars on a wide variety of investment topics. If you prefer the comfort of your own home, you can now borrow videos on many financial subjects from some of the major banks. Moreover, insurance companies that offer mutual funds and the retirement planning representatives and personal investment managers of some financial institutions also make "house calls." In addition, don't overlook your public library. Many branches have quite a wide selection of books and magazines on such topics as personal finance, retirement, and mutual funds.

32

• •

The RRSP Connection

THE FINDINGS OF various surveys by individual financial institutions show that the number of Canadians contributing to a Registered Retirement Savings Plan (RRSP) has fallen significantly. With the recent rounds of corporate downsizing and the continued uncertainty in the labour market, this drop-off in contributions is hardly unexpected. Moreover, according to Statistics Canada numbers, fully *two-thirds* of the Canadian workforce earn less than $30,000 a year. Given these factors, investing for retirement for the majority of Canadians is clearly taking a backseat to paying current living expenses. Under these conditions, perhaps a more realistic and flexible approach to retirement planning is needed — such as investing $25 a month when times are tough and increasing this amount as prospects improve. Regardless of the amount, paying yourself first is still the most effective way to realize your financial goals. Whatever the circumstances, however, it is extremely important that all eligible individuals take advantage of their RRSP entitlement.

What Is an RRSP?

A Registered Retirement Savings Plan (RRSP) is a tax shelter provided under the Income Tax Act (Canada) which gives individuals who file a tax return in Canada and have eligible income the opportunity to save money for their retirement. All monies held in an RRSP, including reinvested income and capital gains, are sheltered from tax until withdrawal. This allows savings to compound tax-free, thereby growing much faster.

Mutual funds offer investors maximum diversification and the opportunity to build a more substantial retirement nest egg at minimum cost and risk. However, whether purchasing mutual funds to be held inside or outside an RRSP, the same general investment rules apply: the further you are from your investment goals, the more growth funds; the nearer you are, the more income funds. In early retirement you may want to consider a 50/50 balance between stocks and bonds, with a gradual increase in the income component as your retirement progresses. However, if you will receive no other benefits and will rely solely on the income from your investments, a more conservative approach would be dictated.

The following key points will put you on the right track.

- The contribution limit is 18% of your previous year's earned income, minus any pension plan adjustments, to a maximum of $13,500 for 1997 plus a carry-forward of unused contribution amounts from 1991. This limit remains until 2003. In 2004, the limit increases to $14,500, and then to $15,500 in 2005. Thereafter, the maximum allowed will be indexed to growth in the average wage. To contribute the current maximum amount of $13,500, you would need to earn $75,000 in the previous year. Confirmation of your RRSP contribution limit appears on your previous year's Revenue Canada Notice of Assessment.
- Contribute as soon as possible, preferably at the beginning of the year or, even better, in monthly payments. Regular payments make a significant difference in the total amount accumulated. Also, one smaller payment made annually will increase faster than a larger contribution made every four or five years.
- Diversify your holdings. Depending on your investment time frame, your retirement expectations, and the degree of risk you are comfortable with, you should hold units in an appropriate mix of domestic and foreign income and growth funds. The current foreign-content limit continues to be 20% of the book value of your total RRSP holdings. Amounts in excess of this limit are subject to a penalty of 1% per month.
- Don't overlook Spousal RRSPs. The more taxable income you have, the higher your tax bracket. You should, therefore, consider allocating

future taxable income as evenly as possible between you and your spouse. You may invest all or a portion of your maximum allowable contribution in your spouse's name. These contributions can be deducted from your taxable income, but the plan belongs to your spouse and the amount contributed will not affect his or her yearly limit. The benefits of a Spousal RRSP are more significant when one partner earns significantly more current income and expects to receive a higher retirement income.

- Your RRSP holding can be transferred on a tax-deferred basis only if you include it in your will or through a Designation of Beneficiary in your RRSP. Otherwise, all RRSP funds will be taxed.

- The maximum lifetime non-deductible overcontribution limit was reduced from $8,000 to $2,000 effective January 1, 1996. If your overcontribution is currently in excess of this amount and was made before February 27, 1995, the excess over $2,000 must be used to fund future contributions. This means that until your existing over-contribution has been reduced to $2,000, no further RRSP contributions will be allowed.

- Previously, contributions to your RRSP were allowed up until the end of the year in which you reached 71. As a result of changes announced in the last federal budget, this age limit has been reduced to 69. This means that individuals who turn 69, 70, or 71 years of age this year must convert their RRSPs into a retirement income option by December 31, 1997. At that time you can either withdraw your RRSP in a lump sum, transfer it to a Registered Retirement Income Fund (RRIF) or a Life Income Fund (essentially a locked-in RIF with annual minimum and maximum with-drawal limits), purchase an annuity, or do any combination of the above.

- Although you cannot claim an income tax deduction for RRSP administration fees paid after March 5, 1996, it is still advisable to pay for these charges by separate cheque. This way, you leave as much money as possible compounding tax free in your plan.

- Seek professional help in building a well-diversified RRSP. You might also want to consider a self-directed plan. This kind of plan gives you much broader investment options such as a more diversified choice of mutual funds, term certificates from a wide range of issuers, and Canadian or foreign stocks and bonds. Consolidation of several RRSPs into a single self-directed plan also allows for easier record keeping.

- Any cash withdrawals from an RRSP are subject to withholding tax at 10% for amounts up to $5,000, 20% for up to $15,000, and 30% for higher amounts.
- Don't forget to review your RRSP holdings at least once a year.

33

• •

Building a Heavy Hitter Mutual Fund Portfolio

WITH OVER 1,400 mutual funds to select from, building an investment portfolio may seem like a next-to-impossible task. However, by concentrating your selection on the Heavy Hitters you dramatically reduce the list of possibilities. Just as important, you also avoid the mediocre and poor performers. With the following step-by-step approach, the entire process becomes manageable and, hopefully, reasonably enjoyable.

Step 1 — Know Your Financial Objectives

A clearly defined plan is the key to financial success. You must know your financial goals, otherwise you may never achieve them. Are you saving for additional retirement income? A down payment on a first home? Putting money aside for a child's education? Once you have identified your financial goal, you must also determine how soon you need to achieve it, and how much risk you are willing to take to get it. The following Investment Profile Quiz will help get you started. Answer the questions honestly, add the points, and move on to Step 2.

INVESTMENT PROFILE QUIZ

How much risk are you comfortable with?

I do not want any drop in value — even temporarily — for most of my investments. (0 points)

I could live with moderate declines of between 10% and 20% in anticipation of potentially higher long-term returns. (5 points)

Declines of 20% or more in the short-term value of my investments would not cause me concern. (10 points)

When will you need your money?

Money intended as an emergency cash fund or for very short-term goals should be held in savings accounts, money-market or T-bill mutual funds, or redeemable GICs.

3–5 years	(0 points)
6–10 years	(5 points)
11+ years	(10 points)

What are your financial goals?

I am most concerned about retaining the value of my investments but would like to keep ahead of inflation. (0 points)

My goal is regular income payments with growth potential. (5 points)

I want long-term growth and am comfortable with market fluctuations. (10 points)

Step 2 — Determining Your Asset Allocation

Every investor wants growth or income or some combination of the two. How much of each, though, will depend on your own unique set of factors such as investment goals, age, net worth, personal circumstances, risk tolerance, return expectations, and more. Since every investor's circumstances and goals are different, there is no one "best" asset allocation. As a general rule, however, you should — since stocks remain the best long-term investment — go with more growth assets if you are far from your chosen goal, and more fixed-income funds if you are closer. The following investment portfolios are intended only as guides, and if you are uncomfortable with any allocation you should move to a lower-risk strategy. Seeking the help of a financial advisor to determine the right combination of funds that are suitable for you is also recommended.

Legend

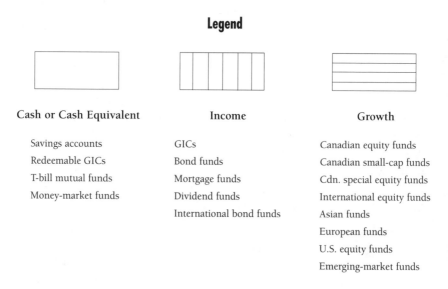

Cash or Cash Equivalent	Income	Growth
Savings accounts	GICs	Canadian equity funds
Redeemable GICs	Bond funds	Canadian small-cap funds
T-bill mutual funds	Mortgage funds	Cdn. special equity funds
Money-market funds	Dividend funds	International equity funds
	International bond funds	Asian funds
		European funds
		U.S. equity funds
		Emerging-market funds

Portfolio I — Preservation of Capital
0–10 points

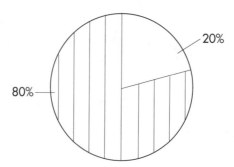

This portfolio reflects the needs of investors who want to guarantee the security of their principal and the interest received. The income component could be split 60% in GICs staggered over various time periods and 20% in suitable bond or mortgage mutual funds. This combination of assets is best suited for investors with no- to low-risk profiles and/or those pursuing short-term goals. Investors who wish to add a growth option should consider 50% in GICs, 20% in income mutual funds, and 10% in a Canadian equity mutual fund that invests in blue-chip companies.

Portfolio II — Income and Growth
15–20 points

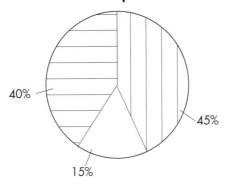

40%

45%

15%

The combination of stock and bond investments in this portfolio reduces volatility but has the potential, over time, to earn returns that will exceed inflation. Options for the income component are GICs — 15%, bond fund(s) — 15%, and dividend fund(s) — 15%. Options for the growth component are 30% in Canadian equity mutual funds and 10% in an international fund. Investors who wish more growth potential could increase the equity component to 45% and reduce the income option to 40%. Individuals with larger amounts of investment dollars could diversify the growth component further by including around 5% in a U.S., European, or Asian equity mutual fund.

Portfolio III — Growth
25+ points

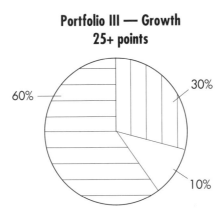

60%

30%

10%

While this portfolio will display volatility from time to time, it also has the potential to provide attractive long-term growth. However, when used for shorter-term goals (under five years) the risk factor will significantly increase. The income component in this portfolio could be allocated as GICs 10%, bond funds 10%, dividend funds 5%, and a global bond fund 5%. Options for the growth component are 30% in Canadian equities, 15% in Canadian small-cap equity mutual funds, and 15% in an international equity fund. More aggressive investors could increase the growth option to 75% or 80% by adding 5% to a fund that invests in a particular region such as the Pacific Rim or Europe and/or a Canadian precious metals fund and 10% in a U.S. fund. Success with this investment strategy requires a longer investment time frame (10+ years) and the ability to resist overreacting to market setbacks.

Step 3 — Selecting the Heavy Hitters

You should now have a better idea of what assets and how much of each should be included in your investment portfolio. Now it's time to choose appropriate Heavy Hitter funds. For a quick overview turn to Chapter 6, "The Heavy Hitters at a Glance." This lists all the Heavy Hitters by fund category and gives you the star ratings for load and no-load funds. Check off the Heavy Hitters that interest you. Next, turn to the appropriate fund chapter(s). Here you will find information on each Heavy Hitter, including how often a fund has beaten its appropriate benchmark, who manages the fund, and what investment style is followed. You will also learn the fund's best and worst returns over the past five calendar years, whether its volatility and management expense ratio are above or below the average for its category, and if any restrictions apply. Now consult that chapter's Rankings/Returns table, which lists all funds alphabetically. This will allow you to quickly and easily compare the rankings and returns of your shortlisted funds over the past one-, three-, and five-year periods. When checking the ranking of a particular fund, don't forget that this ranking is relative to the total number of funds for that time period.

To narrow down your choices you should consider not only returns, but also factors such as sales commissions, management expenses, and volatility. Some funds will automatically be eliminated because of certain restrictions or because they are "capped" — closed to new investors. Before making a final decision, consult the Mutual Fund Company Scorecard (Appendix 3) to see how many Heavy Hitters and Underachievers the fund company holds. This will give you a good fix on the company's overall performance and allow you to make a more informed buying decision. It will also be invaluable for individuals who would prefer to invest with only one or two companies. For ease of reference the Summary table in each chapter lists all funds alphabetically and gives the corresponding fund number for Appendix 3. Finally, read the prospectus and check the latest returns before investing.

Buying Your Funds

Now that you have selected suitable funds for your investment portfolio, the next step is to purchase them. There is, unfortunately, no such thing as one-stop shopping when it comes to buying mutual funds. Some are available only through the fund company itself, while most are sold through brokers and financial planners. Moreover, segregated funds can be purchased only from the insurance company's own sales force. Full-service brokers and the discount brokerage arm, of major banks have the widest selection, but even there the selection is generally limited to around 400 to 500 funds and may not include some of the funds on your buying list. Moreover, many brokers and financial planners promote only a short list of funds from five or six mutual fund companies.

Banks and Trust Companies. Over the last couple of years, financial institutions have upgraded the training requirements for their investment personnel with considerable success. Known as "personal investment managers" or "investment executives," these individuals can give advice on many aspects of personal finance. However, your choice of funds will (in most cases) be limited to their own family of funds.

Full-Service Brokers. Brokers, licensed by the province they practise in, can give advice on matters like asset allocation and tax implications and on a very broad range of investments such as stocks, bonds, stripped bonds, GICs, and mutual funds. Brokers do not receive a salary but rather make their living through the commissions on the investment products they sell. The commission, which is split between the broker and the parent company, compensates them for the investment advice given and the time they spend with a client. A handling fee of between $50 and $100, depending on the amount being invested, may be charged on the purchase of no-load funds.

Discount Brokers offer the same selection of investment products as full-service brokers. But because you receive little or no investment advice, the sales commission for purchasing a load fund is generally 1% for amounts over $25,000 and 2% for amounts under. Some discount brokers charge 2.5% for amounts up to $5,000. If you choose the back-end load option, the fees charged by individual mutual fund companies will apply. When you purchase a no-load fund, a fee of around $40 is usually charged. Most major banks have a discount brokerage arm.

Financial Planners. Make sure they are accredited either as Registered Financial Planners or as Chartered Financial Planners. Some charge an hourly fee to develop a financial plan and do not sell financial products such as mutual funds. Others charge a fee for a financial plan plus a commission for any investment purchased, or provide the plan free if you buy your investments through them.

Mutual Fund Companies. Some funds can be bought on an individual basis from the sponsoring mutual fund company. To do this, call the toll free number listed in Appendix 3. Tell them which fund(s) you are interested in and they will send you the prospectus, application form, and information kit. If you need any help in completing the form, give them another call.

Individuals who are considering investing with only one mutual fund company may find the following points helpful before coming to a final decision.

- Although no mutual fund company has all of its funds in the Heavy Hitter category at all times, some companies certainly have better reputations for consistent above-average performance than others.
- If being able to switch between funds is important, your final choice should be biased towards companies with Heavy Hitters in most asset classes and no Underachievers.
- Some companies have a better performance record in some areas than in others. If you are interested in, say, Canadian equities and are not likely to switch very often, less importance need be given to performance across all sectors.
- Small and large companies usually have different management styles. You may prefer a larger mutual fund company because it has

wider resources or a smaller company because it offers more personal service.

As a final note, once you have purchased your funds, don't forget to monitor their performance on a regular basis. No one else will do it for you.

34

•••••••••••••••••••••••••••••••••

Investment Strategies

Market Timing

BUY LOW AND sell high. A deceptively simple-sounding investment strategy. However, when it comes to mutual funds, many investors do the exact opposite. Lured by advertisements proclaiming returns of 33% or more, they rush to buy. Then, when returns decline, they rush even faster to sell.

Investors who pursue a market timing approach are not so concerned with getting in at rock-bottom prices or selling at the peak. Instead, their aim is to share in most of a bull market while escaping most of a decline. One would aim to invest in equity funds just before an economic recovery starts, move out before the peak, and move into bond funds just as the downturn begins. Of course, in reality, even though you may have judged the business cycle correctly, markets often move down when they are expected to move up and vice versa.

Moreover, there are the added problems of either having too much invested in a particular market when it goes down or being out of a market when it goes up. In addition, many studies have shown that, given sufficient time, the highest returns are most often obtained by investing all of your investment dollars into the stock market as quickly as possible, regardless of the business cycle. However, for all but the most committed investor, it would be unwise to invest a large amount of money in an equity fund if the stock market is at an all-time high and is poised for a correction. When returns plummet, you might be tempted to take your money and run — at a considerable loss.

•The bottom line is that successful market timing is extremely difficult. Perhaps the view of John Bogle, chairman of the Vanguard Group of Investment Companies, sums it up better than most. "In thirty years in this business, I do not know anybody who has done it successfully and consistently, nor anybody who knows anybody who has done it successfully and consistently."

Dollar Cost Averaging

There are many market timing approaches but one of the simplest is "dollar cost averaging." This investment technique also lends itself extremely well to mutual funds. By investing a fixed amount of money at regular intervals, you buy more units in a mutual fund when prices are down and fewer when prices are high. This reduces the average price per unit. The more frequently you invest, such as monthly rather than semi-annually, the better your chances of buying units when prices are especially low. One of the principal advantages of dollar cost averaging is that it does not require large amounts of investment money. Many financial institutions and mutual fund companies allow you to invest as little as $25 on a regular basis. The money is withdrawn automatically from your bank account and invested in the funds of your choice.

Many people use this investment strategy without being aware of it. If, for example, you pay a fixed amount monthly into a company pension plan, or reinvest fund distributions (even though the amounts may vary), you are already dollar cost averaging.

Buy and Hold

This investment strategy involves simply buying assets and keeping them until you reach your financial objectives. It works especially well with equity mutual funds, where an investment time frame of five years or more is generally required in order to capture the high returns. This approach does, however, require a prudent appraisal of the markets and funds before investing. Let's face it, a buy and hold strategy is not in itself going to improve the performance of a fund with a long history of below-average returns.

One of the inherent problems with a buy and hold strategy is the inclination of the riskier assets in your portfolio, over the longer term, to outperform the more conservative ones. Ten years or so down the road this could result in a much riskier portfolio than you would be comfortable with. In order to avoid this scenario, you should review your portfolio at least once a year. By reducing units in the assets that have grown, or adding to others that have lagged, you can rebalance back to your original mix. Moreover, a fund that you considered highly desirable in your 20s or 30s may not have the same appeal when you are in your 50s.

Following a buy and hold strategy does not mean owning units in a fund in perpetuity. If you find your fund's returns, compared to its peers, are continuously declining over a 12-month period or more, it would be wise to call your salesperson. It may be that the manager who generated the above-average returns has left or made a wrong call which may need time to correct, or the investment philosophy of the fund may have changed. If the answers to your questions don't make you feel confident about future performance, you could give it another couple of months and if returns are still headed in a negative direction, you should probably consider moving on.

Asset Allocation

This method of investing involves allocating your money among the following asset classes:

Cash or equivalent — Canada Savings Bonds, term deposits, treasury bills, and money-market funds fit this category because they are easily cashed and low risk.

Fixed income — Investments that provide a fixed rate of return, such as bonds, and regular interest income, such as bond and mortgage funds.

Growth — Investments that provide capital gains, such as common or preferred shares, and equity and special equity funds.

By dividing your investment portfolio among a variety of investments, both domestically and internationally, you not only reduce its level of risk but also ensure being in a market when it takes off. This way losses in Canadian stocks may be offset by gains in bonds or higher returns in overseas markets.

The amount of money you put in each asset class will vary depending on your own personal financial goals, age, risk tolerance, return expectations, and economic conditions. As a general rule, the further you are away from your investment goals, the more growth assets you should hold. The nearer you are, the more fixed income. As you grow older, your asset allocation should become more conservative. Otherwise, you may end up with more money in the stock market than is advisable. However, investors should consider the likelihood of living to at least 80 or 85 and take steps to ensure that their portfolios contain sufficient equities to generate the necessary growth to fund future long-term income needs.

Many financial institutions and mutual fund companies also offer asset allocation mutual funds, which contain a mix of cash, bonds, and stocks in one fund. The amounts held in each asset are changed according to economic conditions and the management team's investment decisions, computer-driven modelling techniques, or a combination. Depending on these factors, some asset allocation funds may hold a higher percentage in stocks than you would be comfortable with.

Most investors use a combination of two or more investment techniques. Regardless of which investment strategy, or combination, you use, you must first clearly define your investment objectives and how much risk you are willing to take to achieve them, and second, ensure that you are investing in funds of well-established companies with proven track records. Overlooking either one of these steps could seriously jeopardize even the most sophisticated investment strategies.

35

● ●

A Look at Indexing

IN ANY GIVEN period some actively managed funds will outperform their relevant index. However, far too many do not. Over the 12-month period ending in May 1997, for example, 65% of all Canadian equity funds failed to match the TSE 300 Total Return Index. For some investors, index funds offer a viable alternative.

What Is Indexing?

"Indexing" describes an investment approach that tries to mirror the performance of a specified stock or bond market benchmark or index, such as the Toronto Stock Exchange (TSE) 300 Composite Index, by investing in the same securities. The TSE 300 is Canada's most broadly based index and tracks the performance of the 300 largest Canadian corporations listed on the Toronto Stock Exchange. It covers a wide range of companies, from banking to telecommunications, and is often referred to as the exchange's bellwether index because it is designed to provide an indication of the general performance of the market at any time. On the fixed-income side, index funds seek to parallel the investment returns of the Scotia Capital Markets Universe Bond Index, the generally accepted benchmark for Canadian bond managers. Investors can also diversify further, through funds that mirror the Standard & Poor's (S&P) 500 Index in the United States and other specific market indices overseas. These funds either invest directly in stocks or combine stock-index futures and cash.

Returns on Index Funds

Although the objective of an index fund is to mirror the performance of a specific benchmark, returns will *always* be lower. How much lower depends on the management fees charged. If, for example, the TSE 300 rises by 14% over a one-year period, the corresponding index fund will rise to nearly 14%. If the TSE 300 falls 14%, the index fund will fall a little more than 14%. The higher the management fees, the greater the difference.

In the United States, the Vanguard Group of Funds, a no-load company, offers U.S. index funds with management fees as low as .20% — 20 cents out of every $100 invested. By comparison, management fees in Canada range from a low of .80% for the National Trust's Canadian Index Fund to a high of 2.64% for Great-West Life's Canadian Equity Index Fund. Because index funds are not actively managed and require no research or stock picking, there is little justification for paying the higher management fee. Clearly, the key for investors is to pick a no-load index fund with low management fees. The lower the fees, the closer the fund's return will match its benchmark. This approach will put you ahead of many actively managed mutual funds.

Advantages of Investing in Index Funds

- Index funds will never beat the market, but they will not dramatically underperform versus it either. For many investors that can be a definite plus.
- Because an index fund employs a "passive" investment approach, there is considerably less buying and selling than in actively managed funds. Fund holdings change only when the index changes. Taxable capital gains, therefore, are usually minimal, and for long-term investors outside a registered portfolio this can be a major consideration.
- A Canadian equity index fund can serve as a good "core" investment, as it gives exposure to a well-diversified mix of consumer goods, industrial products, resources, and interest-sensitive stocks.

Disadvantages of Investing in Index Funds

- Because index funds are fully invested at all times, they will do well in bull markets but will lose ground to funds that maintain or increase cash reserves during market declines.
- Derivative-based index funds can generate higher taxes through income rather than capital gains for investors holding their funds outside a registered plan.
- Some actively managed funds provide exceptional returns over long periods. By investing solely in index funds, you give up the opportunity to benefit from first- or second-quartile performance.

Alternatives to Index Funds

Investors who want the advantages of an index fund but don't want to pay a management fee might want to consider TIPs (Toronto 35 Index Participation units). This product, created by the Toronto Stock Exchange, allows direct investment in the TSE 35. The underlying assets of TIPs are shares in the 35 companies that make up the Toronto 35 Index, the index that tracks the performance of Canada's top blue-chip companies. Another similar investment vehicle is HIPs (TSE 100 Participating units). The TSE 100 Index tracks the performance of the 100 largest companies listed on the Toronto Stock Exchange. Investors can buy either TIPs or HIPs through any full-service or discount broker, just like purchasing any TSE-listed stock, with commissions payable when buying or selling.

APPENDIX 1

•••••••••••••••••••••••••••••••••

Fast Fund Facts

- Total number of funds: 1,431; Canadian: 876; International: 555; Load: 859; No-load: 572
- Total assets under management: $289.8 billion; Canadian: $215.1 billion; International: $74.7 billion
- Total number of Heavy Hitters: 194; Load: 89; No-load: 105
    * Number of Canadian Heavy Hitters: 145; Load: 53; No-load: 92
    * Number of international Heavy Hitters: 49; Load: 36; No-load: 13
- Total number of Underachievers: 176; Load: 109; No-load: 67
    * Number of Canadian Underachievers: 136; Load: 84; No-load: 52
    * Number of international Underachievers: 40; Load: 25; No-load: 15
- Total number of billion-dollar funds: 57; Canadian: 43; International: 14
    * Number of billion-dollar Heavy Hitters: 21; Canadian: 10; International: 11
    * Number of billion-dollar Underachievers: 11; Canadian: 11; International: 0
- Fund company with the most billion-dollar funds: Investors Group (13, of which 2 are Heavy Hitters and 4 are Underachievers)

- Fund company with the most Heavy Hitters:
    * Load: Investors Group (8)
    * No-load: Phillips Hager & North Ltd. (10), McLean Budden Limited (10)
- Fund company with the most Underachievers:
    * Load: Strategic Value Funds Management Inc. (10)
    * No-load: Royal Bank (10)
- Largest fund: Templeton Growth Fund Ltd. ($7.6 billion)
- Most volatile fund: Cambridge Resource Fund (volatility rating 10); Best return: 85.3% (1993); Worst return: -27.8% (1990)
- Least volatile fund: AGF U.S. Dollar Money Market Fund (volatility rating 1); Best return: 8.7% (1989); Worst return: 2.7% (1993)
- Most volatile fund categories: Emerging-market (volatility rating 5.5), Asian (volatility rating 5.5), and special equity (volatility rating 5.3)
- Least volatile fund categories: Canadian money-market (volatility rating 1.0), international money-market (volatility rating 1.1), and mortgage (volatility rating 1.4)
- Number of new funds introduced in the past 12 months: 190; Canadian: 111; International: 79
- Fund with the highest one-year return: AIC Advantage Fund (64.4%); Lowest: Cambridge Special Equity Fund (-52.4%)
- Fund with the highest annualized five-year return: Marathon Equity Fund (37.5%); Lowest: Cambridge Global Fund (-3.9%)
- Fund with the highest management expense ratio: Horizon 1 Multi-Asset Fund Inc. (10.0%)
- Fund with the lowest management expense ratio: Elliott & Page Money-Market Fund (0.26%)

APPENDIX 2

• •

Glossary of Terms

Asset Mix Assets are distributed among stocks, bonds, and money-market instruments (treasury bills, certificates of deposit, short-term government bonds, and commercial paper).

Asset Anything having commercial or exchange value that is owned by a business, institution, or individual.

Back-End Load A charge for withdrawing shares from a mutual fund.

Balanced Mutual Fund An investment fund that usually includes bonds, debentures, or preferred shares, in varying ratios with common stocks.

Bear Market A prolonged period of falling prices. A bear market in stocks is usually brought on by the anticipation of declining economic activity, and a bear market in bonds is caused by rising interest rates.

Bonds Certificates issued by borrowers, usually governments or corporations. A bond will normally have a fixed interest rate and a set maturity date, at which time the principal will be repaid in full. A typical bond will have interest coupons attached which are redeemed annually or semi-annually.

Bond Mutual Fund An investment fund predominantly made up of bonds and debentures.

Broker A person who acts as an intermediary in the purchase of securities or insurance.

Bull Market A prolonged rise in the prices of stocks, bonds, or commodities. Bull markets may last a few months to several years and are characterized by high trading volume.

Appendix 2: Glossary of Terms

Capital Cost Allowance A tax deduction for the depreciation of various types of assets.

Capital Gains The difference between the buy and sell price of an asset. The capital gain on stocks purchased for $1,000 and sold for $1,450 is $450.

Closed-End Mutual Fund A fund in which the total number of shares is fixed. After the initial offer, the shares can be acquired only from another owner. Share prices are set by supply and demand, not net asset value, and are traded on a stock exchange.

Commercial Paper Short-term debt securities issued by corporations, banks, and other borrowers.

Common Share A security representing part ownership in a company, generally carrying the right to vote on major decisions and to receive dividends.

Coupons Certificates attached to a bond that can be redeemed for interest payments at regular intervals.

Debenture General debt obligation backed only by the integrity of the borrower. An unsecured bond is a debenture.

Deposit Insurance Protection of certain types of assets against loss. Bank and trust company deposits are covered by the Canada Deposit Insurance Corporation (CDIC) up to a maximum of $60,000. Mutual funds are not covered by deposit insurance.

Distribution Company A company that has the exclusive right to offer shares of one or more investment funds to the public, directly, or through other investment fund dealers or brokers.

Distribution Fees Assessments levied by some mutual fund companies on the value of units purchased through a back-end load sales option.

Diversification An investment technique intended to minimize risk by placing money in a number of securities. In a diversified portfolio, a decline in the value of one stock, for example, would not dramatically affect the overall value of the holdings.

Dividend Tax Credit A tax credit intended to reduce the effective rate paid on dividend income.

Dividends Payments made to shareholders of a company in the form of cash or additional shares.

Equity Mutual Fund An investment fund consisting primarily of common shares, the objective of which is to participate fully in the growth of an economy.

Equities Common and preferred shares, representing a share in the ownership of a company.

Financial Planners Professionals who specialize in preparing financial programs for individuals, covering such matters as investments, tax planning, retirement preparation, estate planning, and income generation. Some charge an hourly fee while others make their revenue through commissions on the sale of securities, including mutual funds.

Fixed-Income Mutual Fund A fund that invests in securities which pay interest at a fixed rate, such as bonds.

Front-End Load The commission charged when mutual fund units are bought.

Global Mutual Fund A fund that invests in several countries, including its home nation. The fund may specialize in stocks, bonds, or money-market instruments.

Growth Fund An investment fund that seeks growth of capital as its primary objective. This type of fund invests primarily in common stocks and securities convertible into common stocks.

Guaranteed Investment Certificates (GICs) Securities issued by financial institutions, such as banks and trust companies, for a specified term. GICs of up to five years issued by members of the CDIC are covered by deposit insurance up to $60,000.

Hedge A strategy used by fund managers to limit investment risk.

Income Fund An investment fund whose primary objective is current income. Such funds generally invest their assets in government, corporate, or other bonds. Some income funds may include high-yielding common stocks.

International Mutual Fund A fund that invests in many countries but not its own.

Investment Objective A fund's (or investor's) goal. Investment strategies can be designed to generate long-term growth, current income, or other goals.

Investment Portfolio Securities owned by an individual consisting of a combination of stocks, bonds, and other types of securities.

Leveraging The borrowing of money for investment purposes.

Liquidity The ability to convert a security to cash quickly.

Load The fee charged by a mutual fund to investors to buy units (front-end load or acquisition fee) or sell units (back-end load or redemption fee).

Management Company The business entity that establishes, promotes, and manages a fund or funds, each of which is a separate entity with its own board of directors or trustee(s).

Management Fee The fee paid to a fund's manager for investment management and certain administrative services.

Money-Market Mutual Fund An investment fund, the portfolio of which is invested in large denominations of short-term paper (generally maturing in less than six months), designed to provide high yields with no loss of capital.

Appendix 2: Glossary of Terms

Mutual Funds Pools of investment money, managed by professionals, and invested in a wide range of securities.

Net Asset Value (NAV) The value of mutual fund shares. It is normally calculated daily by subtracting a fund's liabilities from its assets and dividing by the number of shares outstanding.

No-Load Mutual Fund A fund offered to the public that carries no purchase fee (front-end load) or redemption fee (back-end load).

Principal The amount of money you invest.

Portfolio The combined holdings of more than one stock, bond, commodity, real-estate investment, cash, or other asset by an individual or institutional investor. The purpose of a portfolio is to reduce risk by diversification.

Prospectus The selling document legally required to be distributed to mutual fund investors. A prospectus describes a fund's investment strategy as well as the risks and costs of the investment.

Redemption The right of a shareholder to sell, at any time, some or all of his or her shares back to the investment fund for cash.

Registered Investment Any security that is held in a tax-sheltered plan approved by Revenue Canada.

Registered Retirement Income Fund (RRIF) A fund set up with proceeds from an RRSP to provide income during retirement.

Registered Retirement Savings Plan (RRSP) A plan registered with Revenue Canada that encourages Canadians to save for retirement by providing tax relief on contributions and earnings.

Return The amount of money earned by an investment.

Risk The measurable possibility of losing or not gaining value. Risk is differentiated from uncertainty, which is not measurable.

Sales Charge The amount of commission paid by an investor to a sales organization.

Share A unit of ownership in a company.

Shareholder Someone who owns one or more shares in a company.

Stock Ownership in a corporation represented by shares that are a claim on the corporation's earnings and assets. Common stock usually entitles the shareholder to vote in the election of directors and other matters taken up at shareholder meetings or by proxy. Preferred stock generally does not confer voting rights but it has a prior claim on assets and earnings (dividends must be paid on preferred stock before any can be paid on common stock).

Switching Moving money from one mutual fund to another.

Total Return The total amount any investment returns, including any capital gains or losses and any dividends or interest.

Transfer Fee   The price charged to transfer your assets to another company.

Treasury Bills   Short-term debt securities issued most commonly by the federal government.

Unitholder   Someone who holds one or more units in a mutual fund.

Volatility   The amount by which a fund's return varies over time; used as a measure of investment risk.

Yield   Income, usually interest, paid by a security on a regular basis.

APPENDIX 3

● ●

Mutual Fund Company Scorecard

THIS APPENDIX ALPHABETICALLY lists all mutual fund companies with a complete list of their funds, both domestic and international. (Companies too new to be alphabetized appear at the end.) It also identifies how many Heavy Hitters (HH) and Underachievers (UA) each company holds relative to its total number of qualifying funds (those with a five-year performance history). Funds without either an (HH) or (UA) ranking have average performance histories.

Funds with less than a five-year history are in italics. This allows investors who are considering one of these newer funds to quickly review a fund company's performance record with its more established funds before making a buying decision. Moreover, although these funds have insufficient performance data to be ranked according to the Heavy Hitter methodology, our research has highlighted a number of promising funds. These funds, with at least a three-year track record, are included in our "Rookie Camp" category and identified as (RC).

Individuals who prefer to invest with only one or two companies will find this section gives them a good overview as to which companies might be suitable. Readers should also use this appendix as an independent means of quickly verifying any investment advice being given. For individual fund performance, readers should consult the Rankings/Returns table in the appropriate chapter in Part Three or Four. The relevant chapter number is listed after each fund in this appendix.

Finally, for ease of reference, we have included whether or not a

Appendix 3: Mutual Fund Company Scorecard

fund company charges sales commissions and if any restrictions apply. Some funds, for example, are sold only in certain provinces, some are restricted to groups of professionals such as dentists or engineers, and some require minimum initial investments of varying amounts. Readers should call the fund management company for details.

(1) ABC Funds

(I. A. Michael Investment Counsel Ltd.)
8 King Street East
Suite 500
Toronto, ON
M5C 1B5
Tel: (416) 365-9696
Fax: (416) 365-9705

Heavy Hitters: 2 Underachievers: 0
Number of Qualifying Funds: 2
Total Number of Funds: 3
No sales commissions, restrictions apply

CANADIAN FUNDS
ABC Fully Managed Fund (HH) ch 14
ABC Fundamental Value Fund (HH) ch 12

INTERNATIONAL FUNDS
ABC American-Value Fund ch 23

(2) Acadia Investment Funds Inc.

295 St Pierre Blvd. West
P.O. Box 5554
Caraquet, NB
E1W 1B7
Tel: (506) 727-1345
Fax: (506) 727-1344
Toll Free: 1-800-351-1345

Heavy Hitters: 0 Underachievers: 0
Number of Qualifying Funds: 0
Total Number of Funds: 4
No sales commissions apply

CANADIAN FUNDS
Acadia Balanced Fund ch 14
Acadia Bond Fund ch 15
Acadia Money Market Fund ch 18
Acadia Mortgage Fund ch 16

(3) AGF Management Limited

Toronto-Dominion Bank Tower
31st Floor
P.O. Box 50
Toronto, ON
M5K 1E9
Tel: (416) 367-1900
Fax: (416) 865-4155
Toll Free: 1-800-268-8583

Heavy Hitters: 6 Underachievers: 5
Number of Qualifying Funds: 18
Rookie Camp Members: 3
Total Number of Funds: 39
Sales commissions apply

CANADIAN FUNDS
20/20 Canadian Resources Fund (HH) ch 19
AGF Canadian Bond Fund (HH) ch 15
AGF Canadian Equity Fund (UA) ch 12
AGF Canadian Growth Fund (UA) ch 12
AGF Canadian Tactical Asset Alloc. ch 14
AGF Dividend Fund (HH) ch 17
AGF Growth & Income Fund ch 14
AGF Growth Equity Fund ch 12
AGF High Income Fund (UA) ch 17
AGF Money Market Account (UA) ch 18
20/20 Managed Futures Value Fund ch 19
20/20 RSP Aggr. Smaller Companies ch 13
20/20 RSP Aggressive Equity ch 13

INTERNATIONAL FUNDS

AGF American Growth Fund (HH)
ch 23
AGF American Tactical Asset Alloc.
(HH) ch 25
AGF Asian Growth Class ch 21
AGF Global Government Bond Fund
ch 26
AGF Japan Class ch 21
AGF Special U.S. Class (UA) ch 23
AGF U.S. Dollar Money Market ($US)
(HH) ch 27
AGF World Balanced Fund ch 25
AGF China Focus Fund (RC) ch 21
AGF European Asset Allocation (RC) ch 25
AGF European Growth Fund ch 22
AGF Germany Class M ch 22
AGF Germany Fund ch 22
AGF Int'l Short Term Income Fund ch 27
AGF International Value Fund ch 20
AGF RSP Global Bond Fund ch 26
AGF RSP Int'l Equity Allocation ch 20
AGF U.S. Income Fund ch 26
AGF U.S. Short-Term High Yield ch 27
AGF World Equity Fund ch 20
20/20 Aggressive Global Stock Fund ch 20
20/20 Aggressive Growth Fund ch 23
20/20 Emerging Markets Value Fund ch 24
20/20 India Fund ch 21
20/20 Latin America Fund (RC) ch 24

(4) AIC Limited

1 Markland Street
Hamilton, ON
L8P 2J5
Tel: (905) 529-5500
Fax: (905) 529-0966
Toll Free: 1-800-263-2144

Heavy Hitters: 2 Underachievers: 0
Number of Qualifying Funds: 2
Total Number of Funds: 7
Sales commissions apply

CANADIAN FUNDS

AIC Advantage Fund (HH) ch 12
AIC Advantage Fund II ch 12
AIC Diversified Canada Fund ch 12
AIC Money Market Fund ch 18

INTERNATIONAL FUNDS

AIC Value Fund (HH) ch 23
AIC Emerging Markets Fund ch 24
AIC World Equity Fund ch 20

(-) AIM Funds Group Canada Inc.

See (69) INVESCO Funds Group
(Canada), Inc.

(5) Allstar Fund Group Ltd.

200 Burrard Street
Suite 320
Vancouver, BC
V6C 3L6
Tel: (604) 682-6446
Fax: (604) 662-8594
Toll Free: 1-800-822-6446

Heavy Hitters: 0 Underachievers: 1
Number of Qualifying Funds: 3
Total Number of Funds: 4
Sales commissions apply

CANADIAN FUNDS
Allstar AIG Canadian Equity Fund ch 12
Allstar Money Market Fund ch 18

INTERNATIONAL FUNDS
Allstar Adrian Day Gold Plus Fund
(UA) ch 23
Allstar AIG Asian Fund ch 21

(6) Altamira Management Ltd.

250 Bloor Street East
Suite 200
Toronto, ON
M4W 1E6

Appendix 3: Mutual Fund Company Scorecard

Tel: (416) 925-1623
Fax: (416) 925-8415
Toll Free: 1-800-262-2824

Heavy Hitters: 2 Underachievers: 5
Number of Qualifying Funds: 12
Total Number of Funds: 25
No sales commissions apply

CANADIAN FUNDS
Altafund Investment Corp. ch 12
Altamira Balanced Fund (UA) ch 14
Altamira Bond Fund (HH) ch 15
Altamira Capital Growth Fund (UA) ch 12
Altamira Equity Fund ch 12
Altamira Growth & Income Fund (UA) ch 14
Altamira Income Fund (HH) ch 15
Altamira Resource Fund ch 19
Altamira Special Growth Fund (UA) ch 13
Altamira Dividend Fund ch 17
Altamira North American Recovery ch 12
Altamira Prec. and Strategic Metal ch 19
Altamira Short Term Gov't Bond Fund ch 315

INTERNATIONAL FUNDS
Altamira Global Diversified Fund (UA) ch 20
Altamira Select American Fund ch 23
Altamira Short Term Global Income ch 27
Altamira Asia Pacific Fund ch 21
Altamira European Equity Fund ch 22
Altamira Global Bond Fund ch 26
Altamira Global Discovery Fund ch 24
Altamira Global Small Co. Fund ch 20
Altamira Japanese Opportunity Fund ch 21
Altamira Spec. High Yield Bond ch 26

(7) AMI Private Capital
26 Wellington Street East
Suite 900
Toronto, ON
M5E 1S2
Tel: (416) 865-1985
Fax: (416) 286-6145
Toll Free: 1-800-880-2412

Heavy Hitters: 4 Underachievers: 0
Number of Qualifying Funds: 4
Total Number of Funds: 4
No sales commissions apply

CANADIAN FUNDS
AMI Private Capital Equity (HH) ch 12
AMI Private Capital Income (HH) ch 15
AMI Private Capital Money Market (HH) ch 18
AMI Private Capital Optimix (HH) ch 14

(8) Association of Public Service Financial Administrators
c/o BPI Capital Management Corp.
BCE Place
161 Bay Street
Suite 3900
Toronto, ON
M5J 2S1
Tel: (416) 861-9811
Fax: (416) 861-9415
Toll Free: 1-800-263-2427

Heavy Hitters: 0 Underachievers: 0
Number of Qualifying Funds: 0
Total Number of Funds: 1
Sale commissions and restrictions apply

CANADIAN FUNDS
VenGrowth Investment Fund Inc. ch 19

(9) Atlas Asset Management Inc.
181 Bay Street
Suite 400
Toronto, ON
M7Y 3M1

Tel: (416) 369-4525
Fax: (416) 369-8176
Toll Free: 1-800-463-2857

Heavy Hitters: 2 Underachievers: 2
Number of Qualifying Funds: 8
Rookie Camp Members: 1
Total Number of Funds: 23
No sales commissions apply

CANADIAN FUNDS
Atlas Canadian Balanced Fund ch 14
Atlas Canadian Bond Fund (HH) ch 15
Atlas Canadian Large Cap Growth ch 12
Atlas Canadian Money Market Fund
   (UA) ch 18
Atlas Canadian T-Bill Fund (UA) ch 18
*Atlas Canadian Emerging Growth Fund
   ch 13*
Atlas Canadian Emerging Value Fund ch 13
*Atlas Canadian High Yield Bond Fund
   ch 15*
*Atlas Canadian Large Cap Value Fund
   ch 12*
Atlas Cdn. Dividend Growth Fund ch 17
Atlas Cdn. Small-Cap Growth Fund ch 13
Atlas Managed Futures Fund ($US) ch 19

INTERNATIONAL FUNDS
Atlas Amer. Large Cap Growth Fund
   (HH) ch 23
Atlas American Money Market ($US)
   ch 27
Atlas Global Value Fund ch 20
Atlas American Advantage Value ch 25
Atlas American R.S.P. Index Fund ch 23
Atlas European Value Fund (RC) ch 22
Atlas Int'l Emerging Mkts. Growth ch 24
Atlas Int'l Large-Cap Growth Fund ch 20
Atlas Int'l R.S.P. Index Fund ch 20
Atlas Latin American Value Fund ch 24
Atlas Pacific Basin Value Fund ch 21
Atlas World Bond Fund ch 26

(10) Bank of Bermuda Ltd.
Compass Point
4th Floor
9 Bermudiana Road
Hamilton, Bermuda
Tel: (441) 299-5600
Fax: (441) 299-6518

Heavy Hitters: 0 Underachievers: 0
Number of Qualifying Funds: 0
Total Number of Funds: 15
Sales commissions and restrictions apply

INTERNATIONAL FUNDS
*Global Manager - German Bund Index
   ch 22*
*Global Manager - German Geared Fund
   ch 22*
*Global Manager - German Index Fund
   ch 22*
Global Manager - Gold Index Fund ch 19
Global Manager - HK Geared Fund ch 21
Global Manager - HK Index Fund ch 21
*Global Manager - Japan Geared Fund
   ch 21*
Global Manager - Japan Index Fund ch 21
Global Manager - U.K. Geared Fund ch 22
*Global Manager - U.K. Gilt Index Fund
   ch 22*
Global Manager - U.K. Index Fund ch 22
*Global Manager - U.S. Bond Index Fund
   ch 26*
Global Manager - U.S. Dollar Cash ch 27
Global Manager - U.S. Geared Fund ch 23
Global Manager - U.S. Index Fund ch 23

(11) Bank of Montreal Investment Management Ltd.
100 King Street West
P.O. Box 1
Toronto, ON
M5X 1A1
Tel: (416) 927-6000 (or any branch)
Fax: (416) 867-7305
Toll Free: 1-800-387-1342

Appendix 3: Mutual Fund Company Scorecard

Heavy Hitters: 2 Underachievers: 1
Number of Qualifying Funds: 5
Rookie Camp Members: 2
Total Number of Funds: 24
No sales commissions apply

CANADIAN FUNDS
First Canadian Bond Fund (HH) ch 15
First Canadian Equity Index ch 12
First Canadian Money Market ch 18
First Canadian Mortgage Fund (HH)
ch 16
First Canadian Asset Alloc. (UA) ch 14
*First Canadian Dividend Income Fund
ch 17*

First Canadian Global Sci. & Tech. ch 19
First Canadian Precious Metals Fund ch 19
First Cdn. Growth Fund (RC) ch 12
First Cdn. Resource Fund (RC) ch 19
First Cdn. Special Growth Fund ch 13
First Cdn. T-Bill Fund ch 18

INTERNATIONAL FUNDS
*First Canadian Emerging Mkts. Fund
ch 24*
*First Canadian European Growth Fund
ch 22*
*First Canadian Far East Growth Fund
ch 21*
*First Canadian International Growth
ch 20*
*First Canadian Japanese Growth Fund
ch 21*
*First Canadian Latin American Fund
ch 24*
*First Canadian NAFTA Advantage Fund
ch 23*
First Canadian U.S. Equity Index ch 23
First Canadian U.S. Special Growth ch 23
First Canadian U.S. Value Fund ch 23
First Cdn. International Bond Fund ch 26
First Cdn. U.S. Growth Fund ch 23

(12) Beutel Goodman Managed Funds Inc.
20 Eglinton Avenue West
Suite 1109
Toronto, ON
M4R 1K8
Tel: (416) 932-6400
Fax: (416) 485-6229
Toll Free: 1-800-461-4551

Heavy Hitters: 3 Underachievers: 0
Number of Qualifying Funds: 6
Rookie Camp Members: 1
Total Number of Funds: 9
No sales commissions apply

CANADIAN FUNDS
Beutel Goodman Balanced Fund ch 14
Beutel Goodman Canadian Equity ch 12
Beutel Goodman Income Fund (HH)
ch 15
Beutel Goodman Money Market Fund
(HH) ch 18
Beutel Goodman Private Balanced (HH)
ch 14
Beutel Goodman Private Bond (RC) ch 15
Beutel Goodman Small Cap Fund ch 13

INTERNATIONAL FUNDS
Beutel Goodman American Equity ch 23
Beutel Goodman International Equity ch 20

(13) Bissett & Associates Investment Management Ltd.
500 Fourth Avenue S.W.
Suite 1120
Calgary, AB
Tel: (403) 266-4664
Fax: (403) 237-2334

Heavy Hitters: 5 Underachievers: 1
Number of Qualifying Funds: 6
Rookie Camp Members: 1
Total Number of Funds: 8
No sales commissions, restrictions apply

CANADIAN FUNDS
Bissett Bond Fund (HH) ch 15
Bissett Canadian Equity Fund (HH)
  ch 12
Bissett Money Market Fund (HH) ch 18
Bissett Retirement Fund (HH) ch 14
Bissett Small Cap Fund (HH) ch 13
Bissett Dividend Income Fund (RC) ch 17

INTERNATIONAL FUNDS
Bissett American Equity Fund
  (UA) ch 23
Bissett Multinational Growth Fund ch 20

(14) BNP (Canada) Valeurs Mobilliers Inc.
Tour BNP
1981 McGill College Avenue
Suite 500
Montreal, QC
H3A 2W8
Tel: (514) 285-2920
Fax: (514) 285-7598

Heavy Hitters: 1 Underachievers: 1
Number of Qualifying Funds: 3
Total Number of Funds: 3
No sales commissions apply

CANADIAN FUNDS
BNP (Canada) Bond Fund (HH) ch 15
BNP (Canada) Canadian Money Market
  (UA) ch 18
BNP (Canada) Equity Fund ch 12

(15) BPI Capital Management Corporation
161 Bay Street
Suite 3900
Toronto, ON
M5J 2S1
Tel: (416) 861-9811
Fax: (416) 861-9415
Toll Free: 1-800-263-2427

Heavy Hitters: 2 Underachievers: 3
Number of Qualifying Funds: 11
Total Number of Funds: 19
Sales commissions apply

CANADIAN FUNDS
BPI Canadian Balanced Fund (UA)
  ch 14
BPI Canadian Bond Fund (UA) ch 15
BPI Canadian Equity Value Fund (UA)
  ch 12
BPI Canadian Small Companies Fund
  ch 13
BPI Dividend Income Fund ch 17
BPI Resource Fund Inc. ch 19
BPI T-Bill Fund (HH) ch 18
*BPI Canadian Opportunities RSP Fund
  ch 12*
BPI High Income Fund ch 17

INTERNATIONAL FUNDS
BPI American Equity Value Fund (HH)
  ch 23
BPI American Small Companies Fund
  ch 23
BPI Global Balanced RSP Fund ch 25
BPI Global Equity Fund ch 20
BPI Asia Pacific Fund ch 21
BPI Emerging Markets Fund ch 24
BPI Global Opportunities Fund ch 20
BPI Global RSP Bond Fund ch 26
BPI Global Small Companies Fund ch 20
BPI U.S. Money Market ($US) ch 27

(16) Brewery General & Professional Association
c/o Spectrum United Mutual
  Funds Inc.
200 King Street West
Suite 1202
Toronto, ON
M5H 3W8
Tel: (416) 598-7777
Fax: (416) 598-7821
Toll Free: 1-800-328-5988

Appendix 3: Mutual Fund Company Scorecard

Heavy Hitters: 0 Underachievers: 0
Number of Qualifying Funds: 0
Total Number of Funds: 1
Sales commissions, restrictions apply

CANADIAN FUNDS
Trillium Growth Capital Inc. ch 19

(17) Caldwell Securities Ltd.
55 University Avenue
Suite 340
Toronto, ON
M5J 2H7
Tel: (416) 862-7755
Fax: (416) 862-2498

Heavy Hitters: 1 Underachievers: 1
Number of Qualifying Funds: 2
Total Number of Funds: 2
Sales commissions apply

CANADIAN FUNDS
Caldwell Securities Associate Fund
  (HH) ch 14

INTERNATIONAL FUNDS
Caldwell Securities International (UA)
  ch 25

(18) Canada Life Assurance Co.
330 University Avenue
Toronto, ON
M5G 1R8
Tel: (416) 597-1456
Fax: (416) 597-9674
Toll Free: 1-800-387-4447

Heavy Hitters: 1 Underachievers: 0
Number of Qualifying Funds: 5
Total Number of Funds: 8
Sales commissions apply
Segregated funds

CANADIAN FUNDS
Canada Life Canadian Equity S-9 ch 12
Canada Life Fixed Income S-19 ch 15
Canada Life Managed Fund S-35 ch 14
Canada Life Money Market S-29 ch 18

INTERNATIONAL FUNDS
Canada Life U.S. & Int'l Equity S-34
  (HH) ch 20
Canada Life Asia Pacific S-38 ch 21
Canada Life European Equity S-37 ch 22
Canada Life International Bond S-36 ch 26

(19) Canada Trust Fund Services Inc.
BCE Place
161 Bay Street
3rd Floor
Toronto, ON
Tel: (416) 361-8000
Fax: (416) 361-5333
Toll Free: 1-800-668-8888

Heavy Hitters: 0 Underachievers: 3
Number of Qualifying Funds: 9
Rookie Camp Members: 1
Total Number of Funds: 18
No sales commissions apply

CANADIAN FUNDS
Canada Trust Everest Balanced Fund
  ch 14
Canada Trust Everest Bond Fund ch 15
Canada Trust Everest Money Market
  (UA) ch 18
Canada Trust Everest Mortgage Fund
  ch 16
Canada Trust Everest Special Equity
  (UA) ch 19
Canada Trust Everest Stock Fund ch 12
Canada Trust Everest Div. Income ch 17
Canada Trust Everest Premium Money
  ch 18
Canada Trust Everest S/T Bond ch 15

INTERNATIONAL FUNDS

Canada Trust Everest Int'l Equity (UA)
ch 20

Canada Trust Everest North American
ch 20

Canada Trust Everest U.S. Equity ch 23

*Canada Trust Everest AmeriGrowth (RC)
ch 23*

Canada Trust Everest AsiaGrowth ch 21

*Canada Trust Everest Emerging Mkts.
ch 24*

Canada Trust Everest EuroGrowth ch 22

Canada Trust Everest Global Growth ch 20

Canada Trust Everest Int'l Bond ch 15

(20) Canadian Anaesthetists Mutual Fund Accumulating Fund Ltd.

94 Cumberland Street
Suite 503
Toronto, ON
M5R 1A3
Tel: (416) 925-7331
Fax: (416) 920-7843
Toll Free: 1-800-267-4713

Heavy Hitters: 0 Underachievers: 0
Number of Qualifying Funds: 1
Total Number of Funds: 1
No sales commissions, restrictions apply

CANADIAN FUNDS
CAMAF (Canadian Anaesthetists
  Mutual Accumulating Fund) ch 12

(21) Canadian Council of Professional Engineers

116 Albert Street
Suite 401
Ottawa, ON
K1P 5G3
Tel: (613) 232-2472
Fax: (613) 230-5759

Heavy Hitters: 0 Underachievers: 0
Number of Qualifying Funds: 3
Total Number of Funds: 6
No sales commissions, restrictions apply

CANADIAN FUNDS
CCPE Diversified Growth Fund R ch 14
CCPE Fixed Income Fund ch 15
CCPE Growth Fund R ch 12
CCPE Money Market Fund ch 18

INTERNATIONAL FUNDS
CCPE Global Equity ch 20
CCPE U.S. Equity ch 23

(22) Canadian Dental Association

100 Consilium Place
Suite 710
Scarborough, ON
M1H 3G8
Tel: (416) 296-9401
Fax: (416) 296-8920
Toll Free: 1-800-561-9401

Heavy Hitters: 1 Underachievers: 1
Number of Qualifying Funds: 4
Total Number of Funds: 13
No sales commissions, restrictions apply

CANADIAN FUNDS
CDA Balanced (KBSH) ch 14
CDA Bond & Mortgage (Canagex) ch 15
CDA Common Stock (Altamira) (UA)
  ch 12
CDA Money Market (Canagex) (HH)
  ch 18
CDA Aggressive Equity (Altamira) ch 13
CDA Canadian Equity (Trimark) ch 12
CDA Special Equity (KBSH) ch 13

Appendix 3: Mutual Fund Company Scorecard

INTERNATIONAL FUNDS
CDA Emerging Markets (KBSH) ch 24
CDA European (KBSH) ch 22
CDA Global (Trimark) ch 20
CDA International Equity (KBSH) ch 20
CDA Pacific Basin (KBSH) ch 21
CDA U.S. Equity (KBSH) ch 23

(23) Canadian Police Association
c/o C.I. Mutual Funds
151 Yonge Street
8th Floor
Toronto, ON
Tel: (416) 364-5181
Fax: (416) 364-6262
Toll Free: 1-800-563-5181

Heavy Hitters: 0 Underachievers: 0
Number of Qualifying Funds: 0
Total Number of Funds: 1
Sales commissions apply

CANADIAN FUNDS
C.I. Covington Labour-Sponsored ch 19

(24) Canadian Venture Opportunities Fund Ltd.
Scotia Plaza
55th Floor
40 King Street West
Toronto, ON
M5H 4A9
Tel: (416) 365-8066
Fax: (416) 365-2558
Toll Free: 1-888-527-4811

Heavy Hitters: 0 Underachievers: 0
Number of Qualifying Funds: 0
Total Number of Funds: 1
Sales commissions and restrictions apply

CANADIAN FUNDS
Canadian Venture Opportunities Fund ch 19

(25) Capstone Consultants Limited
c/o Hughes, King & Company Ltd.
1 University Avenue
Suite 401
Toronto, ON
M5J 2P1
Tel: (416) 863-0005/0687
Fax: (416) 863-0841

Heavy Hitters: 1 Underachievers: 1
Number of Qualifying Funds: 3
Total Number of Funds: 3
No sales commissions apply

CANADIAN FUNDS
Capstone Cash Management Fund
(HH) ch 18
Capstone Investment Trust ch 14

INTERNATIONAL FUNDS
Capstone Int'l Investment Trust (UA)
ch 20

(26) Cassels Blaikie & Co. Limited
1 Adelaide Street East
Suite 200
Toronto, ON
M5C 2W8
Tel: (416) 941-7500
Fax: (416) 867-9821

Heavy Hitters: 1 Underachievers: 0
Number of Qualifying Funds: 2
Total Number of Funds: 2
Sales commissions apply

CANADIAN FUNDS
Cassels Blaikie Canadian Fund (HH)
ch 14

INTERNATIONAL FUNDS
Cassels Blaikie American Fund ($US)
ch 23

(27) Chou Associates Management Inc.

70 Dragoon Crescent
Scarborough, ON
M1V 1N4
Tel: (416) 299-6749

Heavy Hitters: 1 Underachievers: 0
Number of Qualifying Funds: 2
Total Number of Funds: 2
Sales commissions apply

CANADIAN FUNDS
Chou RRSP Fund ch 12

INTERNATIONAL FUNDS
Chou Associates Fund (HH) ch 23

(28) C.I. Fund Management Inc.

151 Yonge Street
8th Floor
Toronto, ON
M5C 2Y1
Tel: (416) 364-1145
Fax: (416) 364-2969
Toll Free: 1-800-653-5181

Heavy Hitters: 3 Underachievers: 3
Number of Qualifying Funds: 9
Rookie Camp Members: 3
Total Number of Funds: 45
Sales commissions apply

CANADIAN FUNDS
C.I. Canadian Sector Shares (UA) ch 12
C.I. Money Market Fund (HH) ch 18
C.I. Short-Term Sector Shares (UA) ch 18
C.I. Canadian Balanced ch 14
C.I. Canadian Bond Fund (RC) ch 15
C.I. Canadian Growth Fund ch 12
C.I. Canadian Income Fund ch 14
C.I. Global Financial Serv. Sector ch 19
C.I. Global Health Sciences Sector ch 19
C.I. Global Resource Sector Shares ch 19
C.I. Global Tech. Sector Shares ch 19

C.I. Global Telecom. Sector Shares ch 19
Monarch Canadian Fund ch 12
Monarch Dividend Fund ch 17
Monarch Cdn. Sector Shares ch 12

INTERNATIONAL FUNDS
C.I. Emerging Markets Fund (UA) ch 24
C.I. Global Fund ch 20
C.I. Global Sector Shares ch 20
C.I. Pacific Fund (HH) ch 21
C.I. Pacific Sector Shares (HH) ch 21
Hansberger European Fund ch 22
C.I. American Fund ch 23
C.I. American RSP Fund ch 23
C.I. American Sector Shares ch 23
C.I. Emerging Markets Sector Shares ch 24
C.I. Global Bond RSP Fund (RC) ch 26
C.I. Global Equity RSP Fund ch 20
C.I. International Balanced Fund ch 25
C.I. International Balanced RSP ch 25
C.I. Latin American Fund ch 24
C.I. Latin American Sector Shares ch 24
C.I. New World Inc. ch 26
C.I. U.S. Money Market Fund ($US) ch 27
C.I. World Bond Fund (RC) ch 26
Hansberger Asian Fund ch 21
Hansberger Asian Sector Shares ch 21
Hansberger Developing Markets Fund ch 24
Hansberger Developing Mkts. Sector ch 24
Hansberger European Sector Shares ch 22
Hansberger Global Small-Cap Fund ch 20
Hansberger Global Small-Cap Sector ch 20
Hansberger Int'l Sector Shares ch 20
Hansberger International Fund ch 20
Hansberger Value Fund ch 20
Hansberger Value Sector Shares ch 20

Appendix 3: Mutual Fund Company Scorecard

(29) CIBC Securities Inc.
Commerce Court Postal Station
P.O. Box 51
Toronto, ON
M5L 1A2
Tel: (416) 980-3863
Fax: (416) 351-4860
Toll Free: 1-800-465-3863

Heavy Hitters: 2 Underachievers: 5
Number of Qualifying Funds: 12
Total Number of Funds: 28
No sales commissions apply

CANADIAN FUNDS
CIBC Balanced Fund ch 14
CIBC Canadian Bond Fund ch 15
CIBC Canadian Equity Fund (UA)
   ch 12
CIBC Canadian T-Bill Fund (UA) ch 18
CIBC Capital Appreciation Fund ch 13
CIBC Dividend Fund (UA) ch 17
CIBC Money Market Fund (UA) ch 18
CIBC Mortgage Fund (HH) ch 16
CIBC Premium T-Bill Fund (HH) ch 18
CIBC Canadian Index Fund ch 12
CIBC Canadian Resource Fund ch 19
CIBC Canadian Short-Term Bond ch 15
CIBC Energy Fund ch 19
CIBC Global Technology Fund ch 19
CIBC North American Demographics
   ch 19
CIBC Precious Metals Fund ch 19

INTERNATIONAL FUNDS
CIBC Global Equity Fund ch 20
CIBC U.S. Dollar Money Market ($US)
   ch 27
CIBC U.S. Equity Fund (UA) ch 23
CIBC Emerging Economies Fund ch 24
CIBC European Equity Fund ch 22
CIBC Far East Prosperity Fund ch 21
CIBC Global Bond Fund ch 26
CIBC Int'l Index RRSP Fund ch 20
CIBC Japanese Equity Fund ch 21

CIBC Latin American Fund ch 24
CIBC U.S. Index RRSP Fund ch 23
CIBC U.S. Opportunities Fund ch 23

(30) Clarington Capital Management Inc.
181 University Avenue
Suite 1010
Toronto, ON
M5H 3M7
Tel: (416) 860-9880
Fax: (416) 860-9884
Toll Free: 1-888-860-9888

Heavy Hitters: 0 Underachievers: 0
Number of Qualifying Funds: 0
Total Number of Funds: 9
Sales commissions apply

CANADIAN FUNDS
Clarington Canadian Balanced Fund ch 14
Clarington Canadian Equity Fund ch 12
Clarington Canadian Income Fund ch 14
Clarington Global Communications ch 19
Clarington Money Market Fund ch 18
Clarington Cdn. Small-Cap Fund ch 13

INTERNATIONAL FUNDS
Clarington Global Opportunities ch 20
Clarington U.S. Equity Fund ch 23
Clarington U.S. Smaller Co. Growth
   ch 23

(31) Clean Environment Mutual Funds Inc.
65 Queen Street West
Suite 1800
Toronto, ON
M5H 2M5
Tel: (416) 366-9933
Fax: (416) 366-2568
Toll Free: 1-800-461-4570

Heavy Hitters: 2 Underachievers: 0
Number of Qualifying Funds: 2
Rookie Camp Members 1:
Total Number of Funds: 4
Sales commissions apply

CANADIAN FUNDS
Clean Environment Balanced Fund
  (HH) ch 14
Clean Environment Equity Fund (HH)
  ch 12
Clean Environment Income Fund ch 15

INTERNATIONAL FUNDS
*Clean Environment Int'l Equity Fund
  (RC) ch 20*

(32) Colonia Life Insurance Company

2 St. Clair Avenue East
Toronto, ON
M4T 2V6
Tel: (416) 960-3601
Fax: (416) 323-0934

Heavy Hitters: 0 Underachievers: 0
Number of Qualifying Funds: 0
Rookie Camp Members: 1
Total Number of Funds: 6
Sales commissions apply
Segregated funds

CANADIAN FUNDS
Colonia Bond Fund ch 15
Colonia Equity Fund ch 12
Colonia Money Market Fund ch 18
Colonia Mortgage Fund ch 16
Colonia Special Growth Fund (RC) ch 13
Colonia Strategic Balanced Fund ch 14

(33) Co-operators Life Insurance Company

130 Macdonell Street
Priory Square
Guelph, ON
N1H 6P8
Tel: (519) 767-3901
Fax: (519) 824-7040

Heavy Hitters: 1 Underachievers: 1
Number of Qualifying Funds: 3
Rookie Camp Members: 1
Total Number of Funds: 4
No sales commissions apply
Segregated funds

CANADIAN FUNDS
Co-operators Balanced Fund ch 14
Co-operators Fixed Income Fund (HH)
  ch 15
Co-operators Canadian Equity Fund
  (UA) ch 12

INTERNATIONAL FUNDS
Co-operators U.S. Equity Fund (RC) ch 20

(34) Cote 100 Inc.

561 Beaumont Street East
St. Bruno, QC
J3V 2R2
Tel: (514) 461-2826
Fax: (514) 461-2177

Heavy Hitters: 0 Underachievers: 0
Number of Qualifying Funds: 0
Rookie Camp Members: 3
Total Number of Funds: 5
No sales commissions apply

CANADIAN FUNDS
Cote 100 REER (RC) ch 12
Cote 100 EXP (RC) ch 12
Cote 100 REA - Action ch 13

Appendix 3: Mutual Fund Company Scorecard

INTERNATIONAL FUNDS
Cote 100 Amerique (RC) ch 23
Cote 100 U.S. ch 23

(35) CSA Management Enterprises Limited
145 King Street West
Suite 2700
Toronto, ON
M5H 1J8
Tel: (416) 865-0326
Fax: (416) 865-9636
Toll Free: 1-800-363-3463

Heavy Hitters: 0 Underachievers: 2
Number of Qualifying Funds: 2
Total Number of Funds: 2
Sales commissions apply

CANADIAN FUNDS
Goldfund Ltd. (UA) ch 19
Goldtrust Fund (UA) ch 19

(36) Deacon Capital Corporation
304 Bay Street
Toronto, ON
M5H 4A6
Tel: (416) 350-3232
Fax: (416) 350-3239

Heavy Hitters: 0 Underachievers: 0
Number of Qualifying Funds: 0
Total Number of Funds: 1
Sales commissions and restrictions apply

CANADIAN FUNDS
Resolute Growth Fund ch 13

(37) Desjardins Trust Inc.
1 Complexe Desjardins
C.P. 34
Montreal, QC
H5B 1E4
Tel: (514) 286-5883
Fax: (514) 843-3328
Toll Free: 1-800-361-2680

Heavy Hitters: 0 Underachievers: 3
Number of Qualifying Funds: 7
Total Number of Funds: 15
No sales commissions apply

CANADIAN FUNDS
Fonds Desjardins Actions ch 12
Fonds Desjardins Environnement ch 12
Fonds Desjardins Equilibre ch 14
Fonds Desjardins Hypotheques (UA)
   ch 16
Fonds Desjardins Monetaire (UA) ch 18
Fonds Desjardins Obligations ch 15
Fonds Desjardins Croissance ch 12
Fonds Desjardins Divers. Ambitieux ch 14
Fonds Desjardins Divers. Audacieux ch 14
Fonds Desjardins Divers. Modere ch 14
Fonds Desjardins Divers. Secure ch 14
Fonds Desjardins Dividendes ch 17

INTERNATIONAL FUNDS
Fonds Desjardins International (UA)
   ch 20
Fonds Desjardins Marche Americain ch 23
Fonds Desjardins Mondial Equilibre ch 25

(38) Directors Guild of Canada
387 Bloor Street East
Suite 401
Toronto, ON
M5C 2Y1
Tel: (416) 972-1158
Fax: (416) 972-0820
Toll Free: 1-800-382-1159

Heavy Hitters: 0 Underachievers: 0
Number of Qualifying Funds: 0
Total Number of Funds: 1
Sales commissions apply

CANADIAN FUNDS
DGC Entertainment Ventures Corp. ch 19

(39) Dominion Equity Resource Fund Inc.
1710 Bow Valley, Square 2
205 - 5th Avenue S.W.
Calgary, AB
T2P 2V7
Tel: (403) 531-2657
Fax: (403) 264-5844

Heavy Hitters: 0 Underachievers: 0
Number of Qualifying Funds: 1
Total Number of Funds: 1
Sales commissions apply

CANADIAN FUNDS
Dominion Equity Resource Fund Inc.
ch 19

(40) Dynamic Mutual Funds
(a division of Goodman & Co. Ltd.)
Scotia Plaza
40 King Street West
55th Floor
Toronto, ON
M5H 4A9
Tel: (416) 363-5621
Fax: (416) 363-1417
Toll Free: 1-800-268-8186

Heavy Hitters: 5 Underachievers: 1
Number of Qualifying Funds: 14
Rookie Camp Members: 2
Total Number of Funds: 23
Sales commissions apply

CANADIAN FUNDS
Dynamic Canadian Growth Fund ch 12
Dynamic Dividend Fund (UA) ch 17
Dynamic Dividend Growth Fund (HH)
ch 17
Dynamic Fund of Canada ch 12
Dynamic Income Fund ch 15
Dynamic Money Market Fund ch 18
Dynamic Partners Fund ch 14
Dynamic Precious Metals Fund ch 19
Dynamic Team Fund ch 14

*Dynamic Global Precious Metals Fund
ch 19*
Dynamic Global Resources Fund ch 19
Dynamic Government Income Fund ch 15
Dynamic Real Estate Equity Fund ch 19

INTERNATIONAL FUNDS
Dynamic Americas Fund (HH) ch 23
Dynamic Europe Fund (HH) ch 22
Dynamic Global Bond Fund (HH) ch 26
Dynamic Global Millennia Fund ch 20
Dynamic International Fund (HH) ch 20
Dynamic Far East Fund (RC) ch 21
*Dynamic Global Partners Fund (RC)
ch 25*

(41) Elliott & Page Ltd.
393 University Avenue
22nd Floor
Toronto, ON
M5G 1E6
Tel: (416) 581-8350
Fax: (416) 581-8428
Toll Free: 1-800-363-6647

Heavy Hitters: 1 Underachievers: 1
Number of Qualifying Funds: 5
Total Number of Funds: 11
Sales commissions apply

CANADIAN FUNDS
Elliott & Page Balanced Fund ch 14
Elliott & Page Bond Fund (UA) ch 15
Elliott & Page Equity Fund ch 12
Elliott & Page Money Fund (HH) ch 18
Elliott & Page T-Bill Fund ch 18

INTERNATIONAL FUNDS
Elliott & Page American Growth Fund
ch 23
Elliott & Page Asian Growth Fund ch 21
Elliott & Page Emerging Markets ch 24
Elliott & Page Global Balanced Fund ch 25
Elliott & Page Global Bond Fund ch 26
Elliott & Page Global Equity Fund ch 20

Appendix 3: Mutual Fund Company Scorecard

(42) Empire Life Insurance Co.

259 King Street East
Kingston, ON
K7L 3A8
Tel: (613) 548-1881
Fax: (613) 548-4104

Heavy Hitters: 3 Underachievers: 2
Number of Qualifying Funds: 7
Total Number of Funds: 9
Sales commissions apply
Segregated funds

CANADIAN FUNDS
Empire Balanced Fund ch 14
Empire Bond Fund (UA) ch 15
Empire Elite Equity Fund 5 ch 12
Empire Equity Growth Fund 3 (HH)
  ch 12
Empire Money Market Fund (UA) ch 18
Empire Premier Equity Fund 1 (HH)
  ch 12
Empire Asset Allocation Fund ch 14

INTERNATIONAL FUNDS
Empire International Fund (HH) ch 20
*Empire Foreign Curr. Cdn. Bond Fund
  ch 26*

(43) Equitable Life Insurance Co. of Canada Ltd.

1 Westmount Road North
Waterloo, ON
N2J 4C7
Tel: (519) 886-5110
Fax: (519) 886-5314
Toll Free: 1-800-387-0588

Heavy Hitters: 2 Underachievers: 0
Number of Qualifying Funds: 2
Rookie Camp Members: 0
Total Number of Funds: 8
Sales commissions apply
Segregated funds

CANADIAN FUNDS
Equitable Life Segregated Accum. Inc.
  (HH) ch 15
Equitable Life Seg. Common Stock
  (HH) ch 12
Equitable Life Asset Allocation ch 14
Equitable Life Canadian Bond Fund ch 15
Equitable Life Canadian Stock Fund ch 12
Equitable Life Money Market Fund ch 18
Equitable Life Mortgage Fund ch 18

INTERNATIONAL FUNDS
Equitable Life International Fund ch 20

(44) Ethical Funds Inc.

510 - 815 West Hastings Street
Vancouver, BC
V6C 1B4
Tel: (604) 331-8350
Fax: (604) 331-8399
Toll Free: 1-800-267-5019

Heavy Hitters: 3 Underachievers: 0
Number of Qualifying Funds: 5
Total Number of Funds: 8
Sales commissions apply

CANADIAN FUNDS
Ethical Balanced Fund ch 14.
Ethical Growth Fund (HH) ch 12
Ethical Income Fund (HH) ch 15
Ethical Money Market Fund ch 18
Ethical Special Equity Fund ch 13

INTERNATIONAL FUNDS
Ethical North American Equity Fund
  (HH) ch 23
Ethical Global Bond Fund ch 15
Ethical Pacific Rim Fund ch 21

(45) Federation of Engineering & Scientific Associations

65 Queen Street West
Suite 1404
Toronto, ON
M5H 2M5
Tel: (416) 362-9009
Fax: (416) 360-8286
Toll Free: 1-800-563-3857

Heavy Hitters: 0 Underachievers: 0
Number of Qualifying Funds: 0
Total Number of Funds: 1
Sales commissions apply

CANADIAN FUNDS
FESA Enterprise Venture Capital ch 19

(46) Fidelity Investments Canada Ltd.

Ernst & Young Tower
222 Bay Street
Suite 900
Toronto, ON
M5K 1P1
Tel: (416) 307-5200
Fax: (416) 307-5508
Toll Free: 1-800-263-4077

Heavy Hitters: 3 Underachievers: 2
Number of Qualifying Funds: 6
Rookie Camp Members: 2
Total Number of Funds: 20
Sales commissions apply

CANADIAN FUNDS
Fidelity Canadian Bond Fund ch 15
Fidelity Capital Builder Fund (UA)
   ch 12
Fidelity Cdn. Short Term Asset Fund
   (UA) ch 18
Fidelity Canadian Asset Allocation ch 14
*Fidelity Canadian Growth Company
   ch 13*
Fidelity Canadian Income Fund ch 15
Fidelity True North Fund ch 12

INTERNATIONAL FUNDS
Fidelity Far East Fund (HH) ch 21
Fidelity Growth America Fund (HH)
   ch 23
Fidelity International Portfolio (HH)
   ch 20
Fidelity Asset Manager Fund (RC) ch 25
*Fidelity Emerging Markets Bond Fund
   (RC) ch 26*
Fidelity Emerging Markets Portfolio ch 24
Fidelity European Growth Fund ch 22
Fidelity Japanese Growth Fund ch 21
*Fidelity Latin American Growth Fund
   ch 24*
*Fidelity North American Income Fund
   ch 26*
Fidelity RSP Global Bond Fund ch 26
Fidelity Small-Cap America Fund ch 23
Fidelity U.S. Money Market ($US) ch 27

(47) First Horizon Capital Corp.

321 Water Street
Suite 504
Vancouver, BC
V6B 1B8
Tel: (604) 688-7333
Fax: (604) 683-4600
Toll Free: 1-800-665-118

Heavy Hitters: 0 Underachievers: 0
Number of Qualifying Funds: 0
Total Number of Funds: 3
Sales commissions apply

CANADIAN FUNDS
Contrarian Strategy Futures L.P. ch 19
Contrarian Strategy RRSP Futures ch 19
Horizons 1 Multi-Asset Fund Inc. ch 19

(48) First Marathon Securities Ltd.

2 First Canadian Place
P.O. Box 21
Suite 3100
Toronto, ON
M5X 1J9
Tel: (416) 869-3707
Fax: (416) 869-3319
Toll Free: 1-800-661-3863

Heavy Hitters: 0 Underachievers: 0
Number of Qualifying Funds: 1
Total Number of Funds: 2
No sales commissions apply

CANADIAN FUNDS
Marathon Equity Fund ch 13
Marathon Resource Fund ch 19

(49) First Ontario LSIF Ltd.

234 Eglinton Avenue East
Suite 310
Toronto, ON
M4P 1K5
Tel: (416) 487-5444
Fax: (416) 487-1345

Heavy Hitters: 0 Underachievers: 0
Number of Qualifying Funds: 0
Total Number of Funds: 1
No sales commissions, restrictions apply

CANADIAN FUNDS
First Ontario LSIF Ltd. ch 19

(50) Fonds des Professionnels du Quebec Inc.

2 Complexe Desjardins
East Tower
Suite 3020
Montreal, QC
H5B 1G8
Tel: (514) 350-5055
Fax: (514) 350-5051
Toll Free: 1-800-363-6713

Heavy Hitters: 1 Underachievers: 2
Number of Qualifying Funds: 4
Rookie Camp Members: 1
Total Number of Funds: 6
No sales commissions, restrictions apply

CANADIAN FUNDS
Fonds de Professionnels Balanced (UA) ch 14
Fonds de Professionnels Bond (UA) ch 15
Fonds de Professionnels Cdn. Equity ch 12
Fonds de Professionnels Short Term (HH) ch 18
Fonds de Professionnels Growth & In ch 14

INTERNATIONAL FUNDS
Fonds de Professionnels Int'l Equity (RC) ch 20

(51) Friedberg Commodity Management Inc.

181 Bay Street
Suite 250
Toronto, ON
M5J 2T3
Tel: (416) 364-1171
Fax: (416) 364-0572

Heavy Hitters: 0 Underachievers: 0
Number of Qualifying Funds: 1
Total Number of Funds: 4
No sales commissions apply

CANADIAN FUNDS
Friedberg Double Gold Plus Fund ch 19
Friedberg Currency Fund ch 19
Friedberg Diversified Fund ($US) ch 19

INTERNATIONAL FUNDS
Friedberg Foreign Bond Fund ch 26

(52) GBC Asset Management Inc.
55 University Avenue
Suite 616
Toronto, ON
M5J 2H7
Tel: (416) 366-2550
Fax: (416) 366-6833
Toll Free: 1-800-668-7383

Heavy Hitters: 2 Underachievers: 1
Number of Qualifying Funds: 5
Total Number of Funds: 5
No sales commissions, restrictions apply

CANADIAN FUNDS
GBC Canadian Bond Fund (HH) ch 15
GBC Canadian Growth Fund (HH) ch 12
GBC Money Market Fund ch 18

INTERNATIONAL FUNDS
GBC International Growth Fund (UA) ch 20
GBC North American Growth Fund Inc. ch 23

(53) Gentrust Investment Counsellors
1100 University Street
9th Floor
Montreal, QC
H3B 2G7
Tel: (514) 871-7171
Fax: (514) 871-7442
Toll Free: 1-800-341-1419

Heavy Hitters: 0 Underachievers: 0
Number of Qualifying Funds: 0
Total Number of Funds: 1
Sales commissions apply

CANADIAN FUNDS
Fonds d'Investissement REA ch 13

(54) Global Strategy Financial Inc.
33 Bloor Street East
Suite 1600
Toronto, ON
M4W 3T8
Tel: (416) 966-3676
Fax: (416) 927-9168
Toll Free: 1-800-387-1229

Heavy Hitters: 1 Underachievers: 3
Number of Qualifying Funds: 5
Rookie Camp Members: 2
Total Number of Funds: 23
Sales commissions apply

CANADIAN FUNDS
Global Strategy Canada Growth Fund (UA) ch 12
Global Strategy Income Plus Fund (HH) ch 14
Global Strategy Money Market Fund ch 18
Global Strategy Bond Fund ch 15
Global Strategy Cdn. Small Cap ch 13
Global Strategy Cdn. Opportunities ch 12
Global Strategy Gold Plus Fund ch 19

INTERNATIONAL FUNDS
Global Strategy Diversified Bond (UA) ch 26
Global Strategy World Bond Fund (UA) ch 26
Global Strategy Asia Fund ch 21
Global Strategy Div Foreign Bond ch 26
Global Strategy Div. Japan Plus ch 21
Global Strategy Divers. World Eq. ch 20
Global Strategy Diversified Asia ch 21
Global Strategy Diversified Europe ch 22
Global Strategy Diversified Latin (RC) ch 24
Global Strategy Europe Plus ch 22
Global Strategy Japan Fund ch 21
Global Strategy Latin America Fund (RC) ch 24
Global Strategy U.S. Equity ch 23

Appendix 3: Mutual Fund Company Scorecard

Global Strategy World Balanced ch 25
Global Strategy World Emerging Co. ch 20
Global Strategy World Equity ch 20

(55) GlobeInvest Funds Management Inc.
20 Queen Street West
Suite 3206
Toronto, ON
M5H 3R3
Tel: (416) 591-7100
Fax: (416) 591-7133
Toll Free: 1-800-387-0784

Heavy Hitters: 0 Underachievers: 0
Number of Qualifying Funds: 0
Total Number of Funds: 2
Sales commissions and restrictions apply

INTERNATIONAL FUNDS
GFM Emerging Markets Country ($US)
ch 24
GlobeInvest Emerg. Markets Country ch 24

(56) Gordon Daly Grenadier Securities
224 Richmond Street West
Toronto, ON
M5V 1V6
Tel: (416) 593-0144
Fax: (416) 593-4922
Toll Free: 1-800-268-9165

Heavy Hitters: 0 Underachievers: 0
Number of Qualifying Funds: 1
Total Number of Funds: 1
Sales commissions apply

CANADIAN FUNDS
First Heritage Fund ch 19

(57) Great-West Life Assurance Co.
60 Osborne Street North
Winnipeg, MB
R3C 3A5
Tel: (204) 946-1190
Fax: (204) 946-8622
Toll Free: 1-800-665-0049

Heavy Hitters: 1 Underachievers: 5
Number of Qualifying Funds: 7
Total Number of Funds: 66
Sales commissions apply on some funds
Segregated funds

CANADIAN FUNDS
GWL Diversified Fund (G) NL (UA) ch 14
GWL Equity/Bond Fund (G) NL (UA) ch 14
GWL Equity Index Fund (G) NL (UA) ch 12
GWL Canadian Equity Fund (G) NL (UA) ch 12
GWL Money Market Fund (G) NL (UA) ch 18
GWL Canadian Bond Fund (G) NL ch 15
GWL Mortgage Fund (G) NL (HH) ch 16
GWL Advanced Portfolio (G) DSC ch 14
GWL Advanced Portfolio (G) NL ch 14
GWL Aggressive Portfolio (G) DSC ch 12
GWL Aggressive Portfolio (G) NL ch 12
GWL Balanced Fund (B) DSC ch 14
GWL Balanced Fund (B) NL ch 14
GWL Balanced Fund (M) DSC ch 14
GWL Balanced Fund (M) NL ch 14
GWL Balanced Fund (S) DSC ch 14
GWL Balanced Fund (S) NL ch 14
GWL Balanced Portfolio (G) DSC ch 14
GWL Balanced Portfolio (G) NL ch 14
GWL Bond Fund (B) DSC ch 15
GWL Bond Fund (B) NL ch 15
GWL Bond Fund (M) DSC ch 15
GWL Bond Fund (M) NL ch 15

GWL Bond Fund (S) DSC ch 15
GWL Bond Fund (S) NL ch 15
GWL Canadian Bond Fund (G) DSC ch 15
GWL Canadian Equity Fund (G) DSC
ch 12
GWL Cdn. Resource Fund (A) DSC ch 19
GWL Cdn. Resource Fund (A) NL ch 19
GWL Conservative Portfolio (G) DSC
ch 14
GWL Conservative Portfolio (G) NL ch 14
GWL Diversified Fund (G) DSC ch 14
GWL Equity Fund (M) DSC ch 12
GWL Equity Fund (M) NL ch 12
GWL Equity Fund (S) DSC ch 12
GWL Equity Fund (S) NL ch 12
GWL Equity Index Fund (G) DSC ch 12
GWL Equity/Bond Fund (G) DSC ch 14
GWL Government Bond Fund (G) DSC
ch 15
GWL Government Bond Fund (G) NL ch 15
GWL Growth & Income Fund (A) DSC
ch 14
GWL Growth & Income Fund (A) NL
ch 14
GWL Growth & Income Fund (M) DSC
ch 14
GWL Growth & Income Fund (M) NL
ch 14
GWL Growth Equity Fund (A) DSC ch 13
GWL Growth Equity Fund (A) NL ch 13
GWL Income Fund (G) DSC ch 15
GWL Income Fund (G) NL ch 15
GWL Larger Co. Fund (M) DSC ch 12
GWL Larger Co. Fund (M) NL ch 12
GWL Moderate Portfolio (G) DSC ch 14
GWL Moderate Portfolio (G) NL ch 14
GWL Money Market Fund (G) DSC ch 18
GWL Mortgage Fund (G) DSC ch 16
GWL N. A. Equity Fund (B) DSC ch 12
GWL N. A. Equity Fund (B) NL ch 12
GWL Smaller Company Fund (M) DSC
ch 13
GWL Smaller Company Fund (M) NL
ch 13

INTERNATIONAL FUNDS
GWL Global Inc. Fund (A) DSC ch 26
GWL Global Inc. Fund (A) NL ch 26
GWL Int'l Equity Fund (P) DSC ch 20
GWL Int'l Equity Fund (P) NL ch 20
GWL International Bond Fund (P) DSC
ch 26
GWL International Bond Fund (P) NL
ch 26
GWL U.S. Equity Fund (G) DSC ch 23
GWL U.S. Equity Fund (G) NL ch 23

(58) Greystone Managed Investments Ltd.
10104 - 103 Avenue
Suite 555
Edmonton, AB
T5J 0H8
Tel: (413) 423-3544
Fax: (413) 426-0506
Toll Free: 1-800-287-5211

Heavy Hitters: 0 Underachievers: 0
Number of Qualifying Funds: 0
Rookie Camp Members: 1
Total Number of Funds: 2
No sales commissions, restrictions apply

CANADIAN FUNDS
Greystone Managed Wealth Fund ch 14

INTERNATIONAL FUNDS
Greystone Managed Global Fund (RC)
ch 20

(59) Groupe Financier Concorde
850 Place d'Youville
Quebec City, QC
G1R 3P6
Tel: (418) 692-1221
Fax: (418) 692-1675

Heavy Hitters: 0 Underachievers: 2
Number of Qualifying Funds: 4
Total Number of Funds: 7
Sales commissions apply

Appendix 3: Mutual Fund Company Scorecard

CANADIAN FUNDS
Concorde Croissance ch 12
Concorde Hypotheques (UA) ch 16
Concorde Monetaire ch 18
Concorde Revenu (UA) ch 15
Concorde Balanced Fund ch 14
Concorde Dividend Fund ch 17

INTERNATIONAL FUNDS
Concorde International Fund ch 20

(60) GT Global Canada Inc.
77 King Street West
Suite 4001
Toronto, ON
M5K 1K2
Tel: (416) 594-4300
Fax: (416) 594-6698
Toll Free: 1-800-588-5684

Heavy Hitters: 0 Underachievers: 0
Number of Qualifying Funds: 0
Total Number of Funds: 15
Sales commissions apply

CANADIAN FUNDS
GT Global Canada Growth Class ch 12
GT Global Canada Income Class ch 14
GT Global Canada Money Market ch 18
GT Global Health Care Class ch 19
GT Global Infrastructure Class ch 19
GT Global Natural Resources Class ch 19
GT Global Telecommunication Class
  ch 19

INTERNATIONAL FUNDS
GT Global - Global Theme Class ch 20
GT Global America Growth Class ch 23
GT Global Growth & Income Fund ch 25
GT Global Latin America Class ch 24
GT Global Pacific Growth Class ch 21
GT Global Short-term Income A ch 27
GT Global Short-term Income B ch 27
GT Global World Bond Fund ch 26

(61) Guardian Group of Funds Ltd.
Commerce Court West
Suite 3100
P.O. Box 201
Toronto, ON
M5L 1E8
Tel: (416) 364-8341
Fax: (416) 947-0601
Toll Free: 1-800-668-7327

Heavy Hitters: 3 Underachievers: 2
Number of Qualifying Funds: 9
Total Number of Funds: 32
Sales commissions apply

CANADIAN FUNDS
Guardian Canadian Balanced Fund A
  (UA) ch 14
Guardian Canadian Money Market A
  ch 18
Guardian Enterprise Fund A (HH) ch 13
Guardian Growth Equity Fund A (HH)
  ch 12
Guardian Monthly Dividend Fund A
  (UA) ch 17
Guardian Canadian Balanced Fund B
  ch 14
Guardian Canadian Income Fund A ch 15
Guardian Canadian Income Fund B ch 15
Guardian Canadian Money Market B
  ch 18
Guardian Enterprise Fund B ch 13
Guardian Growth & Income Fund A ch 14
Guardian Growth & Income Fund B ch 14
Guardian Growth Equity Fund B ch 12
Guardian Monthly Dividend Fund B ch 17
Guardian Monthly High Income A ch 17
Guardian Monthly High Income B ch 17

INTERNATIONAL FUNDS
Guardian American Equity Fund A
  ch 23
Guardian Global Equity Fund A ch 20
Guardian International Income A (HH)
  ch 26

Guardian U.S. Money Market ($US) A
ch 27

Guardian American Equity Fund B ch 23
Guardian Asia Pacific Fund A ch 21
Guardian Asia Pacific Fund B ch 21
Guardian Emerging Markets Fund A ch 24
Guardian Emerging Markets Fund B ch 24
Guardian Foreign Income Fund A ch 26
Guardian Foreign Income Fund B ch 26
Guardian Global Equity Fund B ch 20
Guardian International Balanced A ch 25
Guardian International Balanced B ch 25
Guardian International Income B ch 26
Guardian U.S. Money Market ($US) B
ch 27

(62) Guardian Timing Services Inc.

130 Adelaide Street West
Suite 3303
Toronto, ON
M5H 3P5
Tel: (416) 960-4890
Fax: (416) 364-3752

Heavy Hitters: 0 Underachievers: 3
Number of Qualifying Funds: 3
Total Number of Funds: 3
Sales commissions and restrictions apply

CANADIAN FUNDS
Canadian Protected Fund (UA) ch 12

INTERNATIONAL FUNDS
First American (Guardian Timing)
(UA) ch 23
Protected American Fund (UA) ch 25

(63) Hongkong Bank Securities Inc.

400 - 885 W. Georgia Street
Vancouver, BC
V6C 3E9
Tel: (604) 641-3088
Fax: (604) 641-3096
Toll Free: 1-800-830-8888

Heavy Hitters: 1 Underachievers: 0
Number of Qualifying Funds: 3
Rookie Camp Members: 1
Total Number of Funds: 12
No sales commissions apply

CANADIAN FUNDS
Hongkong Bank Balanced Fund ch 14
Hongkong Bank Equity Fund ch 12
Hongkong Bank Money Market Fund
(HH) ch 18
Hongkong Bank Canadian Bond Fund
ch 15
Hongkong Bank Dividend Income Fund
ch 17
Hongkong Bank Mortgage Fund (RC)
ch 16
Hongkong Bank Small Cap Growth Fund
ch 13

INTERNATIONAL FUNDS
Hongkong Bank Americas Fund ch 29
Hongkong Bank Asian Growth Fund ch 21
Hongkong Bank Emerging Markets Fund
ch 24
Hongkong Bank European Growth Fund
ch 22
Hongkong Bank Global Bond Fund ch 26

(64) HRL Investment Funds

(Hodgson Robertson Laing Ltd.)
1 Queen Street East
Suite 1920
Toronto, ON
M5C 2Y5
Tel: (416) 368-1428
Fax: (416) 869-1653
Toll Free: 1-800-268-9622

Heavy Hitters: 2 Underachievers: 1
Number of Qualifying Funds: 4
Total Number of Funds: 5
No sales commissions apply

Appendix 3: Mutual Fund Company Scorecard

CANADIAN FUNDS

HRL Balanced Fund (UA) ch 14
HRL Bond Fund (HH) ch 15
HRL Canadian Fund ch 12
HRL Instant $$ Fund (HH) ch 18

INTERNATIONAL FUNDS

HRL Overseas Growth Fund ch 20

(65) Imperial Life Assurance Co. of Canada

95 St. Clair Avenue West
Toronto, ON
M4V 1N7
Tel: 9416) 324-1617
Fax: (416) 324-1670

Heavy Hitters: 0 Underachievers: 1
Number of Qualifying Funds: 4
Total Number of Funds: 16
Sales commissions apply
Segregated funds

CANADIAN FUNDS

Imperial Growth Canadian Equity
ch 12
Imperial Growth Diversified Fund
ch 14
Imperial Growth Money Market Fund
(UA) ch 18
Millennia III Canadian Balanced 1 ch 14
Millennia III Canadian Balanced 2 ch 14
Millennia III Canadian Equity 1 ch 12
Millennia III Canadian Equity 2 ch 12
Millennia III Income Fund 1 ch 15
Millennia III Income Fund 2 ch 15
Millennia III Money Market Fund 1 ch 18
Millennia III Money Market Fund 2 ch 18

INTERNATIONAL FUNDS

Imperial Growth North American Eq.
ch 23
Millennia III American Equity 1 ch 23
Millennia III American Equity 2 ch 23
Millennia III Int'l Equity 1 ch 20
Millennia III Int'l Equity 2 ch 20

(66) Industrial Alliance Life Insurance Co.

1080 chemin Saint-Louis
C.P. 1907
Quebec, QC
G1K 7M3
Tel: (418) 684-5000
Fax: (418) 688-0705
Toll Free: 1-800-268-8882

Heavy Hitters: 2 Underachievers: 3
Number of Qualifying Funds: 6
Total Number of Funds: 21
Sales commissions apply
Segregated funds

CANADIAN FUNDS

Industrial Alliance Bond Fund ch 15
Industrial Alliance Diversified Fund
(HH) ch 14
Industrial Alliance Ecoflex Fund M
(UA) ch 18
Industrial Alliance Money Mkt. Fund
(UA) ch 18
Industrial Alliance Mortgage Fund
(UA) ch 16
Industrial Alliance Stocks Fund (HH)
ch 12
Industrial Alliance Bond Fund-2 ch 15
Industrial Alliance Ecoflex Fund A ch 12
Industrial Alliance Ecoflex Fund B ch 15
Industrial Alliance Ecoflex Fund D ch 14
Industrial Alliance Ecoflex Fund H ch 16
Industrial Alliance Stock Fund-2 ch 12
Industrial Diversified-2 Balanced ch 14

INTERNATIONAL FUNDS

Industrial Alliance Ecoflex Fund I ch 20
Industrial Alliance Ecoflex Fund E ch 20
Industrial Alliance Ecoflex Fund G ch 26
Industrial Alliance Ecoflex Fund S ch 23
*Industrial Alliance Emerging Market
ch 24*
*Industrial Alliance Global Bond Fund
ch 26*
Industrial Alliance Int'l Fund ch 20

Industrial Alliance U.S. Stock Fund
ch 23

(67) Infinity Investment Counsel Ltd.
2075 Kennedy Road
Scarborough, ON
M1T 3V3
Tel: (416) 291-4333
Fax: (416) 291-9067
Toll Free: 1-800-835-7131

Heavy Hitters: 0 Underachievers: 0
Number of Qualifying Funds: 0
Total Number of Funds: 5
Sales commissions apply

CANADIAN FUNDS
Infinity Canadian Fund ch 12
Infinity Income Fund ch 17
Infinity T-Bill Fund ch 18
Infinity Wealth Management Fund ch 12

INTERNATIONAL FUNDS
Infinity International Fund ch 20

(68) Integra Capital Management Corp.
55 University Avenue
Suite 1100
P.O. Box 42
Toronto, ON
MJ 2H7
Tel: (416) 367-0404
Fax: (416) 367-0351

Heavy Hitters: 0 Underachievers: 1
Number of Qualifying Funds: 3
Rookie Camp Members: 1
Total Number of Funds: 5
No sales commissions apply

CANADIAN FUNDS
ICM Balanced Fund ch 14
ICM Bond Fund ch 15
ICM Equity Fund (UA) ch 12
ICM Short Term Investment Fund ch 18

INTERNATIONAL FUNDS
ICM International Equity Fund (RC)
ch 20

(69) INVESCO Funds Group (Canada), Inc.
now AIM Funds Group (Canada)
Inc.
150 King Street West
Suite 1802
Toronto, ON
M5H 1J9
Tel: (416) 408-3330
Fax: (416) 408-1228
Toll Free: 1-800-667-2369

Heavy Hitters: 1 Underachievers: 3
Number of Qualifying Funds: 7
Rookie Camp Members: 1
Total Number of Funds: 15
Sales commissions apply

CANADIAN FUNDS
Admax Canadian Performance Fund
  (UA) ch 12
Admax Canadian Select Growth Fund
  (UA) ch 12
Admax Asset Allocation Fund ch 14
Admax Cash Performance Fund ch 18
Admax Global Health Sciences Fund
  (RC) ch 19
Admax Global Technology Fund ch 19

INTERNATIONAL FUNDS
Admax American Growth Fund ch 23
Admax International Fund ch 20
Admax Korea Fund (UA) ch 21
Admax Tiger Fund ch 21
Admax World Income Fund (HH)
  ch 26
Admax Dragon 888 Fund ch 21
Admax Europa Performance Fund ch 22
Admax Global RRSP Index Fund ch 20
Admax Nippon Fund ch 21

(70) Investors Group Financial Services Inc.

One Canada Centre
447 Portage Avenue
Winnipeg, MN
R3C 3B6
Tel: (204) 943-0361
Fax: (204) 943-0021
Toll Free: 1-888-746-6344

Heavy Hitters: 8 Underachievers: 6
Number of Qualifying Funds: 22
Rookie Camp Members: 1
Total Number of Funds: 47
Sales commissions apply

CANADIAN FUNDS
Investors Canadian Equity Fund ch 12
Investors Dividend Fund (UA) ch 17
Investors Government Bond Fund
    (HH) ch 15
Investors Income Plus Portfolio (UA)
    ch 14
Investors Income Portfolio Fund (HH)
    ch 16
Investors Money Market Fund (UA)
    ch 18
Investors Mortgage Fund ch 16
Investors Mutual of Canada ch 14
Investors Real Property Fund ch 19
Investors Retirement Gr. Portfolio
    (UA) ch 12
Investors Retirement Mutual Fund ch 12
Investors Retirement Plus Portfolio
    (UA) ch 14
Investors Summa Fund ch 12
GS Canadian Balanced Fund ch 14
GS Canadian Equity Fund ch 12
IG Beutel Goodman Cdn. Balanced ch 14
IG Beutel Goodman Cdn. Equity Fund
    ch 12
IG Beutel Goodman Cdn. Small-Cap ch 13
IG Sceptre Canadian Balanced Fund
    ch 14
IG Sceptre Canadian Bond Fund ch 15
IG Sceptre Canadian Equity Fund ch 12

Investors Asset Allocation Fund (RC)
    ch 14
Investors Canadian Small-Cap Fund ch 13
Investors Cdn. Natural Resource ch 19
Investors Corporate Bond Fund ch 15
Merrill Lynch Canadian Equity Fund
    ch 12

INTERNATIONAL FUNDS
Investors European Growth Fund ch 22
Investors Global Fund ch 20
Investors Growth Plus Portfolio (HH)
    ch 25
Investors Growth Portfolio Fund (HH)
    ch 20
Investors Japanese Growth Fund (UA)
    ch 21
Investors North American Growth
    (HH) ch 20
Investors Pacific International (HH)
    ch 21
Investors Special Fund (HH) ch 20
Investors U.S. Growth Fund (HH) ch 23
GS American Equity Fund ch 23
GS International Bond Fund ch 26
GS International Equity Fund ch 20
Investors Global Bond Fund ch 26
Investors Latin American Growth ch 24
Investors N. A. High-Yield Bond ch 26
Investors U.S. Opportunities Fund ch 23
Investors World Growth Portfolio ch 20
Merrill Lynch Capital Asset Fund ch 25
Merrill Lynch Emerging Markets Fund
    ch 24
Merrill Lynch World Allocation Fund
    ch 25
Merrill Lynch World Bond Fund ch 26

(71) John D. Hillery Investment Counsel Inc.

2842 Bloor Street West
Suite 203
Etobicoke, ON
M8X 1B1
Tel: (416) 234-0846
Fax: (416) 234-0846

Heavy Hitters: 0 Underachievers: 0
Number of Qualifying Funds: 1
Total Number of Funds: 1
Sales commissions and restrictions apply

INTERNATIONAL FUNDS
Margin of Safety Fund ch 23

(72) Jones Heward Investment Management Inc.

77 King Street West
Suite 4200
Toronto, ON
M5K 1J5
Tel: (416) 359-5000
Fax: (416) 359-5040
Toll Free: 1-800-361-1392

Heavy Hitters: 0 Underachievers: 2
Number of Qualifying Funds: 4
Total Number of Funds: 5
Sales commissions apply

CANADIAN FUNDS
Jones Heward Bond Fund ch 15
Jones Heward Canadian Balanced Fund
    (UA) ch 14
Jones Heward Fund Ltd. (UA) ch 12
Jones Heward Money Market Fund ch 18

INTERNATIONAL FUNDS
Jones Heward American Fund ch 23

(73) Laurentian Bank Investment Services Inc.

130 Adelaide Street West
Toronto, ON
M5H 3P5
Tel: (416) 865-5832
Fax: (416) 947-5161
Toll Free: 1-800-565-6513

Heavy Hitters: 2 Underachievers: 1
Number of Qualifying Funds: 6
Total Number of Funds: 6
No sales commissions apply

CANADIAN FUNDS
Cornerstone Balanced Fund ch 14
Cornerstone Bond Fund ch 15
Cornerstone Cdn. Growth ch 12
Cornerstone Gov't Money (UA) ch 18

INTERNATIONAL FUNDS
Cornerstone Global Fund (HH) ch 20
Cornerstone U.S. Fund (HH) ch 23

(74) Leith Wheeler Management Ltd.

400 Burrard Street
Suite 1500
Vancouver, BC
V6C 3A6
Tel: (604) 683-3391
Fax: (604) 683-0323

Heavy Hitters: 1 Underachievers: 0
Number of Qualifying Funds: 1
Rookie Camp Members: 1
Total Number of Funds: 5
No sales commissions, restrictions apply

CANADIAN FUNDS
Leith Wheeler Balanced Fund (HH)
    ch 14
*Leith Wheeler Canadian Equity Fund
    (RC) ch 12*
Leith Wheeler Fixed Income Fund ch 15
Leith Wheeler Money Market Fund ch 18

INTERNATIONAL FUNDS
Leith Wheeler U.S. Equity Fund ch 23

Appendix 3: Mutual Fund Company Scorecard

(75) Leon Frazer & Associates Ltd.
8 King Street East
Suite 2001
Toronto, ON
M5C 1B6
Tel: (416) 864-1120
Fax: (416) 864-1491

Heavy Hitters: 0 Underachievers: 0
Number of Qualifying Funds: 1
Total Number of Funds: 1
No sales commissions apply

CANADIAN FUNDS
Associate Investors Ltd. ch 12

(76) London Life Insurance Co.
255 Dufferin Avenue
London, ON
N6A 4K1
Tel: (519) 432-5281
Fax: (519) 432-2851

Heavy Hitters: 0 Underachievers: 2
Number of Qualifying Funds: 6
Total Number of Funds: 7
Sales commissions apply
Segregated funds

CANADIAN FUNDS
London Life Bond ch 15
London Life Canadian Equity (UA)
   ch 12
London Life Diversified (UA) ch 14
London Life Money Market ch 18
London Life Mortgage ch 16

INTERNATIONAL FUNDS
London Life U.S. Equity ch 23
London Life International Equity ch 20

(77) Loring Ward Investment Counsel Ltd.
360 Main Street
Suite 1501
Winnipeg, MB
R3C 2Z3
Tel: (204) 957-1730
Fax: (204) 947-2103
Toll Free: 1-800-267-1730

Heavy Hitters: 0 Underachievers: 0
Number of Qualifying Funds: 0
Rookie Camp Members: 4
Total Number of Funds: 6
Sales commissions apply

CANADIAN FUNDS
Optima Strategy Canadian Equity (RC)
   ch 12
Optima Strategy Cdn. Fixed Income (RC)
   ch 15
Optima Strategy Short Term Income ch 15

INTERNATIONAL FUNDS
Optima Strategy Global Fixed Income
   ch 26
Optima Strategy Int'l Equity (RC) ch 20
Optima Strategy U.S. Equity (RC) ch 23

(78) Lutheran Life Insurance Society
470 Weber Street
Waterloo, ON
N2J 4G4
Toll Free: 1-800-563-6237

Heavy Hitters: 0 Underachievers: 0
Number of Qualifying Funds: 0
Total Number of Funds: 6
No sales commissions, restrictions apply
Segregated funds

CANADIAN FUNDS
Lutheran Life Balanced Fund ch 14
Lutheran Life Canadian Bond Fund ch 15
Lutheran Life Canadian Equity Fund ch 12
Lutheran Life Money Market Fund ch 18

INTERNATIONAL FUNDS
Lutheran Life Int'l Bond Fund ch 26
Lutheran Life Int'l Equity Fund ch 20

(79) M. K. Wong & Associates Ltd.
33 Yonge Street
Suite 1050
Toronto, ON
M5E 1S9
Tel: (416) 361-3370
Fax: (416) 361-6345
Toll Free: 1-800-665-9360

Heavy Hitters: 1 Underachievers: 0
Number of Qualifying Funds: 2
Rookie Camp Members: 1
Total Number of Funds: 4
No sales commissions apply

CANADIAN FUNDS
Lotus Balanced Fund ch 14
Lotus Income Fund (HH) ch 18
Lotus Bond Fund (RC) ch 15
Lotus Canadian Equity Fund ch 13

INTERNATIONAL FUNDS
Lotus International Bond Fund ch 26
Lotus International Equity Fund ch 20

(80) Mackenzie Financial Corporation
150 Bloor Street West
Suite M111
Toronto, ON
M5S 3B5
Tel: (416) 922-5322
Fax: (416) 922-0399
Toll Free: 1-800-387-0615

Heavy Hitters: 5 Underachievers: 8
Number of Qualifying Funds: 19
Rookie Camp Members: 5
Total Number of Funds: 56
Sales commissions apply

CANADIAN FUNDS
Industrial Balanced Fund ch 14
Industrial Bond Fund (HH) ch 15
Industrial Cash Management (HH) ch 18
Industrial Dividend Growth Fund Ltd.
(HH) ch 17
Industrial Equity Fund Ltd. (UA) ch 13
Industrial Future Fund ch 12
Industrial Growth Fund (UA) ch 12
Industrial Horizon Fund (UA) ch 12
Industrial Income Fund ch 14
Industrial Mortgage Securities (UA)
ch 14
Industrial Pension Fund (HH) ch 14
Industrial Short-Term Fund (UA) ch 18
Mackenzie Sentinel Canada Equity ch 12
Universal Canadian Resource Fund
(HH) ch 19
Ivy Canadian Fund (RC) ch 12
Ivy Enterprise Fund ch 13
Ivy Growth & Income Fund (RC) ch 14
Ivy Mortgage Fund (RC) ch 16
*STAR Cdn. Balanced Growth & Income
ch 14*
*STAR Cdn. Maximum Equity Growth
ch 12*
*STAR Reg. Balanced Growth & Income
ch 14*
*STAR Reg. Conserv. Income & Growth
ch 14*
STAR Reg. Long-Term Growth ch 14
STAR Reg. Maximum Equity Growth ch 12
Universal Canadian Balanced Fund ch 14
*Universal Canadian Growth Fund Ltd
ch 12*
Universal Precious Metals Fund ch 19
Universal World Science & Tech. ch 19

INTERNATIONAL FUNDS
Industrial American Fund (UA) ch 23
Mackenzie Sentinel Global Fund (UA)
ch 20
Universal Americas Fund ch 20
Universal U.S. Emerging Growth Fund
ch 23

Universal World Equity Fund (UA)
ch 20
Ivy Foreign Equity Fund (RC) ch 20
STAR For. Balanced Growth & Income
ch 25
STAR For. Maximum Equity Growth ch 20
STAR For. Maximum Long-Term Growth
ch 25
STAR Inv. Balanced Growth & Income
ch 25
STAR Inv. Conserv. Income & Growth
ch 25
STAR Inv. Long-Term Growth ch 25
STAR Inv. Maximum Long-Term Growth
ch 25
STAR Reg. Maximum Long-Term Growth
ch 25
Universal European Opportunities ch 22
Universal Far East Fund ch 21
Universal Growth Fund ch 20
Universal Japan Fund ch 21
Universal U.S. Money Market ($US)
ch 27
Universal World Asset Allocation ch 25
Universal World Balanced RRSP (RC)
ch 25
Universal World Emerging Growth ch 24
Universal World Growth RRSP Fund
ch 20
Universal World Income RRSP Fund ch 26
Universal World Tactical Bond Fund ch 26

(81) MagnaTrends Asset Management Inc.
4 King Street West
Suite 301
Toronto, ON
M5X 1J7
Tel: (416) 865-1090
Fax: (416) 363-1954

Heavy Hitters: 0 Underachievers: 1
Number of Qualifying Funds: 1
Total Number of Funds: 1
Sales commissions apply

INTERNATIONAL FUNDS
Century DJ Fund (UA) ch 23

(82) Mandate Management Corporation
1285 West Broadway
8th Floor
Vancouver, BC
V6H 3X8
Tel: (604) 731-2899
Fax: (604) 734-5546

Heavy Hitters: 0 Underachievers: 0
Number of Qualifying Funds: 1
Total Number of Funds: 1
No sales commissions apply

CANADIAN FUNDS
Mandate National Mortgage Corp.
ch 16

(83) Manulife Financial
500 King Street North
Waterloo, ON
N2J 4C6
Tel: (519) 747-7000
Fax: (519) 747-6895
Toll Free: 1-800-661-6464

Heavy Hitters: 1 Underachievers: 9
Number of Qualifying Funds: 15
Rookie Camp Members: 1
Total Number of Funds: 24
Sales commissions apply
Segregated funds

CANADIAN FUNDS
Manulife Vistafund 1 Bond Fund ch 15
Manulife Vistafund 1 Cap. Gains Gr.
(UA) ch 12
Manulife Vistafund 1 Diversified (UA)
ch 14
Manulife Vistafund 1 Equity Fund (UA)
ch 12
Manulife Vistafund 1 Short Term Sec.
(HH) ch 18

Manulife Vistafund 2 Bond Fund (UA)
ch 15

Manulife Vistafund 2 Cap. Gains Gr.
(UA) ch 12

Manulife Vistafund 2 Diversified (UA)
ch 14

Manulife Vistafund 2 Equity Fund (UA)
ch 12

Manulife Vistafund 2 Short Term Sec.
(UA) ch 18

NAL-Canadian Bond Fund ch 15

NAL-Canadian Diversified Fund ch 14

NAL-Canadian Equity Fund ch 12

NAL-Canadian Money Market Fund
(UA) ch 18

NAL-Equity Growth Fund ch 12

NAL-Balanced Growth Fund ch 14

INTERNATIONAL FUNDS

NAL-Global Equity Fund ch 20

Manulife Vistafund 1 Amer. Stock ch 23

Manulife Vistafund 1 Global Bond ch 26

Manulife Vistafund 1 Global Equity ch 20

Manulife Vistafund 2 Amer. Stock ch 23

Manulife Vistafund 2 Global Bond ch 26

Manulife Vistafund 2 Global Equity ch 20

NAL-U.S. Equity Fund (RC) ch 23

(84) Manulife Securities International Ltd.

500 King Street North
Waterloo, ON
N2J 4C6
Fax: 1-800-265-5123
Toll Free: 1-800-265-7401

Heavy Hitters: 0 Underachievers: 0
Number of Qualifying Funds: 0
Total Number of Funds: 7
No sales commissions apply

CANADIAN FUNDS

Manulife Cabot Blue Chip Fund ch 12

*Manulife Cabot Canadian Equity Fund
ch 12*

*Manulife Cabot Canadian Growth Fund
ch 13*

Manulife Cabot Diversified Bond ch 15

*Manulife Cabot Emerging Growth Fund
ch 13*

Manulife Cabot Money Market Fund ch 18

INTERNATIONAL FUNDS

Manulife Cabot Global Equity Fund ch 20

(85) Maritime Life Assurance Company

2701 Dutch Village Road
P.O. Box 1030
Halifax, NS
B3J 2X5
Tel: (902) 453-4300
Fax: (902) 453-7041

Heavy Hitters: 1 Underachievers: 2
Number of Qualifying Funds: 4
Total Number of Funds: 26
Sales commissions apply on some funds
Segregated funds

CANADIAN FUNDS

Maritime Life Balanced - A & C ch 14

Maritime Life Bond - A & C (UA) ch 15

Maritime Life Growth - A & C (HH)
ch 12

Maritime Life Money Market - A & C
(UA) ch 18

Maritime Life Balanced - B ch 14

Maritime Life Bond - B ch 15

Maritime Life Cdn. Equity - B ch 12

Maritime Life Cdn. Equity - A & C ch 12

Maritime Life Dividend Inc. - A & C ch 17

Maritime Life Dividend Inc. - B ch 17

Maritime Life Growth - B ch 12

Maritime Life Money Market - B ch 18

INTERNATIONAL FUNDS

Maritime Life Aggr. Equity - B ch 23

Maritime Life Aggr. Equity - A & C ch 23

*Maritime Life Amer Gr. & Inc. - A & C
ch 23*

Maritime Life Amer. Gr. & Inc. - B ch 23
Maritime Life Discovery - A & C ch 23
Maritime Life Discovery - B ch 23
Maritime Life Eurasia - A & C ch 20
Maritime Life Eurasia - B ch 20
Maritime Life Global Equity - B ch 20
Maritime Life Global Equity - A & C ch 20
Maritime Life Pacific Basin - A & C ch 21
Maritime Life Pacific Basin - B ch 21
Maritime Life S&P 500 - A & C ch 23
Maritime Life S&P 500 - B ch 23

(86) Mawer Investment Management

603 7th Avenue S.W.
Suite 600
Calgary, AB
T2P 2T5
Tel: (401) 262-4673
Fax: (401) 262-4099
Toll Free: 1-888-549-6248

Heavy Hitters: 5 Underachievers: 0
Number of Qualifying Funds: 7
Rookie Camp Members: 2
Total Number of Funds: 10
No sales commissions, restrictions apply

CANADIAN FUNDS
Mawer Canadian Bond Fund (HH) ch 15
Mawer Canadian Equity Fund ch 12
Mawer Canadian Money Market Fund
   (HH) ch 18
Mawer Cdn. Balanced RSP Fund (HH)
   ch 14
Mawer Cdn. Diversified Investment
   ch 14
Mawer New Canada Fund (HH) ch 13
Mawer Canadian Income Fund (RC) ch 15
Mawer High Yield Bond Fund ch 15

INTERNATIONAL FUNDS
Mawer World Investment Fund (HH)
   ch 20
Mawer U.S. Equity Fund (RC) ch 23

(87) Maxxum Group of Funds

(London Fund Management Ltd.)
33 Yonge Street
Suite 320
Toronto, ON
M5E 1G4
Fax: 1-888-629-9861
Toll Free: 1-888-4-MAXXUM

Heavy Hitters: 4 Underachievers: 0
Number of Qualifying Funds: 7
Total Number of Funds: 9
Sales commissions apply

CANADIAN FUNDS
Maxxum Canadian Balanced Fund
   (HH) ch 14
Maxxum Canadian Equity Growth
   Fund ch 12
Maxxum Dividend Fund (HH) ch 17
Maxxum Income Fund (HH) ch 15
Maxxum Money Market Fund (HH)
   ch 18
Maxxum Natural Resource Fund ch 19
Maxxum Precious Metals Fund ch 19

INTERNATIONAL FUNDS
Maxxum American Equity Fund ch 23
Maxxum Global Equity Fund ch 20

(88) McDonald Financial Corporation

40 King Street West
Suite 3910
Scotia Plaza
Toronto, ON
M5H 3Y2
Tel: (416) 594-1979

Heavy Hitters: 0 Underachievers: 0
Number of Qualifying Funds: 0
Total Number of Funds: 7
Sales commissions and restrictions apply

CANADIAN FUNDS
McDonald Canada Plus ch 14
McDonald Enhanced Bond ch 15

INTERNATIONAL FUNDS
McDonald Asia Plus ch 21
McDonald Emerging Economies ch 24
McDonald Euro Plus ch 22
McDonald New America ch 23
McDonald New Japan ch 21

(89) McLean Budden Limited

145 King Street West
Suite 2525
Toronto, ON
M5H 1J8
Tel: (416) 862-9800
Fax: (416) 862-0167

Heavy Hitters: 10 Underachievers: 1
Number of Qualifying Funds: 11
Total Number of Funds: 13
No sales commissions, restrictions apply on pooled funds

CANADIAN FUNDS
McLean Budden Balanced Fund (HH) ch 14
McLean Budden Equity Growth Fund (HH) ch 12
McLean Budden Fixed Income Fund (HH) ch 15
McLean Budden Money Market Fund (HH) ch 18
McLean Budden Pooled Balanced Fund (HH) ch 14
McLean Budden Pooled Cdn. Equity (HH) ch 12
McLean Budden Pooled Fixed Income (HH) ch 15
McLean Budden Reg. Balanced (HH) ch 14

INTERNATIONAL FUNDS
McLean Budden American Growth Fund (HH) ch 23
McLean Budden Pooled American Eq. (HH) ch 23
McLean Budden Pooled Offshore Eq. (UA) ch 20
McLean Budden Global Equity Fund ch 20
McLean Budden Int'l Fixed Income ch 26

(90) MD Management Ltd.

1867 Alta Vista Drive
Ottawa, ON
K1G 3Y6
Tel: (613) 731-4552
Fax: (613) 526-1352
Toll Free: 1-800-267-4022

Heavy Hitters: 3 Underachievers: 0
Number of Qualifying Funds: 4
Rookie Camp Members: 3
Total Number of Funds: 11
No sales commissions, restrictions apply

CANADIAN FUNDS
MD Bond Fund (HH) ch 15
MD Equity Fund ch 12
MD Money Fund (HH) ch 18
MD Balanced Fund (RC) ch 14
MD Bond and Mortgage Fund ch 15
MD Dividend Fund ch 17
MD Select Fund (RC) ch 12

INTERNATIONAL FUNDS
MD Growth Fund (HH) ch 20
MD Emerging Markets Fund ch 24
MD Global Bond Fund ch 26
MD U.S. Equity Fund (RC) ch 23

Appendix 3: Mutual Fund Company Scorecard

(91) Members Mutual Management Corp.
55 Lakeshore Blvd. East
Toronto, ON
M5E 1A4
Tel: (416) 864-2461
Fax: (416) 864-6858
Toll Free: 1-888-560-2218

Heavy Hitters: 0 Underachievers: 0
Number of Qualifying Funds: 0
Total Number of Funds: 1
No sales commissions, restrictions apply

CANADIAN FUNDS
Members Mutual Fund ch 14

(92) Metropolitan Life Insurance Co.
50 O'Connor Street
Suite 1226
Ottawa, ON
K1P 6L2
Tel: (613) 560-6994
Fax: (613) 560-6926
Toll Free: 1-800-267-9375

Heavy Hitters: 0 Underachievers: 4
Number of Qualifying Funds: 4
Rookie Camp Members: 2
Total Number of Funds: 8
Sales commissions apply
Segregated funds

CANADIAN FUNDS
Metlife MVP Balanced Fund (UA) ch 14
Metlife MVP Bond Fund (UA) ch 15
Metlife MVP Equity Fund (UA) ch 12
Metlife MVP Money Market Fund (UA)
   ch 18
Metlife MVP Growth Fund (RC) ch 13

INTERNATIONAL FUNDS
Metlife MVP Asian-Pacific RSP Eq. ch 21
Metlife MVP Global Equity Fund ch 20
Metlife MVP U.S. Equity Fund (RC) ch 23

(93) Middlefield Resource Management Ltd.
One First Canadian Place
58th Floor
P.O. Box 192
Toronto, ON
M5X 1A6
Tel: (416) 362-0714
Fax: (416) 362-7925

Heavy Hitters: 0 Underachievers: 1
Number of Qualifying Funds: 1
Total Number of Funds: 3
Sales commissions apply

CANADIAN FUNDS
Middlefield Growth Fund (UA) ch 12
Middlefield Money Market Fund ch 18
Middlefield Global Technology Fund ch 19

(94) MOF Management Ltd.
Pacific Centre
2020 - 609 Granville Street
P.O. Box 10379
Vancouver, BC
V7Y 1G6
Tel: (604) 643-7416
Fax: (604) 687-6532
Toll Free: 1-800-663-6370

Heavy Hitters: 1 Underachievers: 0
Number of Qualifying Funds: 2
Total Number of Funds: 2
Sales commissions and restrictions apply

CANADIAN FUNDS
Multiple Opportunities Fund ch 13

INTERNATIONAL FUNDS
Special Opportunities Fund (HH) ch 20

Appendix 3: Mutual Fund Company Scorecard

(95) Montrusco Associates Inc.
McGill Tower
1501 McGill College Avenue
Suite 2800
Montreal, QC
H3A 3N3
Tel: (514) 842-6464
Fax: (514) 282-2517

Heavy Hitters: 0 Underachievers: 0
Number of Qualifying Funds: 2
Total Number of Funds: 2
Sales commissions and restrictions apply

CANADIAN FUNDS
Quebec Growth Fund Associates Inc.
ch 13
Teachers RSP-Equity Section ch 12

(96) Morrison Williams Investment Mgmt.
1 Toronto Street
Suite 405
P.O. Box 21
Toronto, ON
Tel: (416) 777-2922
Fax: (416) 777-0954

Heavy Hitters: 0 Underachievers: 0
Number of Qualifying Funds: 0
Rookie Camp Members: 1
Total Number of Funds: 3
No sales commissions apply

CANADIAN FUNDS
Millennium Diversified Fund ch 14
Millennium Next Generation Fund (RC)
 ch 13
Millennium Income Fund ch 15

(97) Mutual Life of Canada
227 King Street South
Waterloo, ON
N2J 4C5
Tel: (519) 888-FUND
Fax: (519) 888-3646

Heavy Hitters: 1 Underachievers: 1
Number of Qualifying Funds: 5
Rookie Camp Members: 1
Total Number of Funds: 13
Sale commissions apply on some funds

CANADIAN FUNDS
Mutual Bond Fund (UA) ch 15
Mutual Diversifund 40 ch 14
Mutual Equifund ch 12
Mutual Money Market ch 18
Mutual Premier Blue Chip Fund (RC)
 ch 12
Mutual Premier Bond Fund ch 15
Mutual Premier Diversified Fund ch 14
Mutual Premier Growth Fund ch 13
Mutual Premier Mortgage Fund ch 16

INTERNATIONAL FUNDS
Mutual Amerifund (HH) ch 23
Mutual Premier American Fund ch 23
Mutual Premier Emerging Markets ch 24
Mutual Premier International Fund ch 20

(98) National Bank Securities Inc.
1100 University Street
4th Floor
Montreal, QC
H3B 2G7
Tel: (514) 871-7530
Fax: (514) 871-4013
Toll Free: 1-800-280-3088

Heavy Hitters: 3 Underachievers: 4
Number of Qualifying Funds: 15
Total Number of Funds: 23
No sales commissions apply

CANADIAN FUNDS
General Trust of Canada Balanced
 ch 14
General Trust of Canada Bond Fund
 ch 15
General Trust of Canada Cdn. Equity
 ch 12

Appendix 3: Mutual Fund Company Scorecard

General Trust of Canada Growth Fund
ch 13
General Trust of Canada Money Mkt.
(HH) ch 18
General Trust of Canada Mortgage
(UA) ch 16
InvesNat Canadian Equity Fund (HH)
ch 20
InvesNat Money Market Fund ch 18
InvesNat Mortgage Fund ch 16
InvesNat Retirement Balanced Fund
ch 14
InvesNat Short Term Government Bond
(UA) ch 15
InvesNat Treasury Bill Plus Fund (HH)
ch 18
InvesNat Canadian Bond Fund ch 15
InvesNat Corporate Cash Mgmt. Fund
ch 18
InvesNat Dividend Fund ch 17

INTERNATIONAL FUNDS
General Trust of Canada Int'l (UA) ch 20
General Trust of Canada U.S. Equity
(UA) ch 23
InvesNat U.S. Money Market ($US)
ch 27
InvesNat Blue Chip Amer Equity ($US)
ch 23
InvesNat European Equity Fund ch 22
InvesNat Far East Equity Fund ch 21
InvesNat International RSP Bond ch 26
InvesNat Japanese Equity Fund ch 21

(99) National Life of Canada
5022 University Avenue
Toronto, ON
M5G 1Y7
Toll Free: 1-800-242-9753

Heavy Hitters: 4 Underachievers: 1
Number of Qualifying Funds: 5
Total Number of Funds: 5
Sales commissions apply
Segregated funds

CANADIAN FUNDS
National Balanced Fund (HH) ch 14
National Equities Fund (HH) ch 12
National Fixed Income Fund (HH) ch 15
National Money Market Fund (UA)
ch 18

INTERNATIONAL FUNDS
National Global Equities Fund (HH)
ch 20

(100) National Trust Co.
One Financial Place
1 Adelaide Street East
Toronto, ON
M5C 2W8
Tel: (416) 361-3863
Fax: (416) 361-5563
Toll Free: 1-800-563-4683

Heavy Hitters: 1 Underachievers: 0
Number of Qualifying Funds: 4
Rookie Camp Members: 1
Total Number of Funds: 13
No sales commissions apply

CANADIAN FUNDS
National Trust Balanced Fund ch 14
National Trust Canadian Bond Fund
(HH) ch 15
National Trust Canadian Equity Fund
ch 12
National Trust Money Market Fund ch 18
National Trust Canadian Index Fund ch 12
National Trust Dividend Fund ch 17
National Trust Mortgage Fund (RC) ch 16
National Trust Special Equity Fund ch 13

INTERNATIONAL FUNDS
National Trust American Equity Fund
ch 23
National Trust Emerging Markets ch 21
National Trust Int'l Equity Fund ch 20
National Trust Int'l RSP Bond Fund ch 26
National Trust U.S. Index Fund ch 23

(101) Navigator Fund Company Ltd.

444 St. Mary Avenue
Suite 1500
Winnipeg, MB
R3C 3T1
Tel: (204) 942-7788
Toll Free: 1-800-665-1667

Heavy Hitters: 0 Underachievers: 0
Number of Qualifying Funds: 0
Total Number of Funds: 5
Sales commissions apply

CANADIAN FUNDS
Navigator Canadian Income Fund ch 15
Navigator Value Inv. Retirement ch 12

INTERNATIONAL FUNDS
Navigator American Value Inv. ch 23
Navigator Asia Pacific Fund ch 21
Navigator American Growth Fund ch 24

(102) NN Life Insurance Company of Canada

One Concorde Gate
Don Mills, ON
M3C 3N6
Tel: (416) 391-2200
Fax: (416) 391-8515

Heavy Hitters: 3 Underachievers: 1
Number of Qualifying Funds: 6
Rookie Camp Members: 2
Total Number of Funds: 13
Sales commissions apply
Segregated funds

CANADIAN FUNDS
NN Asset Allocation Fund (HH) ch 14
NN Bond Fund (HH) ch 15
NN Canadian 35 Index ch 12
NN Canadian Growth ch 12
NN Money Market Fund (HH) ch 18
NN T-Bill Fund (UA) ch 18
NN Dividend Fund ch 17

INTERNATIONAL FUNDS
NN Can-Euro Fund ch 22
NN Can-Emerge Fund ch 24
NN Can-Daq 100 Fund ch 23
NN Can-Asian Fund (RC) ch 21
NN Can-Am Fund (RC) ch 23
NN Can-Global Bond Fund ch 26

(103) North West Life Assurance Co. of Canada

1040 West Georgia Street
Suite 800
Vancouver, BC
V6E 4H1
Tel: (604) 689-1211
Fax: (604) 688-1521

Heavy Hitters: 0 Underachievers: 0
Number of Qualifying Funds: 0
Total Number of Funds: 9
Sales commissions apply
Segregated funds

CANADIAN FUNDS
North-West Life Ecoflex (A)
North-West Life Ecoflex (B)
North-West Life Ecoflex (D)
North-West Life Ecoflex (H)
North-West Life Ecoflex (M)

INTERNATIONAL FUNDS
North-West Life Ecoflex (E)
North West Life Ecoflex (G)
North-West Life Ecoflex (I)
North-West Life Ecoflex (S)

(104) O'Donnell Investment Management Corporation

2 First Canadian Place
Suite 1010
P.O. Box 447
Toronto, ON
M5X 1E4
Tel: (416) 214-2214
Fax: (416) 214-1244
Toll Free: 1-800-292-5658

Heavy Hitters: 0 Underachievers: 0
Number of Qualifying Funds: 0
Total Number of Funds: 10
Sales commissions apply

CANADIAN FUNDS
O'Donnell Balanced Fund ch 14
*O'Donnell Canadian Emerging Growth
  ch 13*
O'Donnell Growth Fund ch 12
O'Donnell High Income Fund ch 15
O'Donnell Money Market Fund ch 18
O'Donnell Short Term Fund ch 18
O'Donnell World Prec. Metals Fund ch 19

INTERNATIONAL FUNDS
O'Donnell American Sector Growth ch 23
O'Donnell U.S. Mid-Cap Fund ch 23
O'Donnell World Equity Fund ch 20

(105) OHA Mutual Fund Services Limited

150 Ferrand Drive
Don Mills, ON
M3C 1H6
Tel: (416) 429-2778
Fax: (416) 429-9198
Toll Free: 1-800-268-9597

Heavy Hitters: 0 Underachievers: 0
Number of Qualifying Funds: 0
Rookie Camp Members: 1
Total Number of Funds: 5
No sales commissions, restrictions apply

CANADIAN FUNDS
OHA Balanced Fund ch 14
OHA Bond Fund ch 15
OHA Canadian Equity Fund ch 12
OHA Short Term Fund ch 18

INTERNATIONAL FUNDS
OHA Foreign Equity Fund (RC) ch 20

(106) Ontario Teachers Group Inc.

57 Mobile Drive
Toronto, ON
M4A 1H5
Tel: (416) 752-9410
Fax: (416) 752-6649
Toll Free: 1-800-263-9541

Heavy Hitters: 3 Underachievers: 0
Number of Qualifying Funds: 6
Total Number of Funds: 6
No sales commissions, restrictions apply

CANADIAN FUNDS
Ontario Teachers Group Balanced (HH)
  ch 14
Ontario Teachers Group Diversified
  ch 12
Ontario Teachers Group Fixed Value
  (HH) ch 18
Ontario Teachers Group Growth ch 13
Ontario Teachers Group Mortgage Inc
  (HH) ch 17

INTERNATIONAL FUNDS
Ontario Teachers Group Global ch 20

(107) Optimum Placements Inc.

425 boul. de Maisonneuve Ouest
Bureau 1620
Montreal, QC
H3A 3G5
Tel: (514) 288-1620
Fax: (514) 288-4280
Toll Free: 1-888-678-4686

Heavy Hitters: 1 Underachievers: 0
Number of Qualifying Funds: 3
Rookie Camp Members: 1
Total Number of Funds: 5
No sales commissions, restrictions apply

CANADIAN FUNDS
Fonds Optimum Epargne ch 18
Fonds Optimum Equilibre ch 14
Fonds Optimum Obligations (HH) ch 15
Fonds Optimum Actions (RC) ch 12

INTERNATIONAL FUNDS
Fonds Optimum Internationales ch 20

(108) Orbit Mutual Fund Management Ltd.
4141 Sherbrooke Street West
Site 303
Montreal, QC
H3Z 1B8
Tel: (514) 932-3000
Fax: (514) 989-2132

Heavy Hitters: 0 Underachievers: 0
Number of Qualifying Funds: 1
Total Number of Funds: 2
Sales commissions apply

INTERNATIONAL FUNDS
Orbit World Fund ch 20
Orbit North American Equity Fund ch 20

(109) Ordre des Ingenieurs du Quebec
2020 University Street
18th Floor
Montreal, QC
H3A 2A5
Tel: (514) 845-6141
Fax: (514) 845-1833

Heavy Hitters: 4 Underachievers: 0
Number of Qualifying Funds: 4
Total Number of Funds: 7
No sales commissions, restrictions apply

CANADIAN FUNDS
Ferique Balanced Fund (HH) ch 14
Ferique Bond Fund (HH) ch 15
Ferique Equity Fund (HH) ch 12
Ferique Short Term Income Fund (HH)
   ch 18
Ferique Growth Fund ch 12

INTERNATIONAL FUNDS
Ferique American Fund ch 23
Ferique International Fund ch 20

(110) Pacific Capital Management Ltd.
666 Burrard Street
Suite 1190
Vancouver, BC
V6C 2X8
Tel: (604) 682-5338
Fax: (604) 682-5339
Toll Free: 1-800-662-5338

Heavy Hitters: 0 Underachievers: 0
Number of Qualifying Funds: 0
Total Number of Funds: 2
Sales commissions and restrictions apply

CANADIAN FUNDS
Pacific Special Equity Fund ch 13
Pacific Total Return Fund ch 12

(111) Peter Cundill & Associates Ltd.
1200 Sun Life Plaza
1100 Melville Street
Vancouver, BC
V6E 4A6
Tel: (604) 685-4231
Fax: (604) 689-9532
Toll Free: 1-800-663-0156

Heavy Hitters: 1 Underachievers: 0
Number of Qualifying Funds: 2
Total Number of Funds: 3
Sales commissions apply

Appendix 3: Mutual Fund Company Scorecard

CANADIAN FUNDS
Cundill Security Fund (HH) ch 12
The McElvaine Investment Trust ch 12

INTERNATIONAL FUNDS
Cundill Value Fund ch 20

(112) Phillips, Hager & North Ltd.
1055 West Hastings Street
Suite 1700
Vancouver, BC
V6E 2H3
Tel: (604) 691-6781
Fax: (604) 685-5712
Toll Free: 1-800-661-6141

Heavy Hitters: 10 Underachievers: 0
Number of Qualifying Funds: 10
Rookie Camp Members: 1
Total Number of Funds: 13
No sales commissions, restrictions apply

CANADIAN FUNDS
PH&N Canadian Money Market (HH)
  ch 18
Phillips Hager & North Bal. Pens. Tr.
  (HH) ch 14
Phillips Hager & North Balanced (HH)
  ch 14
Phillips Hager & North Bond Fund
  (HH) ch 15
Phillips Hager & North Cdn. Equity
  (HH) ch 12
Phillips Hager & North Div. Income
  (HH) ch 17
PH&N Canadian Equity Plus (HH) ch 12
Phillips Hager & North Vintage (HH)
  ch 12
*PH&N Short Term Bond & Mortgage
  ch 15*

INTERNATIONAL FUNDS
PH&N $US Money Market (HH) ch 27
Phillips Hager & North U.S. Equity
  (HH) ch 23

PH&N International Equity Fund ch 20
*PH&N North American Equity Fund
  (RC) ch 20*

(113) Primerica Life Insurance Company of Canada
350 Burnhamthorpe Road
Suite 300
Mississauga, ON
L5B 3J1
Tel: (905) 848-7731
Fax: (905) 270-7096
Toll Free: 1-800-387-7876

Heavy Hitters: 0 Underachievers: 0
Number of Qualifying Funds: 0
Rookie Camp Members: 5
Total Number of Funds: 5
Sales commissions apply
Segregated funds

CANADIAN FUNDS
Common Sense Asset Builder 1 (RC) ch 14
Common Sense Asset Builder 2 (RC) ch 14
*Common Sense Asset Builder 3 (RC)
  ch 14*
*Common Sense Asset Builder 4 (RC)
  ch 14*
Common Sense Asset Builder 5 (RC) ch 14

(114) Professional Association of Foreign Service Officers
60 Queen Street
Suite 1202
Ottawa, ON
K1P 5Y7
Tel: (613) 567-3225
Fax: (613) 567-3979

Heavy Hitters: 0 Underachievers: 0
Number of Qualifying Funds: 0
Total Number of Funds: 1
No sales commissions, restrictions apply
Segregated funds

CANADIAN FUNDS
Capital Alliance Ventures Inc. ch 19

(115) Professional Institute of the Public Service of Canada

c/o Talvest Fund Management
The Exchange Tower
Suite 2200
Toronto, ON
M5X 1B1
Tel: (416) 364-5620
Fax: (416) 368-4243
Toll Free: 1-800-268-0081

Heavy Hitters: 0 Underachievers: 0
Number of Qualifying Funds: 0
Total Number of Funds: 1
Sales commissions apply

CANADIAN FUNDS
Canadian Medical Discoveries Fund ch 19

(116) Puccetti Funds Management Inc.

319 Webb Road, RR 1
Goodwood, ON
L0C 1A0
Tel: (905) 649-5588
Fax: (905) 649-3237

Heavy Hitters: 0 Underachievers: 0
Number of Qualifying Funds: 0
Total Number of Funds: 1
No sales commissions, restrictions apply

CANADIAN FUNDS
The Goodwood Fund ch 12

(117) Pursuit Financial Management Corp.

1200 Sheppard Avenue East
Suite 402
Willowdale, ON
M2K 2S5
Tel: (416) 502-9300
Fax: (416) 502-9394
Toll Free: 1-800-253-9619

Heavy Hitters: 2 Underachievers: 1
Number of Qualifying Funds: 3
Total Number of Funds: 6
Sales commissions apply

CANADIAN FUNDS
Pursuit Canadian Bond Fund (UA) ch 15
Pursuit Canadian Equity Fund (HH)
   ch 12
Pursuit Money Market Fund (HH) ch 18

INTERNATIONAL FUNDS
Pursuit Global Bond Fund ch 26
Pursuit Global Equity Fund ch 20
Pursuit Growth Fund ch 20

(118) Retrocom Investment Management

89 The Queensway
Suite 226
Mississauga, ON
L5B 2V2
Tel: (416) 366-7211
Fax: (416) 366-2700
Toll Free: 1-888-743-5627

Heavy Hitters: 0 Underachievers: 0
Number of Qualifying Funds: 0
Total Number of Funds: 1
Sales commissions and restrictions apply

CANADIAN FUNDS
Retrocom Growth Fund Inc. ch 19

(119) Royal Bank Investment Management Inc.

Royal Trust Tower
77 King Street West
5th Floor
Toronto, ON
M5W 1P9
Tel: (416) 955-3611
Fax: (416) 955-3630
Toll Free: 1-800-463-3863

Appendix 3: Mutual Fund Company Scorecard

Heavy Hitters: 6 Underachievers: 10
Number of Qualifying Funds: 26
Rookie Camp Members: 1
Total Number of Funds: 36
No sales commissions apply

CANADIAN FUNDS
Royal Balanced Fund (UA) ch 14
Royal Energy Fund (HH) ch 19
Royal LePage Commercial Real Estate
 ch 19
Royal Precious Metals Fund ch 19
Royal Trust Advantage Balanced Fund
 (UA) ch 14
Royal Trust Advantage Growth Fund
 (UA) ch 14
Royal Trust Advantage Income Fund
 (UA) ch 14
Royal Trust Bond Fund (HH) ch 15
Royal Trust Canadian Money Market
 (UA) ch 18
Royal Trust Canadian Stock Fund (UA)
 ch 12
Royal Trust Canadian T-Bill Fund ch 18
Royal Trust Growth and Income Fund
 (HH) ch 17
Royal Trust Mortgage Fund (UA) ch 16
RoyFund Bond Fund (HH) ch 15
RoyFund Canadian Equity Fund ch 12
RoyFund Canadian Money Market
 Fund (UA) ch 18
RoyFund Canadian T-Bill Fund ch 18
RoyFund Mortgage Fund ch 16
Royal Canadian Growth Fund ch 13
Royal Canadian Small Cap ch 13
Royal Life Science & Technology ch 19
RoyFund Dividend Fund (RC) ch 17
*Royal Premium Money-Market Fund
 ch 18*

INTERNATIONAL FUNDS
Royal European Growth Fund ch 22
Royal Japanese Stock Fund (UA) ch 21
Royal Trust American Stock Fund (HH)
 ch 23

Royal Trust International Bond Fund
 ch 26
Royal Trust U.S. Money Market ($US)
 ch 27
RoyFund U.S. Dollar Money ($US)
 ch 27
RoyFund U.S. Equity Fund (HH) ch 23
Zweig Strategic Growth (UA) ch 23
Royal Asian Growth Fund ch 21
Royal International Equity Fund ch 20
Royal Latin American Fund ch 24
RoyFund International Income Fund ch 26
Zweig Global Managed Assets ch 25

(120) Royal Life Insurance Company of Canada
277 Lakeshore Road East
Oakville, ON
L6J 1H9
Tel: (905) 842-6200
Fax: (905) 842-6294
Toll Free: 1-800-263-1747

Heavy Hitters: 0 Underachievers: 0
Number of Qualifying Funds: 3
Total Number of Funds: 7
Sales commissions apply
Segregated funds

CANADIAN FUNDS
Royal Life Balanced Fund ch 14
Royal Life Equity Fund ch 12
Royal Life Income Fund ch 15
Royal Life Canadian Growth Fund ch 13
Royal Life Money Market Fund ch 18

INTERNATIONAL FUNDS
Royal Life Int'l Equity Fund ch 20
Royal Life U.S. Equity Fund ch 23

(121) Sagit Investment Management Ltd.

789 West Pender Street
Suite 900
Vancouver, BC
V6C 1H2
Tel: (604) 685-3193
Fax: (604) 681-7536
Toll Free: 1-800-663-1003

Heavy Hitters: 1 Underachievers: 9
Number of Qualifying Funds: 13
Total Number of Funds: 15
Sales commissions apply

CANADIAN FUNDS
Cambridge Balanced Fund (UA) ch 14
Cambridge Growth Fund (UA) ch 13
Cambridge Resource Fund ch 19
Cambridge Special Equity (UA) ch 13
Trans-Canada Bond Fund (UA) ch 15
Trans-Canada Dividend Fund (UA) ch 17
Trans-Canada Money Market (HH) ch 18
Trans-Canada Pension Fund ch 14
Trans-Canada Value Fund (UA) ch 12
Cambridge Precious Metals Fund ch 19

INTERNATIONAL FUNDS
Cambridge Americas Fund ch 20
Cambridge American Growth (UA) ch 23
Cambridge Global Fund (UA) ch 20
Cambridge Pacific Fund (UA) ch 21
Cambridge China Fund ch 21

(122) Saxon Group of Funds

(Howson Tattersall Investment
   Counsel Ltd.)
Cadillac Fairview Tower
20 Queen Street West
Suite 1904
P.O. Box 95
Toronto, ON
M5H 3R3
Tel: (416) 979-1818
Fax: (416) 979-7424
Toll Free: 1-888-287-2966

Heavy Hitters: 2 Underachievers: 0
Number of Qualifying Funds: 4
Total Number of Funds: 4
No sales commissions, restrictions apply

CANADIAN FUNDS
Saxon Balanced Fund (HH) ch 14
Saxon Small Cap ch 13
Saxon Stock Fund (HH) ch 12

INTERNATIONAL FUNDS
Saxon World Growth ch 20

(123) Sceptre Investment Counsel Ltd.

26 Wellington Street East
Suite 1200
Toronto, ON
M5E 1W4
Tel: (416) 866-7496
Fax: (416) 367-5938
Toll Free: 1-800-265-1888

Heavy Hitters: 4 Underachievers: 0
Number of Qualifying Funds: 5
Rookie Camp Members: 1
Total Number of Funds: 6
No sales commissions apply

CANADIAN FUNDS
Sceptre Balanced Growth Fund (HH)
   ch 14
Sceptre Bond Fund (HH) ch 15
Sceptre Equity Growth Fund (HH) ch 13
Sceptre Money Market Fund (HH) ch 18

INTERNATIONAL FUNDS
Sceptre International Fund ch 20
Sceptre Asian Growth Fund (RC) ch 21

(124) Scotia Securities Inc.

40 King Street West
5th Floor
Toronto, ON
M5H 1H1
Tel: (416) 866-2014
Fax: (416) 866-2018
Toll Free: 1-800-268-9269

Heavy Hitters: 2 Underachievers: 7
Number of Qualifying Funds: 12
Rookie Camp Members: 2
Total Number of Funds: 21
No sales commissions apply

CANADIAN FUNDS
Scotia Excelsior Balanced Fund (UA)
  ch 14
Scotia Excelsior Cdn. Blue Chip (UA)
  ch 12
Scotia Excelsior Cdn. Growth Fund
  ch 12
Scotia Excelsior Defensive Income (UA)
  ch 15
Scotia Excelsior Dividend Fund (HH)
  ch 17
Scotia Excelsior Income Fund ch 15
Scotia Excelsior Money Market Fund
  (UA) ch 18
Scotia Excelsior T-Bill Fund (UA) ch 18
Scotia Excelsior Total Return Fund
  (HH) ch 14
Scotia Excelsior Mortgage Fund (RC)
  ch 17
Scotia Excelsior Prec. Metals Fund ch 19
Scotia Excelsior Premium T-Bill ch 18

INTERNATIONAL FUNDS
Scotia Excelsior American Growth (UA)
  ch 23
Scotia Excelsior Int'l Fund ch 20
Scotia CanAm Income Fund (UA) ch 26
Scotia Excelsior European Growth ch 22
Scotia Excelsior Global Bond Fund ch 26
Scotia CanAm Money Market Fund ch 27

Scotia Excelsior Latin American ch 24
Scotia CanAm Growth Fund (RC) ch 23
Scotia Excelsior Pacific Rim Fund ch 21

(125) Scudder Canada Investment Services Ltd.

161 Bay Street
Main Floor
P.O. Box 712
Toronto, ON
M5J 2S1
Tel: (416) 941-9393
Fax: (416) 350-2018
Toll Free: 1-800-850-3863

Heavy Hitters: 0 Underachievers: 0
Number of Qualifying Funds: 0
Total Number of Funds: 7
No sales commissions apply

CANADIAN FUNDS
Scudder Canadian Short Term Bond ch 15
Scudder Canadian Equity Fund ch 12

INTERNATIONAL FUNDS
Scudder Emerging Markets Fund ch 24
Scudder Global Fund ch 20
Scudder Greater Europe Fund ch 22
Scudder Pacific Fund ch 21
Scudder U.S. Growth & Income Fund ch 23

(126) Seaboard Life Insurance Company

2165 West Broadway
P.O. Box 5900
Vancouver, BC
V6B 5H6
Tel: (604) 737-9107
Fax: (604) 737-7207
Toll Free: 1-800-363-2166

Heavy Hitters: 0 Underachievers: 0
Number of Qualifying Funds: 0
Total Number of Funds: 10
Sales commissions apply
Segregated funds

CANADIAN FUNDS
APEX Balanced Allocation Fund ch 14
APEX Canadian Stock Fund ch 12
APEX Equity Growth Fund ch 12
APEX Fixed Income Fund ch 15
APEX Growth & Income Fund ch 14
APEX Money Market Fund ch 18
APEX Mortgage Fund ch 16

INTERNATIONAL FUNDS
APEX Asian Pacific Fund ch 21
APEX Global Equity Fund ch 20
APEX U.S. Equity Fund ch 23

(127) Societe Financiere Azura Inc.
1260 boul. le Bourgneuf
Bureau 206
Quebec, QC
G2K 2G2
Tel: (418) 624-3000
Toll Free: 1-800-231-6539

Heavy Hitters: 0 Underachievers: 0
Number of Qualifying Funds: 0
Total Number of Funds: 5
Sales commissions and restrictions apply

CANADIAN FUNDS
Azura Balanced RSP Pooled ch 14
Azura Conservative Pooled ch 14
Azura Growth RSP Pooled ch 12

INTERNATIONAL FUNDS
Azura Balanced Pooled ch 25
Azura Growth Pooled ch 20

(128) Sogefonds MFQ Inc.
625 rue Saint-Amable
Quebec City, QC
G1R 2G5
Tel: (418) 644-4225
Fax: (418) 528-0457
Toll Free: 1-800-361-8625

Heavy Hitters: 1 Underachievers: 0
Number of Qualifying Funds: 4
Total Number of Funds: 5
Sales commissions and restrictions apply

CANADIAN FUNDS
Fonds Ficadre Actions ch 12
Fonds Ficadre Equilibre ch 14
Fonds Ficadre Money Market (HH)
 ch 18
Fonds Ficadre Obligations ch 15
Fonds Ficadre Hypotheques ch 16

(129) Spectrum United Mutual Funds Inc.
55 University Avenue
2nd Floor
Toronto, ON
M5J 2H7
Tel: (416) 360-2200
Fax: (416) 360-2203
Toll Free: 1-800-263-1851

Heavy Hitters: 2 Underachievers: 5
Number of Qualifying Funds: 18
Rookie Camp Members: 1
Total Number of Funds: 28
Sales commissions apply

CANADIAN FUNDS
Spectrum United Canadian Equity
 (HH) ch 12
Spectrum United Canadian Growth
 ch 13
Spectrum United Canadian Investment
 ch 12
Spectrum United Canadian Portfolio
 ch 14
Spectrum United Canadian Stock Fund
 ch 12
Spectrum United Canadian T-Bill (UA)
 ch 18
Spectrum United Diversified Fund
 ch 14
Spectrum United Dividend Fund (UA)
 ch 17

Spectrum United Long-Term Bond
Fund (HH) ch 15
Spectrum United Mid-Term Bond Fund
ch 15
Spectrum United Savings Fund ch 18
Spectrum United Short-Term Bond
(UA) ch 15
Spectrum United Asset Alloc. Fund ch 14
Spectrum United Cdn. Resource Fund ch 19
Spectrum United Global Telecom. ch 19

INTERNATIONAL FUNDS
Spectrum United American Equity ch 23
Spectrum United American Growth
ch 23
Spectrum United Global Diversified
ch 25
Spectrum United Global Equity Fund
(UA) ch 20
Spectrum United Global Growth Fund
(UA) ch 20
Spectrum United U.S. Dollar Money
ch 27
*Spectrum United Asian Dynasty Fund
ch 21*
*Spectrum United Emerging Markets (RC)
ch 24*
Spectrum United European Growth ch 22
*Spectrum United Global Bond Fund
ch 26*
*Spectrum United Optimax USA Fund
ch 23*
Spectrum United RRSP Int'l Bond ch 26

(130) Sportfund Inc.
c/o Admax Regent International
Management
200 King Street West
8th Floor
Toronto, ON
M5H 3Z8
Tel: (416) 971-8416
Fax: (416) 594-8863
Toll Free: 1-800-970-SPORT

Heavy Hitters: 0 Underachievers: 0
Number of Qualifying Funds: 0
Total Number of Funds: 1
Sales commissions and restrictions apply

CANADIAN FUNDS
Sportfund Inc. ch 19

(131) St-Laurent Financial Corp.
425 boul. de Maisonneuve Ouest
Bureau 1740
Montreal, QC
Tel: (514) 288-7545
Fax: (514) 288-4200
Toll Free: 1-800-361-8100

Heavy Hitters: 1 Underachievers: 0
Number of Qualifying Funds: 3
Rookie Camp Members: 1
Total Number of Funds: 4
No sales commissions, restrictions apply

CANADIAN FUNDS
Batirente - Section Diversifiee ch 14
Batirente - Sec. Marche Monetaire ch 18
Batirente - Section Obligations (HH)
ch 15
Batirente - Section Actions (RC) ch 12

(132) Standard Life Assurance Co. Ltd.
1245 Sherbrooke Street West
Montreal, QC
H3G 1G3
Tel: (514) 284-6711
Fax: (514) 499-4466
Toll Free: 1-800-665-6237

Heavy Hitters: 1 Underachievers: 0
Number of Qualifying Funds: 3
Total Number of Funds: 4
Sales commissions apply
Segregated funds

CANADIAN FUNDS

Standard Life Ideal Balanced Fund ch 14

Standard Life Ideal Bond Fund ch 15

Standard Life Ideal Equity Fund (HH) ch 12

Standard Life Ideal Money Market ch 18

(133) Standard Life Mutual Funds Ltd.

1245 Sherbrooke Street West

Montreal, QC

H3G 1G3

Tel: (514) 284-6711

Fax: (514) 499-4466

Toll Free: 1-800-665-6237

Heavy Hitters: 0 Underachievers: 0

Number of Qualifying Funds: 0

Rookie Camp Members: 3

Total Number of Funds: 10

Sales commissions and restrictions apply

CANADIAN FUNDS

Standard Life Balanced Mutual (RC) ch 14

Standard Life Bond Mutual Fund (RC) ch 15

Standard Life Canadian Dividend ch 17

Standard Life Equity Mutual Fund (RC) ch 12

Standard Life Growth Equity Fund ch 13

Standard Life Money Market Fund ch 18

Standard Life Natural Resources ch 19

INTERNATIONAL FUNDS

Standard Life International Bond ch 26

Standard Life International Equity ch 20

Standard Life U.S. Equity Fund ch 23

(134) Stone & Company Limited

11 King Street West

Suite 1002

Toronto, ON

M5H 1A3

Tel: (416) 363-2822

Fax: (416) 363-7252

Toll Free: 1-800-336-9528

Heavy Hitters: 0 Underachievers: 0

Number of Qualifying Funds: 0

Total Number of Funds: 3

Sales commissions apply

CANADIAN FUNDS

Stone & Co. Flagship Mon. Mkt. ch 18

Stone & Co. Flagship Stock Fund ch 12

Stone & Co. Growth & Income ch 14

(135) Strategic Value Funds Management Inc.

95 St. Clair Avenue West

Toronto, ON

M4V 1N7

Tel: (416) 860-9100

Fax: (416) 860-9090

Toll Free: 1-800-408-2311

Heavy Hitters: 0 Underachievers: 10

Number of Qualifying Funds: 11

Total Number of Funds: 19

Sales commissions apply

CANADIAN FUNDS

Laurentian Canadian Balanced Fund ch 14

Laurentian Canadian Equity Fund Ltd. (UA) ch 12

Laurentian Dividend Fund Ltd. (UA) ch 17

Laurentian Government Bond Fund (UA) ch 15

Laurentian Income Fund (UA) ch 15

Laurentian Money Market Fund (UA) ch 18

Laurentian Special Equity Fund (UA) ch 13

Strategic Value Canadian Equity ch 12

INTERNATIONAL FUNDS

Laurentian American Equity Fund Ltd. (UA) ch 23

Laurentian Commonwealth Fund Ltd. (UA) ch 20

Appendix 3: Mutual Fund Company Scorecard

Laurentian Global Balanced Fund (UA)
ch 25

Laurentian International Fund Ltd.
(UA) ch 20

Laurentian Asia Pacific Fund ch 21
Laurentian Emerging Markets Fund ch 24
Laurentian Europe Fund ch 22
Strategic Value American Equity ch 23
Strategic Value Fund ch 20
*Strategic Value Global Balanced RSP
ch 25*
Strategic Value Global Equity Fund ch 20

(136) Talvest Fund Management Inc.

The Exchange Tower
Suite 2200
Toronto, ON
M5X 1B1
Tel: (416) 364-5620
Fax: (416) 364-4472
Toll Free: 1-800-268-8258

Heavy Hitters: 5 Underachievers: 5
Number of Qualifying Funds: 11
Rookie Camp Members: 1
Total Number of Funds: 19
Sales commissions apply

CANADIAN FUNDS
Hyperion Global Science & Tech. ch 19
Hyperion High Yield Bond Fund (HH)
ch 15
Talvest Bond Fund (HH) ch 15
Talvest Canadian Asset Allocation (UA)
ch 14
Talvest Canadian Equity Value Fund
(UA) ch 12
Talvest Income Fund (UA) ch 15
Talvest Money Fund (HH) ch 18
Canadian Sci. & Tech. Growth Fund ch 12
Hyperion Cdn. Equity Growth ch 12
*Hyperion Small-Cap Canadian Equity
(RC) ch 13*
Talvest Dividend Fund ch 17
Talvest New Economy ch 12

INTERNATIONAL FUNDS
Hyperion Asian Fund (HH) ch 21
Hyperion European Fund (UA) ch 22
Hyperion Value Line U.S. Equity (HH)
ch 23
Talvest Global Asset Allocation (UA)
ch 25
Hyperion Global Health Care Fund ch 23
Talvest Foreign Pay Canadian Bond ch 26
Talvest Global RRSP Fund Inc. ch 20

(137) Templeton Management Ltd.

4 King Street West
P.O. Box 4070
Station A
Toronto, ON
M5W 1M3
Tel: (416) 364-4672
Fax: (416) 364-1163
Toll Free: 1-800-387-0830

Heavy Hitters: 4 Underachievers: 1
Number of Qualifying Funds: 9
Total Number of Funds: 14
Sales commissions apply

CANADIAN FUNDS
Templeton Balanced Fund (HH) ch 14
Templeton Canadian Bond Fund (UA)
ch 15
Templeton Canadian Stock Fund ch 12
Templeton Treasury Bill Fund ch 18
*Templeton Canadian Asset Allocation
ch 14*

INTERNATIONAL FUNDS
Templeton Emerging Markets Fund
(HH) ch 24
Templeton Global Bond Fund ch 26
Templeton Global Smaller Companies
ch 20
Templeton Growth Fund Ltd. (HH)
ch 20
Templeton International Stock Fund
(HH) ch 20

Templeton Global Balanced Fund ch 25
Templeton Int'l Balanced Fund ch 25
Templeton Mutual Beacon Fund ch 23
Franklin U.S. Small-Cap Growth ch 23

(138) The Central Group Ltd.

P.O. Box 7320
Ancaster, ON
L9G 3N6
Tel: (905) 648-2025
Fax: (905) 648-5422

Heavy Hitters: 0 Underachievers: 3
Number of Qualifying Funds: 3
Total Number of Funds: 4
Sales commissions apply

CANADIAN FUNDS
All-Canadian Compound (UA) ch 12
All-Canadian Capital Fund (UA) ch 12
All-Canadian Resources Corporation
  (UA) ch 19
All-Canadian Consumer Fund ch 12

(139) Toronto-Dominion Securities Inc.

Toronto-Dominion Centre
Toronto-Dominion Tower
P.O. Box 100
Toronto, ON
M5K 1G8
Tel: (416) 982-6432
Fax: (416) 982-6625
Toll Free: 1-800-268-8166

Heavy Hitters: 7 Underachievers: 2
Number of Qualifying Funds: 15
Rookie Camp Members: 5
Total Number of Funds: 33
No sales commissions apply

CANADIAN FUNDS
Green Line Balanced Growth ch 14
Green Line Balanced Income Fund ch 14
Green Line Blue Chip Equity Fund
  ch 12

Green Line Canadian Bond Fund (HH)
  ch 12
Green Line Canadian Equity Fund
  (HH) ch 12
Green Line Canadian Gov't Bond Fund
  (HH) ch 15
Green Line Canadian Index Fund (HH)
  ch 12
Green Line Canadian Money Market
  (HH) ch 18
Green Line Canadian T-Bill Fund (HH)
  ch 18
Green Line Dividend Fund ch 17
Green Line Mortgage-Backed Fund
  ch 16
Green Line Mortgage Fund (UA) ch 16
Green Line Short Term Income Fund
  (UA) ch 15
Green Line Energy Fund ch 19
Green Line Health Sciences Fund ch 19
Green Line Precious Metals Fund ch 19
Green Line Real Return Bond Fund ch 15
Green Line Resource Fund (RC) ch 19
Green Line Science & Tech. Fund (RC
  ch 19
Green Line Value Fund (RC) ch 12

INTERNATIONAL FUNDS
Green Line U.S. Money Market ($US)
  ch 27
Green Line U.S. Index Fund ($US)
  (HH) ch 23
Green Line Asian Growth Fund (RC)
  ch 21
Green Line Emerging Markets ch 24
Green Line European Growth Fund ch 22
Green Line Global Government Bond
  ch 26
Green Line Global RSP Bond Fund (RC)
  ch 26
Green Line Global Select Fund ch 20
Green Line International Equity ch 20
Green Line Japanese Growth Fund ch 21
Green Line Latin Amer. Growth Fund
  ch 24

387

Appendix 3: Mutual Fund Company Scorecard

Green Line North Amer. Growth A ch 23
Green Line U.S. Blue Chip Equity ch 23

(140) Tradex Management Inc.
45 O'Connor Street
Suite 1860
Ottawa, ON
K1P 1A4
Tel: (613) 233-3394
Fax: (613) 233-8191
Toll Free: 1-800-567-3863

Heavy Hitters: 1 Underachievers: 0
Number of Qualifying Funds: 2
Total Number of Funds: 3
No sales commissions, restrictions apply

CANADIAN FUNDS
Tradex Bond Fund ch 15
Tradex Equity Fund Ltd. (HH) ch 12

INTERNATIONAL FUNDS
Tradex Emerging Mkts. Country Fund ch 24

(141) Transamerica Life Insurance Company of Canada
300 Consilium Place
Scarborough, ON
M1H 3G2
Tel: (416) 290-2818
Fax: (416) 290-2896

Heavy Hitters: 0 Underachievers: 1
Number of Qualifying Funds: 1
Total Number of Funds: 10
Sales commissions apply
Segregated funds

CANADIAN FUNDS
Transamerica Balanced Inv. Growth (UA) ch 14
Growsafe Canadian Balanced Fund ch 14
Growsafe Canadian Bond Fund ch 15
Growsafe Canadian Equity Fund ch 12

Growsafe Canadian Money Market ch 18

INTERNATIONAL FUNDS
Growsafe European 100 Index Fund ch 22
Growsafe International Balanced ch 25
Growsafe Japanese 225 Index Fund ch 21
Growsafe U.S. 21st Century Index ch 23
Growsafe U.S. 500 Index Fund ch 23

(142) Transportation-Communications International Union
1 University Avenue
Suite 600
Toronto, ON
M5J 2P1
Tel: (416) 362-2929
Fax: (416) 366-5123
Toll Free: 1-800-407-0287

Heavy Hitters: 0 Underachievers: 0
Number of Qualifying Funds: 0
Total Number of Funds: 1
Sales commissions and restrictions apply

CANADIAN FUNDS
Triax Growth Fund Inc. ch 19

(143) Trimark Investment Management Inc.
One First Canadian Place
Suite 5000
P.O. Box 487
Toronto, ON
M5X 1E5
Tel: (416) 362-7181
Fax: (416) 368-6331
Toll Free: 1-800-387-9845

Heavy Hitters: 4 Underachievers: 1
Number of Qualifying Funds: 7
Rookie Camp Members: 1
Total Number of Funds: 14
Sales commissions apply

CANADIAN FUNDS
Trimark Canadian Fund ch 12
Trimark Income Growth Fund ch 14
Trimark Interest Fund (HH) ch 18
Trimark RSP Equity Fund (UA) ch 12
Trimark Select Balanced Fund (HH)
    ch 14
Trimark Advantage Bond Fund ch 15
Trimark Canadian Bond Fund ch 15
Trimark Government Income Fund ch 15
Trimark Select Canadian Growth Fund
    ch 12

INTERNATIONAL FUNDS
Trimark Fund (HH) ch 20
Trimark Select Growth Fund (HH)
    ch 20
Trimark - The Americas Fund (RC) ch 20
Trimark Discovery Fund ch 20
Trimark Indo-Pacific Fund ch 21

(144) Trust General du Canada
1100 University Street
Montreal, QC
H3B 2G7
Tel: (514) 871-7530
Fax: (514) 871-8525
Toll Free: 1-800-280-3088

Heavy Hitters: 1 Underachievers: 0
Number of Qualifying Funds: 1
Total Number of Funds: 1
No sales commissions apply

INTERNATIONAL FUNDS
Vision Europe Fund (HH) ch 22

(145) Trust Pret & Revenu du Canada
850 Place d'Youville
Quebec City, QC
G1R 3P6
Tel: (418) 692-1221
Fax: (418) 692-1675
Toll Free: 1-800-667-7643

Heavy Hitters: 1 Underachievers: 1
Number of Qualifying Funds: 6
Total Number of Funds: 9
No sales commissions apply

CANADIAN FUNDS
Trust Pret & Revenu Bond Fund ch 15
Trust Pret & Revenu Canadian Fund
    (HH) ch 12
Trust Pret & Revenu H Fund ch 16
Trust Pret & Revenu Money Market
    ch 18
Trust Pret & Revenu Retirement Fund
    ch 14
Trust Pret & Revenu Dividend Fund ch 17

INTERNATIONAL FUNDS
Trust Pret & Revenu American Fund
    (UA) ch 23
Trust Pret & Revenu International ch 20
Trust Pret & Revenu World Bond Fund
    ch 26

(146) University Avenue Management Ltd.
40 University Avenue
Toronto, ON
M5J 1T1
Tel: (416) 351-1617
Fax: (416) 351-8225
Toll Free: 1-800-465-1812

Heavy Hitters: 0 Underachievers: 2
Number of Qualifying Funds: 2
Total Number of Funds: 3
No sales commissions apply

CANADIAN FUNDS
University Avenue Canadian Fund
    (UA) ch 12
University Avenue Bond Fund ch 15

INTERNATIONAL FUNDS
University Avenue Growth Fund (UA)
    ch 23

(147) Value Contrarian Asset Management Inc.
1155 Metcalfe Street
Suite 1810
Montreal, QC
H3B 2V6
Tel: (514) 398-0808

Heavy Hitters: 0 Underachievers: 0
Number of Qualifying Funds: 0
Total Number of Funds: 1
No sales commissions apply

CANADIAN FUNDS
Value Contrarian Canadian Equity ch 12

(148) Westbury Canadian Life Insurance Co.
21 King Street West
Hamilton, ON
L8N 3R5
Toll Free: 1-800-263-9241

Heavy Hitters: 0 Underachievers: 1
Number of Qualifying Funds: 3
Total Number of Funds: 3
No sales commissions, restrictions apply
Segregated funds

CANADIAN FUNDS
Westbury Canadian Balanced Fund
ch 14
Westbury Canadian Bond Fund (UA)
ch 15
Westbury Canadian Equity Fund ch 12

(149) Working Opportunity Fund Ltd.
Royal Centre
1055 West Georgia
Suite 2901
P.O. Box 11170
Vancouver, BC
V6E 3R5
Tel: (604) 688-9631
Fax: (604) 669-7605

Heavy Hitters: 0 Underachievers: 0
Number of Qualifying Funds: 1
Total Number of Funds: 1
No sales commissions, restrictions apply

CANADIAN FUNDS
Working Opportunity Fund ch 19

(150) Working Ventures Investment Services Inc.
65 St. Clair Avenue East
9th Floor
Toronto, ON
M4T 2Y3
Tel: (416) 922-5479
Fax: (416) 929-4390
Toll Free: 1-800-268-8244

Heavy Hitters: 0 Underachievers: 1
Number of Qualifying Funds: 1
Total Number of Funds: 1
Sales commissions and restrictions apply

CANADIAN FUNDS
Working Ventures Canadian Fund Inc.
  (UA) ch 19

(151) Corporation Financier LaSalle Inc.
7676 rue Edouard
LaSalle, QC
H8P 1T4
Tel: (514) 365-8006
Fax: (514) 365-8006

Heavy Hitters: 0 Underachievers: 0
Number of Qualifying Funds: 1
Total Number of Funds: 2
Sales commissions and restrictions apply

CANADIAN FUNDS
LaSalle Balanced Fund ch 14
LaSalle Equity Fund ch 12

(152) Gestion de Placements Valorem Inc.

850 Ave Ernest Gagnon
Suite 160
Quebec, QC
G1S 4S2
Tel: (418) 527-2880
Fax: (418) 527-3883

Heavy Hitters: 0 Underachievers: 0
Number of Qualifying Funds: 0
Total Number of Funds: 5
Sales commissions apply

CANADIAN FUNDS
Valorem Canadian Bond-Value ch 15
Valorem Canadian Equity-Value ch 12
Valorem Demographic Trends Fund ch 19
Valorem Diversified ch 14

INTERNATIONAL FUNDS
Valorem U.S. Equity-Value ch 23

(153) Centrefire Capital Management Inc.

141 Adelaide Street West
Suite 277
Toronto, ON
M5H 3L9
Tel: (416) 777-0707
Fax: (416) 777-0706
Toll Free: 1-888-777-2949

Heavy Hitters: 0 Underachievers: 0
Number of Qualifying Funds: 0
Total Number of Funds: 1
Sales commissions and restrictions apply

CANADIAN FUNDS
Centrefire Growth Fund Inc. ch 19

(154) International Federation of Professional & Technical Engineers

c/o University Avenue
  Management Ltd.
40 University Avenue
Toronto, ON
M5J 1T1
Tel: (416) 351-1617
Fax: (416) 351-8225
Toll Free: 1-800-465-1812

Heavy Hitters: 0 Underachievers: 0
Number of Qualifying Funds: 0
Total Number of Funds: 1
Sales commissions and restrictions apply

CANADIAN FUNDS
B.E.S.T. Discoveries Fund ch 19

(155) Quebec Federation of Labour

8717 rue Berri
Montreal, QC
H2M 2T9
Tel: (514) 383-8383
Fax: (514) 383-2552
Toll Free: 1-800-361-5017

Heavy Hitters: 0 Underachievers: 0
Number of Qualifying Funds: 0
Total Number of Funds: 1
Restrictions apply

CANADIAN FUNDS
*Fonds de Solidarite des Trev. du Quebec
  ch 19*

ABOUT THE AUTHOR
● ●

RANGA CHAND IS recognized both domestically and internationally as one of Canada's leading economists and mutual fund analysts. Professionally, he held senior positions with Canada's Department of Finance, then served as a director of the Conference Board of Canada, before joining a major stock brokerage firm. He has also taught economics at the University of Waterloo, published extensively in the field of economics, and represented Canada at numerous economic forums, including the OECD in Paris, the United Nations, and the World Institute of Economics in Germany.

Much in demand by organizations, industries, and associations throughout North America, Ranga Chand is well known for his down-to-earth, clear, and informative presentations on the subjects of the global economy and investing. He frequently appears on major network TV shows and is interviewed regularly by radio and the national print media. *Ranga Chand's Getting Started in Mutual Funds*, his companion guide to the *World of Mutual Funds*, is also a bestseller across the country.

Ranga Chand is founder and president of the Oakville, Ontario, research firm Chand Carmichael & Company Limited, and is an advisor to Scotiabank, which based its Scotia Leaders mutual fund program on his objective research methodology.

> Ranga Chand is always interested in hearing from his readers and may be reached by writing to: Ranga Chand, Chand Carmichael & Company Limited, Suite 622, 268 Lakeshore Road East, Oakville, Ontario, L6J 7S4.
>
> If you would like information on Ranga Chand's customized seminars and workshops for corporations and associations, please telephone (905) 844-6708, e-mail chand@idirect.com or fax (905) 844-6458.